KV-621-281

Communitarian International Relations

In Emanuel Adler's distinctive constructivist approach to International Relations theory, international practices evolve in tandem with collective knowledge of the material and social worlds. This book—a selection of his journal publications, a substantial new introduction and three previously unpublished articles—points IR constructivism in a novel direction, characterized as 'communitarian.'

Adler's synthesis does not herald the end of the nation-state; nor does it suggest that agency is unimportant in international life. Rather, it argues that what mediates between individual and state agency and social structures are communities of practice, which are the wellspring and repositories of collective meanings and social practices. The concept of communities of practice casts new light on epistemic and security communities, helping to explain why certain ideas congeal into human practices and others do not, and which social mechanisms can facilitate the emergence of normatively better communities.

This book will be of interest to students and scholars in International Relations theory and particularly those interested in constructivism.

Emanuel Adler is the Andrea and Charles Bronfman Professor of Israeli Studies at the University of Toronto and Professor of International Relations at the Hebrew University of Jerusalem. He is also the author of *The Power of Ideology* and editor, with Michael Barnett, of *Security Communities*.

The New International Relations
Edited by Barry Buzan and Richard Little
London School of Economics and the University of Bristol

The field of International Relations has changed dramatically in recent years. This new series will cover the major issues that have emerged and reflect the latest academic thinking in this particular dynamic area.

International Law, Rights and Politics
Developments in Eastern Europe and the CIS
Rein Mullerson

The Logic of Internationalism
Coercion and accommodation
Kjell Goldmann

Russia and the Idea of Europe
A study in identity and International Relations
Iver B. Neumann

The Future of International Relations
Masters in the making?
Edited by Iver B. Neumann and Ole Wæver

Constructing the World Polity
Essays on international institutionalization
John Gerard Ruggie

Realism in International Relations and International Political Economy
The continuing story of a death foretold
Stefano Guzzini

International Relations, Political Theory and the Problem of Order
Beyond International Relations theory?
N.J. Rengger

War, Peace and World Orders in European History
Edited by Anja V. Hartmann and Beatrice Heuser

European Integration and National Identity
The challenge of the Nordic states
Edited by Lene Hansen and Ole Wæver

Shadow Globalization, Ethnic Conflicts and New Wars
A political economy of intra-state war
Dietrich Jung

Contemporary Security Analysis and Copenhagen Peace Research
Edited by Stefano Guzzini and Dietrich Jung

Observing International Relations
Niklas Luhmann and world politics
Edited by Mathias Albert and Lena Hilkermeier

Communitarian International Relations

The epistemic foundations of
International Relations

Emanuel Adler

Routledge
Taylor & Francis Group

LONDON AND NEW YORK

First published 2005
by Routledge
2 Park Square, Milton Park, Abingdon, Oxon OX14 4RN

Simultaneously published in the USA and Canada
by Routledge
270 Madison Ave., New York, NY 10016

Routledge is an imprint of the Taylor & Francis Group

© 2005 Emanuel Adler

Typeset in Garamond by Taylor & Francis Books
Printed and bound in Great Britain by TJ International Ltd,
Padstow, Cornwall

British Library Cataloguing in Publication Data
A catalogue record for this book is available from the British Library

Library of Congress Cataloging in Publication Data
A catalog record for this title has been requested.

ISBN 0–415–33590–6 (hbk)
ISBN 0–415–33591–4 (pbk)

To the late Ernst (Ernie) Haas

Contents

Illustrations

Figures

Tables

Series editor's preface

Nearly two decades ago, theorists in international relations slowly began to take on board the implications of a social constructivist approach to the discipline. The timing for the introduction of this new theoretical approach could not have been more opportune. International theory had been developing under the shadow of the Cold War and there is no doubt that the chronic tension between the United States and the Soviet Union had a significant impact on the discipline and helped to privilege the view that conflict is a defining feature of international relations and that it is naive or utopian to envisage the emergence of a peaceful world. Although this view was constantly challenged throughout the Cold War, the image of international relations being conducted within a rigidly structured anarchic arena persisted as the frame of reference for both realists and neoliberal institutionalists, who provided the dominant theoretical approaches to the study of international relations. The end of the Cold War and the eventual collapse of the Soviet Union, posed a problem for most international relations theorists, therefore, not only because there had been almost a universal failure to predict these developments, but also because the main theories were not well-equipped to explain these developments even after they had occurred. Against this background, the effect of constructivism on the way that we now think about international relations has been little short of revolutionary.

Social constructivism provides a new way of looking at and conceptualising the world that, potentially, has significant consequences for all ongoing theories in international relations. From a social constructivist perspective, many of the long-established debates in the social sciences, between, for example, rationalism and reflectivism, materialism and idealism, structure and agency, facts and values, and holism and individualism, all build on false dichotomies. It follows that social constructivists see themselves occupying the middle ground in all of these debates and, more important, possessing the capacity to build bridges that make it possible for advocates of the competing positions in these debates to make contact with each other via constructivism and then to engage in some form of dialogue. Given this ambition, however, it is almost inevitable that social constructivism is also becoming a very broad church and that competing views are beginning to open up within it. In particular, conventional constructivists are seen by more radical constructivists to have been coopted, in effect, by the mainstream approaches in international relations, such as realism and neoliberal institutionalism.

How much substance there is to this radical critique of the conventional constructivists remains open to debate. But, in any event, it is now very widely acknowledged that even conventional constructivists have irrevocably changed the way that most theorists think about international relations. They have dealt a fatal blow to the erstwhile, received view that in conducting international relations states are driven by objective interests that are defined by the material circumstances that underpin the state. Constructivists postulalate that although interests do take account of these material circumstances, they are also profoundly influenced by normative and ideational factors. Because norms and ideas are amenable to dramatic transformation, social constructivists have demonstrated that international relations, in theory and practice, can be subject to profound change. But they have also demonstrated that for change to take place, there must be a shift in the established intersubjective and epistemic understanding of the world and this requires a degree of cognitive evolution that is not always easily achieved.

Emanuel Adler has been at the forefront of the revolution precipitated by social constructivism from the start and he has made some very significant theoretical and empirical contributions to the approach. This book brings together published and unpublished essays, written from a social constructivist perspective. By drawing these essays together, it becomes easier to identify the distinctive nature of Adler's contribution. Central to this contribution has been his emphasis on epistemic and security communities. A key presumption is that both knowledge and security are social constructions that are constituted by and are associated with specific communities. These communities can be national, international or transnational. When communities are brought into contact with each other, or membership of communities overlap, then the norms and ideas that constitute one community can leak into another. Adler's analysis of how the idea of arms control helped to constitute an epistemic community in the United States and how the idea was then transferred to the Soviet Union and helped to reconstitute how the Soviets conceptualised weapons provides a classic illustration of how social constructivism works and it opens up, in a very illuminating way, one of the most important political developments in the Cold War era.

For Adler, the idea of arms control provides an excellent example of cognitive evolution. Someone had to come up with the idea in the first instance and then others had to be convinced of its viability by argument and persuasion. As this process developed, an epistemic community came into existence. But only after the epistemic community had succeeded in convincing policy makers of the relevance of arms control did the idea start to affect policy practice. By understanding the nature of this process, however, it becomes possible to appreciate how the policy process might be pushed in new and more peaceful directions. At the end of this book, Adler extends his thinking into the context of the Middle East conflict. The final two chapters were first presented as talks, one in Israel and the other in Canada. Both focus on the need for Israelis to reconstitute themselves by establishing a new set of identities as a necessary step to bringing peace to the region. Constructivism is here being used not just as a tool to understand social reality, but also as a mechanism to transform reality.

Richard Little

Preface and acknowledgements

It was in the course of my intellectual and professional growth that I 'stumbled' on an IR constructivist communitarian approach that emphasizes the evolutionary interconnection between the social construction of knowledge and the construction of social reality. My first understanding that social reality is socially constructed came not only from the sociology of continental post-structuralists and post-modernists, but also, by way of analogy, from how scientific knowledge and theories evolve. Lectures by such giants as Michel Foucault, Jürgen Habermas, and Ilya Prigogine, which I attended while a graduate student in Berkeley, provided material that later became fundamental building blocks of my approach: for example, the relation between 'epistemes' and politics (Foucault), a pragmatist approach in the social sciences (Habermas), and a nonlinear understanding of change (Prigogine). The late Ernst Haas, my mentor, who was extremely well read in the philosophy of science and the sociology of knowledge, encouraged me not only to do good social science and empirical research, but also to think about the metaphors that science and its evolution suggest for the subject of IR change. He introduced me to Donald Campbell's work on cognitive evolution and evolutionary epistemology and (if memory does not fail me) I introduced him to Stephen Toulmin's *Human Understanding*. Together we analyzed the work of Karl Popper, Imre Lakatos, Thomas Kuhn, Larry Lauden, and Erich Jantsch, all of whom understood the evolution of knowledge, including scientific knowledge, from an evolutionary perspective. In short, the philosophy of science taught me not only that knowledge is a social construction, but also that socially constructed knowledge co-evolves with and is a necessary condition for the construction of social institutions and practices.

I owe my understanding of social epistemology as applied to International Relations, as well as almost everything else I have done in my academic career, to Ernst Haas. Ernie was not only a mentor, my most severe critic, and sometimes an enthusiastic supporter, but also a model I have tried to emulate in my writing and teaching throughout my career. It was from him that I first learned the constructivist approach that I have called, along with others, 'modernist.' In countless conversations, Haas taught me an approach that builds on Immanuel Kant, Max Weber, and Habermas, who strongly affected his own work. I came out of this process with a pragmatist understanding of International Relations that is based on learning and highlights the dynamic social processes by which collective meanings evolve within communities of the like-minded, become attached to material objects, and persist in time as new and renewed social institutions and practices. My collaborations, with Peter Haas on epistemic communities, Beverly Crawford on progress in International Relations, and Michael Barnett on security communities, added substantially to my understanding of social and international change. I am deeply indebted to all of them. In retrospect, I now understand that, for me, these collaborative endeavors were part of a quest for the building blocks of a synthetic approach about 'cognitive evolution' and 'communities of practice' that places social construction and evolutionary epistemology at center stage, and which this book only partially and incompletely reflects.

A Spanish saying, *dime con quien andas y te dire quien eres* (tell me who you hang out with and I'll tell you who you are), pretty much summarizes this book's background. This book, and my small contribution to constructivist IR theory, would have been impossible without my sometimes deliberate but frequently unintended *encounters with smart people*, too many to list here. I would nevertheless like to mention Karl Deutsch, Peter Katzenstein, Joseph Nye, John Ruggie, Thomas Schelling, and Janice Stein, whose inspiration and support were critical at different stages of the conception of ideas expressed in this book. And there is no better proof that ideas evolve in communities of the like-minded and professional practice than the wisdom, insights, and experience I accumulated while collaborating with so many of my colleagues, especially Barnett, Crawford, Haas, and Charles Kupchan.

But it is my past and present students in Israel, Canada, and the United States to whom I owe the most and about whom I thought while working on this book. As a mental exercise, I would suggest to my future students the following ten books (in alphabetical order by author), which I would take with me to a desert island to begin writing this book from scratch all over again: (1) Kenneth Boulding, *Ecodynamics*; (2) Karl Deutsch *et al.*, *Political Community*; (3) Ludwik Fleck, *Genesis and Development of a Scientific Fact*; (4) Ernst Haas, *When Knowledge Is Power*; (5) Robert Pirsig, *Zen and the Art of Motorcycle Maintenance*; (6) Karl Popper, *The Open Universe*; (7) Ilya Prigogine, *From Being to Becoming*; (8) Thomas Schelling, *The Strategy of Conflict*; (9) John Searle, *The Construction of Social Reality*; and (10) Stephen Toulmin, *Human Understanding*.

The articles that make up this book were written over a period of two decades; inevitably, some modifications (mainly stylistic) proved necessary before their republication here. I would like to thank Barry Buzan and Richard Little, editors of Routledge's *The New International Relations* series, for giving me the opportunity to do this book and for their confidence and support throughout the publication process. I would also like to thank my colleague and friend Michael Barnett, who urged me to publish this book and read and commented on its material from the beginning. In addition, I am grateful to two anonymous referees and to Routledge's editor, Heidi Bagtazo, production editor, Tony Phipps, editorial assistant, Grace McInnes, and Belinda Latchford for their thorough professional help and support. I would also like to thank Lenn Schramm, who not only did a superb job as my editor during the years when these essays were written, and in the process taught me some English, but was also often one of my severest critics and thus prevented me from making unnecessary serious mistakes. Needless to say, the responsibility for the book's content is entirely mine. I am grateful to the Department of Political Science at the University of Toronto for financial assistance to cover editorial expenses. Last but not least, I would like to thank my wife Sylvia, my daughter Shirli, my sons Nadav and Jonathan, and my parents, Abraham and Eva, for providing me with broad shoulders on which to stand, for their love and understanding, and for their patience during the times I was 'missing in action.'

The author and Routledge thank the original copyright holders for permission to reproduce material in this book. The following articles are reproduced with the permission of the publishers:

'Cognitive Evolution: A Dynamic Approach for the Study of International Relations and Their Progress', in Emanuel Adler and Beverly Crawford, eds, *Progress in Postwar International Relations* (New York: Columbia University Press, 1991) © Columbia University Press, 1991.

'Seizing the Middle Ground', *European Journal of International Relations* 3(3) (September 1997), 321–63. © Sage Publications Ltd, 1997.

'Ideological "Guerrillas" and the Quest for Technological Autonomy': Brazil's Domestic Computer Industry,' *International Organization* 40(3) (Summer 1986), 673–705. © MIT Press Journals, 1986.

'The Emergence of Cooperation: National Epistemic Communities and the International Evolution of the Idea of Nuclear Arms Control', *International Organization* 46(1) (Winter 1992), 101–45. © MIT Press Journals, 1992.

'Imagined (Security) Communities: Cognitive Regions in International Relations', *Millennium: Journal of International Studies* 26(2) (1997), 249–77. © Millennium, London School of Economics, 1997.

'Condition(s) of Peace', *Review of International Studies* 28(5) (1998), 165–92. © Cambridge University Press, 1998.

The lyrics to the song 'Winter of Seventy-Three' by Shmuel Hasfari, printed in chapter 10 of this volume, are reproduced with the permission of the copyright holders © Shmuel Hasfari and ACUM Ltd.

Part I
Introduction

1 Communities of practice in International Relations

This introduction, written especially for this volume, suggests a theoretical communitarian approach to International Relations, one whose foundations lie in the epistemic condition of social—and thus also international and transnational—life. Most of my published and still unpublished work has explicitly or implicitly followed such an approach. I begin this introduction by differentiating between analytical and normative communitarian approaches. Toward the end of the chapter I also propose ways to synthesize between them. I then introduce the concept of communities of practice, which, suggesting a unifying and comprehensive way of understanding the role of transnational communities in International Relations, helps explain how social learning occurs and how international and transnational practices evolve.

Introduction

The present volume, which contains both selected journal articles published over the past twenty years and previously unpublished material, highlights a constructivist approach to International Relations (IR). This approach emphasizes dynamic 'epistemic' features of international social reality and takes social learning as an attribute of 'communities of the like-minded.'[1] By focusing on social epistemology, the role of collective knowledge in international social life, and the communities in which knowledge originates and is then diffused, politically selected, and institutionalized, this approach helps explain where international practices and institutions—more broadly, global governance[2]—come from and why certain ideas congeal into human practices and institutions whereas others do not. The main thrust of this opening chapter, however, is to shed new light on the epistemic and communitarian IR constructivist school of thought by synthesizing the discipline's understanding of international and transnational communities and consolidating it around the concept of 'communities of practice.'[3]

Until a few years ago, a communitarian approach to IR existed mainly in the normative IR theoretical debate between cosmopolitans, most of whom hold a liberal theory of justice and employ a rationalist or individualist methodology,[4] and communitarians, who take communities, groups, and societies as the key to understanding moral action.[5] But ever since constructivism penetrated IR theory, the communitarian approach has become a leading contender in analytic IR theory.[6] Because constructivism highlights the dynamic role played by the social construction of knowledge in the construction of social reality,[7] the new turn to communitarian IR has meant, not only that political communities and their potential transformation are studied in more appropriate and global perspectives, but has also highlighted the 'community-shared background understandings, skills, and practical predispositions without which it would be impossible to interpret action, assign meaning, legitimate practices, empower agents, and constitute a differentiated highly structured social reality.'[8] In other words, the turn to communitarian IR is an attempt to make knowledge, along with the communities within which it develops and evolves and from which it diffuses, one of the leading ontological factors in the study of IR. For a communitarian IR approach, *knowledge* means not only information that people carry in their heads, but also, and primarily, the intersubjective background or context of expectations, dispositions, and language that gives meaning to material reality and consequently helps explain the constitutive and causal mechanisms that participate in the construction of social reality.

Not only is the new turn to communitarian IR, spurred by constructivism, enlivening and driving the quest for a synthesis of traditional cosmopolitan and communitarian approaches;[9] it is also making room for a more ambitious synthesis of normative IR theory and analytic IR theory. In a nutshell, because constructivism relies in part on an argument about the co-constitution and evolution of intersubjective social structures and agents,[10] a constructivist synthesis may avoid one of the problems that has divided cosmopolitans from communitarians; namely, whether agents or structures should be the starting point and focus. Communitarian IR may also help introduce to mainstream IR theory the role of knowledge communities, communities of discourse, and, more generally, 'communities of the like-minded' in the structuration[11] and dynamic evolution of social reality. Moreover, because a communitarian turn to IR theory accents the notion that similar if not identical ontological (structure and agency) and epistemological (truth, the nature of social knowledge) issues inform the disagreements and debates among normative IR theorists and among analytic IR theorists, communitarian IR could point to a synthesis that includes both normative IR theory and analytic IR theory. For example, Fearon and Wendt,[12] referring to the socially constructed nature of agents or subjects, and especially the notion that 'one cannot be a certain kind of subject … unless others in the society make it possible,' argue that the question of whether agents or structures are the starting point is not merely epistemological but 'ultimately a political question of whether society can be normatively grounded on the liberal conception of the individual as some kind of natural baseline.' Such a synthesis could accordingly be instrumental in grounding constructivism in political philosophy and in conferring on constructivism what it currently lacks most: a theory of politics. It also could provide normative IR theory with the ontological and epistemological tools for bridging the gap between the present reality and the desired human condition.

In the next section I will describe briefly the main characteristics and problems of communitarian approaches in general, and point out how the new strand of constructivist communitarian IR has tried to overcome their inherent problems. The second section describes and compares the normative communitarian IR approach and the newer analytic communitarian IR approach, which is informed by constructivism. Its main thrust is to trace the evolution of contemporary communitarianism in the IR literature, show that the debates between the different types of communitarianism (normative and analytic) are informed by similar ontological and epistemological issues, and argue that a synthesis is possible, not only between the parties to the normative and analytic debates, but also between normative and analytic communitarian approaches in IR theory. In the third section I portray the various communities and networks featured by the communitarian turn in IR—notably security communities,[13] epistemic communities,[14] and transnational advocacy networks[15]—as different interpretations of communities of practice. This section also briefly describes the community of practice concept as it applies to IR. In the fourth section I revisit our understanding of collective learning through the concept of communities of practice. I argue here that cognitive evolution is the type of collective learning that best describes the evolution of practices. The fifth section analyzes the main characteristics of communities of practice, including their epistemic and normative structure, the importance of identity for their existence and evolution, and their boundaries. This chapter winds up with a brief concluding section on a communitarian synthesis.

Communitarian approaches

Communitarian approaches may share some or all of the following attributes. First, human beings are members of multiple and sometimes overlapping communities, whose lowest common denominator consists of a shared identity or 'we-feeling,' shared values and norms, and face-to-face interactions—or, at least, a discourse, practice, moral conviction, or some combination thereof that is shared with other people and differentiates the group from other groups. Second, from an analytic perspective, a communitarian approach assumes that individuality and subjectivity depend on the social context[16] and, at the same time, that they contribute to the reproduction[17] and transformation[18] of communities. It also involves the notion that collective learning originates, takes place, and acquires its social import in communities of the like-minded. Furthermore, because individual cognition evolves together with intersubjective understandings, communities of the like-minded, which are the physical and practical instantiation of intersubjective understandings, constitute an ontological bridge between individuals and their ideas, on one side, and social structures and social systems, on the other.

From a normative perspective, a communitarian approach stresses the moral integrity of communities and the notion that, by becoming part of and identifying with communities, 'subjects are included within moral calculations or within the range of moral considerateness.'[19] Thus if, along with normative IR theorists, we take moral calculation or considerateness as one of several paths to individual and collective knowledge of the world and other people, and at the same time, along with (analytic-oriented) constructivists, we take social institutions as the result of the co-constitution of subjectivity and community by means of practice and discourse, it follows that we may also conceive of communities as fields of practice and discourse in which humans learn their social, political, and moral meanings and their capacity to act as social and moral agents.

Communitarian approaches, however, are not without problems.[20] They suffer from vagueness as to the nature, shape, and extent of the communities under study.[21] This problem is complicated by the notion that people simultaneously participate in various overlapping communities whose boundaries are sometimes indistinct. In addition, the argument that communities constitute individuals is not always made clearly.[22] What is constituted, individuals' identities and interests or the content of their thinking? If the latter, what room is left for subjective cognitive factors, such as individual beliefs, motives, and emotions? And even though it is true, as communitarians argue, that individuals enter a previously existing society and draw on its understandings to know how to be agents, society is nevertheless constituted by human beings. Hence, as in methodological individualism[23] and liberalism,[24] they must be taken as the basic units of analytic and moral inquiry. Again, communitarian approaches necessarily raise the prospect of relativism; that is, that values are relative to community and that truth exists only within communities. Finally, communitarian approaches emphasize the differences that divide people, rather than the physical, ideational, and moral factors that bring them together as humans.

These are serious criticisms that cannot be dismissed. What I hope to demonstrate in this book, however, is that the new communitarian turn in IR is aware of and receptive to most if not all of the above criticisms. What is more, constructivism aspires and to some extent has managed to find a middle ground[25] between a rationalist perspective that focuses on individuality and universality and an interpretive perspective that takes contextual knowledge, contingency, and human interpretation to be the hallmarks of social reality. This middle ground can be found in constructivists' attempts to highlight: (a) the role of agency (individuals and states) in the construction of social reality;[26] (b) the global or cosmopolitan context within which transnational communities develop;[27] (c) the importance of general normative principles that can be learned by communities through the logic of communicative argument and persuasion;[28] (d) the notion that even though, as Ashley[29] has argued, the practical community in IR may be the transnational community of realists, it is also true that in the last several decades a competing community of liberals has arisen (mainly in Europe) that opposes the realists and endeavors to make liberal international practice a self-understood reality; and (e) the argument that social practice[30] helps bridge between the ideational and discursive world and the material world.

Normative communitarian approaches and constructivist-led communitarianism in IR theory

Normative IR theory

The main question posed in the debate between cosmopolitans and communitarians in normative IR theory concerns the possibility of a moral community beyond the state and the qualities and characteristics of such a community [31] In liberal discourse, the question deals with the possibility of international justice and the debate is whether justice can be explained,[32] as it is by liberals,[33] from the perspective of individuals who rationally choose among neutral and universal principles of justice or, as it is by communitarians,[34] from a context-dependent perspective of differing cultures and communities.

Liberals, according to Morrice, 'stress individualism as against collectivism; self-interest as against the common good; government limited to protecting individual rights and liberties as against a strong state; and the role of the market and consumer choice rather than state regulation in the distribution of goods.'[35] Behind this political and economic doctrine lies liberalism's assumption that individuals possess 'an identity and value prior to, and independent of, society,'[36] its model of voluntary or contractual association or 'gesellschaft,'[37] and its commitment to explaining macro-social phenomena or 'wholes' in terms of micro-level phenomena or 'component parts' and of universal principles of causation or determination.[38] From a liberal perspective,[39] morality makes sense only within the bounds of a cosmopolitan and thus universal community of the human species, in which individuals make a rational choice to pursue universally applicable principles of justice. States are free to pursue their interests as they care to define them, but only as long as they abide by 'universal' (Western liberal) principles of justice.[40]

Communitarians, on the other hand, because they defend the view that the 'common good or community interest ... is greater than individual goods and interests,'[41] argue that justice is possible only within the boundaries of a differentiated community. This view, which usually means that individuals can fulfill themselves as moral subjects only within states, relies on several assumptions. First, 'communitarians argue that individuals are constituted by the communities in which they live, and [that] the values which influence individuals' behavior, together with the meanings by which they make sense of their lives, derive from their community.'[42] Second, the normative communitarian perspective rests on a notion of association based on solidarity or *gemeinschaft*.[43] Third, subjectivity and the content of individuals' beliefs do not exist in isolation from communities and their conventions.[44] Finally, social knowledge stresses interpretation over determination.[45] Although communitarians portray the state as the sphere in which moral community can best be expressed,[46] some communitarian IR scholars have argued that communities and citizenship may be able, through open dialogue and persuasion, to expand to the transnational level (or are already in the process of doing so).[47]

Despite the apparent differences between liberal cosmopolitanism and communitarianism, in practice it is difficult to establish a clear distinction between them.[48] For example, some communitarians accept the notion that moral community has a potential beyond the Westphalian state;[49] other communitarians stress the importance of the state for the evolution of a moral global community.[50] Post-modern communitarians like Richard Rorty[51] identify themselves as liberals but do not accept liberal individualist methodology and objective epistemology. Theorists of the English school[52] maintain that, at the international and global levels, common norms and values are mediated by conceptions of international society and world society, which represent a mixture of *gesellschaft* and *gemeinschaft* types of association.[53] In light of the problematic dichotomy[54] established by the debate between liberal cosmopolitans and communitarians, some scholars have sought a synthesis between the two approaches, which highlights individuals and universality on the one hand, and communities and particularity on the other. To show that a synthesis in normative IR theory is related and similar to the middle-ground analytic approach I advocate in this book, let us look briefly at attempts at such synthesis by Mervyn Frost and Richard Shapcott as well as by Mark Neufeld, Andrew Linklater, and Richard Ashley (all of them with a critical-theory orientation).

Relying on insights from analytic constructivist theory about the socially constructed nature of subjectivity, Frost used 'an universalized account of agency and subjectivity'[55] to argue that people reason and engage in moral argumentation when they participate in communities of discourse in which language and normative understandings are shared. According to Frost, individuals 'are constituted within a system of mutual recognition which includes within it the institutions of the family, civil society, the state and the system of sovereign states.'[56] Although the national society is the most important community for realization of the individual, the state, which is the highest form of community in which individual realization occurs, is also constituted intersubjectively within a society of states.[57] Thus, just as domestic communities help constitute the normative understanding of individuals within states, the community of states helps constitute normative discussion among states. From this perspective, a discourse of rights—which 'are envisaged as what people come to recognize one another as having within the context of a community with specified social and political institutions'[58]—and a discourse of sovereignty are complementary and together constitute the individual's subjectivity.

Shapcott has also tried to incorporate the best from liberal-cosmopolitan and communitarian conceptions into an approach that 'requires the attempt to conceive of the 'we' as a potential community of concrete agents engaged in a search for understanding.'[59] In Shapcott's view, expanding the boundaries of community to the universal level depends on a practice and ethics of communication that

> takes from the ... Kantian tradition the project of universal community, to treat all others in a moral fashion regardless of natural or communal boundaries. From the communitarian position it takes the premise that treating others in a moral fashion requires paying attention to their particularity and that such particularity may place (flexible) limits on the possible 'thickness' of any larger community.[60]

Following H. G. Gadamer's hermeneutic account of communication,[61] Shapcott's synthesis holds that mutual recognition, taken to be the key to justice, is most successfully achieved through acts of communication and understanding. A generalized practice of communication and conversation may make it possible to expand the community to the universal level, with no need to diminish or eliminate 'the other' in the process. While communication may not be able to achieve universal community, to which liberals aspire,[62] by achieving mutual recognition, it may still create a community thick enough to solve the problem of justice in world politics. Moreover, inasmuch as Shapcott's approach[63] suggests the possibility of expanding the realms in which conversation and learning can take place and reason be applied to the universal level (on which just relations founded on mutual recognition are based), it addresses the important notion that creating a cosmopolitan order that does not exclude membership in particular communities is predicated on the evolution of community practice and discourse.

Probably more than any other approach, critical theory has left its mark by attempting to build a synthesis based on both cosmopolitan and communitarian considerations. For example, Neufeld defended the Aristotelian view that the normative task in IR is to enlarge the *polis*—a political space within which the 'good life' can take place through persuasion and through the pursuit of liberty and equality—to the global level.[64]

Andrew Linklater,[65] probably the theorist who has gone the farthest toward a compromise between cosmopolitan and communitarian approaches, argues that the 'key problem of community in IR is how to promote universality which respects difference, and how to give expression to cultural differences without encouraging and unleashing extreme particularism.'[66] In his view, achieving this requires reconstitution of political community by a learning process that involves open dialogue.[67] Far from being utopian, this process may have already begun. Globalization-led pacification in the industrial world and increased sensitivity to the moral problem of the use of force show that like-mindedness can become the basis of political community at the international and transnational levels.[68] These developments point in the direction of the expansion of community and citizenship and of the concomitant transfer of authority to the transnational and sub-national levels.[69]

Linklater, who follows Jürgen Habermas' critical approach,[70] in which communicative action makes the existence of a universal dialogical community possible, considers that a 'post-Westphalian cosmopolitan community' will be 'constituted discursively as one in which all humans have the opportunity for equal participation in a conversation, and thereby of determining their own lives.'[71] Thus, according to Linklater, 'a post-Westphalian framework can develop where like-minded societies are keen to establish closer forms of political cooperation to integrate shared ethical norms into the structure of social and political life.'[72] Linklater's critical approach further exemplifies the crucial importance of community in IR. Not only do learning and the fixation of meaning occur within expanding communities of discourse and practice; what is more, a cosmopolitan order may be achieved thanks to the transformation of political community at the transnational and sub-national levels.

One of the earliest (and most successful) attempts by critical theorists to change the terms of the normative debate in IR was Ashley's argument that the sole existing international community is the community of realist practitioners. Its members accept the Western rationalist conception of community as universal and timeless, while denying the possibility of its existence at the international level, thus denying their own existence and identity as a real and practical transnational realist community. According to Ashley, the

> dominant mode of international political community is already present … in the dispositions, techniques, skills, and rituals of realist power politics. It is present, in other words, on the surface of a transnational discourse of power politics whose every breath denies the positivity of international community as such. That we do not or cannot recognize it as international community is not proof of international community's absence. It is a testament to the power of a realist community of statesmanship.[73]

Thus the challenge faced by critical theory is to emancipate the theory and practice of the 'double move' of realist practitioners and to move toward international (security) communities, which can advance the cause of justice and peace. In addition to his critical-theory message, Ashley has made points that are of profound importance for communitarian IR; namely, that transnational or international communities are communities in, and of, *practice*, that there can be more than one transnational or international community, that transnational or international communities carry the collective understandings that may eventually become the patrimony of all mankind, and that they are accordingly learning communities. It is from this practical, contextual, and discursive perspective that we can reasonably consider the possibility of the evolution of a liberal community of practitioners to universal proportions.

Constructivism and the analytic move to communitarian IR

Constructivism describes the dynamic, contingent, and culturally based condition of the social world. Unlike positivism[74] and materialism,[75] which take the world as it is, constructivism sees the world as a project under construction, as *becoming* rather than *being*. Unlike idealism[76] and post-structuralism and post-modernism,[77] which take the world *only* as it can be imagined or talked about, constructivism accepts that not all statements have the same epistemic value and consequently that there is some foundation for knowledge.

Constructivism stresses the reciprocal relationship between nature and human knowledge. It suggests a view of the social sciences that is contingent, partly indeterminate, nominalist,[78] and to some extent externally validated.[79] All strands of constructivism converge in an *ontology* that depicts the social world as intersubjectively and collectively meaningful structures and processes. In this world, subjectivity is constituted by social structures; consequently, 'material resources only acquire meaning for human action through the structure of shared knowledge in which they are embedded.'[80] This means that social facts, because they depend on the attachment of collective meaning to physical reality and thus on human consciousness and language, are real objective facts only by human agreement.[81] It also means that, although individuals carry knowledge, ideas, and meanings in their heads, they also know, think, and feel only in the context of and with reference to collective or intersubjective understandings, including rules and language.

Constructivists consider the mutual constitution of agents and structures, or structuration, to be part of constructivism's ontology. Structuration theory, as sustained by the principle of the 'duality of structure,' maintains that 'structures, as rules and resources, are both the precondition and the unintended outcome of people's agency. ... People draw upon structures to proceed in their daily interaction.'[82] Thus, when people act, they reproduce these structures. 'Structure allows for agency, which in turn makes for the unintended reproduction of the very same structures.'[83] Unlike structuration, the theory of cognitive evolution, which I feature in this book, is not only about the co-reproduction of agents and structures, in a vicious circle, but is also about transformation—in particular, the institutionalization of novel ideas and knowledge as social practices. The key point to remember about the co-constitution of agents and structures, however, whether in the structuration or the cognitive-evolution version, is that it occurs in and through practice. Communities of practice, therefore, play a crucial role in the mutual constitution of agents and structures.

Constructivists share, at least to some extent, an *epistemology* in which interpretation is an intrinsic part of the social sciences and emphasizes contingent generalizations. Contingent generalizations do not freeze understanding or bring it to closure; rather, they open up our understanding of the social world. Moreover, most constructivists agree that, even if it were possible to grasp social reality's minimalist foundations and thereby inch toward truth, theories would remain far from being true pictures of the world.

In addition, constructivists eschew the 'methodological individualism' on which most other approaches to politics are based—for example, rational choice, bureaucratic politics, social-psychological decision-making models, and so on—which reduces political analysis to its micro foundations, i.e., individuals and their relationships. Instead, constructivists adopt the 'methodological holistic'[84] view that individuals' identities and interests do not make sense outside the communities to which they belong and thus apart from the collective understandings, discourse, and practice by virtue of which communities exist and their members' subjectivities are constituted. Taking a methodological holistic view also means not only searching for causal mechanisms (e.g., socialization) that enter into the construction of social reality, but also, and in particular, establishing the 'conditions of possibility for objects and events by showing what they are made of and how they are organized. As such, the object or event in question is an "effect of the conditions that make it possible, but it does not exist independent of them,"'[85] as in causal theory.

This ontology and epistemology shapes distinctive features of the constructivist approach. First, constructivism considers communities' inter-subjective knowledge and ideas to have constitutive effects on social reality and its evolution. When individuals draw on collective understandings and discourse to give meaning to the material world, consciousness is awakened, reasons emerge, and people act intentionally on behalf of these reasons.

Second, constructivism does not share the conservative outlook with which the communitarian normative view is usually identified. On the contrary, constructivism takes a dynamic view of social life in which new practices, institutions, identities, and interests emerge with new constitutive rules[86] and newly evolving social structures.[87] Moreover, constructivism's attention to sociocognitive changes, along with its critical theory component,[88] emphasizes the notion that the study of change, including change for the better,[89] is central to the constructivist research program.

Third, constructivists do not accept the notion that rationality means only instrumental rationality.[90] As a result, they advance the notion of *practical* or *communicative rationality*, which, though sometimes calculating and choice-related, is also sensitive to historical, social, and normative contexts and emphasizes the communicative and persuasion logic of social theory.

Fourth, constructivism takes language as the vehicle for the diffusion and institutionalization of ideas within and between communities, as a necessary condition for the persistence over time of institutionalized practices, and as a mechanism for the construction of social reality. Moreover, the communities around which knowledge evolves, which play a crucial role in the construction of social reality, are constituted by language. First and foremost, therefore, they are 'communities of discourse'; that is, 'communities of competing producers, of interpreters and critics, of audiences and consumers, and of patrons and other significant actors who become the subject of discourse itself. It is only in these concrete living and breathing communities that discourse becomes meaningful.'[91] Thus discourse and practice cannot easily be separated.[92]

Constructivism and normative communitarian IR compared

Eight differences can be enumerated between constructivism and the normative communitarian approach. First, unlike the latter, constructivism is agnostic about whether there is a community interest that is greater than the individual interest and whether the state should uphold this common good rather than remain neutral.[93] Instead, constructivism takes community interests and individual interests as ontologically complementary; that is, community interests require the fulfillment of individuals' interests and vice versa.

Second, the analytic community turn does not establish the priority of good over right, or vice versa. It posits rather that good and right are mutually constituted and inseparable.

Third, although the two communitarian approaches share the epistemological view that objectivity is unachievable and that the epistemological task accordingly depends on interpretation rather than proof, constructivism adopts the notion that pragmatic and contingent knowledge is achievable and desirable and that, in association with conditions that can be clearly specified and understood, the communities within which knowledge develops may become transnational or even global.

Fourth, constructivism has yet to provide clear statements about the quality and content of the knowledge that enters into the construction of social reality and about whether the construction of governance institutions and practices should aim, as Hedley Bull[94] argued, at maintaining international order or, as Beitz[95] held, at achieving global justice. On the other hand, it has been developing the analytical tools—dealing, for example, with causal socialization and constitutive mechanisms involving narratives,[96] discourse,[97] and practice[98]—without which it would be difficult for normative IR theorists to envision a way to bridge between the present situation and a desired future reality.

Fifth, constructivism's community turn is more explicit than was the 'old' communitarianism about the role of power in changing the international and transnational reality. By 'power' I mean not only the possession of material capabilities, but also the ability to impose meanings, status, or functions on material objects by collective agreement. One can also find power in speech acts,[99] hegemonic discourses,[100] dominant normative interpretations and identities,[101] and moral authority.[102]

Sixth, constructivism takes the possibility of moral dialogue and communication as part of a wider and intricate process of social communication through which community meanings are selected and institutionalized. Through social communication, communities expand and enlarge their membership, perhaps to global proportions. Expanding community provides a foundation for the diffusion of normative and political principles and thus for the achievement of normative cosmopolitan objectives.

Seventh, unlike the normative communitarian project, which privileges differences of national identity, the new community turn points to the dynamic attributes of identity, which may lead to the creation of transnational identities and security communities[103] of various sizes and composition. Moreover, constructivism emphasizes humanity's common traits, such as trust and learning, which can trigger the development of security communities. Although people may not trust other people, under certain conditions they can probably recognize one another as potentially trustworthy and capable of trusting.

Finally, although the construction of social reality entails a community or *gemeinschaft* type of association, in which people are bound by solidarity links and 'we-feeling,'[104] as in the oft-cited 'logic of appropriateness,'[105] constructivism also highlights conditions that make certain contractual or *gesellschaft* types of association possible, as well as the role of self-interested purposeful actions aimed at constructing social reality in ways that serve instrumental goals.

New communitarian IR: communities of practice

With the help of the concept of communities of practice, I endeavor to make explicit what constructivists have so far left mostly implicit; namely, that IR constructivism is not only a sociological critique of rational choice approaches or a synonym for norm-oriented research, but also the epistemological and ontological foundation of a reformulated IR 'communitarian approach.' This approach does not herald the end of the nation-state or underscore the unimportance of individuals and agency in international life. Rather, it argues that what mediate between state, individuals, and human agency, on the one hand, and social structures and systems, on the other, are communities of practice.

The IR literature includes various interpretations of communities of practice: 'epistemic communities'[106] and 'security communities,'[107] which I have studied in the past, as well as 'transnational advocacy networks'[108] 'networks of knowledge and practice,'[109] 'critical communities,'[110] and 'communities of discourse.'[111] Other communities described in the social sciences may be taken as conceptual variants of communities of practice. These include 'imagined communities'[112] in political science, 'communities of print'[113] in sociology, and 'interpretive communities' in literary studies[114] and legal studies.[115]

Communities of practice

Communities of practice 'consist of people who are informally as well as contextually bound by a shared interest in learning and applying a common practice.'[116] More specifically, they are a configuration of a *domain of knowledge*, which constitutes like-mindedness, a *community of people*, which 'creates the social fabric of learning,' and a *shared practice*, which embodies 'the knowledge the community develops, shares, and maintains.'[117] The knowledge domain endows practitioners with a sense of *joint enterprise* that is constantly being renegotiated by its members. People function as a community through relationships of *mutual engagement* that bind 'members together into a social entity.' Shared practices, in turn, are sustained by a *repertoire of communal resources*, such as routines, words, tools, ways of doing things, stories, symbols, and discourse.[118]

'Communities of practice,' says Wenger, 'are everywhere. We all belong to a number of them—at work, school, at home, in our hobbies. Some have a name, some don't. We are core members of some and we belong to others more peripherally.'[119] Moreover, communities of practice have no fixed membership; people 'move in and out' of them.[120] Wenger, who, together with anthropologist Jean Lave, introduced the concept of community of practice more than a decade ago,[121] has dealt mainly with domestic or national communities of practice. There is no reason, however, why we should not be able to identify transnational or even global communities of practice. The closer we get to the level of practices, in fact, the more we can take the international system as a collection of communities of practice; for example, communities of diplomats, of traders, of environmentalists, and of human-rights activists.

Communities of practice cut across state boundaries and mediate between states, individuals, and human agency, on one hand, and social structures and systems, on the other. It is within communities of practice that collective meanings emerge, discourses become established, identities are fixed, learning takes place, new political agendas arise, and the institutions and practices of global governance grow. Communities of practice are not international actors in any formal sense, but coexist and overlap with them. In fact, state and other non-state actors do or practice what communities of practice first bring to collective consciousness and attention. Because people do what they do partly because of the 'communities of practice' they happen to form and sustain, when communities of practice expand across institutional and national boundaries, their own intersubjective knowledge and identity help structure an ever-larger share of people's intentional acts at the regional or global level, thereby sustaining practices that are institutionalized across time and space. Normative ideas diffuse the same way. Hence explaining the evolution of practices and institutions requires identifying how, in and through communities of practice, ideas become attached to physical objects, are diffused across national borders, and, after having been subjected to authoritative cultural and political selection, become discursively and institutionally established.

Any discussion of communities of practice raises several obvious points about structure and agency, change and stability, and boundaries.

First, communities of practice are intersubjective social structures within which meaning is fixed, learning takes place, and practices evolve. Because they are structures, communities of practice constitute the normative and epistemic ground for reasoned political action. At the same time, communities of practice are also agents, consisting of real people who affect the course of political, economic, and social events via network channels, across national borders, over organizational divides, and in the halls of government. Therefore, when IR scholars study communities of practice they have a firm basis in actual communities of people, their material and institutional resources, and their reasoned actions.

Second, as persistent patterns or structures, communities of practice retain their collective understandings, despite the constant turnover of members, as long as social learning and evolutionary processes do not lead to the replacement of the patterns or structures.

Third, the boundaries of practices are directly related to the scope of the community's expansion.

Epistemic communities, security communities, critical communities, and global policy networks as communities of practice

Most of the transnational communities described in the IR literature—for example, epistemic communities, security communities, and critical communities—are in fact species of communities of practice. The argument that security communities[122] are communities of practice is simple but noteworthy. To understand this argument, however, we must begin by viewing security communities as transnational regions whose members/inhabitants *practice* peaceful change; in other words, whose collective understanding that conflicts in the region should be solved by peaceful means and that the use of force has become unimaginable has been internalized by individuals and embedded in practices. From this perspective, peace is neither the absence of war, as realists maintain, nor an idealistic goal to which nation-states aspire but never achieve. Rather, peace is the practice of a security community. In other words, security communities are communities whose members have learned to practice peaceful change, have internalized a peaceful identity (unlike the 'other fellows out there,' who make war), and who accordingly practice peace. Security communities are marked by a domain of knowledge, a community of people, shared practices, and a sense of joint enterprise, all of them sustained by a repertoire of ideational and material communal resources.

The concept of epistemic community makes little sense unless it is understood as a vehicle of new scientific interpretations that serve as the basis for the construction of new practices. Although all communities of practice engage in knowledge exchange, diffusion, selection, and institutionalization, not all of them also engage in knowledge validation.[123] Hence epistemic communities should be considered to be a special kind of community of practice. Epistemic communities are actors or agents; they make things happen. But they are also communities of practice, which, starting from small and local beginnings—sometimes only a few persons—may expand to global proportions (e.g., the ban on landmines[124]), thus becoming a vehicle for global consciousness and practices.

Epistemic communities are important not only as catalysts of change in political behavior or as the workers of 'policy coordination' between states.[125] Rather, their most far-reaching effect is cognitive evolution, i.e., the constitution of new practices that may be used by both present and future generations of practitioners and may constitute the basis of the transformation of the identities and interests of an increasing number of people.

Like all other communities of practice, epistemic communities bargain about meanings and thus socially construct knowledge, including scientific knowledge. In fact, the interesting question about epistemic communities is not whether the scientific knowledge on which they base their action is objectively true: much of what passes for the scientific knowledge of epistemic communities can hardly be considered objective, because it is usually amalgamated with social knowledge that can rarely allege truthfulness. The interesting question is this: what difference does it make for political and social reality that the socially constructed knowledge applied to reality by communities of practice is scientific—i.e., produced in the laboratory by people wearing white coats and enjoying firm social legitimacy—rather than normative or ideological?

If we want to think about epistemic communities as communities of practice, then we should view science not only as understandings of cause–effect relationships in nature, but also as a constitutive norm that socially constructs the practices, identities, and interests of modern rulers. Consequently, modern rulers rely increasingly on science not so much out of calculated choice but rather because science has become part of their modern identity. On those occasions when epistemic communities diffuse, through the institutions of state and society, a new scientific orthodoxy—for example, about the global environment—both the new norms and their carriers may help work a transformation of environmental practices, identities, and interests.

All of this means that the difference between epistemic communities and what Rochon has called 'critical communities'[126] is one of emphasis rather than of substance. According to Rochon, the main differences between critical communities and epistemic communities are that the former help develop alternative knowledge frameworks, may increase policy uncertainty, and do not exhibit some of the formal and informal links characteristic of epistemic communities.[127] Epistemic communities, however, are also 'critical,' because their members act with the conviction that their actions will change something in the world for the better, making it more just or more efficient. In fact, both epistemic communities and critical communities are communities of practice, because they are characterized by social communication, learning, and the construction of new identities around particular practices.

It is social communication—i.e., the transmission of meanings,[128] rather than the mere transmission of information—that allows communities of practice to evolve and interact with other communities. This feature helps differentiate communities of practice from networks. Whereas networks are the interpersonal, intergroup, and inter-organizational relationships through which information flows, communities of practice, in addition to their networking capacity, also involve social communication through which practitioners bargain about and fix meanings and develop their own distinctive identity and how to practice it.[129]

So a case can be made that distinctive types of transnational networks that have been prominently featured in the IR literature, such as 'global public policy networks'[130] and TANs,[131] are also communities of practice[132] whose identity derives from their capacity for learning, social communication processes, and practices. For example, the Global Development Network, a global association of researchers, think tanks, and other institutions, established by the World Bank around the idea of promoting global development,[133] is in the business not only of transmitting information, but also of teaching economic development practices to people in developing societies, who lack the knowledge required to engage in these practices.

Moreover, TANs are really communities of practice because a knowledge domain—for example, human rights—constitutes their like-mindedness and practices. True, the network metaphor lends itself to describing how otherwise unrelated units or actors interrelate and are mobilized by and for a common purpose.[134] But TANs consist of individuals, who converge on governmental offices, street rallies, and Internet chats not only because of what they believe, but also because of what *they do*, sometimes in close personal interaction.

Second, the practices of TANs are sustained by a repertoire of communal resources and their members have a sense of joint enterprise.

Third, as with epistemic communities, TANs are not only agents that persuade or socialize other agents to see the world their way; they are also the builders of an 'episteme'[135] on which future agents will draw to get their bearings. Fourth, TANs 'influence discourse, procedures, and policy' by becoming part 'of larger policy communities that group actors working on an issue from a variety of institutional perspectives.'[136] Finally, because TANs can 'talk' only about, rather than for, science, their growth and expansion must include scientific experts who lend scientific legitimacy to their norms.

Communities of practice and collective learning in a social context

According to Richard McDermott,

> knowledge belongs to communities. The idea that knowledge is the stuff 'between the ears of the individual' is a myth. We don't learn on our own. We are born into a world already full of knowledge, a world that already makes sense to other people. ... We learn by participating in these communities and come to embody the ideas, perspectives, prejudices, language, and practices of that community.[137]

In the following pages I will show how this view can contribute to our understanding of social change in general and of IR change in particular. I will argue that learning occurs in and by means of communities of practice. Construing practices[138] as a learning process makes communities of practice emergent structures, which, 'neither inherently stable nor randomly changeable,'[139] evolve with new knowledge, discourses, and identities. The reified products of communities of practice, such as diplomatic practices, warfare practices, global financial practices, and transnational human-rights practices, cannot be separated from the learning processes that produced them.[140]

There are almost as many understandings and definitions of learning as there are dimensions and factors that enter into the constitution of social action and social change.[141] It is not surprising, therefore, that few concepts in the social sciences are as contested and multifaceted as learning.

Most common is the *'bucket' view of learning*,[142] in which people add knowledge and skills to the mind as if it were a bucket.

From a behaviorist perspective, learning means both: (1) modification of behavior in response to some stimulus or change in the environment; and (2) selective reinforcement. This, in brief, is how IR realists and rational choice scholars view learning—as the responses by states to environmental changes or as an adjustment of their behavior to suit changes in the pay-off matrix.[143]

Trial-and-error learning amounts to a variation of the same 'tune'; people learn as a result of failed behaviors.[144]

Learning-by-doing (or Bayesian learning) emphasizes the ability of people to modify a course of action on the basis of experience.[145]

Although its name may indicate otherwise, *social learning* emphasizes individual social-psychological changes, the result of people's interactions with other people.[146] Although the most popular *psychological* understanding of learning in IR has been as changes in individual beliefs,[147] a *cognitive* learning perspective, which focuses on changes in cognitive structures and their effects on information processing, has been making inroads in recent decades.[148] Closely connected to the latter perspective is *constructivist* learning, an approach made famous by Jean Piaget.[149] This emphasizes how people construct new mental structures when they interact with their environment.

Sociological learning perspectives have highlighted socialization and organizations. *Socialization-based learning*,[150] which IR constructivists have used lately,[151] focuses 'on the acquisition of membership by newcomers within a functionalist framework, where acquiring membership is defined as internalizing the norms of a social group.'[152] The view that people are socialized and in fact persuaded when they interact and argue with other people assumes a mechanism by which ideas somehow jump from mind to mind. *Organizational* learning theories 'concern themselves both with the ways individuals learn in organizational contexts and with the ways in which organizations can be said to learn as organizations.'[153] Even here, however, scholars treat organizations as if they were individuals or an aggregation of individuals.[154]

It follows that none of these conceptions of learning is truly collective or social. None of them takes learning as a change in background knowledge, which, residing not only in people's minds, but also in human practices, constitutes the communities people belong to, as well as their identities.

Hence the notion of communities of practice may shed new light on processes of social change in general and on the concept of learning in particular. In short, learning means participation in[155] and engagement with the meanings, identities, and language of communities of practice and their members.[156] To put this another way, learning is 'what changes our ability to engage in practice, the understanding of why we engage in it, and the resources we have at our disposal to do so.'[157]

For individuals, learning means redefining reality by means of contextual 'community' knowledge, from which they borrow in order to get their bearings. Practitioners arrive at their outlook and do what they do, consciously and knowledgeably, because they draw upon the community's collective knowledge. They also contribute to the practices of their communities.[158] As such, individuals acquire their knowledge when they learn to participate in the knowledge of others.

From the perspective of a community of practice, learning means the evolution of background knowledge (intersubjective knowledge and discourse that adopt the form of human dispositions and practices) or the substitution of one set of conceptual categories that people use to give meaning to reality for another such set. Learning thus requires the creation, diffusion, selection, and institutionalization of new knowledge. It takes place as a result not only of the internalization of new knowledge by individuals, but also, and mainly, when a growing number of individuals become acquainted with and disposed to use a new practice. Thus understood, we may see organizations as the venues used by members of communities of practice in order to institutionalize their practices.

This interpretation of social learning has a number of implications. First, although social change begins and takes place in people's minds, it also resides in and is an attribute of the background knowledge that constitutes communities of practice and their specific practices. As the background knowledge on which individuals draw changes, they modify their understandings of reality and their discourse and thus may be able to participate in new practices. Communities of practice thereby help create, diffuse, select, and institutionalize knowledge that becomes the background of new practices. To put this another way, when individuals draw on background knowledge that has cognitively evolved, their dispositions and skills—indeed, their practices and behavior—also evolve. Preferences in general and national interests in particular are socially constructed on the basis of what communities of practice have become through learning.

Second, a 'communitarian' interpretation of social learning also means that not only present-day but also future individuals can draw upon an evolving structure of background knowledge in order to formulate their own individual expectations, dispositions, and intentional acts. This means that the capacity for rational thought and behavior is not only an individual, but also and above all a background, capacity.[159] Rationality lies less in the act of instrumental choice between alternatives on the basis of true theories than in acting in ways that 'stand to reason' given people's background expectations and dispositions.

Third, most of the background knowledge that ends up informing individuals how to organize political units, what goals they should pursue, what rules of engagement should exist between them, and so on, begins as critical knowledge generated by communities of practice, sometimes quite small, which then expand, sometimes to global proportions. In proportion as a community of practice has more members and its selectively retained institutionalized collective knowledge is taken for granted, knowledge is increasingly represented in the material world as practices and these practices selectively survive in individuals' minds. I call this interpretation of social learning *cognitive evolution*.

Cognitive evolution may be defined as a collective learning process that constitutes the practices of social and political communities. In contrast to the individual-oriented concepts of 'learning' I have reviewed above, cognitive evolution takes social change as the innovation, diffusion, political selection, and institutionalization of collective intersubjective structures or 'epistemes,'[160] which congeal in human practices and constitute agents' transformed expectations and dispositions to act. Cognitive evolution, therefore, means not only learning something new, but also altering 'the conceptual categories with which we give meaning to reality. ... What was unthinkable is now seen as thinkable.'[161] Thus, we can best understand the innovation, diffusion, political selection, and institutionalization of collective understandings as the growth or expansion across time and space of communities of practice. To become international practices and constitute national interests, ideas must not only be granted social legitimization and taken as part of 'the natural order' within states; they must first gain control over communities of practice and the institutional and material resources associated with them.

The main characteristics of communities of practice

To better understand communities of practice as learning communities and the role they play in cognitive evolution we should describe their main characteristics. The following discussion, however, is no more than a first step in the conceptualization of communities of practice in IR. For it is one thing to describe and explain, for example, the evolution of claim processors[162] and another to show how global anti-terrorist practices evolve around one or several (probably competing) communities of practice. Hence this introductory description will have to be supplemented not only by additional theoretical analysis, but also by empirical research. In a few places I will illustrate some of my conceptual points with examples drawn from global governance practices, especially international security.

The epistemic and normative nature of communities of practice

The joint enterprise of members of a community of practice does not necessarily mean a common goal or vision, although in most cases it does. 'In fact, in some communities, disagreement can be viewed as a productive part of the enterprise.'[163] Members of a community of practice, however, must share collective understandings that tell their members what they are doing and why. In some cases, as in epistemic communities, the episteme may be primarily scientific. In other cases, such as TANs and security communities, the episteme may be primarily normative. At the same time, communities of practice may be either national or transnational, which can make for interesting combinations. In chapter 5, for example, I describe national communities of practice that I call 'anti-dependency guerrillas.' Drawing on an episteme that combines technical and normative, as well as tacit and explicit, knowledge, intellectual 'guerrillas' created the necessary conditions for the development of the technological and industrial sector in Argentina and Brazil. Chapter 6 describes a community of US strategic and arms control experts whose cause-and-effect and normative interpretation of the arms race was transmitted to the Soviet Union, thus creating the structural basis for arms control treaties during détente and, eventually, the end of the Cold War. Chapters 7 and 8 describe security communities that, being transnational and constituted primarily around a normative episteme, help explain the stable peace in Europe since World War II and the nature of the practices that Europe is now keen to apply in the Mediterranean region.

Although peace, happiness, and harmony need not characterize communities of practice[164]—which are neither necessarily about good practices nor about socially deplorable practices—some global-governance communities of practice have cognitively evolved to practice 'good practices.'[165] In this respect communities of practice, which embody collective understandings of fairness and legitimacy, differ from epistemic communities and TANs and may accordingly be called 'communities of (good) practice.' In recent years, with the aim of empowering communities in the Third World, communities of good practice have developed within the World Bank, which has actually adopted the term 'communities of practice.'[166] The practices of these communities not only embody a moral critique of the status quo, they also turn fairness, responsibility, and justice into self-evident reasons for action. Although to date the discourse of good practice has been restricted mainly to international political economy, it would not be difficult to find a desire for practices that are not only efficient, but also fair and legitimate, in the security field. For example, cooperative security practices,[167] which developed in the last fifteen years in Europe and later in other regions, are intended not only to enhance state security most efficiently, but also, and primarily, to achieve a level of human security and international cooperation that is based on mutual accountability and transparency, mutual responsibility, and fairness.

Identity

According to Wenger, building an identity 'consists of negotiating the meanings of our experience of membership in social communities,'[168] which is achieved mainly through processes of engagement,[169] imagination,[170] and alignment.[171] Engagement is what allows individuals to conform to the norms of the community and to negotiate their participation in it. Imagination allows its members to link their experience with that of others. Alignment, in turn, allows them to combine their material and ideational resources for the sake of what they jointly practice. Regardless of other types of identification practitioners may have with, for example, their family or nation, their engagement in a common practice makes them share an identity and feel as a 'we.' At times, some very strange bedfellows may align themselves to create a 'we.' A movement such as environmentalism, for instance, is constituted by a collection of motivations, beliefs, and passions that may have different origins for different participants. Yet the act of imagination, which leads disparate groups of people—such as scientists, holistic fundamentalists, and anti-globalization demonstrators—to believe they are a 'we,' and alignment behind the idea of preserving the environment created a vast community united by a common purpose.[172] As communities of practice grow or diminish, members' joint notion of 'we'—who is inside and who is outside—also expands or contracts. Forty years ago, one could find only the seeds of global environmental practices, and only in a few developed countries in North America and Europe. Today, global environmental practices reach all corners of the world and there is hardly a state that does not have a ministry of environmental affairs.

Boundaries

People belong to many communities of practice; some of them overlap, while others stand in a hierarchical relationship. Since the boundaries of communities of practice are determined by people's knowledge and identity and the discourse associated with a specific practice, communities of practice are not necessarily 'congruent with the reified structures of institutional affiliations, divisions and boundaries.'[173] For example, although members of a security community, who practice cooperative security, may not share the same national or bureaucratic allegiances and may never meet one another, they nonetheless all know about Confidence Building Measures (CBMs) or multilateral humanitarian intervention, talk the language of cooperative security, identify with other practitioners who talk the way they do, and apply their knowledge when considering courses of action.

As boundaries form in and around practice,[174] communities of practice link up with their social environments and with other communities of practice. For example, in order to halt the flow of money used by global terrorist networks, security strategists cooperate with banking communities to develop capital-transfer practices and money-laundering controls. We may be able to document overlapping communities of practice—such as diplomats and security analysts or brokers and financial consultants—that produce distinctive community constellations,[175] as in the security field. The practice of cooperative security in Europe, for instance, helps sustain a contemporary constellation of regional military, economic, political, and cultural practices. Moreover, communities of practice may be hierarchically related to one another. For example, during the Cold War, the nuclear-arms control community was embedded in a community of nuclear deterrence practice.[176]

Structure

Communities of practice may be viewed as being composed of three concentric circles.[177] Practices are brought into existence in the first or inner circle. For example, a look at cooperative security and the role of the Conference on Security and Cooperation in Europe (CSCE) in the evolution of this practice shows that the Helsinki Final Act and subsequent normative injunctions and practices, such as CBMs, were developed in the inner circle of CSCE practitioners. In an intermediate circle we find people, who, due to expertise or normative commitment, help diffuse the practice. This would include the CSCE experts, the Helsinki Human Rights groups, and European political leaders, who assimilated cooperative practices, diffused them more widely, and brought them to their respective domestic systems.[178] The outer circle is made up of all those experts, practitioners, and activists who adopt and help implement such practices beyond their original functional and geographical boundaries. In our case, this includes people from the North Atlantic Treaty Organization (NATO), the Association of Southeast Asian Nations (ASEAN), and the Euro-Mediterranean Partnership (EMP) or Barcelona Process. Hence the expansion of communities of practices may also be understood as their centrifugal enlargement from the core outward.

Some communities of practice are tightly coupled; practitioners know one another personally and their practices are confined to a specific action. For example, UN weapons inspectors all know one other and their practices are well defined and localized. Other communities of practice—for example, cooperative security—are loosely coupled. Few practitioners know one another, they perform a plethora of distinct activities, and the boundaries of their community are likely to transcend organizational lines.

Agency

Although individuals' reasons, dispositions, and intentional acts are partly derived from the intersubjective understandings of communities of practice, they are not determined by them. More often than not, people act purposefully, with judgment and emotional drive on the basis of beliefs and interpretations of reality. This is why individuals' actions often surprise us. To put this another way, reasons are sensitive to interpretation and reflexivity. This means that reasons do not spring directly from the material world, but from the meaning, value, and function with which material objects are endowed. What agents think they are doing must be a cause of what they actually do.[179] But what they actually think they are doing and, thus, what they do is constituted or made possible by the episteme.

Power, governance, and authority

It is as members of communities of practice that people exercise one of the highest forms of power: determining the meanings and discourses that produce social practices. Because the meanings and discourses of communities of practice are negotiable, when practitioners negotiate meanings and discourse they also exercise power. For example, what does cooperative security mean? The answer is that it means different things to different people. Academics, members of regional security organizations, diplomats, and journalists who have been involved in an incipient cooperative security community of practice over the last fifteen years bargain about the meanings of cooperative security. This bargaining, however, has not been an academic exercise. Practitioners who were able to set the meanings of regional and global security for international organizations such as NATO, the European

Union, and the Organization for Security and Cooperation in Europe exercised one of the highest forms of power.

The exercise of power in communities of practice is mainly an issue of authority and, ultimately, of governance. Paul Miller has recently argued that governance within communities of practice can be traced to norms, the coupling of impersonal and personal authority, and trust. As communities expand, norms and identities also expand, thus creating the cognitive alignment between the personal and community purposes of an increasing number of practitioners across space and time. More specifically, shared norms facilitate the cognitive alignment of practitioners during processes of norm selection and coordinate the evolution of norms.[180]

Because norm-based governance has its limitations, however, personal agency and authority, which rely on trust, may influence social communication and affect the twin processes of norm selection and norm evolution.[181] Personal authority enters through roles and positions in a bureaucratic and policy hierarchy. Thus the addition of key decision-makers to communities of practice can turn the knowledge, identity, and social learning of an otherwise small and localized community of practice into a national interest. As communities of practice expand and 'induct' policymakers into their ranks, the material and organizational resources and political power of policymakers become part of the repertoire of expanded communities of practice, which structure the practice of entire bureaucracies, governments, nation-states, and international coalitions. Personal authority also enters through agents' ability to affect the environment in ways that makes it more conducive to the expansion and evolution of communities of practice. This ability can (but need not) be correlated with bureaucratic or political power. But it may also be related to intellectual innovation, the diffusion of ideas through the mass media, economic entrepreneurship, and the shaping of public opinion.

Interest

It would be wrong to think that the different types of communities of practice I have described above are functional and nonpolitical. On the contrary, behind every political or military practice, old or new, stands a community of practice that keeps changing with changes of knowledge, identity, and interests. It would be equally wrong, however, to think that policy-oriented communities of practice develop only around group interests. In fact, group interests and interest groups develop primarily because a community of practice has first attempted to influence the conceptual framework used to think about interests.[182] As communities of practice expand, interests acquire a political and sometimes even a global dimension, and cognitively evolve into established practices. Thus, for example, what started in the mind of some academics and diplomats as the CSCE process and later crystallized into the 1975 Helsinki Final Act[183] has become a cooperative security practice that has been adopted, at least in part, in various regions and by diverse multilateral institutions—for example, Asia and ASEAN.[184]

The authority to determine what the interest of a community means and is depends not only on material and organizational resources but also on the ability to attach one's meanings to material objects in ways that permit them to survive processes of diffusion, selection, and institutionalization. But people learn about their 'real' interests only as they are revealed in the 'heat of the battle'—in political campaigns, negotiations, and collective action. In other words, interests emerge when people have to bargain about meanings, justify their aptness to particular situations, and create narratives through which they can control their social environment. The negotiations about meaning that occur within and between communities of practice eventually define the communities' boundaries. Once the cognitive-evolution process is under way, communities of practice diffuse the political innovations that have been selectively retained to state and non-state actors.

Conclusion

In this chapter, I have argued that constructivism has not merely enlivened IR theoretical debates. It has also introduced a new communitarian approach for which the social construction of knowledge and the construction of social reality take place within communities of the like-minded—most of which can be characterized as communities of practice. On one level, this communitarian approach can contribute to an understanding of social change and of international and transnational reality. Taking real and practical communities as the ontological ground and level of analysis that mediates between individuals and social structures helps overcome the epistemological and methodological problems associated with using ideas to explain social phenomena as well as the agent–structure dilemma. As I have tried to show in this chapter, however, it also helps to explain the relevance of both collective learning for IR theory and the communitarian sources of social change. On another level, the communitarian approach advanced in this chapter provides us with a better understanding of the mechanisms and processes involved in normative change and of the notion that some of the tough questions currently being debated in analytical IR theory may be intrinsically related to normative issues about liberal order, its variants, and its alternatives.

So this chapter points toward the development of a double synthesis. The first blends normative IR theory with constructivist–analytic IR theory, both of which have been debating the role of communities in international life and their value as a key concept in IR theory. The English school has tried, with some success, to achieve such a synthesis.[185] Although not all IR theorists adopt this school's main theories, discourse, and findings, they can profit greatly from its example.

Once we realize that the ontological and epistemological terms of the debates in normative IR theory and in analytic IR theory are similar, we can move along to a second and more ambitious synthesis. This blends the liberal–rationalist argument—which emphasizes the individual, the micro foundations of change, methodological individualism, and a cosmopolitan society as a normative goal—with the normative and analytic communitarian argument—which locates social change in communities, emphasizes the macro foundations of change, and holds that moral life is possible only within communities. If the discipline moves in the direction of the latter synthesis, normative IR theorists will be able to ground their work on the evolving common ground between constructivism and rationalism. For example, learning the conditions and circumstances in which instrumental action and practical or communicative rationality complement each other in the construction of social reality[186] may enlighten normative IR theorists about how communitarian and cosmopolitan notions of normative change can be combined to explain normative evolution toward larger, procedurally better, and more just communities.

At the same time, constructivists and rationalists, who have been concerned mainly with ontological, epistemological, and methodological questions, will be able to ground their understanding of social and international reality on normative foundations of the nature of knowledge, social association, rationality, social change, and human progress. Then we will be able to start speaking the same 'language' and tackle the task of imagining together how to transcend our present situation and move in the direction of a global security community in which, peaceful change having been guaranteed, issues of fairness, transparency, responsibility, and mutual dignity can become the new terms of political discourse and practice.

One question that most theorists can debate, regardless of their persuasion, is whether a more just society and a more efficient system of global governance can evolve from existing social structures and practices, or whether the cause of peace and justice will have to wait for a larger transformation of social epistemology, practice, and organization. In the former case, one way of evolving in that direction would be the enlargement of the emerging European liberal order. It is hard to imagine, however, that this will happen in the short term. Another way of evolving toward a normatively and procedurally better, albeit 'thinner,' system of governance would be via partnerships of different normative orders—for example, Western liberal and Islamic—and of their related communities of practice. Although these partnerships would not prod political, cultural, and religious communities to abandon their separate understandings of the social world, they could nevertheless advance a moral cause by establishing the conditions of peaceful change (e.g., the rule of law, sustainable development, institutionalized dialogue, international cooperation) in which fairness and mutual respect can more readily develop.

Part II
Cognitive evolution

2 From being to becoming

Cognitive evolution and a theory of non-equilibrium in International Relations

Written when I still was a graduate student at Berkeley, this 'relic' manuscript was the starting point of my ideas about the construction of social reality, cognitive evolution, and IR change. At a time when the concept of complexity theory was only beginning to be known, I used the work of Ilya Prigogine, one of its fathers, to develop a theory of non-equilibrium in IR, identifying the evolution of collective knowledge as the key for understanding the transformation of International Relations. At William Thompson's insistence, I overcame my reluctance to publish this 'relic' and, allowing for editorial changes, publish it as first written. The chapter's value, I think, lies in its ideas as they were presented then. Its significance, however, transcends historical or sociological curiosity and lies in the articulation of a theoretical framework for understanding IR change.

Today, of course, I would write the chapter very differently. First, the constructivist approach is in full bloom and we now know much more about the importance of norms, identities, and knowledge in general in the construction of social reality. Second, we now have a much better understanding of nonlinear and emergent processes, which lie at the core of complexity theory. Today I would be more careful about borrowing from Prigogine's non-equilibrium theory, although doing so put me on the road to understanding IR from a constructivist perspective. Third, I am now much more wedded to a sociological approach to social change than I was when I wrote this paper; my understanding of cognitive evolution has moved closer to a synthesis between methodological individualism and what Alexander Wendt called 'methodological holism.' My current synthetic thinking, I believe, owes much to an understanding of community, which I lacked back then. Fourth, since I wrote this paper, I have radically revised my understanding of the international system and power—I am much more critical of functional structural systemic thinking than I was then—and would not call my approach 'social relativity,' although, essentially, the seeds of my constructivist approach were embedded in the meaning and content I gave to this concept. I feel as uncomfortable with radical historicist and relativistic perspectives today as I felt then; thus my insistence on working toward an interpretive epistemology that leaves some room for material reality, people's choices and intentional acts, and explanatory dynamic mechanisms. Fifth, I would have organized the manuscript differently and would probably have articulated the theory in ways more consonant with contemporary theoretical debates. Finally, some of the illustrations are based on international events of years past; readers may find them amusing or, worse, annoying. If so, they should skip pages 48–56.

Unpublished manuscript, 1981

> There rolls the deep where grew the tree
> O earth, what changes hast thou seen!
> [...]
> The hills are shadows, and they flow
> From form to form, and nothing stands;
> They melt like mist, the solid lands,
> Like clouds they shape themselves and go.

Tennyson, *In Memoriam*

Introduction

The objective of this study is to give a 'push' to ideas of 'becoming' rather than of 'being'—Heraclitus' *panta rei* (everything is in flux): the ideas of permanent change, non-equilibrium, and evolution as applied to International Relations. The method used will involve a discussion of what others have meant and what I mean by the concept of international system and then a presentation of a theory of change based upon the ideas of flow and non-equilibrium. This will be followed by some illustrations of the theory and some suggestions about an evolutionary approach that encompasses the cognitive sources and dynamics of change in International Relations.

The IR discipline, to put it mildly, has been reluctant to deal with evolution. The thin boundaries between evolution and the ideologically unwelcome ideas of revolution and drastic change have prevented scholars from dealing with change—with 'becoming'—from a scientific, non-normative perspective. Furthermore, it sometimes takes many generations to change the dominant ideas and scientific conceptions of an epoch. Perceptions, images, and expectations about nature and society are the result of social activity, of interaction between human beings—mainly scientists and intellectuals. Ludwik Fleck[1] has called the vehicle for the evolution of ideas the 'thought collective,' which he defined as a community of persons exchanging ideas or maintaining intellectual interaction that provides the special 'carrier' for the historical development of any field of thought, as well as for the given stock of knowledge and level of culture.

In order to be transformed, the IR thought collective requires of its members introspection at the deepest and most abstract levels regarding International Relations. At the root of the difference between 'being' and 'becoming' lie two images and sets of perceptions about causality and about phenomena in general, and international phenomena in particular, which are broader than the concept of paradigm.[2] These images can be seen more as ideologies of causality, as a set of beliefs about causality, about the nature of phenomena, and about change, which affect the paradigms we subscribe to and thus every theoretical proposition we develop.

Although its scope and reach appear to be 'grandiose,' this study attempts only to be heuristic. I will build on the intellectual achievements of the field and add some insights into the main body of knowledge. Although some of the metaphors, ideas, and insights are taken from the hard sciences, this study will by no means reduce social phenomena to the laws of physics. The scientific models and systems of physics, chemistry, and biology alluded to will only be sources for metaphorical thinking to replace other metaphors now dominant, which are also based on scientific and philosophical models. Although I am presenting the idea of non-equilibrium as the mechanism for explaining change, as a more adequate metaphor for the analysis of International Relations, I am not arguing against the concept of scientific equilibrium. It is the static connotations of the metaphor as applied to International Relations that trouble me. Nor am I rejecting equilibrium from an ideological or moral ground, as, for example, Marxists tend to do. My idea of evolution is devoid of teleological and final-state elements. The fact that static models have been used to back ideological positions of status quo and that dynamic models have been used to back ideological positions of revolution should not prevent us from dealing with the question in a scientific way, once we are aware and have made it clear to others that our position is not normative and prescriptive but is driven by our desire to understand phenomena as we perceive them and not as we would like them to be.

International Relations theory and 'the international system'

The evolution of the study of systems in International Relations

I will start with a very short review of the literature of international systems and international regimes. Early, good, short, and concise reviews of the literature are those by James Dougherty and Robert Pfaltzgraff[3] and by Kenneth Waltz.[4] Newer accounts are those of Waltz[5] and of Ole Holsti *et al.*[6] Morton Kaplan,[7] George Modelski,[8] Charles A. McClelland,[9] Richard Rosecrance,[10] and Kenneth Waltz[11] are some of the theorists who built the international systems literature in the 1960s. Kaplan, for example, defined the international system as 'a set of individual variables to a combination of external variables.'[12] For McClelland, a system was an outcome of the interaction between states conceived as 'black boxes,' which received 'inputs' and elicited 'outputs.'[13] Modelski believed that an international system has to have structural and functional requirements,[14] and Rosecrance described a system in terms of disturbance inputs, a regulator, and environmental constraints, which he induced from the study of nine historical situations.[15] Waltz, in turn, emphasized structural change, the structure being the outcome of the stratification of power of the actors. Thus, according to him, a system and its structure can be bipolar, multipolar, etc.[16]

What characterizes most of these studies, and many more, to a greater or lesser extent, is that the systems devised by these theorists 'behave' according to rules reified from the theorists' original assumptions, such as Kaplan's;[17] in some cases these systems were conceived as black boxes interacting with one another, such as McClelland's;[18] some were teleological, heading in the direction of equilibrium, such as Waltz's.[19] Some were deterministic and tautological.[20] These systems approaches tended to be static, even if the theorists were concerned with their transformation. Thus they neglected the process of feedback and the actors' capacity for self-transformation.[21]

To be sure, there were harsh critiques of this kind of systemic thinking, such as those by Stanley Hoffmann[22] and by Knorr and Rosenau.[23] But to my mind, there were only two early attempts, different from the above type of systems thinking, that should have become—but were only partially successful in becoming—the philosophical and epistemological foundation for the evolution of systems thinking in International Relations. I refer to Karl Deutsch[24] and Ernst Haas.[25] Both were heuristic conceptualizations of International Relations characterized by a dynamic approach; both were Heraclitean thinking. They stressed the individual as a learning actor, as reacting and adapting through processes of positive and negative feedback. Deutsch emphasized the flow of communication in the system and its cybernetic characteristics.[26] Haas defined the international system as a 'concrete actor-oriented abstraction on recurrent relationships that can explain its own transformation into a new set of relationships, i.e., into a new system,'[27] a system without needs and *telos*.

By the end of the 1960s this type of international systems thinking had come to an end. That which followed arose not only out of the previously described failure but also as a consequence of events that occurred in the 'real world' and enhanced the perceptions of complexity and interdependence, as well as a consequence of the failure of other theories such as integration theory.[28] The offspring was international regimes, which, in contrast to preceding theories, focused on smaller units of analysis where interdependencies abounded and thus facilitated the understanding of their causes and consequences.

In the literature of international regimes, Robert O. Keohane and Joseph Nye's *Power and Interdependence*[29] and Haas's 'Is There a Hole in the Whole?'[30] are good examples of theoretical attempts to grasp international phenomena from the systemic point of view. They have led to a deeper understanding of the interdependencies that characterize these regimes and have transcended the realist paradigm, which was so important for systems thinking in the 1960s. One of the distinctions between the realist paradigm based on the rational behavior of black-boxed states, which maximize their power in the search for equilibrium, and the interdependence/international regimes approach is that the latter allows for understanding of what goes on inside the black boxes and among international actors, other than the state itself, and for international activities other than war and peace. The realists criticized these approaches, arguing that explanation of the international system and the prediction of its transformation would be better served by placing the emphasis on the stratification of power, because all the issues that were not power-oriented were in fact subsumed under the all-encompassing power variable. Thus the issues of interdependence would remain redundant and unnecessary.[31] The literature of international regimes and interdependence also came under attack from those who argued that the Less Developed Countries (LDCs) were left out of the picture for too long.[32] The argument was that the theory of interdependence in fact legitimized the relations of dependency between the North and the South. But in fact, by the middle of the 1970s, systemic theorizing was leaning toward the study of asymmetrical interdependence or dependence, leading to distinctions such as between 'dependence' and 'dependency.'[33] Thus for the first time questions of equality were added to those of complexity.

'Being': equilibrium

The idea of equilibrium—sometimes used merely as metaphor, sometimes taken in a literal sense—has been prevalent in International Relations theory. In most cases the equilibrium image has been translated into the descriptive, explanatory, and prescriptive concept known as 'the balance of power.' Kenneth Waltz, one of the strongest supporters of this concept, has argued that balance of power is the most developed theory in international politics.[34] A quick glance at some relevant IR issues shows how deeply rooted this conception is.

National security

Theories of national security, of military and strategic relations, and of deterrence, all of them prevalent in American strategic thinking since the 1950s, are based on the concept of balance of power. A strategic balance of power can be either stable or unstable. For example, a new defensive weapon such as the antiballistic missile (ABM) or a more accurate missile can upset the 'balance' and disrupt the 'stability' of the system. When a change in the balance of power occurs, homeostasis, the mechanism that restores equilibrium, occurs. The balance of power, then, is most of all a prescriptive image, which indicates that, when a change leads to an imbalance, an offsetting action should be taken to restore 'balance' or equilibrium. From this perspective, a relationship can be reversible.

International systems theory (macro)

This subdiscipline fell for the image of equilibrium, defined by Kaplan as a steady state or homeostatic condition, which maintains the stability of selected variables as the consequence of changes in other variables. Kaplan described the balance of power as an international social system, composed of national actors, that generates 'essential rules,' which are themselves in equilibrium. This not being enough, he claimed that two additional kinds of equilibrium characterize the international system: that between the set of essential rules and the variables of the international system and that between the international system and its environment or setting.[35] Waltz and Richard Rosecrance also looked for the determinants of stability, the former emphasizing that a bipolar balance of power is more conducive to stability, the latter stressing the role of the 'balancer,' a key role filled by one actor of the system, that helps to maintain it in equilibrium.[36]

Foreign policy (micro)

In the realm of foreign policy, George Liska is on a 'quest for equilibrium' for the United States: the country should plan an 'orderly retreat from empire to equilibrium' and the initial step is to identify 'the main kinds of equilibrium from which to choose.'[37] Henry Kissinger not only wrote his classic study on the balance of power,[38] but also, during the period from 1969 to 1976, as a practitioner, led the mightiest world power in the 'quest for equilibrium.' His foreign policy aimed at equilibrium in various regions as well as between the superpowers.

International organization

In this realm Leon Lindberg and Stuart Scheingold, for example, stressed the fact that 'equilibrium occurs when an area of activity is routinized or institutionalized. Rules are established and recognized and there is little need for intergovernmental bargaining.'[39]

International political economy

In the area of international regimes, one of the most important theories of the 1970s that accounts for the development and demise of international regimes is 'hegemonic stability,' as exemplified in the studies of Charles Kindleberger,[40] Robert Gilpin,[41] and Stephen Krasner.[42] Keohane explained it as follows: 'According to this theory, strong international economic regimes depend on hegemonic power. Fragmentation of power between competing countries leads to fragmentation of the international economic regime; concentration of power contributes to stability.'[43] The conclusion is that where there is a hegemon there is stability. If the hegemon is absent, so is stability. Power becomes the variable that introduces stability and prevents change from occurring.

World systems and world futures

In the realm of world systems and world futures, in which 'ecoholists'[44] are in abundance, one of the most recurrent theoretical assertions is that growth should be brought into equilibrium with nature, that equilibrium should be restored through 'steady-state' or 'non-growth' societies.[45]

Additional examples are available, but I believe they are unnecessary. Even if the concept of equilibrium is defined in the 'dynamic sense' of a steady state, it represents a static definition of movement, one that is time-less and time-reversible. Homeostasis maintains the values of key systemic variables within certain limits that allow the system to survive. These systems are characterized by equifinality, meaning that many types of responses can lead in the same direction: toward steady-state equilibrium. The idea of dynamic equilibrium was mainly developed following vitalist ideas, which 'bought' the metaphor of the body with its potential for growth. But this image did not prevent the theorists from imagining the body and growth in a state of equilibrium.

> From two quite different images of society—the organic and the mechanical—then, there emerged a common strand of theory. Whether the product of organic cooperation or of the pressures of conflicting groups, equilibrium tendencies were presumed to characterize social relations. Equilibrium, in both cases, implied stability. And stability, by tacit agreement, was ever a desirable condition.[46]

Not only is equilibrium the most deeply rooted image in IR theory; it also has the same status in the practice of international politics by political leaders. The effects of this paradigmatic way of thinking on policymaking and international politics have been little considered or understood. When decision-makers are driven in their decisions and actions by the image of the balance of power, by the idea, perception, and expectation of reversibility, by the idea that equilibrium can be created, they are likely to omit from their cognitions the element of time, the cross-catalytic influences across time, and the long-range future implications of their actions. For example, policy-makers of a nation in conflict with another who follow the balance-of-power image will disregard events and relationships that are not related to or do not enhance the balance of power. The neglect of certain events will never-theless have some effect on that nation's relationships, effects that are unpredictable and unmanageable.

It is the gap between the idea and perception of equilibrium and stability, on the one hand, and the reality of continuous fluctuations and evolution, on the other, that should be blamed for the relative lack of explanatory and predictive power of our theories and for the 'surprises' we encounter in the real world of international politics day after day.

'Becoming': a system in flux

I believe that the concept of an international system should be an analytical, heuristic construct, built inductively from the evolution of knowledge and the behavior of human beings; it should be an open system based on the idea that all is in flux and should be studied with attention to cybernetic processes. From this perspective we should especially emphasize the flow of knowledge, which generates mechanisms of positive and negative feedback responsible for the amount and scope of change. International system thinking should also look at the hierarchies that result from the interaction of the system's actors, be they international organizations or the international economic 'system.'

Whereas the approach of the 1960s and the 1970s was to observe the international system and its offspring, the international regime, and deduce change from their properties and behavior, I suggest observing change and explaining the international system from its causes, its consequences, and especially its 'mechanisms.' I define the international system as agents interacting in a steady state of fluctuation; system change, as the evolution to a different pattern of relationships with a distinctive steady state of fluctuation. As we will see in the rest of this study, both analytical abstractions—that of the system, and that of systemic change—are the result of the relative nature of the phenomena that result from human relations, due to changing cognitions and the behavior they generate. It is the observer who analytically perceives systemic change and decides when an evolution in pattern interaction is large enough to be referred to as such. Leaders, bureaucrats, the people in the street—all perceive 'plain' change. Analysts perceive systemic change, for only they are conscious of this analytical and perceptual construct.

Change within the international system is immanent, caused by transformations in the relations among individuals; but it is also imposed upon them and their interactions by the environment. I consider an environment to be made up of a changing physical context (materials, resources, energy, physical conditions such as pollution, natural disasters, etc.) and a changing social context (culture, values, and science and technology). The environment has always changed; the difference now is that the rate of change has increased.

> The growth, expansion, competitions and conflicts of society are all human undertakings, which would not take place if people did not make them take place. But it is also true that changes in both the natural environment and social environment affect the way people think, feel and act, just as the way people think, feel and act affects the natural and social environment.[47]

The physical and social environments are real, but it is our perceptions and cognitions of them and their changes that affect our choices and our behavior, and thus the changing systemic interactions.

The hierarchy of interactions

Because we are referring to systems as analytical constructs, which are abstractions of the interaction of real people, their ideas, knowledge, ideologies, and actions, I suggest breaking up the concept of system into 'international dimensions,' functional areas that are broader than international regimes. These dimensions are: international stability, international equality, international development, international security, and international post-industrial corrections.[48] International dimensions are not 'structures' or 'wholes'; neither are they geographical entities or economic, political, or military issue areas. Rather, they are analytically separated sets of interactions.

The international dimensions are broader than issue areas as described in the literature;[49] in fact, they are the greatest common denominator of all the issue areas that can be said to pertain to a distinctive set of interactions. On the other hand, they are smaller than the 'international system.'

The usefulness of boundaries broader than those of an international regime is that more than one regime deals with a distinctive set of interactions. Haas[50] has shown how and why issues can and are being linked in different ways for the creation of an international regime. An 'international dimensions approach' facilitates the study of linkages among issue areas that transcend one or more regimes and also allows the study of linkages between functional areas. For example, analysis of the evolution of *international equality* would include North–South relations, the New International Economic Order (NIEO), the Group of 77, transnationalism (especially multinational corporations (MNCs)), etc., and the interdependencies of international inequality with other functional areas. The study of *international security* would entail analyzing crises, conflicts, wars, military alliances, arms control and disarmament, nonproliferation matters, and the interdependencies of these problems with the other four functional areas, such as the connections with East–West and North–South questions.

From this point of view, each international dimension has its own dynamic, its own set of changes. But at the same time, all are interdependent with the others. Each international dimension would be something similar to a 'nearly decomposable system.'[51] The international economic system, for example, could be conceived as a higher level of abstraction of the relationships of some of these five dimensions, while the international system could be seen as all five dimensions in continuous interaction and evolution.

Ilya Prigogine's theory of non-equilibrium and 'order through fluctuations'

An evolutionary approach to the study of International Relations requires replacing the concept of equilibrium with the concept of non-equilibrium.

The image of non-equilibrium provides a much better mental tool, a better metaphor, to describe and explain change in International Relations.

The essence of the theory to be presented here is that the key to understanding the appearance of the stability that we sense, in spite of continuous change, and of the creation of cooperative phenomena and order lies in fluctuations that arise in a condition of non-equilibrium.

The theoretical ideas of systemic change in open systems and in conditions of non-equilibrium will be presented on the basis of insights drawn from a theory developed in the physical and chemical sciences by 1977 Nobel Laureate Ilya Prigogine and his followers.[52] Again I must emphasize that I possess neither the knowledge nor the desire to apply a physical theory directly to social phenomena; I merely borrow some insights that allow me to frame international-politics knowledge in a different way to those who use equilibrium as the dominant metaphor.

It was Prigogine's conviction that non-equilibrium may be the source of order and organization 'that become the foundation for a nonlinear thermodynamics of irreversible processes now permitting the description of phenomena of spontaneous structuration.'[53] Prigogine's theory is about the self-organization of evolving systems in the face of permanent instabilities and fluctuations. The theory encompasses two central ideas: 'dissipative structures' and 'order through fluctuations,' based on the following assumptions:

1   An evolving system, in contrast to the notions of classical thermodynamics, can only be an open system, i.e., in continuous relationship with its environment.
2   Processes are irreversible.
3   Fluctuations are basically random and in most cases emerge as a consequence of auto- or cross-catalytic steps.
4   The system is in a situation far from equilibrium (classical thermodynamics deals only with equilibrium systems, which evolve toward equilibrium and stay there).
5   The system is 'autopoietic.' The Chilean biologist Humberto Maturana argues that a system is autopoietic when its function is primarily geared to self-renewal.[54]

The Second law of Thermodynamics states that the evolution of a physicochemical system leads to an equilibrium state of maximum disorder. In an isolated system, which cannot exchange energy and matter with the surroundings, this tendency is expressed in terms of the function of the macroscopic state of the system: its entropy.[55]

Prigogine[56] has formulated an extended version of the Second Law that applies to open systems. The main point is the inequality governing the variation of entropy during a time interval (dS), which takes the form $dS = deS + diS$ ($diS \geqslant 0$), where deS is the flow of entropy due to exchanges with the surroundings and diS the entropy production due to irreversible processes inside the system. Although diS is never negative, the flux term deS has no definite sign. As a result, during evolution a system may reach a state where entropy is smaller than at the start. Moreover, this state can be maintained indefinitely, provided the system can reach a steady state such that dS = 0 or deS = −diS ≤ 0. Thus in principle, at least, if we supply a system with a sufficient amount of negative entropy flow, we can maintain the system in an ordered state. This supply must occur under non-equilibrium conditions, otherwise, diS and deS would vanish identically.[57]

In most of the phenomena studied in classical physics, fluctuations play only a minor role. This is the case in the entire domain of classical equilibrium thermodynamics (on which IR theory has always been based). On the other hand, the study of nonlinear systems in conditions far from equilibrium leads to new situations in which fluctuations play a central role. It is the fluctuations that can force the system to leave a given macroscopic state and move to a new state that has a different spatiotemporal structure.[58]

Dissipative structures

Dissipative structures illustrate precisely this type of behavior. They are so called because they maintain continuous entropy production, which is more than compensated for by the flows of matter or energy from the environment; that is, these systems dissipate the accruing entropy.

> A 'non-equilibrium system' moves through a sequence of mutatory transitions to new regimes, which, in each case, generate the conditions for renewed high entropy production within a new regime, and thus open up the possibility for the continuation of metabolizing activity. ... Such systems are characterized by a high degree of energy exchange with the environment and are therefore called *dissipative structures*.[59]

Let us take the system in question to be a city, for example. Without compensating for its needs (due to its increase in size and necessities) by drawing energy and materials from the environment, the city will decay and die. The fluctuations of the system are therefore dissipated to the environment, which compensates for them.

From the point of view of dissipative structures, entropy becomes an uphill process rather than the hypothesized downhill slide in nature. (This may explain how, even under the conditions of the 'mighty' Second Law, life evolved to high levels of complexity.) By gaining vigor and complexity from the downhill slide, dissipative structures dump their own decay into the environment.[60]

Order through fluctuations

Prigogine shows that partially open systems in a state of sufficient non-equilibrium try to maintain their capability for energy exchange with the environment by switching to a new dynamic regime whenever entropy production becomes stifled in the old regime. This is the principle of 'order through fluctuations,' which reverses some of the dynamic characteristics holding for closed systems and systems near equilibrium. 'In general,' says Prigogine, 'fluctuations play a minor role in macroscopic physics, appearing only as small corrections that may be neglected if the system is sufficiently large. However, near bifurcations [thresholds] they play a critical role because there the fluctuation drives the average. This is the very meaning of *order through fluctuations*.'[61]

The theory's micro dimension describes the formation of fluctuations. It takes chance into account by generally considering the occurrence and the kind and size of fluctuations as random.[62] From this perspective, fluctuations may appear small in comparison to the system as a whole, but when the instabilities approach a threshold they may drive the system to change.[63]

The theory's macro dimension describes how the system as a whole is forced into a new structural–functional order. This new order is not predetermined, for fluctuations are random. The only deterministic element of the theory, from the macro perspective, is the determinism to change to a new order of things (structural–functional). (See Figure 2.1)

Non-equilibrium and 'order through fluctuations' as applied to International Relations theory

Applying the concepts of non-equilibrium, dissipative structures, and order through fluctuations to international systems theory makes the latter sensitive to learning and adaptation to change. We also become aware that the system can achieve a new functional and structural order, not only in spite of, but also because of permanent change. When changes are small or moderate and actors are able to control them, the system is maintained in a state of 'stable' fluctuations (fluctuations below the threshold). But when

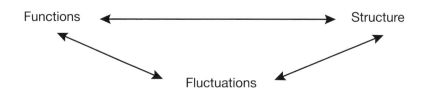

Figure 2.1 'Dissipative Structures'

Source: Adapted from Ilya Prigogine, 'Order through Fluctuation: Self Organization and Social System,' "in Erich Jantsch and Conrad H. Waddington, eds, *Evolution and Consciousness: Human Systems in Transition* (Reading, MA: Addison-Wesley, 1976), p. 94

large fluctuations take place and actors cannot control them, even a small change can drive the system's actors to change functions and structures and to perceive that a dramatic transformation has occurred.

Fluctuations (diS and deS) are triggered at the actor's level by human action (micro level). Thus, the study of the origin of change in International Relations should center on foreign policy, foreign policymaking, on the actors' perceptions, images, and expectations, and on the attributes of the societies in question. This is the 'diS' source of fluctuations. At the same time, the study of change should also focus on how a self-transforming pattern of interactions is affected by the physical and social environments. This is the 'deS' source of fluctuations.

Thus we come back to the formula diS + deS = dS (entropy change = fluctuations). As 'diS' and 'deS' change, people's images, perceptions, and expectations also evolve. With them, new political choices arise and political actions occur. The more interdependence there is among the actors, the faster is the change, because the environment provides the energy, materials, and knowledge to replace those 'used up' by the actors and to help the actors adapt to new situations.

An international dissipative system results from the above process of change. Today the system is characterized by increasingly complex interdependence and an increased number of fluctuations and discontinuities among the five dimensions mentioned before, as well as by increasing complexity and uncertainty as perceived by the actors.

The threshold that I believe takes us to a different kind of system is cognitive. A cognitive threshold is reached when changes affect the relationship between actors in such a way that they lead to perceptual recognition of the need for new types of relations, organizations, and means to allocate values in and between societies. The fluctuations can be very large, like a world war, or the system can be driven to change by small fluctuations if its functions and structures have already been severely disrupted by a series of cumulative changes. In such an event, even a small country can precipitate changes that are disproportionate to its size or its role and importance in the international system. In most cases the cross-catalytic influences of change within and between several actors have a random effect. Some changes, however, are not accidentally originated but result from purposeful action by individuals for the sake of personal, class, or national goals.

Order through fluctuations: a new order is created in response to instabilities and fluctuations (non-equilibrium) because the human mind experiences new ideas and knowledge. Fluctuations are the origin and driving force of new orders, but these actually 'become' because the human mind is creative, because it has the capability to learn and to adapt to changes. New systems arise because of political, social, and institutional innovations that start in the minds of policymakers and their advisers.

I will now describe in more detail the two components of fluctuations: 'diS' and 'deS.'

First, 'diS' refers to the fluctuations originating within the system, due to the actors' choices and actions as well as to chance. Chance, as Democritus said many centuries ago, 'is a cause, but it is inscrutable to human intelligence.' In my explanation of change in International Relations, chance reflects unexpected events or a succession of events.[64] These are occurrences that have nothing to do with human choice, not even with automatic mechanisms of regulation. The death of a leader that affects some incident in the international arena can be an example of chance.

With regard to human choice and action, 'diS' refers to the fluctuations that originate in the lack of absolute control over the outcome of the actions undertaken by the actors. Fluctuations also occur because policymakers learn and acquire new information that keeps generating new initiatives and responses. I will leave the explanation of cognitive change for a later section of this study. Controls, both within a nation and between nations—such as laws, threats, promises, and force—are not enough to prevent the occurrence of actions and events that conflict with the actors' will. In other words, policymaking processes and the actions and events they trigger are characterized by at least some measure of positive feedback that leads to actions with a life of their own.

Figure 2.2 describes this concept. It shows a process of positive feedback in which, for lack of control in the foreign policymaking process of one nation, each new decision leads to an action that differs from the original intention. After a certain period of time, actions, and consequently events, occur that were not intended in the first place. For example, an American foreign policy that originally sets out to back a friendly government in Latin America may after a while become involved in unwanted belligerent acts and intervention, involve other Latin American nations in these actions, produce responses in other parts of the world (Soviet actions in Eastern Europe, for example), and cause reactions to the policy that may eventually affect its own outcome. This has happened in Latin America (e.g., the Dominican Republic and Chile) and in Southeast Asia (Vietnam and Cambodia) and it can happen again in the future (e.g., in El Salvador).

But to get a more accurate picture of the system and its complexity we must multiply the process described above for one country by 155 (the approximate number of countries). The more free will that exists, both among the actors in each system and in the relationships among them, the more fluctuations are likely. Free will means that more human beings try to pursue their own purposes (relatively) undisturbed, creating a larger and richer set of cognitions and attitudes and thus more fluctuations, more complexity, and more uncertainty. When more individuals pursue their own goals within and across nations, it is more likely that the net result of the interactions, i.e., their catalytic effect, will tend to raise problems and create discontinuities within and between the stability, economic development, equality, security, and post-industrial correction dimensions.

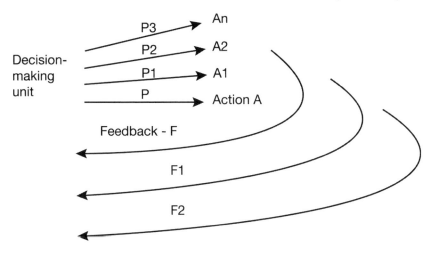

Where P is the decision and implementation process

F = feedback

P = A

A + F + P1 = A1

A1 + F1 + P2 = A2

A2 + F2 + P3 = An

A ≠ An

Figure 2.2 Positive feedback

On the other hand, a planned society, whether national or international, may in the short run be able to control and slow down fluctuations originating from positive feedback mechanisms. But the possibilities of adaptation will be smaller than under free will, because planned national or international societies are like horses with blinders, which can look only ahead and not to the side, sensing only themselves and their goal and unable to see other roads.

Now we come to 'deS.' Whether we are talking about the international system as a whole or international cognitive dimensions and international regimes, they are in constant relation with their physical and social environment through positive and negative feedback. The learning processes that take place in reaction to environmental sources can be characterized by two integrative processes: horizontal—learning that occurs from one cognitive dimension to another; and vertical—learning that occurs within the same cognitive dimension.

Adaptations to a changing environment do not occur only as a response to images and perceptions of the past and the present, as might well happen with a technological innovation or the realization that there is no longer enough oil to go around. They are also likely to occur because of expectations of the future, regardless of whether they might actually come true. Because of their sense of anticipation, self-reflective human beings react and/or adapt to a situation expected to happen in the future and thus irreversibly change the course of events today. The expectation that oil will run out in twenty-five years, for example, would give rise to adaptive measures which would lead to new functions, new structures, and new interactions that did not previously exist.

Furthermore, environmental changes can drive the system to the perceptual threshold. For example, as actors acquire new cognitions and knowledge about scientific and technological issues, the notion of cost-free progress and infinite material and technical growth (economic development dimension) is overlapped by cognitions and knowledge that weigh the above objectives against the consequences of technological development and growth for the system's actors. This dimension is what I have called 'post-industrial corrections.' Being dynamic, this overlap can reach a threshold at which the behavior of the actors in science and technology issues would drastically change. This in turn would demand new approaches, new functions, and new organizations to deal with the changes. Thus, a new regime/dimension/system would be cognitively recognized.

Overall change of a system is much less common than permanent incremental change below the threshold. Thus we need to deal with the mechanisms that explain how fluctuations are controlled and maintained below the threshold. It is the changes themselves—the new technological advances, the new weapons invented, and the changes that occur within each nation and among nations—that drive human beings to 'invent' new social devices, to organize in such a way as to control the changes.

The devices responsible for maintaining a system in a steady state of fluctuation are *homeorhesis* and *resilience*. These are macro variables that describe a pattern of interaction in flow. But, as should be clear by now, such variables can be understood only by taking into account the micro origin of fluctuations and the choices made there with regard to their control.

Homeorhesis

This concept, coined by C. H. Waddington,[65] will be used to replace the mechanistic term homeostasis, which, as we have seen, means a return to equilibrium (see Figure 2.3a). Homeorhesis, instead, is a return to a stable flow. What is maintained constant is a time-expanded course of change. The main characteristic of homeorhesis is that disturbances are counteracted so as to bring the process back, not to where it was when disturbed but to where it would have progressed if left undisturbed.[66] Homeorhesis thus ensures the continuation of a given (metastable) type of change.

Homeorhesis applies to all five cognitive dimensions. As an example, however, I will briefly discuss it in terms of the international security

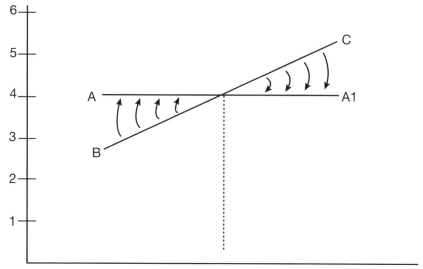

Figure 2.3a Homeostasis

dimension—in particular, balance-of-power theory. The problem with balance-of-power theory has been its inability to account for the international system's dynamic stability, i.e., a stable non-equilibrium of power.[67] Assuming a situation of non-equilibrium, represented by the solid line in Figure 2.3b, then, to be stable, a flow that was characterized by homeorhesis would return to C, the point to which the flow would have continued if undisturbed, and not to A, the initial point where the disturbance occurred. Thus, for example, should the US–USSR balance of power be disturbed by the Soviets attaining strategic superiority, a stable flow pattern would be restored, not to the exact situation that existed before the Soviets attempted to attain strategic superiority, but to the point to which the balance of power would have evolved had the disturbance not occurred. The important point I would like to emphasize, thus, is the replacement of a stable point with a stable flow; the fewer the fluctuations, the more stable the flow and the more homeorhesis or dynamic stability.

Resilience

This is the measure of the ability of the system to absorb change-driving variables and parameters and survive.[68] The existence and function of cooperative phenomena indicate the resilience of the system but do not in themselves prevent or stop change. Large-scale cooperation is in itself a source of fluctuations, which is controllable and therefore desirable in the eyes of the policymakers.

We can illustrate resilience with international economic issues. But, as with homeorhesis, resilience is applied to all types of interactions. Policymakers'

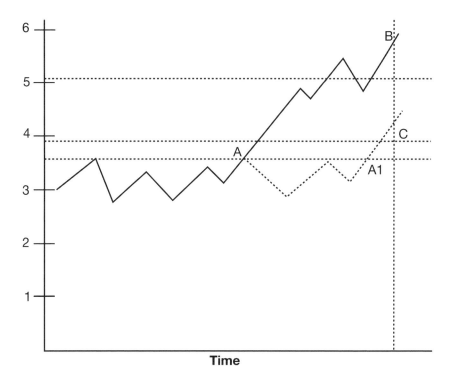

Fluctuations are brought back to C, not to A

A - Point of disturbance
B - The path, following disturbance
C - Where it would have gone if left undisturbed

Figure 2.3b Homeorhesis

perceptions, expectations, and predictions concerning North–South relations and their multiple variable and multi-level issues fluctuate continuously. The fluctuation itself is highly important, because it is what makes for resilience. Under a system with few or no fluctuations, resilience—the absorption of change through new functions, organizations, and regimes—would be minimal. Thus, due to increasing interdependence and the North–South problems, new and different kinds of functions, organizations, issue linkages, and planning at the global level—such as international 'codes of conduct' and the NIEO—are arising to absorb change. This is an example of the resilience process. On the other hand, fluctuations can be amplified to a point where resilience becomes ineffective, a threshold is reached, and fluctuations are amplified to a new dynamic pattern of relationships. (See Figure 2.4.)

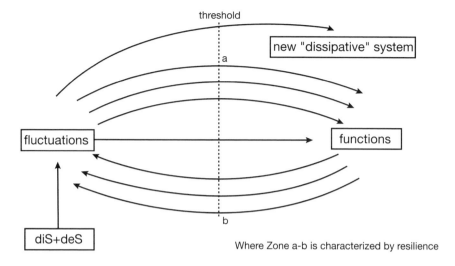

Figure 2.4 Resilience

Illustrations

The foregoing ideas should be followed by well-researched, detailed cases dealing with some or all of the perceived international dimensions; but this cannot be done within the framework of this study. Instead, I will choose several issues to illustrate a few applications of some of the theoretical insights presented up to this point. Given the degree of perceived complexity and the growing number of issues, relevance becomes an essential cognitive property. I have thus chosen to deal with: (1) system transformation; (2) nuclear proliferation and nuclear 'balance of power'; (3) change in the international monetary regime; and (4) the question of interdependence and self-reliance that divides North from South.

System transformation

Discussion in this area has frequently focused on the differences between scholars who stress structural explanations, emphasizing power and its stratification, and scholars who stress process, interactions, and interdependencies.[69] Some of the theoretical arguments suggested in the previous sections transcend the discussion in the literature by suggesting a process–structure explanation of system transformation that combines the micro and macro levels of theory.[70] For example, by studying the nature of the fluctuations, their timing, their cross-catalytic influences, and their effect on both conflictual and cooperative behavior and on various types of human organization, we can learn about macro developments such as the transformation of one international dimension or all of them (the international system) once cognitive thresholds are crossed. We can also learn about macro variables, such as homeorhesis and resilience, that maintain change in these cognitive dimensions below the cognitive threshold.

Figure 2.5 shows that by juxtaposing these two macro variables we obtain four possibilities or conditions, which can help us explain past transformation and, depending on changes in the two variables, predict the probability of system transformation.[71]

When the pattern of interaction is characterized by strong homeorhesis and large resilience, the system is in a state of stable flow (Box 1). The system between 1945 and the early 1960s may be characterized as such. A stable flow of change was maintained because the system had fewer actors, lesser degrees of perceived interdependence, and fewer discontinuities than today's international system has.

When the pattern of interaction is characterized by weak homeorhesis and resilience is small, it is likely that the fluctuations will reach the threshold and a dissipative system will be transformed into a new dynamic pattern of interaction (Box 4). Whereas in Box 1 fluctuations are below the threshold, in Box 4—a situation that can be exemplified by the period preceding World War II—the weak homeorhesis and small resilience mean that fluctuations exceed the threshold, thus leading to systemic change.

Box 3 reflects the possibility that, despite weak homeorhesis (high instability in the fluctuations), the system can still be preserved through resilience. As I have argued above, the fluctuations themselves prompt a search for new functions, organizations, and regimes, which help absorb the impact of change. The present international system (1981) reflects this configuration. Fluctuations are high because, due to complex interdependence, the US cannot control them as before. But the system maintains itself through resilience processes.

Box 2, on the other hand, reflects the possibility that, given strong homeorhesis, there is no immediate need for large resilience. That is, there is no need for major adaptation to change because fluctuations are not large. But if a random and sudden change occurs, states and international institutions may not be strong enough to contain it; the system reaches the threshold rapidly, thus leading to systemic change. For example, the sudden changes that afflicted the international system between 1870 and 1918, starting with the Franco-Prussian War and ending with World War I, represented amplified fluctuations that crossed the threshold, thus bringing about abrupt system change.[72]

Nuclear proliferation and the nuclear balance of power

One of the most remarkable accomplishments of the fight against nuclear proliferation is that since the Big Four (the United States, the Soviet Union,

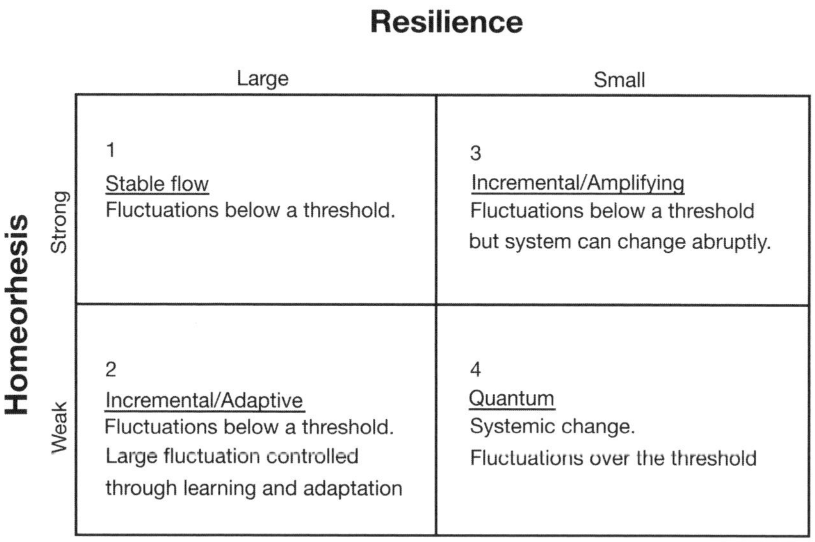

Resilience

		Large	Small
Homeorhesis	Strong	1 <u>Stable flow</u> Fluctuations below a threshold.	3 <u>Incremental/Amplifying</u> Fluctuations below a threshold but system can change abruptly.
	Weak	2 <u>Incremental/Adaptive</u> Fluctuations below a threshold. Large fluctuation controlled through learning and adaptation	4 <u>Quantum</u> Systemic change. Fluctuations over the threshold

Figure 2.5 System transformation

the United Kingdom, and France) acquired their nuclear military capability more than two decades ago, only two other countries have joined the nuclear club: China and India. The Nuclear Test Ban Treaty and the Nuclear Nonproliferation Treaty (NPT) gave the system a measure of resilience, probably attesting to the fact that for the majority of states the risks and pain of going nuclear outweighed the benefits. But nuclear proliferation remains an immense threat to world peace. Several countries could go nuclear in half an hour should they decide to do so; several others are on the brink of acquiring the capability in a matter of months or years.[73]

Recognizing the danger, several American administrations have tried to put a lid on the transfer of nuclear technology and material, with varying degrees of success. President Carter's nuclear nonproliferation policy was the strongest of all; it prohibited the export of enriched uranium and uranium-enrichment facilities that could be used to manufacture an atomic bomb.[74] But the Reagan administration has been considering the revision of that policy. Some officials and experts have proposed that the ban on the export of nuclear materials be lifted,[75] proposing instead to rely on the Nuclear Nonproliferation Treaty (NPT) and the International Atomic Energy Agency (IAEA), whose success depends on the cooperation and good will of the countries involved. If there is any definitive policy in the works, its details are not well known, so no objective analysis can be made. Furthermore, the Israeli raid on the Iraqi nuclear facility in June 1981 may affect the course of policymaking and the final outcome with regard to nuclear proliferation policy.

As the White House considers renewing the export of nuclear materials, decision-makers consciously and unconsciously weigh several contrasting values: What is more important for the US? What is more urgent? What is more secure? What is more profitable? What is more politically remunerative? What is ethically more sound? Decision-makers must also take account of pressures from Congress, public opinion, and private interests. In addition, they probably have some expectations or 'predictions,' if not computerized forecasts, about the policy's outcome. This is where the 'being' image rests.

Thinking in equilibrium terms, however, and perceiving 'stability' where there is none, decision-makers may irreversibly affect their immediate future in ways that that are inconsistent with their own objectives. The decision to renew the export of nuclear materials could have immediate and future cross-catalytic influences that are far from predictable or even imaginable. In fact, even if a decision such as this is later reversed, the lapse of time before implementation would have an irreversible effect on the capabilities, policies, and mutual relations of 'buyers' and 'sellers' and perhaps on the stability of the international system.

For example, Third World countries that buy these nuclear materials may have political objectives unknown to American officials or could develop them after they achieve nuclear capability. The rapid turnover of ideologies and political regimes in these countries (to which a nuclear capability might be a contributing cause) is a source of unrest and danger for the world community in general and for the United States in particular. Furthermore, many Third World countries are or will be involved in regional conflicts, thus increasing the danger that nuclear weapons might be used. Those who think the NPT and IAEA are enough to control nuclear proliferation believe the resilience of the system is adequate to keep fluctuations of this type in a manageable state of flow. When we are dealing with nuclear proliferation, however, one large fluctuation can bring us to the brink. In the case of nuclear proliferation, then, strengthening the homeorhesis and resilience of the system requires not only thinking and deciding on the basis of extremely dynamic models, but also replacing the image of equilibrium with that of non-equilibrium.

It has been argued, for example, that the Middle East conflict could be 'stabilized' by nuclearizing the belligerent countries and creating a 'stable' balance that would deter any party from launching an attack on another. Recently, for instance, there has been a lively discussion in Israel about the prospect of 'going nuclear' or admitting that Israel already has the bomb and about formulating a nuclear doctrine that would create a deterrent effect. This, it has been argued, would allow Israel to withdraw from the West Bank, remain secure within recognized boundaries, and restore its diminishing national consensus.[76]

Any Middle Eastern country, however, that decided to go nuclear would create major fluctuations and lead to irreversible changes in the region. By going nuclear, Israel would obviously hasten the nuclearization of Arab countries, thus leading to changes that Israel could neither predict nor control. Nuclear military power can have a tremendous effect on the political elites and political objectives of all the countries concerned and could change the power elites in some countries. It could also spur other international conflicts that are only latent or do not even exist today. Environmental and safety problems related to nuclear energy would also be increased. Most ominously, of course, it would make nuclear war more likely.

In a volatile conflict situation where stakes of national survival may be high for both sides, the likelihood of the use of nuclear weapons or of nuclear 'accidents' increases considerably.

Since the Middle East conflict is between Israel and several Arab countries, any Arab state that went nuclear would likely cause Israel to perceive the balance of power as having been upset, leading to countermeasures that would fuel a spiral of escalation and a multilateral nuclear arms race. Because the process is irreversible and constantly changing, there would be no return to the original positions; the best attainable situation would be a metastable type of flow. The asymmetries referred to above would create enormous obstacles to strong homeorhesis and would probably produce large fluctuations in a situation where resilience is very low. This, in turn, would mean that even a small systemic fluctuation could push the whole system beyond the cognitive threshold and to the brink of nuclear war.

If Israel, therefore, decides to go nuclear, it is unlikely to achieve a stable nuclear equilibrium. Instead, it will make the non-equilibrium pattern of fluctuations much less stable. Policymakers should be aware of the processes they are initiating, their catalytic nature, and the difficulty of predicting and controlling them. This applies not only to Israel, but also to the Arab countries.

The international monetary regime and its transformation

I will use the international monetary system to illustrate two elements from our previous theoretical discussion— 'order through fluctuations' and the cognitive dimension of the threshold. Quoting Otto Pohl, Fred Bergsten wrote that the 'emergence of a multiple-currency reserve system may well be the least noticed, and yet the most spectacular result of the evolutionary process of international monetary reform that succeeded the abortive effort to set up a new world monetary order within the framework of the IMF in the early 1970s.'[77]

According to Bergsten, the international monetary system is being transformed from a dollar-based system into one characterized by the salience of other currencies, the 'multiple reserve currency system.' Hence, Bergsten concluded, 'it seems appropriate to refer to today's international monetary standard as increasingly becoming a "multiple reserve currency system."'[78]

The question that interests me is, when do people start perceiving that the system is changing or *becoming* something different? When do they perceive that the 'system' or 'regime' has already 'changed'? In other words, where does the perceptual threshold lie?

Bergsten believes that the decisive element in the evolution of the multiple-currency system is the advent of flexible exchange rates, which may lead to the use of multiple currencies and, due to perceived currency instability, may also affect the portfolio management of national reserves. As these changes multiply and intensify, more fluctuations occur near the threshold and it becomes more likely that even a minor and most likely random fluctuation may create the perception of a new 'order': 'A shift of a major country from dollar-pegging or SDR-pegging [Special Drawing Rights] to free floating ... could over a few years produce a substantial shift from dollars into other currency holdings by that country.' He believes that in practice there is little scope for this, because there are only a few major reserve-holders pegging to the dollar (Iraq, Libya, and Venezuela) or to SDRs (Iran). In fact, it is the changes in the arrangements of other countries, such as the eight members of the European Monetary System, the twenty-one countries pegging to a currency basket other than SDRs (including Austria, Kuwait, Malaysia, Norway, and Sweden) and another forty-eight not pegging at all (including Brazil, India, Japan, Mexico, Nigeria, Spain, the UAE, and the United Kingdom) that 'could most rapidly lead to changes in the overall composition of international currency reserves.'[79]

The new emerging regime overlaps with the old one; many countries have not yet stopped pegging to the dollar and holding SDRs. So when do we say that a new order, a new regime, or a new system has been created? This is entirely a cognitive matter, determined by the actors' perceptions and expectations. Where new functions and new international institutions are created they serve as signals and indices of change. But new international arrangements alone do not make for a change in regime, because new functions and structures continue to overlap with old ones. But when enough analysts and policymakers perceive that the regime has indeed changed, we can say that a new one has been created.

When enough actors have perceived macro change, it does not necessarily mean that 'equilibrium' and 'stability' have been achieved. On the contrary, actors will also start perceiving the new fluctuations that are above the threshold:

> The early period [after the fluctuations above the threshold have been perceived] offers financing advantages at a time when the individual currency comfortably meets the criteria for playing a major international role. As time progresses, however, the very evolution of the role itself jeopardizes the currency's continued position and adjustment constraints begin to set in. Thus the cost–benefit ratio shifts toward the negative over time, certainly from the standpoint of the key-currency country

and probably—depending on the available alternatives—to the system as a whole.[80]

The international monetary system, with its continuous transformation, thus provides an example of evolutionary change, of fluctuations below a perceived threshold, and of the transition across it after fluctuations become large and catalytic. Awareness of the change by analysts and policymakers sets the limits and determines what was 'old' and what is 'new.' The process, which is characterized by learning and adaptation to the new situation, does not stop once the threshold is crossed, but goes on indefinitely. New functions and new institutions result from these processes of learning and adaptation, and new levels of homeorhesis and resilience set in.

International economic development and equality: interdependence or self-reliance?

The last illustration serves to emphasize: (1) the usefulness of looking at international politics from a cognitive dimension; and (2) the evolutionary character of the processes involved.

The relations of individuals across societies—whether directly, through institutions and organizations, or, more commonly, through the interaction of their governments—have been, still are, and probably will continue to be deeply influenced by modernization and its consequences. The consistent development of knowledge and its applications, the need to increase capabilities for production and domination, and the increase of constraints have generated a system of relationships based on trade, exchange, communication, movement, and diffusion: in other words, an interdependent system. The 'journeys toward progress'[81] are perceived not only as linked, but also as 'meeting' at intersections; some argue that they have been waiting too long for a 'green light.' Interdependence has produced many of the benefits promised by liberal philosophy, but it has also meant problems and conflicts. The problems and their solutions have transcended the nation-state.

The perception by many Third World leaders and intellectuals of dependency and their positing of a 'theory of dependency' are one of the reactions to interdependence. Those who perceive dependency see it as an explanation for underdevelopment and inequalities that characterize the Third World. They differ, however, about the meaning and effects of dependency. For some it is a question of asymmetry in interdependent relations. For others, dependency is perceived as a singular phenomenon in the history of the Third World, which is condemned to stagnation due to the advance of international capitalism. Still others accept the latter definition while admitting that dependency need not necessarily lead to stagnation and underdevelopment, but can also result in economic growth.[82]

Most of those who today perceive Third World countries as being 'dependent' on international capital, on MNCs, and on foreign technology have gone through a process of cognitive evolution about interdependence and its effects. The evolution has consisted of a movement away from perceiving interdependence (dependency) as something passive and beneficial (some would say also naïve) to perceiving it as a threat. Before cognitive evolution occurred, dependency was a non-issue; there was no awareness of it. But once the cognitive threshold was crossed, nothing was the same in relations between poor and rich countries, and the idea of self-reliance was born.

Self-reliance is a reaction by some political leaders and intellectuals in LDCs against what they consider to be the inequality, sense of degradation, and frustration that an interdependent economic and political system has placed upon them. Allowing for some nuances, self-reliance does not call for outright autarky but for autonomy and self-determination (nationalism), on the one hand, and for the redistribution of wealth at the national and international levels (equality), on the other.

Thus interdependence and self-reliance represent distinct and contrasting futures. Modernization processes will take different directions as a result of choices between interdependence and self-reliance. Self-reliance appeals to nationalists who have a perception of the inequalities both within and among nations, because self-reliance means more effective control of the process of change in which they are involved. It is a way to deal not only with inequality but also with complexity. Interdependent development means that, even if some of the inequality and nationalist feelings can be resolved, the development of new knowledge in one country (which implies change) induces change in other countries as well. Interdependent development means a more complex world. It follows that the choice between interdependence and self-reliance implies one of two different paths of action and interaction, which would lead each nation and the community of nations in different directions. For some, 'reinventing the wheel' to calm nationalistic overreactions and the haste to solve the problems of inequality seem wasteful and ill advised. For others, without autonomy and equality there is nothing to lose. Obviously it is an ideological question; the interaction of ideologies in the political realm leads to unpredictable paths. But actors, if aware of this, may be able to manage the interactions and outcomes, accommodating interests and improving their present collective situation.

Evolution, overlap, and social relativity

Throughout this study I have referred to cognitive change and alluded several times to evolution. But I have not stated how they are connected.

So much has been written about evolution, and the term has been applied so loosely to so many fields, that some clarifications are called for. Since Darwin's days, evolution has dramatically changed thinking about the physical, natural, and later the social worlds.

The theory of evolution was first applied to the social realm around 1860. The argument, based on the concept of the 'survival of the fittest,' was that the competitive struggle between races and nations is the key to the survival of some cultures and the extinction of others—i.e., the key for 'social evolution' and 'progress.' The fact that this 'Social Darwinism' was later instrumental in the development of the Fascist and Nazi ideologies led to its demise. Theories of social and cultural evolution continued to flourish in the twentieth century in sociology and anthropology, but without the survival-of-the-fittest argument.[83] These approaches, however, have been hindered by the difficulty of determining what really evolves, as well as by the fact that in most cases evolution is viewed as a teleological concept.

Ideas of finality, determinism, and unidirectional evolution are characteristic of Marxist thinking, according to which societies evolve because the ownership of the means of production passes from one class to another. Marx and his followers (with many nuances, of course) see this evolution as leading to the triumph of the proletariat and later to the classless society. Some intellectuals, including Teilhard de Chardin,[84] Kenneth Boulding[85] and Erich Jantsch,[86] have tried to unite natural realms—physical, biological, and social—into all-embracing theories of evolution, in which the processes evolve in an interconnected way toward some final stage: God for Chardin, ethics for Boulding, and self-transcendence for Jantsch. Other more recent teleological and deterministic 'evolutionary' approaches picture our changing world as moving toward decadence, depletion of resources, and the disruption of the environment—described with the metaphor of increasing entropy. The message is clear: something must be done to stop and/or redress this process of evolution if we want to save the world.[87]

My ideas of evolution, as applied to social science in general and to International Relations in particular, have no relation to the approaches described above. The idea of evolution provides our discipline with a different way to ask questions, expecting different answers. Isomorphism from the biological sciences would be misleading and self-defeating. Hence I do not mix biology and politics, as some have tried to do.[88] I borrow from the theory of evolution an insight, an idea, and a set of concepts that, combined with the knowledge available in our discipline, can shed some new light on international politics. My ideas of evolution are thus an exercise of metaphor. Although evolution is a paradigm[89] that is not empirically demonstrable, theories based on this paradigm should be testable.

What evolve are cognitions, ideas, and knowledge. These are politically relevant when their evolution serves as the basis for political decisions and actions that incrementally transform people, their interactions, and their environment. When we suddenly become aware of something; when we suddenly feel that we know something we did not know before; when we have an awareness of our awareness, i.e., when we have consciousness and rationally adjust our conscious insights to our previous consciousness; when consciousness becomes learning; when a non-issue becomes an issue: that is when we have taken a step forward, when our cognition has evolved. This is cognitive evolution.[90] When it occurs in the political realm, it changes ideas and ideologies about progress, development, distribution, conflict, and cooperation, thereby shaping the way in which societies are stratified, how 'pies' are divided, the reasons people go to war, the way they relate to each other, etc. Thus cognitive evolution determines how people interact across societies in a given functional dimension.

In *An Imagined World*, June Goodfield deals with the fascinating world of scientific creativity that culminates in the 'flash' or insight that influences the evolution of science. She quotes a scientist she calls 'Anna': 'I was looking at [certain cells] three weeks ago ... and I missed ... them because I was not looking for them. Now I am, and I see them. *But they were there all the time!* And what has changed? Only my thoughts.'[91] This illustrates that even the discovery of scientific facts is the result of cognitive evolution and that the object being observed and the observer are in interaction. This realization has begun to affect physics and biology today;[92] I propose that it is also valid in social science in general and in International Relations in particular. What this means is that the objects and the processes we study in International Relations emerge as 'phenomena' and 'relations' when we *become* conscious of their existence, when we learn about them.

Thus cognitive evolution helps unravel the old dilemma of what really changes—the objects, the 'systems,' or their representation in our minds. Knowledge in general—especially scientific knowledge—constitutes an irreversible and extremely important element in the cognitive-evolutionary process. After knowledge is created, diffused, and assimilated, it is indestructible, for it unites the past with the present and creates expectations and images of the future. This helps explain the difference between cognitive evolution and cognitive change. Once we know something, it cannot be erased from our minds.

We can better understand the evolutionary characteristic of cognitions and knowledge by means of the concept of overlap. Cognitive evolution may shake ideologies and well-rooted political assumptions about issues related to international conflicts, crises, wars, cooperation, and economic development. But the new ideas, cognitions, and images do not replace the old ones in a revolutionary way; they tend instead to emerge and coexist for a time with the old ones. This overlap is not static; rather, it changes continually, as ideas continue to flow. New ideas tend to push aside old ones, which no longer look the same; knowledge has been added irreversibly. This process in turn affects political decisions and actions in a continuous process of transformation. The overlap represents evolution in its deepest sense: in the overlap lies the mixture of the past, the present, and the future. The present holds the memories of what has been learned from the past as well as a sense of the future.

In order to survive, the results of cognitive evolution must be communicated and diffused; otherwise they can fade away and disappear, as species have. Knowledge and ideas never really disappear (except in cataclysmic circumstances). Nevertheless, ideas influence other ideas; when some are 'rediscovered' after a long period of 'non-existence', the past persists in the present.

Thus, once cognitive evolution has taken place, the cognitive results of evolution, in order to survive, must compete with other cognitions and knowledge in one's mind and in the cognitions and knowledge of others. This knowledge persists when it is able to affect something, whether other ideas and knowledge or social processes. In other words, to maintain the metaphorical development path that cognitive evolution has revealed, some change must be effected. For example, when cognitive evolution helps change political, economic, and social reality, the resulting changes will persist in the future. To be politically relevant, cognitive evolution has to influence the policymaking process and those involved in it.

But once cognitive evolution has occurred and once political events have happened, nationally and/or internationally, they have some effect, even if it is delayed until years after the events themselves. In fact, some changes take a long time to affect International Relations, because of the overlap discussed above. What overlap means in this context is that changes must deal with the 'inertia' caused by previous and present policies, relationships, functions, and organizations. Thus an apparent regression in a particular trend, whether ideological or material, may be only temporary if the effects of whatever caused this trend can become reality only after a long period of time. For example, the 'French revolution at first led back to a monarchy and at least 150 years were needed to fulfill some of its essential demands.'[93]

This brings us to a crucial point about cognitive evolution. Cognitive evolution and its communication and diffusion, the development path started by cognitive evolution, are open-ended. This is because they are determined by the experiences of the past (cognitive evolution is pushed from behind), which differ from one individual to another and from one nation to another, and because they are pulled forward by the actors' images of the future, i.e. by their expectations of the future—for example, about progress, modernization, and economic development[94]—which also differ from person to person and from nation to nation. Thus the direction of evolution is determined by the past, by images of the future, and by political choices in the present.

To elaborate on this point: systems, nations and other abstractions devised by the human mind to understand phenomena do not have a purpose. Human beings do. Once these purposes are translated into policy and action, their outcomes may not necessarily reflect the original intentions. As is well known in economics, there is a wide gap between 'micromotives' and 'macrobehavior.'[95] This is even more evident in politics, which is based on give and take, bargaining, accommodation, and bureaucratic interests and constraints.

The outcome of the interaction among international actors may not reflect only one ideological trend; it will probably reflect a process of adaptation and accommodation to one another's purposes. But each new ideological trend makes a difference. Cognitive evolution is the catalytic element in this process, for new knowledge, new ideas, and the change of ideologies affect the process of interaction and its ultimate outcome.

Cognitive evolution begins with ideas, which can be amplified though a social-change reaction that can transform policy and action. John Platt has coined the term 'seed operations' to describe the function of those who generate the ideas and knowledge. By generating the seeds (ideas) and then planting them, and by working indirectly and directly in the political process, they induce chain reactions that amplify ideas into a potential (policy) that bears some fruit from the cognitive point of view (cognitive evolution) and occasionally from the political point of view (the transformation of policies and change). 'Seed operations' are performed mainly but not exclusively by intellectuals.[96]

The idea of evolution is closely linked with that of complexity; many evolutionists, in fact, believe that evolution tends toward complexity. Viewed from an evolutionary perspective, complexity can shed some light on the relations between observed phenomena and the observer. To illustrate this point, we can define perceived international complexity as an increase in the number of actors, increased differentiation, increased interdependence, and plurality in the interactions among societies and across national borders. Note that complexity, from this point of view, is not a system or a 'whole.' It is real people—decision-makers, intellectuals, even the man in the street—who perceive complexity, for complexity is only an image in our minds.[97]

Harlan Wilson has defined *situational complexity* as the perception of many interdependent facts that are seen as essential for determining the course of action.[98] The perceiver is the decision-maker. Perceptual situational complexity has a direct impact on the choices of interdependence. *Analytical complexity* refers to the perception of a set of interrelated elements, as perceived by the observer of action. The observer selects the actions, relations, and structures he/she wants to study. The more actions, relations, and structures to choose from, the more complex the situation seems. The perceiver is usually the intellectual, the scholar, the political adviser and/or the scholar/decision-maker, who tries to make some sense of the 'reality' out there. He/she merely deals with a higher level of abstraction than the actor or decision-maker.

The act of selecting the variables on which the abstraction is based is very relevant, for the 'analytical structure' the theorist builds will always be partial, just one among many possibilities of 'complex reality.' 'The only limits to selection,' writes Wilson, 'are the ingenuity of scientific observers and the scientific, political, ideological, etc. criteria that govern selection.'[99] This is extremely important if we accept the proposition that analytical complexity influences choice and action by the interaction of intellectual activity and political actors and political action. For in contrast to remote galaxies, which are not changed by being studied, political thinking, political ideologies, and political behavior are influenced and changed when studied.

To put it graphically, when observers select A, B, and C among A, B, C, D, E, and F to describe some kind of international complexity, it means that D, E, and F vanish from their cognitive awareness of the problem or situation. Thus the more complexity we perceive in the object we are trying to make sense of, such as the international system, the more elements it has and the more difficult the choice becomes; but at the same time, the more elements are left out.

As complexity grows, our perceptual reality of the system of relations between actors decreases. As complex international interdependence grows, so do the issues and their interrelatedness; factors, events, and choices are lost from our awareness and perceptions. But the fact that we lose sight of these events and issues does not mean they actually disappear. They continue to be 'out there' and they continue to influence change. This, in part, explains the 'surprises' in International Relations when, suddenly, 'out of the blue,' something unanticipated occurs. Were we able to perceive the connections that lead to such a surprise event, we would not be surprised; if we do something to prevent it, it may not even occur. If we add to this factor the proposition that the actors who relate across boundaries are not only states but also corporations, institutions, organizations, and individuals, in many different arrangements and ways, the issue of complexity and unintended causes and consequences is even more striking.

Social relativity

The notion of cognitive evolution and its consequences leads to the conclusion that, in their own dimension, social phenomena are as relative as the relationship between space and time. Because individuals' interactions across borders and their structures depend on cognitive evolution, and because cognitive evolution leads to complexity, turbulent environments,[100] uncertainty, and partly indeterminate change, I call a social explanation of individuals' behavior and of its effects on the international field *social relativity*. There is nothing new about a phenomenological theory of causation; nor is it new in International Relations theory to focus on human beings' perceptions and expectations rather than on 'rational states balancing each other.' It is only when we connect these theoretical insights with the concept of evolution and the changing nature of knowledge, when we link it with non-equilibrium and change, and when we focus on the resulting evolution of interactions and structures that we arrive at the notion of indeterminism, open-ended processes, stochastic processes, and social relativity.

Social phenomena are relative because knowledge is constantly expanding. Our conditions and interactions with others keep changing all the time because of expanding knowledge and cognitive evolution; but there is more and more to learn and more and more we want to know. Social phenomena are also relative and diverse because they are the outcome of how different people think, what they know and choose, how they apply this knowledge, and how fast they interact among themselves.

A current of thought known as 'relativism' characterized the early part of the twentieth century. As then understood, relativism posited 'the infinite plasticity of the human self, or personality, which it sees as the effect of historical and cultural conditioning. Thus, for relativism there was no fixed human nature. Its emphasis was on the changing and variable determinants of personality and behavior.'[101] This philosophy was closely related to historical relativism, better known as 'historicism.' Largely a nineteenth-century product, historicism 'exulted in the infinite variety of historical phenomena, in the uniqueness of each successive age and culture'; consequently it opposed abstract generalizations.[102] Relativism and historicism were vehemently disputed,[103] but this dispute has almost faded away. Because of the rigidity of both supporters and detractors of relativism and historicism, I identify with neither of them.

Social relativity, as I conceive it, is an *ideology of causality*, so we cannot 'prove' it through positivist methods of inquiry. Also, social relativity is not 'relativistic' in the sense of deducing social phenomena from people's personalities. It is not historicism, because it is a set of abstractions about what causes phenomena and how they change across time. Thus social relativity is not just an abstraction and a generalization; it is the highest level of abstraction and generalization. On the other hand, socially relative theories—in particular, about International Relations—can be constructed and studied using empirical methods. In order to build such theories we need to identify the actors and their ideologies; we need to focus on their evolving images, perceptions, and expectations; we need to see how cognitive evolution affects policymaking and how relationships, policies, and events are shaped. We also need to see how policies of one actor interact with those of another, how one adapts to a change by another, and how these relationships change over time.

IR theories that develop from this ideology of causality would have to concentrate to a great extent on choices, which are what drive actors to change and their relationships to fluctuate. Choice from this perspective involves two sets of variables: (1) the cognitive, affective, and evaluative dimension of the human mind; and (2) reason (present), memory (past), and imagination and creativity (future). It is in their interdependence and combination that a theory of choice can be developed.

Illustration: social relativity and the idea of progress

The idea of progress is subjective; it is ideological. A particular set of beliefs leads some people to see material wealth, technological change, and economic growth as the elements needed to improve the human condition. Others ask: 'Improvement for whom? What kind of improvement?' Progress is the perceived terminus toward which we are traveling and which, if reached, seems to generate more stations down the line. Progress can be efficiency, security, basic human needs, power for the sake of power, equality, a combination of the above, and many other ideas as well. Values and beliefs about progress lead to an image of the future that leads policymakers to set objectives and means to turn the image into reality.

The variations and differences among individuals are sufficient reason to make the idea of progress relative; but there is more. The material or spatial dimension of progress, such as well-being (for the individual (liberalism), for the class (Marxism), or for the nation (nationalism)), or technological development can be truly understood only with the addition of the *time dimension*, i.e., the projection of our images of the past and the future onto the present. This projection affects the choices we make about progress. In other words, progress becomes a self-fulfilling prophecy.

For example, the image of the future can be optimistic: 'human creativity, imagination, ingenuity, engineering, etc., can solve all problems'; or it can be pessimistic, evoking images such as 'entropy, social decay, the discovery of limits, spaceship Earth,' etc. These time-based projections largely determine people's images, perceptions, and expectations about spatial–material objects: wealth, technology, and well-being. Material well-being is thus relative to our time dimension of progress; time and space meet in the concept of progress and overlap.

Conclusion

I will conclude this essay by pointing to one major implication of my approach. Our discipline has so far had little success in predicting future events. We have tried to predict crises and wars; but events usually surprised us nevertheless. The notions of evolution and non-equilibrium, as explained in this essay, should sensitize us to the idea that a complex system of relationships generated by human beings—who have contrasting images, perceptions, expectations, and ideologies—cannot lead to easy predictions. According to David Park,

> The great difference between our understanding of past and future is a difference in the complexity of the guessing games they offer. ... The past presents relatively few choices—with a small amount of information we can make a good guess at what it was. For the future, we would need absurd quantities of data to rule out the alternatives. How is this? The amount of data you need before you can say you know something is a measure of the complexity of the alternatives offered. ... [A world without living beings] ... will remain almost constant in complexity. Then the future will be known almost as well as the past. How can this be? Simply because since nothing will be happening, there will be nothing to remember or predict. It is the tremendous rate at which the

world changes now, even our little corner of it, that makes prediction hard. There are other lives and deaths possible for the world than mere equilibrium.[104]

Our discipline will have to show innovative and creative approaches to deal with change and adaptation to change. We need to know much more about why and how these processes occur, what affects these processes, and how they can be managed. We need to add techniques and methodologies to our study of International Relations and systems. One beneficial method, for example, is scenario-building—scenarios constructed not only on the basis of our cognitions, but also on what we believe are the ideologies, perceptions, and expectations of others. The 'becoming' and social-relativity approach invites us to place ourselves in someone else's shoes and to try harder to understand the behavior of other countries, people, and cultures. In fact, it can be argued that the measure of realism this approach would create would compensate for the uncertainties and unpredictability inherent in our social relations.

We should also take account of as many cross-catalytic influences as possible, and always assume fluctuation and change, rather than equilibrium and stability, in our systems and our environment. When building scenarios, we should realize that the future and images of the future are as important as the present and the very short-run consequences of our actions. This is not an idealist position, for we not only owe it to future generations (we 'construct' their future), but we also owe it to ourselves to take the future into account in our theories. In sum, our most important policy-relevant contribution should be not trying to predict the unpredictable but affecting the process of cognitive evolution with our ideas and our scientific knowledge.

The essential message of social relativity, of open-ended evolution, and 'order through fluctuations' is one of guarded optimism. There is no deterministic road down the slope of history toward entropy, decay, disorder, and annihilation. But there is also no determined process toward improvement and nirvana. The future will depend on our perceptions, expectations, and images of the future; it will depend on the choices of decision-makers and on the cross-catalytic effects of those choices. Human beings have the capability to shape their own future in the present: they can be creative, cooperative, adaptive, imitative, self-reflective; but they can also be destructive. I will consider that this essay's objectives have been achieved if, at least for a few scholars, it becomes a source of *cognitive evolution*.

3 Cognitive evolution

A dynamic approach for the study of International Relations and their progress

This was the first published presentation (other than my dissertation) of my theory of cognitive evolution. Cognitive evolution describes a process of collective learning in which innovative ideas preferentially survive processes of political selection and institutionalization and thus become the foundation of new international practices and national interests. This article explores whether a change of practices and interests can be progressive for International Relations. It also introduces the concept of epistemic communities and illustrates the theory with a case of social innovation that became institutionalized: the post-World War II system of economic governance. In its original form the article also included a case study on nuclear arms control. Because I cover this subject more exhaustively in chapter 6, I have excised that section from this chapter.

Originally published in Emanuel Adler and Beverly Crawford, eds,
Progress in Postwar International Relations
(New York: Columbia University Press, 1991, 43–88)

Being and becoming

A hunter sees a live duck. He makes a 'rational' prediction of its speed and movement, wind speed, and other physical conditions; aims at the point where he figures it will be when his shot reaches it; shoots … and misses. But the same hunter aiming at a duck in a shooting gallery at a county fair will most likely 'kill.' The difference lies in the fact that live ducks can suddenly turn to the right, to the left; they can back or tumble; they can move in undeterministic and unpredictable ways. Ducks have reflexes and they can surprise us.

The contrast between the target duck and the live duck can illustrate the difference between 'being' and 'becoming.' 'Being' is a prevalent notion that sees everything in nature and society as static and mechanistic—including change. The idea of 'becoming' considers everything to be in flux, as a permanent process of change and evolution, even that which appears to be static.

Galileo, Descartes, and Newton can be mentioned as 'intellectual parents' of being. In their concepts of nature (and philosophy), 'space and time were absolute, in the sense of existing objectively and of being completely independent of any physical content. Matter, to be sure, occupied, and moved in, space, but space itself remained ... "always similar and immovable." ' [1] Since then, science and the arts have evolved considerably from being to becoming, over a period of several centuries. For example, Voltaire, Rousseau, Kant, and Hegel can be seen as links in this chain of the transformation of ideas. But becoming grew stronger as we approached the twentieth century. The most important transformation occurred in the second half of the nineteenth century and the beginning of the twentieth because of the work of Charles Darwin, Herbert Spencer, Henri Bergson, and Albert Einstein, among others. The philosophical ideas about becoming promoted developments in physics, which at the same time influenced the former. The formulation of quantum theory by Max Planck and the theory of relativity by Einstein fueled philosophical ideas of becoming.[2]

International Relations theories, mainly of the realist and neorealist strands, are still based on the image of being.[3] International systems and their components have been perceived as Newtonian elements, 'suspended in space'; time has little to do with them and movement and change are linear, just like the ducks in the shooting gallery. This kind of theory studies International Relations and international phenomena according to the metaphors of equilibrium and balance of power: It looks for the recurrent, for 'stability,' and tries to predict the future from past events. International Relations theory thereby fails to grasp the nature of the phenomena it tries to describe and explain, which are in flux and evolution. It therefore has been and still is basically shooting at live ducks as if they were the predictable ones that rhythmically move along the gallery track.

Kenneth Waltz's *Theory of International Politics* and Robert Gilpin's *War and Change in World Politics*[4] are among the best illustrations of being. Waltz's theory deals with structural continuity,[5] yet continuity here means change within a similar pattern rather than the absence of change itself. (Without any change there would be no reason for theories.) However, to catch the essence of change within a pattern—wherein anarchy and the stratification of power determine 'broad expectations about the quality of international–political life'—Waltz has portrayed an international system and a concept of change that strikingly resemble Newton's astronomical universe.[6] He has taken space and time—indeed the international system itself—as absolute, in the sense of existing objectively and of being independent of the content of units and their attributes. Waltz has therefore portrayed a predictable and static balance-of-power system, in which movement is linear and change automatic.[7] Emphasizing equilibrium, he has looked for the recurrent; stressing material power alone, he has overlooked the capacity of humans to change the meaning and understanding of power with a change in expectations and values, which occurs at the unit level— the 'ultimate source of systemic change.'[8] The crux of the matter, however, is that expectations, whether general or specific, are not 'readily amenable to cause and effect "clocklike" models or metaphors. ... The actors in politics have memories; they learn from experience. They have goals, aspirations, and calculative strategies. Memory, learning, goal seeking and problem solving intervene between "cause" and "effect," between independent and dependent variable.'[9]

Gilpin's *War and Change* proposes an elegant and provocative theory of change. To Gilpin, however, change means only the rearrangement of things:

> In every international system there are continual occurrences of polit-
> ical, economic and technological changes that promise gains or threaten
> losses for one or another actor. ... As a consequence of the changing
> interests of individual states, and especially because of the differential
> growth in power among states, the international system moves from a
> condition of equilibrium to one of disequilibrium.[10]

Equilibrium must be restored because a disjunction has been created between the existing, basically unchanged, social system—the hierarchy of prestige, the division of territory, the international division of labor, and the rules of the system—and the redistribution of power, which now favors those actors that would benefit most from a change in the system, and that disjunction has weakened the foundations of the existing system. Although the resolution and restoration of equilibrium may happen peacefully, the 'principal mechanism of change throughout history has been war.'[11] Change in world politics, therefore, turns out to be the perpetual rise and decline of hegemons; political, economic and social changes are important only insofar as they fuel the differential growth process that leads to mechanistic alter-ations in the positions of things; and war is mostly determined in the 'celestial' mechanics by which the system rearranges itself.

Because states move deterministically like the ducks in the shooting gallery, caught as it were in the equilibrium–disequilibrium–equilibrium movements caused by differential growth, their interests, as well as their motivations, are predetermined, and changes in the nature and quality of things are ruled out unless and until we 'learn to develop an effective mecha-nism of peaceful change.'[12] But Gilpin's approach does not provide us with the tools and incentives to inquire how, why, and when an effective mecha-nism of peaceful change may develop. Thus, for example, his theory cannot show under what conditions Great Powers will choose peaceful change, even when there are structural opportunities to win a hegemonic war.

My critique is not based on a radical historicist and reflectivist view of International Relations,[13] for it 'is far from clear on what grounds history and historicism can provide an adequate alternative to the structuralist turn.'[14] The alternative, therefore, is to look at International Relations as partly determinate or '*intermediate* in character between perfect chance and perfect determinism—something intermediate between perfect clouds and perfect clocks,'[15] and to adopt a becoming epistemology that would be able to catch both *historical* and *structural* forces, explaining change in a dynamic way. This epistemology would have to bridge an ontology based upon a strong element of intersubjectivity and an epistemology that has circumvented the actors and looked for explanations exclusively at the structural level.[16]

Following and trying to build on the work of Ernst Haas, I claim that the bridge can be built with the aid of an epistemology that Donald T. Campbell called evolutionary,[17] which, consistent with a contemporary interpretation of science[18] and evoking what Campbell called 'epistemic humility,'[19] makes the intersubjective level of analysis more 'real' or 'objective' and more amenable to generalization, and our epistemological assumptions less cast-iron and more dynamic.

To Haas, an evolutionary epistemology has meant that politics is a historical process that changes with physical changes and with the evolution of meanings. When applying evolutionary thinking to the study of international regimes, Haas has argued that emphasis should be placed on learning and on the collective understandings of political choices, which depend on how we think about nature and culture.[20] Learning thus is a creative process by which individuals and organizations reevaluate cause–effect relationships and arrive at new interpretations of the social world; these interpretations are then injected back into the historical process, where they affect political action and events.[21]

Evolutionary epistemology

The evolutionary epistemology Haas is using to grasp the dynamic nature of International Relations can be traced back to Popper's understanding of the process by which knowledge grows[22] and to a group of philosophers and psychologists who have followed Popper's insights. This is true with Campbell's ideas on cognitive evolution, Thomas Kuhn's insight about paradigms and their evolution, and Stephen Toulmin's idea of the evolution of concepts and disciplines.[23] These ideas, paradigms, or concepts have something in common: they refer to interpretative practices and collective meanings and understandings, neither valid nor true *a priori*, that evolve into the collective expression of human understanding at a particular time and place, after being selected by authoritative processes.

What the group mentioned earlier has found in the realm of scientific growth and human behavior to be similar or compatible (but not isomorphic) to natural selection processes, I find it useful to describe and explain as the evolution of common understandings in International Relations, which I see as a condition for change and for progress. The main insight that I carry over from natural selection processes to International Relations, by way of the philosophical understanding of scientific growth, is that at any point in the time and place of a historical process, international actors, mainly nation-states, may be affected by politically relevant collective sets of under-standings of the physical and social worlds that are subject to political selection processes and thus to evolutionary change.

Popper's evolutionary epistemology can be summarized as taking a succession of theories in science as similar to the process of selective elimi-nation in nature. According to Popper, the highest creative thought, like animal adaptation, is the product of 'blind variation' and 'selective reten-tion,' or to use his own terminology, a product of trial and error, or of conjectures and refutations.[24] This means that science is never free from assumptions, and at every instant it presupposes a horizon of expectations or a frame of reference that precedes and confers meanings or significance on our experience, actions, and observations. As hypotheses are falsified and replaced by others, so are the meanings we confer on experience, on action, and on observations. From this point of view, therefore, science is a 'shot in the dark,' a bold guess that goes far beyond the evidence and to which justification is less important than the viability of the mutation. The problem of whether a theory is 'true' or not is resolved by exposing the 'mutations' to the processes of selection, or attempted criticism and refutation. Survival in this process does not justify the survivor, either; a species that has survived for thousands of years may nevertheless become extinct. A theory that has survived for generations may eventually be refuted.[25]

To show that his theory of 'conjectures and refutations' does not turn science into a subjective and relativist enterprise, Popper introduced the notion of 'World 3,' which, in contrast to 'World 1' (the physical universe) and to 'World 2' (the subjective experience of individuals), encompasses the products of the human mind, such as art, scientific theories, technologies, institutions, plans, stories, and myths. These may be autonomous of any knowing subject, once they are communicated, that is, once they have become part of a collective understanding or culture.[26] World 3, thus, is the world of the logical content of books, computers, and institutions; it is 'real' because, once communicated to and shared by other individuals, it can affect the physical environment through all manner of intended and unintended consequences.[27]

Following Popper, one can turn the understanding of International Relations into a problem of control; that is, the 'control of behavior and other aspects of the physical world by human ideas.'[28] In contrast to the cast-iron control one gets from a deterministic and mechanistic episte-mology, an evolutionary epistemology offers the alternative of 'plastic control,' which, by combining notions of freedom and control, enhances our understanding of how such nonphysical things as plans, decisions, theories, intentions, and values can play a part in bringing about physical changes in the physical world.[29]

Kuhn's concepts of 'paradigms' and 'scientific revolutions' help explain the organizing effect of World 3 'products' that transcend the subjective minds of particular individuals and thus highlight the effect of shared understanding in International Relations and their evolution. Kuhn has shown that in any type of scientific discipline a collectively agreed-upon set of concepts and epistemological understandings creates the framework for research by structuring the activities of science and scientists. The bulk of 'normal' science, according to this view, consists of solving problems within the paradigm, which indicates what 'makes sense,' what phenomena are important, what questions to ask, and what inferences to draw. Most important for our purposes, the paradigm leads scientists to flatly reject evidence that is fundamentally out of line with the expectations it generates.[30] It follows, then, that scientific communities give meaning to data and evidence in accordance with the paradigms that govern periods of 'normal' science. However, during scientific revolutions, those critical moments when belief about scientific phenomena changes—much as during changes in beliefs about religion or politics or among aesthetic interpretive communities—one paradigm replaces another, and a new period of normal science commences.[31]

The notion that scientific paradigms structure the development of scientific concepts and make nature intelligible is not alien to Toulmin, for whom science progresses not by recognizing the truth of new observations but by making sense of them.[32] Taking evolution as a shift in the composition of a gene pool shared by a population, rather than as specified in an individual, Toulmin creates an explicit analogy between population genetics and the evolution of concepts that I find congenial with Popper's interpretation of the evolution of science and with Kuhn's concept of paradigmatic change. Substituting competing intellectual variants for genes, and indicating the *collectivity* of scientists as being the carriers of selective variants, Toulmin explains that, through processes of selective diffusion and retention, some intellectual variants eventually become predominant, others are completely eliminated, and still others do not remain viable but do not disappear and may come back as circumstances change.[33] Science progresses—and social processes evolve—through intellectual innovation and authoritative selection; what survives is collective understandings as embedded in institutions.

Like Toulmin, Campbell uses the evolutionary metaphor and relies on processes of innovation and selection for explaining how ideas, beliefs, and behavior change, but he goes further than the authors previously mentioned in explaining learning and creative learning, which he conceptualizes as cognitive evolution. The three requirements for evolution are: (1) mechanisms for replication or reproduction; (2) variety in whatever is reproduced; and (3) mechanisms for selection that consistently favor one type of variation over others. In cognitive evolution, learning provides the mechanisms for replication. Our ideas, beliefs, and behavior are learned from other people. When variation is introduced into this learning process, creativity results.[34]

Cognitive evolution

I will present here a theory of collective learning in International Relations that follows my evolutionary epistemological principles. The theory interprets foreign policy as a process by which intellectual innovations are carried by domestic institutions and selected by political processes to become the descriptive and normative set of understandings of what it takes to advance the nation's power, influence, and wealth. Likewise, the theory interprets international politics as a process of diffusion of domestic initiatives and innovations through agenda setting, strategic interaction, negotiation, and intersubjective processes involving socialization and learning. My argument is that we can find the sources of collective learning in International Relations at the national level—more precisely, in processes of intellectual innovation and political selection—and that, with increasing interdependence and diplomatic, political, economic, and cultural contacts, nations transmit to each other the political innovations that have been selectively retained at the national level. Power plays a crucial role in both domestic selection and international diffusion processes. I also argue that, once values and expectations that affect concepts and understandings in International Relations are shared, they help condition or structure International Relations. The latter part of my theory builds on a concept developed by James Rosenau that he called 'aggregative processes,' a dynamic or set of dynamics whereby individual actions are summed and thereby converted into collectivities and then at subsequent points of time converted over and over again into more or less encompassing collectivities.[35]

Robert Putnam describes international politics as a 'two-level game.' He suggests that at the

> national level, domestic groups pursue their interests by pressuring the government to adopt favorable policies, and politicians seek power by constructing coalitions among those groups. At the international level, national governments seek to maximize their own ability to satisfy domestic pressures, while minimizing the adverse consequences of foreign developments.[36]

I argue, in addition, that the two-level games are not only about fixed interests and power, but also about the selection, retention, and spread of expectations and values at national and international levels. The domestic game therefore refers to how expectations and values enter into the political process through the active participation of political groups with a stake in them, and how through the political process (e.g., coalition building) these ideas help define the national interest, which then becomes a conceptual and normative input to the international game. In the international game, governments act not only out of concern for the domestic political environment, but are also motivated by solutions—whether through conflict or cooperation—to problems, solutions whose interpretation and meanings are embedded in the national interest. As part of this game, governments transmit expectations and values that compete to become the basis of international behavior.

I operationalize this theory by showing how national interests are born, how they become part of a general *domestic* political understanding that helps create political agendas, policy options, and bargaining positions, and how such understanding can have both interactive and structural effects at the international level. My approach therefore captures the essence of creativity in International Relations, when new alternatives are generated and when political actors suddenly become aware of something new. Understanding how change in International Relations occurs, therefore, entails grasping how national interests are created and how their essence is transmitted to other nations.

Thus, a structural theory of International Relations calls equally for a theory of cognitive and institutional change as its natural complement. We need to learn how cognitive and institutional variants make their appearance in the first place, how they show their merits as solutions to outstanding international problems, and how they succeed—given favorable conditions—in spreading and establishing themselves more widely. We therefore must pay attention not only to the distribution of power and to the structural–functional aspects of institutions, but also to the historical processes by which political innovations demonstrate their validity as solutions to domestic and international problems.[37]

The searching theory of learning

Realists view learning as a response to structural changes in the environment or, in game-theory terms, as adjustment of state behavior to changes in the pay-off matrix.[38] But game-theoretical approaches, as well as others that deal with cooperation from a realist perspective,[39] say very little about the sources of preferences, how interests are created in one area and not in another, why at a certain time and not before or later, and whether there is creative learning.

I define learning as the adoption by policymakers of new interpretations of reality, as they are created and introduced to the political system by individuals and institutions. This implies that national policymakers are subject to absorbing new meanings and interpretations of reality, as generated in intellectual, bureaucratic, and political circles, and therefore are subject to changing their interests and ability and/or willingness to consider new courses of action. Seen in this light, learning increases the capacity and motivation to understand competing alternatives to a currently entertained inference and becomes a creative process by which alternatives and preferences or 'interests' are generated. The capacity to generate new cognitions is related not only to the acquisition of new information about the environment but also to new and innovative ways of drawing linkages between causes and effects and between means and ends.

This last point is crucial if we are to understand International Relations from an evolutionary epistemology perspective. Most of the notions of learning used in the literature do not lend themselves to such study because they are informed by what Popper called the 'bucket theory of science.' According to this theory, most, if not all, of what we learn is by the entry of experience into our sense openings, so that all knowledge consists of information received by experience. Our mind is a 'bucket,' originally more or less empty, into which material enters, and where it accumulates and becomes digested.[40]

Popper believes this theory is wrong. Instead, he offers a 'search-light theory of science,' wherein experience or observations are secondary to the theories or hypotheses people already have in their minds. These theories color, inform, and even determine the kind of observations and anticipations we make.[41] For learning to occur, therefore, we need to change not only our 'knowledge' base but also our underlying theories. In any social context, consensus over these theories is also necessary. Thus, without an assessment of the theories and hypotheses and of the ideological barriers that impede trans-ideological communication, 'lessons' from experience may have very little impact, falling, as it were, in the 'bucket.'

The theories or hypotheses people have in their minds we call 'expectations.' Human knowledge consists of linguistically formulated expectations that are continually submitted to critical assessment and reality tests.[42] Thus an expectation can be described as an image of the future bounded by what is physically, humanly, and socially possible. To expect is to imagine situations and events that seem possible, given a certain act. Popper's theory of learning therefore assumes that learning consists in the modification or rejection of expectations. He backs his arguments with a logical exercise: expectations could not arise just from experience because experience presupposes repetition; repetition presupposes similarity, and similarity presupposes a theory or an expectation. Thus, any observation is always preceded by a question, a problem, something theoretical, that carries expectations.[43]

In this sense all knowledge, including scientific knowledge, is subject to bias;[44] therefore, regardless of the content of knowledge, the difference between facts and hypotheses is assumed to be one of subjective confidence rather than of objective truth.[45] It follows, then, that, depending on the conditional 'if–then' linkages (major premises) that individuals happen to form, several conclusions or inferences can be deduced from a piece of 'evidence,' and in this sense any conclusion or inference inevitably goes 'beyond the information given.'[46]

When we apply this interpretation to International Relations, it follows that: (1) the environment does not 'instruct' policymakers, but challenges them; and (2) scientific knowledge is not a sufficient condition for international learning because it can be subject to bias, sometimes as much as nonscientific knowledge. The capacity of institutions in different countries to learn and to generate similar interests, therefore, will depend not only on the acquisition of new information, but also on the political selection of similar cause–effect premises. The political importance of these premises lies not in their being 'true,' but in their being shared across institutions and nation-states. Learning in International Relations takes place as biases or collective understandings (as World 3 phenomena) become selected, anchored,[47] established, and spread across institutions in different nation-states. I will show that this approach may have profound implications for how we think about progress in International Relations. If the key to change lies in the sharing of 'biases' or expectations that need not be *a priori* valid or 'true,' then scientists, *their values*, and the institutions they help build or in which they participate may play a political role in the process of change equal to or even greater than knowledge itself.

Cognitive evolution

Cognitive evolution is the process of innovation and political selection, occurring mainly within and between institutional settings, that creates the 'objective' collective understanding that informs the interests of government. A cognitive evolutionary approach requires that new or changed ideas be communicated and diffused and that political stakes be created that political groups and institutions and other interest groups may then help maintain through the use of power. To be politically relevant, cognitive evolution must be backed by enough power to invalidate and make people set aside competing expectations and values.

Cognitive evolution is politically relevant because it replaces cause–effect and end–means relationships that collectivities accept as true, thus leading to new political, military, and economic strategies and to the channeling of action in new and different directions. This in turn will most likely lead to the creation of new interests, institutions, and interest and pressure groups, which will further create new paths and alternatives. As each new path is taken, others will be abandoned, and the world out there will never be the same. For once

> a critical choice has been made it cannot be taken back; ... once a path is taken it canalizes future developments. Sidney Verba has referred to this conceptualization as the branching tree model of sequential development. A critical choice forecloses other options in part because the 'choice to set up a program in relation to a particular problem area may lead almost inevitably to the maintenance and even expansion of the program because of the vested interests it creates.'[48]

Cognitive evolution and branching-tree models may imply some kind of historical irreversibility, but what is really irreversible? A revolution may topple a democratic regime, but democracy may be restored. Nations go to war, but they later make peace; progress is reversible, and so is regress. Cognitive evolution is irreversible only in the sense that it adds new meanings and understandings to collective experience.[49]

Crises may play an important role in cognitive evolution because change in political processes tends to be episodic. 'The importance of crises,' says John Ikenberry,

> stems from the intransigence of political institutions and relations. Politicians and administrators are continuously engaged in coping with socioeconomic challenges; responses are channeled through existing institutions. At particular moments, however, these challenges call into question existing rules of the game and the repertories of state action.[50]

Thus, dramatic events such as war, depression, acute hunger, or a large environmental accident such as Chernobyl may have the effect of a 'cognitive punch,' making apparent to political actors that existing institutions and types of political behavior have become dysfunctional and can no longer deal with the situation in the old ways. A crisis is thus an environmental incentive to hasten the process of reevaluation and change from one set of collective understandings or 'paradigms' to another. It helps show, in fact, that policies based on old analogies to the past are likely to have deleterious consequences.[51]

Cognitive evolution therefore is a useful corrective to institutional approaches that have used a branching-tree model but disregarded the cognitive factor. Although historical circumstances and institutional realities may tend to limit, delay, and even prevent institutional change,[52] the latter does sometimes take place. And when it does, it is most likely to be the result of a dynamic process of change in collective understandings.

Cognitive evolution involves three processes:

Innovation—the creation of new expectations and values that become collective within institutions.

Selection—political processes that determine which policies are effectively adopted and therefore which expectations and values are selected to be tested in politics, in both national and international arenas. Political selection then determines which expectations and values become at least temporarily perpetuated: 'The continuing emergence of intellectual innovation is thus balanced against a continuing process of critical selection.'[53]

Diffusion—the spread of expectations and values to other nations. As international negotiations agendas are created on the basis of new expectations and values and as negotiation and diplomatic processes begin, diplomats, acting on behalf of a set of ideas as well as a set of policies, 'communicate to the leaders of other states their 'theoretical' understanding ... in addition to signaling their intent on the particular issue at hand.'[54]

Innovation

New or radically different theories, expectations, and values may occasionally arise that 'represent the acquisition of a new understanding.'[55] Innovation occurs when new meanings and interpretations are generated by individuals within institutional structures. The realization of conceivable expectations depends largely on their practical application, on their timing, and on the ability of those individuals who urge a particular interpretation of the national interest to anticipate the exigencies and needs of the political structures involved in the selection process. From this point of view, innovation is not 'blind' but is in a sense preselected; innovators have to bear in mind the requirements for selection.[56]

Personal originality, of course, plays an important role in the innovation process as collective understanding is realized through the intellectual performances of individuals; but what matters is that meanings and interpretations are shared. Epistemic communities, defined loosely as a group of intellectuals sharing a common causal understanding on a particular subject and who organize to turn this understanding into action strategies,[57] can play an important role in the innovation process, especially when issues depend on some kind of technical knowledge, as most issues now do.

Selection

The actors, structures, and processes of the political system determine which expectations and values are turned into policies. The policymaker, in principle at least, serves as judge, jury, and, if necessary, executioner for the professional output of expectations developed at the institutional level.[58] Expectations and values can thus be satisfied only through policy decisions. Those selected are the ones that pass the test of domestic politics. Given that no political idea, whatever its origin or content, is valid *a priori* but is validated only by the political process, domestic institutions must persuade other actors, especially those at the top of the political hierarchy, of the validity of the ideas advanced by the institutions. What we must ask now is: on what occasions and by what processes and procedures are institutional expectations and values discredited and abandoned in favor of new or new/old sets of expectations and values?

My view of the selection process requires a fresh look at the concept of state and the role of institutions, one that transcends the idea of state used by realists and neorealists of the systemic and game-theoretical strands. In my view, states are still the essential actors of International Relations; they are made up of many institutions and entities competing for authority, each with its own 'embedded orientations or dispositions to act'[59] and each able to learn different 'lessons.' The state is not, however, merely an aggregation of bureaus acting according to their 'standard operating procedures,' as the various bureaucratic and bureaucratic–organizational models often suggest,[60] but a historical entity represented by institutions, each with a particular collective understanding or set of expectations and values. Some institutions will undoubtedly carry more power than others in the selection process and make the critical choices in the international arena, but those choices will be affected by conceptions and understandings developed, in and through politics, by institutions that 'work together, neither "for good" entirely nor "for ill" entirely, but simply as their joint histories dictate.'[61]

The state should not be presumed to be 'rational.' Rationality must be asserted and proved in every instance, according to the ability of the state to change expectations and values and select political solutions that deal effectively with problems. Thus, the rational state is a historical entity that—pregnant with new and old expectations arising from various groups and institutions that respond in different ways to real problems—is able to learn by selecting political solutions that can deal with problems better.

Two important implications follow from my conceptualization of the state. First, progress in International Relations will depend on the extent to which the state can solve problems in such a way as to enhance security, welfare, and human rights across national borders. Second, the national interest is the intersubjective consensus that survives the political process, given the distribution of power in the society. The 'objective' national interest is therefore a World 3 product that, once produced, can have various real intended and unintended consequences. The key question from a becoming perspective, then, is how to effect changes in ideational and ideological assumptions. The preliminary answer is through the creation of new formal or informal institutions that incorporate a new set of expectations and values.[62]

Diffusion: international cognitive structures

International collective understandings are constituted and international organization may even take place when institutions of different countries share and coordinate their expectations and values. 'The world indeed becomes more organized when participants of the processes build consensus on what factors have caused what events, what has gone wrong, and what has to be done to resume the correct order.'[63] The study of International Relations then deals with processes by which governments seek to establish their understanding of the world and of phenomena and coordinate their behavior according to a set of causal understandings. Thus, when states negotiate and renegotiate their respective interests, they also implicitly negotiate and renegotiate meanings and understandings. Nations that get together in direct negotiations or that are brought together by strategic interaction and are linked by security, economic, and technological interdependence will affect each other's intentions, plans, expectations, and policies. One way this can happen is by what Robert Legvold has called 'interactive' learning, which occurs when one society learns from another.[64] This has been the case with the gradual acceptance by the Soviets of the importance of having secure second-strike, or retaliatory, nuclear forces, which may have been influenced, if not directly affected, by theories of deterrence developed in the United States and by American strategic behavior. [65] Processes of interactive learning and socialization imply, then, that as individuals and institutions transmit to each other their expectations and values, they also transmit *descriptive and normative conceptions of the national interest.*

We can describe the World 3 theoretical understanding of social phenomena that conditions the convergence of expectations of those states that share it as a 'cognitive structure.'[66] A related though not similar concept is that of the 'thought collective,' developed by Ludwik Fleck.[67] Cognitive structures generate the 'evidence' that confirms their validity, and treat those actions that can be considered anomalous to the collective understanding as 'errors.' Collective understandings can be based either on scientific knowledge or on interpretation of historical events. Cognitive structures, like scientific paradigms, have conditioning and constraining effects on what people consider 'right' or 'wrong,' where they place their attention, and what expectations they develop. Several cognitive structures may coexist at any given time, and power may play a major role in determining which ones will survive.

Because World 3 products produce observable effects, we can justify their importance as ontological constructs. In this sense, I adhere to the observation made by Alexander Wendt in his justification of the ontological status of non-observable structures, to the effect that even if unobservable, social structures (or in my case international cognitive structures) can produce observable effects and their manipulation can affect the observable world.[68]

Cognitive structures organize rather than constrain behavior; in other words, they apply plastic control to a situation. These structures are 'generative,'[69] but only in the sense that they generate foreign policy as if International Relations were structured as thought.[70] The world is made sensible by interpreting agents who create collective understandings that acquire a life of their own as 'objective' products, thus generating policy responses, institution-building, and agendas across national borders.

My theory could be portrayed as structurationist,[71] to the extent that institutional agents play a role in effecting broader collective understandings, at both the domestic and the international level, and subsequently these collective understandings help organize relations and condition, in part, the behavior of institutions. I am reformulating somewhat the structuration concept, however. First, my theory deals with two sets of agent–structure relations. In my 'national game,' institutions are the agents and the structure is trans-institutional. In my 'international game,' states are the agents and the structure is transnational. Second, the structures I refer to *do not generate* the agents and their behavior;[72] they acquire their causal efficacy as World 3 products once they become part of international political agendas and negotiation processes. Third, agents and structures are not codetermined;[73] rather, the agent, through political processes, succeeds (or fails) in introducing its innovation and turning it into a World 3 product. Later this innovation may have organizational effects on the motivation and behavior of national actors. In other words, the structures I am describing are part of the historical process, explain the actual, and do not fully determine behavior. My theory, then, does not have to deal with structural and historical research simultaneously,[74] because structures and history are complementary.

Cognitive evolution, values and progress in International Relations

A national interest will emerge, or be transformed, because of a combination of descriptive–explanatory understandings with normative judgments.[75] For progress in International Relations to take place, the normative content of such national interest as is spread internationally must place a high value— relative to other values—on human beings, regardless of their nationality. Progress in International Relations will depend less on the advancement of science *per se*, or on the cunning of reason, than on the political selection, retention, and diffusion of values that tend to enhance security, welfare, and human rights across borders.

Values

Realism takes values as unproblematic and constant; for example, values are given in game-theoretical studies. Yet how 'values are developed, maintained, and changed may be crucial to international politics, and may strongly influence the extent of cooperation'[76] and the prospects for progressive change in International Relations.[77] It is meaningful to speak about terminal or end values and instrumental values, as it is to speak about institutional values, which Milton Rokeach defined as socially shared cognitive representations of institutional goals and demands.[78]

Values are mixed with varying amounts of knowledge, beliefs, and expectations, because our judgments of what should be are related to our judgments of what is.[79] Thus, although values are backward-looking in their frequent justification of past conduct, they also guide anticipatory and goal-directed behavior (i.e., they are linked to expectations).[80] Indeed, the relation between values and expectations did not escape Haas and Whiting and Karl Deutsch *et al.*,[81] who saw the evolution toward an international community as resulting from a joint transformation of values and expectations.

Emergence and evolution of values and interests

Human values affect action by influencing our definition of a particular situation and by directing our choice of relevant 'facts'[82] or 'interests' ('a disciplined understanding of what it takes to advance one's power, influence and wealth'). [83] The interdependence of facts and values implies a constant shifting between empirical and normative elements in decision-making. Values therefore affect international political behavior, and the transformation of interests, by defining the gratification that establishes and reinforces those interests and the sources of this gratification.[84]

Values emerge in the political system along with problems.[85] In the last forty years the superpowers may have come to value peace more than war, not as a result of a new ethical or moral stand, but because they had to face the problem of nuclear surprise attacks and inadvertent and unintended nuclear war. [86] Certain problems, which can become more perceptually acute through crises, may help turn previously fringe or 'eccentric' values—such as environmental concerns—into more durable and central values.[87] Thus, cognitive evolution may help turn valueless objects or interests into politically valuable and durable objects and interests.[88]

Domestic institutions may help inject into the political process objectives and interests that reflect new values or new combinations of values. Values become politically relevant when they are backed by institutional power, legitimacy, and authority and are most effective when they are not held merely in abstract terms, but are incorporated in political institutions and in habits of political behavior that permit them to be acted on in such a way as to strengthen people's attachment to them.[89]

For example, expectations of peaceful change, coupled with a strong valuation of peace (or a strong negative valuation of war), may help create an interest in measures such as arms control that may be perceived to enhance the prospects of peaceful change. An interest in arms control then becomes a way to organize values and expectations of international security. Arms control becomes a 'searchlight' or 'map' that affects attention, diplomacy, and political actions and reactions. Once the habit of arms control becomes established (i.e., when expectations and values become routinized and are taken for granted), we can say that it has become a national interest for countries x, y, and z to pursue arms control agreements. Interests are therefore not antithetical to ideational or normative phenomena; they are, in part, ideational and normative phenomena and they can be molded, albeit with many constraints.

Progress in International Relations

There are two necessary conditions for progress in International Relations: (1) the emergence of new values, the redefinition of old values, and a change in the context of valuing that advances human interests across national borders without creating an unbearable harm to other values or human interests; and (2) a change in expectations regarding the quality of the outcomes for the agent, including a redefinition of what exists, what can exist, what causes what, what the concomitants of desired actions are, and the like. [90]

The key question is what causes expectations and values that enhance human interests across national borders to be politically selected, maintained, and spread at domestic and international levels. There is probably no single answer, and generalizations would require the study of many cases and comparison of political processes that have led to a reevaluation of a situation and to new expectations. In general, however, we can raise the hypothesis that progress in International Relations may take place when interdependence, rising to the level of political collective understanding, helps break previously held expectations and values about political autonomy in the international arena and triggers a reevaluation process that causes old interests to veer away from war, poverty, and human-rights violations because they have suddenly become dysfunctional. After World War II, for example, values and expectations of peace and war changed through a combination of learning, modernization, technological changes, and growing security interdependence that challenged some governments to alter the way they advanced their power and influence.

Learning does not take place without some active persuasion of decision-makers and governmental institutions; deals may need to be cut, alliances may need to be formed before a certain set of values and expectations can win the day. Growing interdependence may persuade policymakers of the need to reevaluate national interests. But mediating between interdependence and progress are institutions that introduce to the political system theoretical and normative views regarding the implications of interdependence for the national interest. Thus, they create possibilities for progressive change, which must be actualized by political decision.

Treating learning as a necessary condition of progress raises the question, however, whether, as Haas argued,[91] increasing consensual *scientific* knowledge in a context of growing interdependence will lead to the creation of new interests or to the reevaluation of old interests in ways that collective solutions to problems are preferred over unilateral solutions. Although consensual scientific knowledge can be conducive to progress in highly technical international fields, consensual scientific knowledge is neither a necessary, nor a sufficient, condition of progress in International Relations. For scientific knowledge (e.g., physics, economics, strategy) can be manipulated to produce several ways to explain the same physical and social phenomena. In the most demanding case, the issue of war and peace,

> we have reason for pessimism, for it is not clear what kinds of information or knowledge we could gather or what kinds of scientific research we could undertake that would make it easier than it now is to penetrate the confusions and complexities of policies for maintaining peace. It is particularly difficult if we have several goals, as most of us have.[92]

The picture is not very different in the economic realm. Because the operation of the economy depends critically on human expectations about the future and human reactions to those expectations,[93] it is very difficult for economists to provide the kind of consensual knowledge that can bridge different ideologies.

Scientists (in contrast to 'science' itself), however, can play an instrumental role in producing shared understandings that can lead to progressive changes. Armed with the authority and legitimacy conferred to them by society, and equipped with a unique understanding in their area of expertise, scientists and other experts, when organized into epistemic communities, can play an important role in the process of intellectual innovation and political selection of ideas and understandings. On the one hand, epistemic communities can provide decision-makers with new answers to old questions and help them redefine and reconceptualize problems. Epistemic communities do not necessarily provide decision-makers with 'the truth,' which, because it is 'true,' helps turn political wheels. They can nevertheless be very influential because they may provide a solution or a key—in the sense that any key mutually recognized as the key becomes the key.[94] On the other hand, together with their innovations, epistemic communities also introduce values and visions that can catch the imagination of decision-makers who then, on the basis of their new understanding, may redefine strategic and economic interests so as to enhance human interests across national borders.

Epistemic communities can do much to affect the political selection process. They can help create new institutions or use old ones to push ideas within the government; they may help gain media and public opinion support for their ideas, which can then help persuade decision-makers and legislators; and they may be actively involved in creating and participating in coalitions that will promote their innovations.

The success of epistemic communities is historically contingent. Historical contingency is provided by the state of technology; the distribution of power in the international system; domestic political and administrative structures and procedures; and political, economic, and military events. Historical events such as international crises, wars, new technologies introduced into the economy or the military, and perceived changes in economic, political, and military power may help decision-makers see what they were not able to see before. In other words, as the historical context changes, theories or policy proposals that previously did not make any sense to politicians may suddenly acquire a political (perhaps even urgent) meaning, thus becoming politically viable.

However, the chances of success of an epistemic community will be enhanced when: (1) some of its members are brought into state institutions as officials, technocrats, or consultants, who can then affect the political process from within; (2) structures and procedures of government and administration facilitate the persuasion task of experts by protecting or insulating them from opposing individuals and institutions holding different interests and points of view; (3) there is an ideological affinity between experts and key policymakers; (4) once inside the government, experts are given enough time to formulate their ideas into policies and to implement them; (5) experts formulate their ideas in ways such that policymakers can see their practical application; (6) the ideas advanced address the policy-makers' main concerns and interests and give a new meaning to their past experience; (7) the community members are trusted as bearers of legitimate knowledge; (8) key decision-makers are willing and able to use their leader-ship in the political system on behalf of the ideas; and (9) the ideas strike a balance, or find a common denominator, between competing positions within the government and in society, thus helping break domestic political deadlocks and creating a *temporary* consensus that enables the implementa-tion of these ideas. (Once implemented, however, they may acquire a life of their own and transcend and outlast the temporary consensus that cleared the way for their promotion by the epistemic community.)

The next section, which focuses on the development of a new economic order after World War II, illustrates the creation, selection, retention, and spread of conceptual and normative 'keys' or understandings, which through socialization and interactive learning processes became part of a collective understanding that transcended national borders and resulted in progressive change. Although American hegemonic power played an important role in the diffusion of institutional innovation, the latter originated from seem-ingly 'scientific' understandings. The case illustrates cognitive evolutionary processes that resulted in *instrumental progress*, which refers to international regimes[95] or cooperative frameworks and institutional structures that nation-states jointly create to deal with problems that, given their nature and scope, are perceived as not solvable by unilateral actions alone.

Emergence of the national interest: postwar international economic order

The emergence of the postwar international economic order has been recounted more than adequately by others;[96] my short account of the subject is not the first to focus on ideas.[97] The point, however, is to show the unfolding and changing of International Relations as a result of innovation, selection, and diffusion processes. The economic order that emerged after World War II was born in the minds of a small group of key US economists and officials, working mainly at the Treasury Department and operating under the leadership of Undersecretary Harry Dexter White,[98] whose efforts were being replicated on the other side of the Atlantic, especially in Great Britain. For example, the idea for a financial international order can be traced back to two plans, one developed in the United States under White's leadership and the other engineered by John Maynard Keynes in Great Britain. However, the expectations and values that emerged from this intel-lectual process, and that provided intellectual guidance to political intentions and policies, were negotiated twice: first, in the domestic game, where processes of coalition-building, persuasion, and the elimination of plausible alternatives determined the survivors to a large extent; second, in the international game between the Americans, the British, and other European countries in such a way as to reflect not only the original intentions of the innovations but also the preferences and needs of those who were supposed to buy these ideas. Thus, the ensuing understandings, which amounted to a cognitive structure and even international institutions such as the International Monetary Fund (IMF), the World Bank, and the General Agreement on Tariffs and Trade (GATT), resulted in part from cognitive evolution processes.

The international regimes literature has rightly pointed out that the multilateral order that gained acceptance after World War II owed much to American hegemonic power.[99] John Ruggie has enriched our understanding on the subject, adding that the 'authority relations that were instituted in the international regimes for money and trade reflected a new balance of state–society relations that expressed a *collective* reality.'[100] This collective or intersubjective understanding, which Ruggie called 'embedded liberalism' and which anticipated the content and purposes of the new international order, was a compromise between economic nationalism and liberalism: unlike the economic nationalism of the 1930s, embedded liberalism was multilateral. Unlike the liberalism of the gold standard and free trade, its multilateralism was predicated upon domestic interventionism.[101]

The novel conceptual and normative aspects of the American interest in multilateralism, as they emerged and evolved in the postwar era, arose from a need and desire to create an alternative to the past era of economic nationalism and were directly affected by the last war and by the unique moment of transition from war to peace that helped direct the attention of experts and politicians (increasingly exposed to Keynesian ideas) to efforts of reconstruction and therefore of innovation. The growing preoccupation with the spread of Communism in Europe was crucial in persuading political actors in America and Europe to back ideas of embedded liberalism. Expectations also reflected a certain exuberance that evidenced the self-perception of the United States as a hegemonic power, because few Americans anticipated that the powers bestowed upon international institutions could one day be exercised against the United States. Richard Gardner also points out that the architects or innovators zeroed in on a detailed plan for the construction of an economic order and institutions because they remembered the chaos that followed World War I and the negative implications of the US failure to join the League of Nations; they interpreted the breakdown of the last peace settlement as a result of inadequate handling of economic problems.[102]

These architects, expressing much genuine idealism, generated a vision of peace and prosperity and expectations of interdependence not shared by all American elites. Nor was this vision readily embraced in Europe. The vision had to survive the hurdles of domestic and international politics before it could be accepted as being in the interest of the states involved. Indeed, given the strong isolationist and nationalist ideas of many Americans and the strong political interests and ideological biases against multilateralism of both the right and the left in Europe, it would have been impossible for the original ideas that motivated the emerging international order to become the basis of international behavior. This is why

> Bretton Woods' sails had to be trimmed to the point where public and Congressional acceptance might be possible—but only after a life and death fight. ... The package was wrapped in the glittering generalities of a hard political fight designed to get public acceptance and force Congressional approval.[103]

The crystallization of multilateral policies in the United States owed a great deal to the action of individuals and institutions in three nongovernmental areas: (1) gaining public support for a view that was being sold to the world, including the idea of containment; (2) intense personal and informal coordination with Congress; and (3) private and international consultation with other countries, with feedback to the domestic political arena.[104] Groups at State and Treasury who were committed to the idea of multilateralism toured the country explaining, persuading, and putting forward their expectations until the banking community, which formed the strongest opposition to the Bretton Woods agreement, was isolated. Also critical was the creation of a coalition between very strange bedfellows who shared a notion of peace through open markets and thus were receptive to embedded-liberalism ideas. The domestic political structure was also an important factor. With respect to trade, Raymond Vernon and Debra Spar stress the fact that, because

> Congress periodically has exhibited a willingness to delegate the political burden of dealing with the costs and benefits of trade policy, it has been possible for a leader inside the bureaucracy to take on the task of seeking presidential approval for a new trade program and then shepherding it over the domestic and international hurdles.[105]

The British had their own reasons for going along with the American proposals[106] and were careful to draft clauses in such a way that their own interpretations would be represented. Yet at the same time a broad range of ideas was negotiated before the countries could reach a consensus. 'A process of socialization, furthered by the modification of these normative principles and the cooptation of a variety of European domestic groups, did result in the legitimation of hegemonic power.'[107] Socialization, however, was accompanied by active arm-twisting, bargaining, persuasion, and promises of economic aid and protection on the part of the United States. The loss of power by European rightist and leftist groups opposing embedded-liberalism ideas was also consequential.[108]

Once the principle of cooperation had survived these processes of innovation, selection, and diffusion, it became habitual and normal. Although several of the original institutions failed to work at first, like the IMF, or never materialized, like the International Trade Organization (ITO), 'other institutional innovations appeared,'[109] providing continuity to the original understandings and purposes, which were renegotiated at both the domestic and international levels. This continuity was especially evident in the monetary and trade regimes.[110] Once the collective ideas became embedded in institutions and as the latter adapted to changing situations[111] and arrived at new understandings of the situation,[112] these entities acquired new and different functions.

Postwar international institutions originally conceived to manage interdependent relations between developed countries increasingly developed new goals and means to deal with Third World debt, development, and poverty problems and, more recently, with the global environment,[113] and started to reallocate resources to poorer, or even to the poorest, countries.

Also, in its attempt to reform (rather than replace) the postwar economic order, the Third World added new ideas and institutions to old ones and thus unintentionally bestowed on the old order a minimal measure of legitimacy. Thus, elites from the 'North' and the 'South' used existing understandings and institutional arrangements to exchange and renegotiate their positions and visions, as well as the normative and epistemic notions on which their respective sets of interests were based.

While certainly not the 'best,' or a moral, solution from a global perspective, and always subject to setbacks and failure, the postwar order that followed cognitive evolutionary processes produced a very imperfect order, but one that 'may be superior to politically feasible alternatives'[114] and that may have helped improve the welfare of *some* human beings, mainly in developed, but increasingly also in Third World, countries.[115]

Minimalist progress in the management of international political–economic relations, then, should be measured neither against an abstract and utopian idea of global welfare nor against the notion that in two generations humanity can solve the problem of justice, but against what could have happened to the welfare and security of individuals across national borders if either more radical *laissez-faire* policies or economic nationalism had continued to be the only intellectual source of 'wisdom' on which international economic policies were based.

Humanist realism

The approach I develop in this study does not challenge realism; it does challenge the structural determinist notions that realists and neorealists have used to make sense out of realist assumptions. From my critique a more dynamic approach emerges, which for lack of a better term I call humanist realism. Humanist realism offers a pragmatic middle ground between the view that nothing changes (which would be debilitating and lead to despair) and the view that everything is possible (which would be utopian). It blends power structures, interests, and pessimism with bounded optimism, a dynamic view of international politics, and the conviction that some choices do exist and that change can, at times, lead to the enhancement of human interests across borders.

A research program using a humanist–realist approach should therefore be based on the following assumptions, which qualify and amend those framed by Keohane.[116]

(1) States are still seen as the principal actors in world politics, although the origins of policies must be traced to domestic institutions. More emphasis is placed on the relation between state and human beings, who play a crucial double role: they shape interests, policies, international agendas, and therefore international negotiations and outcomes, and themselves become the recipients of the 'fruits' of progress or the victims of its absence. Without abandoning the nation-state view of International Relations, analysts can and should take human interests into account when describing and explaining international politics.

(2) Questions of rationality are rephrased to fit a dynamic evolutionary perspective. Rationality is discovered rather than assumed and concerns the condition and manner in which governments are prepared to change their expectations and values as time goes on.[117]

(3) Power is complementary to values, and behavior is a combination of both. States, representing different cultures, employ numerous ways to interpret, apply, and enhance power (which can be interpreted from more aspects than simply the physical—i.e., military—capabilities). According to the principle of complementarity, which is a central tenet of humanist realism, reality in International Relations can be seen as an accommodation of opposites,[118] as constituted by different aspects of reality that exclude one another yet add to our understanding of the phenomenon as a whole.[119] In a dialectical fashion, the presence of anarchy and the increase of disorder are both needed to bring about management and order. Tensions are reduced because they are caused. Adaptation takes place because there is change. Innovative ideas that can change the way actors relate to each other grow from failure and disappointment. Improvements are made because of dissatisfaction with the present condition. Power and values therefore express two views of the same international reality: power determines the range of possible outcomes and the human mind determines what is good, bad, rational and irrational.

I cannot improve upon Charles Sabel's explanation of how this complementarity works:

> It is true that the initial distribution of power and interests between contestants sets broad limits on the possible outcomes of a struggle. But given those limits, the ultimate result depends on the contestants'

tactical skill and programmatic boldness, as well as on the web of human sympathy or mistrust that binds or separates allies on both sides. This necessity to maneuver makes possible the transformation of interest in the midst of conflict. ... A group ... may gradually revise its claims by applying them to the new circumstances, amalgamating them with those of an ally, or radically extending them in the enthusiasm or desperation of battle.[120]

(4) Cognitive phenomena and history are integrated into scientific analysis, based on an epistemology of science attuned to scientific understanding, mainly in the physical sciences and biology, as it has evolved in the twentieth century. This epistemology, by suggesting a partly indeterminate and emergent physical and social universe, does not give scientists a license to abandon formal scientific research. It instead guides research, armed with a much more dynamic set of concepts and frameworks.

(5) It is understood that preference changes result not only from environmental alterations but from human adaptive creativity as well. Therefore, learning processes and outcomes—whether individual, institutional, or international—must be studied.

(6) We must understand the intersubjective meanings that international political actors give to situations and events, and how human values, beliefs, and expectations come into play through the meanings and interpretations of actions and events.[121] Humanist realism thus is open to the interpretative kind of work that Haas has pioneered, and should not be confused with approaches that analyze the role of perceptions and misperceptions in world politics.[122] Instead, it means penetrating to the sources of collective human understandings, to the processes that generate them, and to the reasons they so often fail to take shape.

(7) The concept of national interest must be more dynamic and plastic and concerned with how interests are born, how they evolve, and what their descriptive and normative characteristics and qualities are.

(8) Finally, a humanist–realist approach will open the door to the study of progress in International Relations. The realist side warns us to be very cautious and to expect at best minimalist progress. The humanist side, however, gives us some hope. For it is ironic that, as the Enlightenment idea of progress has all but lost its prestige—gone as it were, down the drain of history—it has taken with it the notion that sometimes, somewhere, changes away from 'the worst' can and do occur and that human beings and their values may contribute to such occurrences. It is this idea that should be salvaged, interpreted, and analyzed within the perspective of International Relations. Progress in International Relations, therefore, can be likened to climbing a precipice: slow, painfully difficult, fraught with setbacks, yet still humanly possible. In International Relations we seldom climb toward the top, but mainly away from the abyss.

4 Seizing the middle ground

Constructivism in world politics

This is a widely cited article in which I argue that constructivism occupies the middle ground between rationalist approaches and interpretive approaches and creates new areas for theoretical and empirical investigation. The bulk of the article lays out the social epistemological basis of the constructivist approach; juxtaposes constructivism to rationalism and post-modernism and explains its advantages; presents the concept of cognitive evolution as a way of explaining the social construction of reality; and suggests ways of expanding constructivist research agendas. Although many of the citations in this article make reference to the epistemological middle ground that constructivism later came to occupy in mainstream IR theory, its main value, I think, lies in laying the foundation for a pragmatist way of doing social science, of which cognitive evolution is a striking example. So the details here are at least as important, if not more so, than the general argument.

Originally published in the *European Journal of International Relations* 3(3) (1997): 319–63

> In our highly complex organic state we advanced organisms respond to our environment with an invention of many marvelous analogues. We invent earth and heavens, trees, stones and oceans, gods, music, arts, language, philosophy, engineering, civilization and science. We call these analogues reality. And they **are** reality.
>
> Robert Pirsig, *Zen and the Art of Motorcycle Maintenance*

In recent years, a great deal has been written in the scholarly literature about the role of ideas in International Relations. This scholarship has sparked a theoretical debate between 'rationalists'[1] (mainly realists, neorealists and neoliberal institutionalists) and adherents of interpretive epistemologies (post-modernists and post-structuralists, critical theorists in the Frankfurt School sense,[2] and feminist theorists) about the nature of international reality and how scholars should go about explaining it. Increasingly, however, the debate has come to concentrate on and be influenced by the arguments of the constructivist approach.

The constructivist approach has been described and explained,[3] applied empirically[4] and contrasted to other International Relations approaches.[5] Nevertheless, there is very little clarity and even less consensus as to its nature and substance. The reliance of constructivist International Relations theory on interpretive social theory and vocabulary; the mistaken belief that constructivism, post-structuralism and post-modernism are all varieties of the same 'reflectivist' approach; the relative scarcity of early constructivist empirical research; and, most important, the debates within constructivism itself as to 'what constructivism is really about'—all these have tended to obscure constructivism's scientific basis, its preference for ontology and epistemology over methodology, and its potential contribution to a better understanding of International Relations.

It is therefore imperative to attempt to pull together the pieces and provide a synthetic explanation of the constructivist approach. It is equally imperative to justify the constructivist approach on ontological and epistemological grounds and show how these lead to new theoretical and empirical ways of understanding international reality. Moreover, there is a real need to distinguish between the claims of constructivism and those raised by more radical interpretivists and/or by rationalist (mostly neoliberal) renditions of the role of ideas in International Relations. To date, most constructivist descriptions have failed to emphasize the importance of *sociocognitive* factors and have only just begun to reconcile *systematic* social-science theory and research with the role played by interpretation in social life.

Finally, it is crucial to make it clear, once and for all, that the core of the debate about constructivism is not science versus literary interpretation or 'stories,' but the nature of social science itself and, therefore, of the discipline of International Relations. In other words, the issue pits a naturalist conception of science, almost entirely based on contested philosophies of science and on physical concepts and theories that physics has long since abandoned, against a concept of social science that is *social*. A metaphor may help to illustrate this point.

Suppose you toss a rock into the air. It can make only a simple response to the external physical forces that act on it. But if you throw a bird into the air, it may fly off into a tree. Even though the same physical forces act on the bird as on the rock, a massive amount of internal information-processing takes place inside the bird and affects its behavior.[6] Finally, take a group of people, a nation, or various nations and metaphorically toss them in the air. Where they go, how, when, and why, is not entirely determined by physical forces and constraints; but neither does it depend solely on individual preferences and rational choices. It is also a matter of their shared knowledge, the collective meaning they attach to their situation, their authority and legitimacy, the rules, institutions and material resources they use to find their way, and their practices or even, sometimes, their joint creativity.

The first section of this chapter provides a brief introduction to constructivism as the 'middle ground' approach in International Relations. The next section lays out the social and epistemological basis of the constructivist approach. The issues I discuss in this section do not deal only with ontology and epistemology; they also have much to say about how we think about the world. In section three, I juxtapose constructivism with rationalism and post-structuralism and justify its claim to the middle ground. I also show that there are adequate methods for empirical research on the social construction of International Relations. In the fourth section I show how cognitive evolution—a dynamic application of constructivist thought to International Relations—may enhance our understanding of the world. Finally, I offer some suggestions for a constructivist research agenda.

Constructivism: the middle ground

Realists[7] and neorealists,[8] undisturbed by the seasonal 'idealist' offensives that punctuate International Relations debates, and empowered by positivist[9] and exclusively materialist philosophies of science,[10] have been reluctant to engage in ontological and epistemological polemics. They prefer to explain International Relations as simple behavioral responses to the forces of physics that act on material objects from the outside.[11]

On the other side of the divide, post-modernists and post-structuralists,[12] critical theorists,[13] and feminist theorists[14] build on a relativist philosophy of science[15] and interpretivist sociology of knowledge;[16] they propose to debate the nature of international social relations and discuss ways for studying it, because, in the social and interpreted world in which (as they see it) we live, only ideas matter and can be studied.

The key epistemological and ontological dilemma raised by relativist approaches is described by the 'hermeneutical circle'—whenever people try to establish a certain reading of a text or expression, they allege other readings as the ground for their reading. Thus we can never provide a rational explanation for a social situation and are condemned to appeal to common understanding of the language involved. Empirical data—what Charles Taylor called 'brute data'—become just one more interpretation, open to question by other interpretations or readings.[17]

Neoliberal institutionalists cleverly circumvent this dilemma by following the Weberian maxim that material and ideal interests, rather than ideas, directly govern people's conduct. Frequently, though, 'the "world images" that have been created by ideas have, like switchmen, determined the tracks along which action has been pushed by the dynamic of interest.'[18]

Like realists, neoliberal institutionalists consider behavior to be affected by outside physical forces. Like interpretivists, however, they make a concession to 'ideas,' which they define, following the lead of psychological (mainly cognitive) approaches,[19] as 'beliefs held by individuals.' Next, taking a rational-choice approach to information-processing, they explain how individuals' beliefs can affect policy choices and outcomes.[20] Thus, by turning individuals' ideas and knowledge into 'variables' that may have causal effects on political choices, neoliberal institutionalists believe they can seize a middle ground between realist (positivist) and interpretive (relativist or post-positivist) approaches.

This article maintains that the true middle ground between rationalist and relativist interpretive approaches is occupied neither by an interpretive version of rationalism, nor by some variety of 'reflectivism,' as described by Keohane,[21] nor even by all sorts of critical theories as imprecisely portrayed by Mearsheimer,[22] but by *constructivism*.[23]

Constructivism is the view that *the manner in which the material world shapes and is shaped by human action and interaction depends on dynamic normative and epistemic interpretations of the material world.*

Constructivism shows that even our most enduring institutions are based on collective understandings; that they are reified structures that were once upon a time conceived *ex nihilo* by human consciousness; and that these understandings were subsequently diffused and consolidated until they were taken for granted. Moreover, constructivists believe that the human capacity for reflection or learning has its greatest impact on the manner in which individuals and social actors attach meaning to the material world and cognitively frame the world they know, experience, and understand. Thus collective understandings provide people with reasons why things are as they are and indications as to how they should use their material, abilities and power.

Constructivism's importance and its added value for the study of International Relations lie mainly in its emphasis on the ontological reality of intersubjective knowledge and on the epistemological and methodological implications of this reality. Constructivists believe that International Relations consist primarily of social facts, which are facts only by human agreement. At the same time, constructivists are 'ontological realists'; they believe not only in the existence of the material world, but also that 'this material world offers resistance when we act upon it.'[24] Thus constructivism is an attempt, albeit timid, to build a bridge between the widely separated positivist/materialist and idealist/interpretive philosophies of social science.[25]

Constructivism, unlike realism or liberalism, is not a theory of politics *per se*. Rather, it is a social theory on which constructivist theories of international politics—for example, about war, cooperation, and international community—are based. Constructivism can illuminate important features of international politics that were previously enigmatic and have crucial practical implications for international theory and empirical research.

Constructivism challenges only the ontological and epistemological foundations of realism and liberalism. It is not anti-liberal or anti-realist by ideological conviction; neither is it pessimistic or optimistic by design. Consequently, constructivism represents the first real opportunity to generate a synthetic theory of International Relations since E. H. Carr[26] laid its foundations, just before World War II.[27] If a persuasive case can be made that normative and causal collective understandings are real, insofar as they have consequences for the physical and social worlds, it will be much easier to claim that both an understanding of world politics and the progress of the discipline may depend on the construction of a sociocognitive synthesis that draws on the material, subjective, and intersubjective dimensions of the world.[28]

Social epistemology and International Relations

Materialism and idealism

Steve Woolgar describes three approaches to the ontological and epistemological debate about the reality of ideas: (1) the reflective; (2) the constitutive; and (3) the mediative.[29] For reflectivists, reality is independent of cognition but can be accurately represented in true descriptions. Constitutivists, on the other hand, while not denying the existence of material reality, believe that it cannot be known outside human language. Since 'we have no way of deciding whether statements correspond to reality except by means of other statements, it makes no sense to assume the independent existence of an external reality to begin with.'[30] Hence constitutive philosophers and sociologists adopt the relativist stance in which only the organization of discourse really matters.

Finally, 'mediativists' are ontological realists who believe that reality is affected by knowledge and social factors. 'Reality exists independently of our accounts, but does not fully determine them.'[31] More specifically, a mediative approach means that social reality emerges from the attachment of meaning and functions to physical objects; collective understandings, such as norms, endow physical objects with purpose and therefore help constitute reality.

Most scholars of International Relations follow Woolgar's first approach;[32] they are materialists and positivists who, like Stephen Krasner,[33] believe that ideas do not construct and structure social reality, but only reflect the material world and serve to justify material causes. Other scholars, like Goldstein and Keohane,[34] suggest that, within this material world, beliefs held by individuals may partly determine political outcomes.

Students of International Relations who identify themselves as post-modernists and post-structuralists embrace the constitutive position and propose textual and discourse analysis as the basis for understanding International Relations.[35] Thus, reality 'can be nothing other than a text, a symbolic construction that is itself related to other texts—not to history or social structure—in arbitrary ways.'[36]

On the other hand, constructivists who (like post-modernists and post-structuralists) follow an interpretive approach embrace the mediative position. While accepting the notion that there is a real world out there, they nevertheless believe that it is not entirely determined by physical reality and is socially emergent.[37] More importantly, they believe that the identities, interests, and behavior of political agents are socially constructed by collective meanings, interpretations, and assumptions about the world.

Individual vs. social origins of human action: Elster, Durkheim, and Giddens

The debate surveyed above raises another question—if ideas affect physical reality and do not merely reflect it, is cognition grounded in the individual level or the social level? The answer to this ontological question will probably determine the answer to the following epistemological question: do we explain human action on the basis of individual motivation and the causal interaction of intentional agents,[38] or do we explain individual cognition and action as a function of social forces or social structure?[39]

Jon Elster, for example, has made the case for individualism not only at the methodological but also at the ontological and epistemological levels.[40] 'The elementary unit of social life,' he argues, 'is the individual human action. To explain social institutions and social change is to show how they arise as the result of the action and interaction of individuals.'[41] For him, explanation in the social sciences, which is best achieved by a combination of rational choice and game theory, involves the intentional explanation of individual actions alongside causal explanation of the interaction between individuals. It also involves sub-intentional causality—processes that explain 'mental operations not governed by will or intention.'[42]

Emile Durkheim, on the other hand, thought that ideas like 'religious representations are collective representations which express collective realities.'[43] In short, Durkheim believed that social facts could not be reduced to individual cognition and demanded a social explanation.

Structuration theory, however, argues that 'the properties of agents and of structures are both relevant to explanations of social behavior.'[44] It explains social institutions and social change as the result of the 'duality of structure,' i.e., 'the essential recursiveness of social life, as constituted in social practices: structure is both medium and outcome of the reproduction of practices. Structure enters simultaneously into the constitution of the agent and social practices, and 'exists' in the generating moments of this constitution.'[45]

Anthony Giddens' agents are far from being structural 'idiots,' however. They are the social constructors of their own practices and structures, and bear identities, rights, and obligations (to name a few) in their own consciousness. These agents act according to institutionalized rules, but also according to their interests.[46]

Constructivists, too, believe that 'ideas' have structural characteristics. First of all, ideas—understood more generally as collective knowledge, institutionalized in practices—are the medium and propellant of social action; they define the limits of what is cognitively possible and impossible for individuals. Concurrently, knowledge-based practices are the outcome of interacting individuals who act purposively on the basis of their personal ideas, beliefs, judgments, and interpretations. The main goal of constructivism, therefore, is to provide both theoretical and empirical explanations of social institutions and social change, with the help of the combined effect of agents and social structures.

Verstehen *as epistemology and as reality*

I have established that, with regard to both ontology and epistemology, constructivists stand at two intersections—that between materialism and idealism, and that between individual agency and social structure. Another factor that enables constructivists to seize this middle ground is their notion of intersubjectivity. To shed light on this notion we must start with interpretation or *Verstehen*. Max Weber's notion of *Verstehen* located the problem of explaining social action in an interpretive setting, which requires us to 'specify that there is meaning both in "the behavior of others" and in the "account" which the acting individual takes of it. That leads directly to the central hermeneutic theme that *action must always be understood from within.*'[47]

Rationalists, like Goldstein and Keohane,[48] as well as students of political psychology like Robert Jervis,[49] who, along with Weber, recognize the necessity of studying meaning, or 'what is in people's heads,' take *Verstehen* as an epistemological problem. Hence they define it as 'the interpretation of meaning through empathetic understanding and pattern recognition' by an observer.[50] The problem, however, soon becomes one of explanation and of methodology, because 'unless the interpreter's judgments are evaluated according to systematic standards for assessing the quality of inferences, they remain only the personal view of the observer.'[51]

Relativist philosophers and sociologists,[52] by contrast, do not believe the problem of interpretation to be solvable by means of systematic social-science methods. If 'our idea of what belongs to the realm of reality is given for us in the concepts we use,'[53] we cannot know the world independently of the language we use. It follows that social scientists are condemned to interpret discourses, considered to be the only points of entry to hermeneutical circles or shared understandings—or, in Wittgenstein's words, 'forms of life.'[54] Postmodernists, in particular, subscribe to the view that if people cannot know that there is an objective reality, they should not waste their time looking for it.[55]

Constructivism does not build on the relativist implications of interpretive epistemology, but on the ontological implications of *Verstehen*.[56] To understand the ontological implications of *Verstehen*, we must start with the notion that what social scientists want to know, interpret, or explain has already been interpreted in the social world. *Verstehen* is, thus, not just a method used by the social scientist, but also the collective interpretations, practices and institutions of the actors themselves.[57] *Verstehen*, in fact, *is* social reality. It can be a set of norms, or consensual scientific understandings, or the practice of diplomacy, or arms control. All these knowledge structures are continually constituted and reproduced by members of a community and their behavior. At the same time, however, they determine the boundaries between what these agents consider to be real and unreal.

Intersubjectivity

It follows from the ontological implications of *Verstehen* that intersubjective meanings are not simply the aggregation of the beliefs of individuals who jointly experience and interpret the world. Rather, they exist as collective knowledge 'that is shared by all who are competent to engage in or recognize the appropriate performance of a social practice or range of practices.'[58] This knowledge persists beyond the lives of individual social actors, embedded in social routines and practices as they are reproduced by interpreters who participate in their production and workings. Intersubjective meanings have structural attributes that do not merely constrain or empower actors. They also define their social reality.[59]

At the same time, the concept of intersubjectivity neither assumes a collective mind nor disavows the notion that individuals have purposes and intentions. Rather, it is based on the notion that, although 'each of us thinks his own thoughts; our concepts we share with our fellow-men.'[60] Similarly, when doing something together, 'the individual intentionality that each person has is derived from the collective intentionality that they share.'[61]

Intersubjective reality thus exists and persists thanks to social communication. The social world 'is intersubjective because we live in it, ... understanding others and being understood by them.'[62] Karl Deutsch's notion of security communities[63]—groups of people who share a communication environment and, accordingly, share values, with mutual responsiveness (a 'we-feeling,' of sorts) and mutual trust—comes close to the idea of intersubjectivity. So does Benedict Anderson's reference to nations as 'imagined communities.'[64] 'Imagined communities' are not merely the sum of the beliefs of some national group; regardless of the physical existence of the individuals, they exist in symbols, practices, institutions, and discourses. From the perspective of their consequences for the subjective world of the members of the community, as well as for the physical world, they are real.

Here I cannot improve on Karl Popper's depiction of intersubjective reality and his notion of 'World 3.' Popper divided the universe into three sub-universes, which he called World 1, World 2, and World 3. 'World 1 is the world of all physical bodies and forces and fields of forces; also of organisms, of our bodies and their parts.' World 2 is the subjective world 'of conscious experiences, our thoughts, our feelings of elation or depression, our aims, our plans of action.' World 3 is the world of culture, or of the products of the human mind, 'and especially the world of our languages: of our stories, our myths, and our explanatory theories, ... of our technologies, ... of architecture and of music.' World 3 acquires its ontological reality because 'a thought, once it is formulated in language, becomes an *object* outside ourselves. Such an object can then be inter-subjectively *criticized*— criticized by others as well as by ourselves.'[65] Once the objects in World 3 are collectively generated, their reality is also predicated on the fact that they can have real consequences, both intended and unintended.

The key to understanding the reality of World 3 (Searle calls it institutional or social facts) is the 'collective intentional imposition of function on entities that cannot perform those functions without that imposition.' [66] Thus, God could not see money or private property. Instead he would see '*us treating* certain objects' as money and private property. In other words, Searle makes the obvious yet usually unrecognized point that 'there are portions of the real world, objective facts in the world, that are only facts by human agreement.'[67]

World 3 objects cannot exist without World 1 objects—'just about any sort of substance can be money, but money has to exist in some physical form or another.'[68] At the same time, however, the move from World 1 to World 3 is a linguistic one, because once a function is imposed on a physical entity 'it now symbolizes something else. ... This move can exist only if it is collectively represented as existing. The collective representation is public and conventional, and it requires some vehicle.'[69]

Moreover, Searle argues, 'institutional facts exist only within systems of constitutive rules.'[70] For example, when we say that 'such and such bits of paper count as money, we genuinely have a constitutive rule, because ... "such and such bits of paper" [are not sufficient to be considered as money, nor do they] specify causal features that would be sufficient to enable the stuff to function as money without human agreement.'[71]

Constructivism's approach to science

Based on a pragmatist philosophy of science,[72] constructivism turns interpretation into an intrinsic part of a scientific enterprise that seeks to explain the social construction of reality. This pragmatism, which should be even more relevant for the social sciences than it is for the natural sciences, dismisses the Cartesian notion that we must choose between objectivism and relativism. It underscores the role of choice, deliberation, judgment, and interpretation by communities of scientists who immerse themselves in a type of rational persuasion that must aspire to, but cannot always be assimilated with, models of deductive proof or inductive generalization.[73]

Constructivists believe that 'reason is a practice imbedded in science; when scientists argue about truth, they refer not to some supra-social reality but to this imbedded reason—to "the best possible scientific reasons that can be given."'[74] Unlike ideologues, however, scientists make decisions about beliefs according to fairly rigorous rules, norms, and definitions.[75] Thus, like people in general, who can accept rules as binding not simply because they wish to be understood but because they recognize their validity, scientists can also reasonably recognize the validity of scientific traditions.[76] Reason can guide scientists to dive at some point of the hermeneutic circle and produce the best explanation available.[77]

Pragmatism is a useful corrective to attempts by relativists to delegitimize science altogether. But it is also a useful corrective *vis-à-vis* positivists,

who judge constructivism on criteria that favor rationalism and are themselves the target of constructivist criticism.[78]

Constructivism's sociological approach[79] is consistent with pragmatism.
To begin with, constructivism means studying how what the agents themselves consider rational is brought to bear on collective human enterprises
and situations. This position commits 'us to finding out what the actors on
the international stage think they are doing.'[80] But because people's intentions and motives are affected by what they intersubjectively believe, any
'attempt to understand the intersubjective meanings embedded in social life
is at the same time an attempt to explain why people act the way they do.'[81]

This raises the issue of causality. In the physical world, causal relations
connect entities and occurrences into structures and patterns. In the social
world, however, deterministic laws are improbable; the heroic leap of faith
that social forms 'determine' human action, or the ontologically incomplete
assumption that individual action 'determines' social forms, must both be
rejected.[82] Constructivism subscribes to a notion of social causality that
takes *reasons as causes*,[83] because 'doing something for reasons means
applying an understanding of "what is called for" in a given set of circumstances.'[84] However, because people do 'what is called for' on the basis of
'norms and rules emerging in historical and cultural circumstances,'[85]
norms and rules structure and therefore *socially constitute*—'cause'—the
things people do; that is, they provide actors with direction and goals for
action.[86]

It follows that causality in social science involves specifying a time-
bounded sequence and relationship between the social phenomena we want
to explain and the antecedent conditions, in which people consciously and
often rationally do things for reasons that are socially constituted by their
collective interpretations of the external world and the rules they act
upon.[87] This relationship is demonstrated on the basis not only of logical
persuasion, but also of detailed historical narratives that involve analysis of
agents and their reasons and the sociocognitive structures that help constitute their practices and behavior. Learning both the actors' reasons and the
rules that govern a practice 'enable[s] us to improve predictions of the
behavior of those acting in accordance with it. So determining the meaning
of actions provides some knowledge of causes.'[88]

Constructivism's middle ground between rationalist and relativist International Relations theories

By way of summarizing the argument so far about constructivism's claim to
the ontological middle ground, and to set the stage for comparing constructivism to rationalist and relativist theories of International Relations, I
suggest a revision of Alexander Wendt's two-by-two matrix of International
Relations theories,[89] in which the discriminants are realism (materialism) or
idealism and holism or individualism. In this matrix, Wendt places

constructivism alongside post-modernism and post-structuralism, all of them occupying the same structuralist–idealist box. Constructivism seizes the middle ground because it is interested in understanding how the *material*, subjective, and intersubjective worlds interact in the social construction of reality and because, rather than focusing exclusively on how structures constitute agents' identities and interests, it also seeks to explain how *individual agents* socially construct these structures in the first place. Consequently, constructivism belongs in the center of the matrix, the dense dot where all the lines intersect (see Figure 4.1).

The realist, neorealist, and dependency theories of International Relations in the two left-hand quadrants are grounded on a purely materialist (structural or individualist) ontology; hence they do not concern us here. Neoliberal theories, however, which reside primarily in the bottom right quadrant, suggest that individuals' ideas do matter. Acting in the background of the fixed essences of material interests, ideas affect the choices

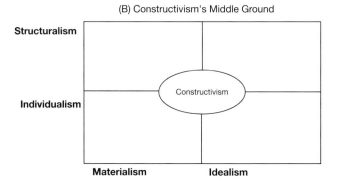

(A) Alex Wendt's Map of International Theory

Holism		
	World Systems Theory	Gramscian Marxism
		English School
	Security Materialism	World Society
		Postmodernism
		Constructivism
	——— Neorealism ———	
Individualism		Domestic Liberalism
	Classical Realism	Neoliberalism
		Ideas Liberalism

Realism   **Idealism**
(Materialism)

(B) Constructivism's Middle Ground

Structuralism

Constructivism

Individualism

Materialism   **Idealism**

Figure 4.1 The ontological position of constructivism

that states make and sometimes help overcome collective-goods problems and lead to international cooperation.[90] Neoliberalism's ontological assumptions, however, beget a *minimalist* and therefore weak epistemological approach. According to neoliberalism, ideas work within structural constraints, such that they can affect choices about the material world only; interests are exogenous to interaction. Accordingly, neoliberal epistemology misses most of 'the action,' namely, the constitution of actors' identities and interests by collective cognitive structures.

Neoliberal epistemology is also hampered by its exclusive reliance on methodological individualism.[91] For example, Goldstein and Keohane defend their analytical distinction between interests and ideas on individualist methodological grounds. They argue that the distinction is required to know whether, all else being equal, a variation on individuals' beliefs is causally related to a change in political behavior. The problem with this argument is that, as Friedrich Kratochwil and John Ruggie have argued perceptively, studying behavior with strict positivist methods that separate between 'objects' and 'subjects' cannot lead to an understanding of the intersubjective ontological nature of meaning.[92] If constructivists are right, and cognitive as well as material structures play a role in constituting the identities and interests of actors, as well as the boundaries between them—international reality itself—empirical research must study ideas and interests as part of a unitary process of the creation of social reality.

For example, although Kathryn Sikkink skillfully shows 'the power of ideas to reshape understandings of national interest,'[93] she follows the rationalist path of assuming material interests as given and employs ideas as intervening variables between interests and political behavior. The adoption of normative beliefs that contradict material interests would have provided rationalism with reliable evidence for the independent power of ideas about human rights. But this would be like looking at the contents of a room through a tiny window. For what is at stake here is actually the construction, by collective beliefs about human rights, of Western countries' identities, and the explanation of the role of social actors, such as non-governmental organizations (NGOs), in constructing these identities in the first place. The interesting question is whether and how human-rights norms are becoming not only regulative injunctions designed to overcome the collective- action problems associated with interdependent choice, but also constitutive, a direct reflection of the actors' identity and self-understanding.

The top right quadrant takes us to constitutive ontology and epistemology; in this short article I cannot do justice to the variety of post-modern, post-structuralist, critical theory, and (post-modern) feminist theory[94] approaches and nuances. My primary goal is to distinguish between these approaches and the constructivist approach, because much of the confusion about constructivism lies in the conflation of constitutive and mediative epistemologies.

The proposition common to the majority of constitutive approaches in International Relations is that reality in its objective form (truth) cannot be known outside human language; thus, inexorably, reality must be a constitutive effect of discourse. [95] Constitutivists, however, concede too much to ideas; unless they are willing to deny the existence of the material world, they should recognize, as constructivists do, that 'a socially constructed reality presupposes a nonsocially constructed reality' as well[96] and that, consequently, the question of how the material world affects and is affected by the conceptual world is crucial for social science.

Some post-modernists, such as Baudrillard,[97] go so far as to turn not only truth, but also reality itself, into linguistic conventions.[98] This proposition is untenable, however. Statements are turned into facts not only by the power of discourse, but also by gaining control over the social support networks and the material resources of organizations and networks. Facts emerge when social and material resources 'make it too difficult and costly to deconstruct the statements supported by them.'[99] In other words, epistemic authority also has a material basis.

Constitutive perspectives, mainly post-structuralism and post-modernism, are also problematic because, although they concede that discourse practices are produced and reproduced by subjects, they nevertheless argue that individual subjectivity is completely constituted by discourse structures. *In their world* the subject, in its atomistic sense, causes nothing.[100] Hence, despite the post-structuralists' and post-modernists' respect for the agent/structure paradox 'as an opposition in which it is never possible to choose one proposition over the other,' they are able only to *describe* histories of discursive practices; whereas history is understood 'in its intrinsic pluralness, as a boundless text of countless texts.'[101]

If, on the other hand, *in our world*, subject and structure constitute each other with the help of and in the background of *material* resources, it may prove difficult to explore the subject's production and reproduction of inter-subjectivity and the latter's constitution of the subject 'from anywhere but within modernity.'[102] For example, taking agency and structure as different levels of stratified social reality,[103] constructivist scholarship of the 'morpho-genetic' tradition has enhanced our understanding of the dynamic social structuration of international reality and led to scientifically progressive explanations of foreign policy.[104]

Because of their ontological stand, constitutivists are too ready to 'abandon the search for causes and objective [i.e. intersubjective] truths to celebrate semantic instability and interpretive multiplicity.'[105] Post-modernists in particular advocate an 'intertextual' approach to International Relations[106] and argue that 'without deconstruction there might be no questions of ethics, identity, politics, or responsibility.'[107] Moreover, the main objective of inquiry, for constitutivists, is emancipation from oppressing discourses, power structures, ideologies, and theories (critical theory) and the unmasking of 'the way power is used in all of society's sites' (post-modernism/post-structuralism).[108]

A constructivist 'mediative' epistemology, on the other hand, is interested neither in emancipation *per se*, nor exclusively in uncovering the power structures that affect the marginalized in history, but in providing better explanations of social reality. Unlike post-structuralists and post-modernists, who are 'not especially interested in the meticulous examination of particular cases or sites for purposes of understanding them in their own distinctive terms,'[109] constructivists *do* want to know, *in detail*, how norms constitute the security identities and interests of international and transnational actors *in particular cases*.[110]

The above does not mean, however, that constructivists are blind to ideas of progress in International Relations[111] or that they do not care about improving the world just as much as Habermas[112] and other critical theorists do.[113] For most constructivists, however, it does mean that progress: (1) is not based only on what theorists say but also, and primarily, on what political actors do; (2) occurs through the redefinition of identities and interests of the actors themselves; and (3) is inescapably about universal normative ideas, even if their meaning varies from time to time and place to place. Thus a constructivist theory of progress in International Relations, which explains the emergence and consolidation of practices that enhance human interests within and across political communities—including the manner in which theoretical knowledge intervenes in struggles over meaning and reflectively affects these processes[114]—offers a better, more pragmatic and more even-handed alternative to critical theories that mark their favorite discourses for emancipation.

Finally, constructivist theory can be both 'critical' and 'problem-solving,' in Robert Cox's sense. 'It is critical in the sense that it stands apart from the prevailing order of the world and asks how the order came about.' But it is also problem-solving, in the sense that, once institutions and practices are reified, 'it takes the world as it finds it ... as the given framework for action.'[115] For example, although Wendt explains self-help as a socially constructed institution rather than a deterministic outcome of anarchy, he nevertheless sees the prevailing problem of predation as the explanation for the pervasive resilience of anarchical self-help.[116]

Constructivism, then, is an evolving *modernist* enterprise that blends 'understanding' and 'explaining' to create a sociologically sensitive scientific approach to International Relations.[117] Constructivism, for example, can accept the view that

> science ... and interpretation are *not* fundamentally different endeavors aimed at divergent goals. Both rely on preparing careful descriptions, gaining deep understandings of the world, asking good questions, formulating falsifiable hypotheses on the basis of more general theories, and collecting the evidence needed to evaluate those hypotheses.[118]

Moreover, some constructivists rely on precise comparisons [119] and covariation between material and ideational factors. [120] And when corroborating or cross-validating a theoretical or descriptive argument, constructivists may call on statistical and other quantitative methods [121] and make good use of historical counterfactuals. [122]

Constructivism can do *more*, not less, than other scientific approaches in explaining International Relations because, in addition to relying on logical–deductive and inductive means for knowing and verifying, it *also* invokes a variety of interpretive methods, such as narratives [123] and thickly described 'histories'[124] of sociocognitive processes to uncover collective meaning, actors' identities, and the *substance* of political interests.

I am aware, however, that not all constructivists will agree with the modernist portrayal of constructivism; the constructivist landscape is much more variegated than these paragraphs suggest. The diversity of approaches within constructivism reflects disagreements about the extent to which structure or agents are more important and about whether discourse should take precedence over material factors. Furthermore, it is sometimes hard to tell constructivists from post-modernists.[125] All constructivists do, nonetheless, share the mediative approach.

Thus, to build on a recent categorization by Cecelia Lynch and Audie Klotz[126] and shed some light on the differences within the constructivist camp, we can think about constructivism as divided into four different groups demarcated chiefly by methodological disagreements. Scholars of the first, 'modernist,' camp believe that, once ontological extremism is removed, there is no reason to exclude the use of standard methods alongside interpretive methods.[127] Within the modernist group, we can also distinguish state-centric constructivists[128] from constructivists who take the main actors of International Relations, such as nations and ethnic groups, as emergent features rather than as reified categories.[129]

A second group of constructivists, prominently represented by Onuf [130] and Kratochwil,[131] uses insights from international law and jurisprudence to show the impact on International Relations of modes of reasoning and persuasion and of rule-guided behavior. This approach shifts 'the focus explicitly toward a non-positivist epistemology, emphasizing the point that "large-scale historical change cannot be explained in terms of one or even several causal factors but through an analysis of conjectures."'[132] Rey Koslowski and Friedrich Kratochwil, for example, have used this approach to show the constitutive effect of normative change on the transformation of the international system in the late 1980s.[133]

A third group[134] emphasizes narrative knowing. Particular attention has been given to gender-based narratives,[135] actions of agents such as social movements,[136] and the development of security interests.[137] Finally, the scholars of the fourth camp do not shy away from techniques developed by post-modernists. Some constructivists have used Foucault's genealogical method;[138] others have engaged in the 'deconstruction of sovereignty'[139] by means of a detailed history of the delegitimation of non-Western polities by Western states. Deconstruction, in this sense, was only the preamble for the 'reconstruction of sovereignty' 'in the face of unambiguous opportunities for colonial imperialism.'[140]

Nothing said so far invites the conclusion that constructivism is merely a theory of global peace and harmony.[141] If international reality is socially constructed, then World War II, the Holocaust, and the Bosnian conflict must also have been socially constructed, just as arms control and environmental agreements and the end of the Cold War and collapse of the Soviet empire were socially constructed. In other words, constructivism is a set of paradigmatic lenses through which we observe *all* socially constructed reality, 'good' and 'bad.'

It also follows that power must play a crucial role in the construction of social reality. Power, in short, means not only the resources required to impose one's view on others, but also the authority to determine the shared meanings that constitute the identities, interests, and practices of states, as well as the conditions that confer, defer, or deny access to 'goods' and benefits. Because social reality is a matter of imposing meanings and functions on physical objects that do not already have those meanings and functions, the ability to create the underlying rules of the game, to define what constitutes acceptable play, and to be able to get other actors to commit themselves to those rules because they are now part of their self-understandings is perhaps the most subtle and most effective form of power.[142] This means that there is a very strong relationship between knowledge and power; knowledge is rarely value-neutral but frequently enters into the creation and reproduction of a particular social order that benefits some at the expense of others. In this reading, power is primarily institutional power to include and exclude, to legitimize and authorize.[143] Also, in this sense, international organizations *are* related to power, because they can be sites of identity and interest formation and because states and sometimes individuals and other social actors can draw on their material and symbolic resources.

In addition, there is hardly any concept that is more sensitive and amenable to constructivist logic and to the notion of power presented above than 'the national interest.' Constructivism seizes the middle ground because it integrates knowledge and power as part of an explanation of where interests come from.[144] National interests are not merely the collective interests of a group of people; nor, with rare exceptions, are they the interests of a single dominant individual. Rather, national interests are intersubjective understandings about what it takes to advance power, influence, and wealth—understandings that survive the political process, given the distribution of power and knowledge in a society. In other words, national interests are facts whose 'objectivity' relies on human agreement and the collective assignment of meaning and function to physical objects. 'The social construction of identities ... is necessarily prior to more obvious conceptions of interests: a 'we' needs to be established before its interests can be articulated.'[145] Constructivism is thus conducive to the empirical study of the conditions that make one particular intersubjective conception of interest prevail over others. In sum, constructivism is equipped to show how national interests are born, how they acquire their status of general political understandings, and how such understandings are politically selected in and through political processes.[146]

Constructivist dynamics: cognitive evolution

A dynamic theory of institutional selection is the natural complement of constructivism. Because interpretation is involved in the social construction of international reality, constructivist theory must be able to address the question of which and whose interpretations become social reality. In other words, why do certain ideas and concepts acquire epistemic, discursive, and institutional authority?[147] More specifically, which norms, and whose, come to constitute the games nations play?[148] Finally, how and why do certain collective expressions of human understanding, neither valid nor true *a priori*, develop into social practices, become firmly established within social and political systems, spread around the world, and become reified or taken for granted?

Critical, post-modernist, and post-structuralist theories are not very helpful in answering these questions. Although they enhance our understanding of *how* people go about creating consensus around meanings,[149] they fail to explain *why* social reality evolves around one particular set of interpretations as opposed to another. Neorealism[150] does even worse, because it lacks a theory of institutional evolution and the state. Drawing on an analogy between organisms and states and insisting that material power is the single arbiter of the selection of states, neorealism suggests that states must choose to survive or be marked for destruction by powerful systemic constraints. George Modelski's 'long-cycles' evolutionary theory[151] is not very helpful either, because it highlights the selection of global political systems by systemic war, that is, by material power only.

Neoliberals, on the other hand, are not oblivious to institutional selection and ideas. Following rational choice theory, however, they concentrate on institutional efficiency in providing material benefits.[152] For example, although Peter Hall[153] develops an elegant explanation of why Keynesian economic ideas became politically, administratively, and economically viable, he remains firmly grounded in rational choice, because he aims to determine the structural conditions that affected the choice of Keynesian ideas in different countries.

Hendrik Spruyt[154] suggests a different neoliberal explanation of institutional selection. Trying to overcome the fallacy that the existence of the institution derives from the functions it performs,[155] he focuses on the selection of the sovereign territorial state from among its rivals. Spruyt contends that the sovereign state was selected because 'it proved more effective at preventing defection by its members, reducing internal transaction costs, and making credible commitments to other units.'[156] Spruyt's account of 'selection' is still insufficient, however.

First, Spruyt reduces a rich history of the structuration between thinking and judging agents and intersubjective and social structures to material factors. Second, a true explanation of the selection of the sovereign territorial state must draw a feedback loop to cognition. Third, it cannot avoid the notion that intersubjective and social structures may 'engineer the selection process'—in other words, that intersubjective structures may partly determine the range and the nature of the choices and socially construct the 'proof' invoked by judging agents to choose among alternatives. Thus, while Spruyt is right when he points to the empirical usefulness of history, history is needed to show not only what alternatives could have been chosen, but also *how* and *why* human agents arrived at those alternatives and at the criteria for choosing among them.

A history of the selection of institutions should include an account of the agents, the innovators, the carriers of collective understandings who socially construct the alternatives, and the 'proofs' that legitimate the choices. It should also study the institutions that promote and socialize other actors to collective understandings and help to create social reality. Moreover, this history should account not only for processes of emulation, as in Spruyt's work,[157] but also for processes of active persuasion and recruitment. In order to answer at least some of the questions raised at the beginning of this section, we need to know how cognitive and institutional variants make their appearance in the first place, how they display their merits as solutions to international problems, and how—given favorable conditions—they spread and establish themselves. This suggests a theory of cognitive evolution.

Cognitive evolution is a 'homologous'[158] type of theory; it holds that the way social facts become established in the social world is relevant to the way they exert their influence.[159] Thus cognitive evolution has history and historicity[160] built into the theory; it is interested in the origins of social or institutional facts, such as identities, interests, practices, and institutions.

Cognitive evolution[161] means that at any point in time and place of a historical process, institutional or social facts may be socially constructed by collective understandings of the physical and the social world that are subject to authoritative (political) selection processes and thus to evolutionary change. Cognitive evolution is thus the process of innovation, domestic and international diffusion, political selection, and effective institutionalization that creates the intersubjective understanding on which the interests, practices, and behavior of governments are based.

A cognitive evolutionary theory is structurationist to the extent that individual and social actors successfully introduce innovations that help transform or even constitute new collective understandings, which, in turn, shape the identities and interests, and consequently the expectations, of social actors. Collective understandings, such as norms, are not sufficient cause for actions; individual agents must act according to their identities and as their interests dictate. Domestic and international politics, however, may sometimes keep them from acting in this way. Sometimes domestic politics is the arena in which cognitive structures are politically and institutionally empowered, before they can make their mark on the international scene. At other times, cognitive structures develop at the international level before leaving their mark on the domestic scene of individual states. In any case, a cognitive evolutionary approach requires that new or changed ideas be communicated and diffused and that political stakes be created, which political groups may then help maintain through the use of power.

Cognitive evolution is a theory of international learning, if we understand learning as the adoption by policymakers of new interpretations of reality, as they are created and introduced to the political system by individuals and social actors. The capacity of institutions in different countries to learn and to generate similar interests will depend not only on the acquisition of new information, but also on the political selection of similar epistemic and normative premises. The political importance of these premises lies not in their being 'true,' but in their being intersubjectively shared across institutions and nation-states. Seen in this light, learning increases the capacity and motivation to understand competing alternatives to a currently entertained inference and becomes a creative process through which alternatives and preferences or 'interests' are generated.

For example, fifty years ago there was no political value, and thus no interest, in arms control, sustainable development, and universal human rights. Today, both the value of and interest in all three are intersubjectively taken for granted—international security has come to depend on arms control practices. Domestic and international economic and environmental decisions are increasingly shaped by our relatively recent 'discovery' of the finite nature of our global environment. Human rights have become a central factor in the interests of democratic nations because they increasingly define their social identities.

Because we 'invent concepts and categories that we use to carve up the world ... and find ourselves categorized as well,'[162] the key demand made of the theory of cognitive evolution is to explain how institutional facts become *taken for granted*. To be taken for granted, institutional facts need to be 'naturalized,' that is, to be taken as part of the natural order of the universe. Thus, to be 'politically selected' an institution must gain legitimacy by being grounded in nature and reason. Next, it provides its members with a set of analogues with which to explore the world and justify the naturalness and reasonableness of the institutionalized rules.[163] The 'taken-for-grantedness' process implies that, as certain ideas or practices become reified, competing ideas and practices are delegitimized.

Second, unlike rationalist thought, a cognitive evolutionary approach maintains that it may not be the best-fitted ideas, nor the most efficient institutions, that become 'naturalized' or reified, but those that prove most successful at imposing collective meaning and function on physical reality. I have in mind ideas that help produce a balance or temporary consensus between competing trends within governments and societies, and between them, and that may serve as a rallying point for the formation of dominant coalitions.

Third, to be taken for granted, institutional facts must be backed by power; in other words, intersubjective ideas must have authority and legitimacy and must evoke trust.[164] Institutional facts are more likely to become established when agents, acting on their behalf, manage to frame reality around authoritative meanings (scientific or not) and/or gain control of the social support networks of politics, making it too difficult and costly for opponents to deconstruct institutionalized intersubjective ideas.[165]

Fourth, institutional selection is not an arbitrary act in a subjective sense, nor does it take place in an 'instant' of rational choice. It is rather the continuous rational institutionalization of a tradition that provides new or improved understandings of reality.

Fifth, political selection is driven by political leaders' intersubjective expectations of progress, that is, by ideas and institutions that conform to concepts that have been brought to public awareness as involving new and/or progressive solutions to critical political problems. Expectations of progress can be based on experience, scientific understandings, and even myths. Thus political selection becomes a function of what is collectively regarded as 'better' or 'worse,' which in turn depends on intersubjective understandings and prior social agreements about 'good' and 'bad.' What leaders can or cannot 'see' depends on collective normative and causal understandings about what is needed and about which needs should be promoted to the level of interests.

Sixth, institutional facts acquire prominence when people are collectively aware of the problem in practical terms. Institutions dispose individuals to follow the rules because they can intervene in the world to solve a problem. It is only in and through practice that social facts acquire self-criticism and transformation procedures that make the whole process 'rational.'[166]

Finally, institutional facts collectively emerge both from socialization processes that involve the diffusion of meanings from country to country and from political and diplomatic processes that include negotiation, persuasion, and coercion. Particularly noteworthy is the role of persuasion. Persuasion is a struggle to define mutual understandings 'that underpin identities, rights, grievances, ... interests, [and] attempts to control behavior through a wide range of social sanctions, only one of which is the use of force.'[167] When political actors interact, cooperatively or otherwise, they may be able to affect each other's understanding so that they can have a shared definition of their situation; they can collectively identify beneficial courses of action and recognize them as norms; and they can try to persuade each other to enact such norms through symbolic communication that threatens or enhances 'face' or 'dignity.'[168] For example, one of the most relevant roles of the Conference on Security and Cooperation in Europe during the Cold War was to serve as a forum where shared meanings between East and West were socially constructed by means of persuasion.

A constructivist research agenda

The descriptions, explanations and hypotheses produced by constructivism and cognitive evolution are oriented toward empirical research. Although constructivists were initially slow to develop research programs based on their approach,[169] the discipline is now bursting with constructivist studies.[170] In the pages below, I suggest ways of broadening and deepening constructivist research agendas.

Change in International Relations as cognitive evolution

A constructivist approach can go a long way toward a systematic explanation of change in International Relations. To a certain extent, the social construction of reality that assigns changes in collective meaning and purpose to physical objects is itself an important component of the process of change. Take, for example, the end of the Cold War, a powerful event that traditional approaches have found difficult to explain and certainly did not predict. It has become increasingly clear that events and phenomena that seemed to be 'systemically' unimportant, such as the Soviet dissident movement, which helped fuel the international delegitimation of the Soviet Union, and the Chernobyl nuclear accident, which brought home the horrors of uncontrolled nuclear power, gave rise in a few years to far-reaching and unpredictable consequences.

Koslowski and Kratochwil[171] have shown that changes in the political context and normative environment, that is, in the political conventions and practices of the Communist world, took place before the changes in the material environment. The overall change in intersubjective understandings that led to the delegitimation of Eastern European Communism in 1989, the hollowing of the Warsaw Pact, the subsequent delegitimation of Soviet Communism and imperialism, and, finally, the revival of nationalism and movements of self-determination in the Soviet Union,[172] all contributed to the deterioration of Soviet capabilities. Much work remains to be done, however, to understand the end of the Cold War. For example, we need to understand better how institutions such as the Helsinki process (the Conference on Security and Cooperation in Europe) helped create the standards that led actors to discover new preferences.[173]

A constructivist approach can also explain changes in the international political economy. For example, because it can show that changing collective understandings of technology and national and global economies may have direct material effects on the wealth of nations, constructivism may do a better job of explaining North–South relations than rational explanations that focus chiefly on material objects[174] and than post-modern explanations that focus exclusively on discursive changes.[175]

The evolution of international environmental policy offers another fertile ground for constructivist research. Take, for example, the concept of 'sustainable development.' Physical conditions led individuals to develop this normative and causal concept in their minds. After the concept was circulated extensively, it was officially adopted by the World Commission on Environment and Development in 1987, and later by the 1992 Rio Conference. UN institutions emerged to implement policies of sustainable development; even the United States adopted the concept as official policy on the environment. In the wake of all this, sustainable development became an intersubjective understanding on the basis of which problems and solutions regarding the environment and development are analyzed and repertoires for action formulated.[176] Because there is more than one interpretation of sustainable development, and some of them conflict, a consensual intersubjective definition is developing only in and through practice; this allows material factors to leave their mark. In any case, this understanding has begun to determine policies that act on the material world, affecting the physical environment, people, and their well-being.

Epistemic communities and the construction of social facts

The study of epistemic communities[177] does not make much sense unless it follows the constructivist approach. Epistemic communities are not a new actor on the international scene or an interest group. They are rather a vehicle of collective theoretical premises, interpretations, and meanings; in some cases they help construct the social reality of International Relations. NGOs, social movements, international organizations, and domestic institutions may play a similar role.[178] All these actors are significant for a broader theoretical understanding of the social construction of International Relations by intersubjective knowledge. In other words, constructivism broadens our understanding of the relationship between scientific knowledge and International Relations outcomes with the argument that International Relations in general, whether cooperative or conflictual, are framed and socially constructed by all classes of knowledge, scientific and other.

The interesting question about epistemic communities, from a political perspective, is not whether scientific knowledge is objectively true or not—much of what passes for the scientific knowledge of epistemic communities can hardly be considered truly objective, for the simple reason that in most cases it is amalgamated with social knowledge that can rarely allege truthfulness. The interesting question is how the effect on political and social reality of socially constructed scientific knowledge, produced 'in the laboratory' by people wearing white coats and adorned with a large dose of social legitimation, differs from that of socially constructed knowledge that does not claim to represent reality or that is accompanied only by normative, and not causal, claims.

While it is important to describe the ways in which dominant epistemic beliefs emerge from social interaction within a scientific group or community, it is equally important to study how *politically* dominant ways of framing issues emerge in interactions among political groups. We must look at the entire cognitive evolutionary process, trying to explain how knowledge is constructed twice—first by members of epistemic communities and later by individuals and institutions interacting in domestic and international political systems. Because mainstream ideas have a better chance of surviving the political selection process, epistemic communities that succeed in bringing mainstream ideas to public awareness may have a better chance of emerging as winners.

More broadly, constructivism can enlighten us about the role played by epistemic communities in bringing about major changes in the ways political leaders think about science and its consequences. To see how this may happen, think about science as a *constitutive norm* that socially constructs the identities, interests, and practices of modern rulers. Consequently, modern rulers can be thought of as increasingly relying on science not so much as the result of a calculated choice as because science has become part of their modern identity. On those rare occasions when epistemic communities diffuse a new normative view of science and of the global environment through the institutions of state and society, both the norms and their carriers may help bring about a transformation of political actors' identities, interests, and practices. These changes can be empirically documented.

Seen this way, normative ideas of science—carried by epistemic communities—may be more than just a resource that encourages states to act in a way that is consistent with the norms (e.g., cleaning up a polluted environment) and the transnational impact of these norms may go beyond helping to bring about 'policy coordination' between states.[179] Rather, their most far-reaching effect—in other words, the 'constructivist-dependent variable'—may be *the transformation of identities and interests*. The social construction of International Relations by epistemic communities may thus consist of the diffusion and internalization of new constitutive norms that end up creating new identities, interests, and even new types of social organization.

The emergent nature of political actors: security communities

The more we buy into the notion that international security is increasingly associated with the establishment of a security community[180] and that the boundaries of security communities are ideational, the more plausible it becomes 'that regions are socially constructed and are susceptible to redefinition.'[181] The research task, then, is to trace the social construction of security communities through history and compare them across areas.[182]

A security community agenda recognizes the social character of world politics; consequently it can make a major contribution to the constructivist research program by exploring the relationship among structures (defined in material and normative terms), the practices that are made possible and imaginable by these structures, the security orders that are rendered accessible within that field, and how those security orders regulate or extinguish the use of force. Thus, understanding security must begin not just with a set of previously constructed and thus reified categories, but also, and primarily, with the recognition that policymakers may have the ability to act upon the world with new knowledge and new understandings about how to organize security.

A research agenda on security communities requires identifying those interstate practices and transnational forces that create the assurance that states will not settle their differences through war. It also entails the notion that states govern their domestic behavior in ways that are consistent with the community. Said otherwise, membership in the community is shaped not only by the state's external identity and associated behavior but also by its domestic characteristics and practices.[183] For example, it would be very difficult for a European state to consistently abuse human rights and still be deemed to belong to contemporary 'Europe.'

This research agenda also requires studying the role that international and transnational institutions play in the social construction of security communities. By establishing, articulating, and transmitting norms that define what constitutes acceptable and legitimate state behavior, international organizations may be able to shape state practices. Even more remarkable, however, international organizations may encourage states and societies to imagine themselves as part of a region. This suggests that international organizations can be a site of interest and identity formation. Particularly striking are those cases in which regional organizations have been established for instrumental reasons, later and unexpectedly gaining an identity component by becoming a new site for interaction and source of imagination.

National security and the social construction of 'the strategy of conflict'

Peter Katzenstein and his colleagues[184] have conclusively shown that a constructivist approach can be very useful in explaining the normative underpinnings of national security, primarily security cooperation. This line of research, however, should be supplemented with the study of the social construction of conflict and war. On this issue, recent scholarship that emphasizes the cultural aspects of decisions about the use of force in war,[185] military doctrine,[186] military strategy,[187] and war proneness[188] suggests a fruitful research direction for constructivists to take.

Military strategy is a particularly promising field for constructivist research because the structural situation in which the actors find themselves in a strategic game situation—characterized by interdependent reciprocal expectations [189]—results not only from material objects or independent subjective beliefs, but also from dynamic intersubjective understandings based on shared historical experience, epistemic criteria, expectations of proper action, and, most importantly, the existence or lack of mutual trust.

A constructivist reading of Schelling's theory should emphasize the role played by social communication—and by the transfer from nation to nation of meanings, concepts, and norms—in socially constructing the intersubjective understandings and the focal points that make a peaceful solution to the strategic game possible. As Schelling himself remarked,

> the players must *bargain* their way to an outcome. ... They must find ways of ... communicating their intentions. ... The fundamental psychic and intellectual process is that of participating in the creation of *traditions*, and the ingredients out of which traditions can be created, or the materials in which potential traditions can be perceived and jointly recognized, are not at all coincident with the mathematical contents of the game.[190]

Because strategic knowledge can become part of reality and its unfolding, constructivists should also study the effect of military traditions and military academic knowledge on the social construction of military strategy and international affairs. For example, a shared set of epistemic criteria, together with convergence on a common practice of arms control—which Schelling and his colleagues helped to socially construct—enabled the United States and the Soviet Union to develop a coordination game and discover the extent to which its symbolic contents suggested compromises, limits, and regulations.[191] In this case, academic theoretical knowledge was neither just 'reasoning' about an external reality, as positivists would have it, nor simply a practice produced to discipline society to the rituals of power, as post-modernists might interpret it. Rather, strategic theory, by contributing to intersubjective understandings about strategic and arms control practices, provided 'reasons' to actors and thus affected the material world.

It is also remarkable how little appreciation there is in the International Relations literature of the fact that, like any other social institution, war is socially constructed and consequently depends partly for its persistence on collective ideas about the inevitability of war and its desirability for achieving political gain, riches, and glory. Constructivists should be able to test John Mueller's theory of 'the obsolescence of major war'[192] by showing whether, as a practice, war is collectively being redefined as inefficient, undesirable, and normatively unacceptable. Constructivists can try to show whether and how changes in nuclear technology[193] and values of war[194] are helping to constitute anti-war identities that promote the development of war-prevention national interests and strategies. [195]

Finally, although the notion that the social construction of an enemy ('the other') as part of the development of identities of 'self' has been validated by social identity theory[196] and analyzed by post-modern scholars,[197] constructivists have yet to develop research projects that can show how enemies and military threats are socially constructed by both material and ideational factors.

The social construction of the 'democratic peace'

The 'democratic peace' cries for a constructivist explanation. The leading neoliberal explanations of the democratic peace[198] share a combination of rationalistic and normative claims about the incentives and restraints imposed on state leaders by their societies and the international system. The 'democratic peace,' however, is neither about constraints nor solely about the subjective beliefs of particular individuals. Nor should we take liberalism as a fundamental determinist variable. Instead, the democratic peace is about the historical development and spread over part of the world of an intersubjective liberal identity that, cutting across national borders, becomes an identity marker and indicator of reciprocal peaceful intentions. In other words, the democratic peace is about the social construction of a transnational 'civic culture'[199] that engenders mutual trust and legitimacy. Needless to say, this hypothesis requires additional refinement and examination.

Furthermore, research can also follow the lead of Thomas Risse-Kappen,[200] who recently examined the social construction of a community of liberal values among North Atlantic democracies in the postwar era, and of Ido Oren, who has shown that the democratic peace is only a social construction of American social scientists, whose selection of empirical criteria 'is consistent with the dominant image of democracy in current American culture.'[201]

Conclusion

I hope that the present essay has shown that knowledge and interpretation are not only compatible with good social science, but are in fact indispensable for understanding and explaining the social construction of international reality. Constructivism may hold the key for developing dynamic theories about the transformation of international actors, institutionalized patterns, new political identities and interests, and systems of governance. It also establishes new areas of empirical investigation—nonexistent for realists, overlooked by liberals, and unimportant to psychological approaches—namely, the objective facts of world politics, which are facts only by virtue of human agreement.

I also hope I have shown that constructivism does not mean abandoning reason or rationality, but rediscovering how rational considerations are brought to bear in collective human enterprises and situations.[202] With constructivism prudently located in the middle ground, the 'Third Debate'[203] can now begin—not as a means to 'celebrate' dissent, but chiefly as part of the common enterprise of developing a sociocognitive theory of International Relations.

Part III
Epistemic communities

5   Ideological 'guerrillas' and the quest for technological autonomy

Brazil's domestic computer industry

This article is one of my earliest accounts of epistemic communities, written at a time when—as in my book The Power of Ideology *(1987)—I still referred to epistemic communities as 'intellectual guerrillas.' The article documents how and why ideologically motivated technocrats used their positions in state bureaucracies to convince policymakers of the viability of Brazil's infant computer industry and to establish institutions that would defend the Brazilian science-and-technology autonomy model and turn a sector-oriented policy into a national policy. This article shows how the realization of Brazil's autonomy policy depended on an epistemic community of ideologically oriented technocrats who, moving from ideological inclinations to the political process, briefly led Brazil to develop its own domestic computer policy. Brazil's computer autonomy policy and market reserve system came to an end in 1992. Although the autonomy policy helped generate technological development in, and technology transfer to, Brazil, it proved unable to withstand globalization pressures. The Brazilian computer market was liberalized and only a few domestic computer-hardware companies have survived foreign competition.*

Originally published in *International Organization* 40(3) (1986): 673–705

Why and how was Brazil—which has suffered from many 'classic dependency syndromes'[1]—successful in implementing a computer policy that explicitly aimed to reduce technological dependency on outside sources? Why and how did it establish a domestic computer industry that excluded international computer giants such as IBM from Brazil's lucrative micro- and minicomputer markets? To answer these questions, I shall analyze the economic, technological, and political factors that were partially responsible for overcoming some obstacles associated with technological dependency. For example, an 'economic miracle' in Brazil produced the capital necessary for industrial and technological development, and a balance-of-payments crisis forced its leaders to impose import controls and step up import substitution. Furthermore, since 1964 Brazil had experienced some measure of political stability, allowing for policy continuity. Most significant was the revolution that occurred in the technology of microelectronics, which decreased the costs and increased the simplicity of computer production.

At the same time, I shall show that a causal analysis based only on structural opportunities and/or constraints is insufficient because it does not account for the interaction of process-oriented and material factors: structural constraints and opportunities are not the only factors that matter, and motivated behavior is not merely behavior in the 'national interest.'

In the case of Brazilian computers, technological dependency could not be overcome until the dependency had been perceived and identified and solutions examined and selected. This process required the mobilization of ideological and institutional resources that, while they do not by themselves provide sufficient conditions for human behavior, do stimulate change by increasing the available solutions. The literature on bargaining theory claims that dependence on foreign sources of capital and technology,[2] even in high-technology sectors, can be partially overcome with time. The developing country, learning from experience, eventually gains access to sources of bargaining power earlier controlled by multinational corporations (MNCs), thereby shifting the balance in its favor.[3] I shall argue that, though accurate, the bargaining explanation is incomplete because it ignores the cognitive, mainly ideological, factors that inform capabilities and attributes.

Any learning or bargaining process is necessarily cognitive in that it involves beliefs, perceptions, and motives. These cognitive factors should not be taken for granted. Institutions that act to acquire the know-how necessary to force the balance of power to shift in their favor do not act as machines programmed to overcome MNCs' control of capital and technology but as purposive and sometimes even voluntaristic groups. Believing dependency to be the key development problem their countries face, such groups view autonomy from the MNCs as the most natural solution. The absence of such ideologically motivated groups might prevent a country from taking action to reduce dependency. A successful bargain was made possible in the Brazilian case partly because an ideology based on a 'theory' of dependency was turned into a strategy for achieving change, that is, for overcoming dependency.

In this study I will identify a 'pragmatic anti-dependency' school of thought, prevalent among the Brazilians responsible for Brazil's computer policy, which views dependency as a problem and which also believes that such dependency can be reduced through learning, control of foreign technology and investment, development of a domestic capacity for innovation, and direct state intervention aimed at linking domestic industry with the scientific and technological infrastructure.

This pragmatic anti-dependency approach refutes classic Marxist structural dependency theory, which, accepting only global and structural solutions to what are diagnosed as global and structural problems, concludes that developing countries are unable or unwilling to reduce their dependence on MNCs. The anti-dependency approach is attuned to bargaining theory in that it claims bargaining can take place beyond marginal issues, that dependency can be reduced sooner rather than later, and that developing countries are therefore not condemned to eternal dependency. Both pragmatic anti-dependency and bargaining theories reject structural determinism. Pragmatic anti-dependency is influenced by an eclectic Latin American ideology that I call *egalitarian nationalism*, a mixture of nationalist beliefs (which reject internationalism in both their pure liberal and Marxist versions) and Marxist humanitarian and egalitarian values, which derives from a strong indigenous statist tradition.[4]

The cognitive factor

Ideologies, as specific sets of ideas, can be powerful because they tell actors (including institutions and groups within institutions) what their goals should be, the importance of these goals compared to other goals, how to pursue these goals, and who their friends and enemies are. Ideologies can be important for understanding politico-economic behavior because they have origins that cannot be reduced to material developments ... [and that] can have substantial and independent effects,' as well as the 'obvious potential to develop into potent political forces. This happens when a set of political doctrines is adopted by a group of people, assumes a critical position in their belief systems, and then becomes a guiding force behind their actions.'[5]

I shall refer to political ideologies as doctrines or strategies that embody a consensus on causes and effects, antecedent conditions, and preferred outcomes that motivate individuals and groups to effect political, economic, and social change. Two major implications follow from this definition. First, because individuals and groups attach the label 'real' only to those situations that are both perceived and interpreted,[6] strategies for achieving change vary according to how a situation is understood, evaluated, and decoded. Whereas structural factors may generate the potential for events to happen in a certain way, human intervention (i.e., interpretation of reality) may cause the events to happen quite differently.

> All but the most extreme policy situations seem highly complex and uncertain; policy makers typically disagree among themselves as to diagnosis and prescription, or later analysts uncover evidence and reasoning that support more than one plausible interpretation of the national interest. Conflicting schools of thought cutting across interest groups, political parties, and bureaucracies are often evident. Policies sometimes seem to vary to a greater extent with the rotation of these schools of thought through the offices of government than with other variables. The cognitive analyst may argue that for a given case, a change in reigning ideas would have made a greater difference for a policy content than conceivable changes in other factors. Situational factors may explain the rejection of an old policy, the timing of a policy change, or the degree of policy coherence, but contain no explanation for the choice of a new policy from among the alternatives.[7]

Second, the consensus embodied in political ideologies can be achieved only in the light of mutual understanding among people within groups and institutions. Therefore, a cognitive explanation is by no means an alternative to an institutional explanation. The actors I characterize in this study as sharing a strategy for achieving change succeeded within and through institutions. Institutions are 'carriers' for ideologies that may compete with other ideologies both inside and outside the institutions. This study suggests that institutions integrate certain constellations of collective understanding and that these constellations may remain intact even if the institutions later cease to depend directly on them. By helping to set up goals and direct attention to political processes and resources, these constellations may become a precondition for institutional and policy change.

Inherent in the cognitive factor, however, are certain epistemological dangers; for example, the claim that ideas matter may be taken for granted, or the cognitive perspective may be so overstated that it becomes a truism.[8]

Nevertheless, these dangers should not discourage the search for an understanding of how cognitive and structural factors interact. The Brazilian computer case illustrates this interaction and proves that the point is not self-evident.

For the most part, Brazil's political, economic, and, to some degree, military elites regarded with skepticism the idea that Brazil could develop a computer industry without the participation of MNCs, especially IBM. A group of ideologically motivated actors who enjoyed the support of scientific and technological institutions and funds established in the late 1960s to develop Brazil's technological potential attempted to convince the elites otherwise. These actors included scientists, technologists, and technocrats, who, for the sake of their ideas and ideology, elected to act as political and ideological 'guerrillas' within public institutions. By placing their ideas about technological autonomy on high-level agendas, by keeping their ideas there, and by proving the economic viability of their ideas, they finally induced political leaders to give them a chance.

This group of what I term *pragmatic anti-dependency guerrillas* used their scientific, technological, and managerial knowledge, as well as their access to political power, to mobilize not only the *know-how* and *know-what* but also the *know-where-to* regarding computers. They were benevolent conspirators, who maintained belief in the possibility of a domestic computer industry even when the technological means to fulfill their vision were still minimal. And they continued to fight for their idea in the face of opposition from the politico-economic leaders.

The guerrillas' actions point up the importance of the cognitive approach in our understanding of state intervention in industrialization processes in the Third World. For, although a 'long history of economic dependence' can have 'a deleterious impact on domestic private enterprise, in terms both of its ability to accumulate capital and of its development of technology[,] ... a choice has to be made between direct state or parastatal intermediation and reliance on foreign entrepreneurship.' The ideological choice that Third World countries must make should not be taken for granted: whether to let MNCs run the show in the course of industrialization processes, or whether to allow the 'nationalist logic of external benefits and long-range returns' to lead toward state intervention.[9]

Research on the Third World ought to include studies on what enables one particular ideology and its institutional carriers to overcome alternative ideologies and their carriers. The Brazilian computer case would make an ideal subject for such a study, for it shows how the ideologically oriented pragmatic anti-dependency guerrillas induced and even co-opted the economic and political elites (who favored partnership with MNCs) to accept a market reserve that enabled the industry to develop. Any such study, however, must place cognitive and institutional factors in the context of the political, economic, and technological capabilities that influence elite behavior.

Brazil's computer market and the growth of its domestic computer industry

In the early 1970s the Brazilian computer market was already the twelfth largest in the world. While the world market was growing at a rate of about 20 percent a year, the Brazilian data-processing market was growing at a rate of 30 to 40 percent, second only to Japan. Growth rates were still high in the mid-1970s, between 20 and 30 percent. By 1975, when the national computer policy went into effect, Brazil had become the tenth largest data-processing market; by 1976 the market was worth about US$1.4 billion, or 1 percent of the Gross Domestic Product (GDP).[10]

By 1982 the value of installed computers in Brazil had reached US$2.8 billion.[11] In dollar terms the computer industry grew 64 percent between 1979 and 1980, 26 percent between 1980 and 1981, and 51 percent between 1981 and 1982 (the last after adjusting for 100 percent inflation). Growth for 1979–80 reflects the entrance of new domestic enterprises into the market; the 1981–82 figure represents a real growth in sales. The market was expected to reach US$5 billion by 1985.[12]

The growth in the number of installed computers between 1970 and 1982 is set forth in Table 5.1, which is broken down into the six categories adopted by the Brazilian Special Secretariat of Informatics (SEI).[13]

Between 1970 and the appearance of the first Brazilian computers in the marketplace in 1978, the number of computers in the country grew almost fourteenfold. Even discounting microcomputers, the number of computers increased by 270 percent between 1973 and 1978 and 673 percent between 1973 and 1982. The number of installed computers grew by 71 percent in 1981–82 alone.

The data indicate a very dramatic change in the market between 1970, when small and medium-sized computers accounted for 99 percent of all computers, and 1978, when micro- and minicomputers made up 71 percent

Table 5.1 Number of installed computers in Brazil, 1970–82, by size

Class	1970	1971	1972	1973	1974	1975	1976	1977	1978	1979	1980	1981	1982
Micro	*	*	*	586	1,514	2,143	3,131	3,846	4,290	4,791	4,722	8,756	17,702
(%)	*	*	*	(38)	(54)	(56)	(60)	(64)	(62)	(60)	(53)	(61)	(73)
Mini	*	*	*	19	81	173	265	356	656	1,015	1,675	2,719	3,571
(%)	*	*	*	(1)	(3)	(4)	(5)	(6)	(10)	(13)	(19)	(19)	(14)
Small	378	403	454	639	775	1,057	1,309	1,296	1,378	1,494	1,688	1,858	1,950
(%)	(75)	(70)	(68)	(40)	(27)	(27)	(25)	(21)	(20)	(18)	(19)	(13)	(8)
Medium	122	163	184	250	288	327	338	353	370	377	388	408	400
(%)	(24)	(28)	(28)	(16)	(11)	(9)	(7)	(6)	(5)	(5)	(5)	(3)	(2)
Large	2	2	10	45	72	82	99	122	166	226	248	374	544
(%)	(0)	(0)	(1)	(3)	(3)	(2)	(2)	(2)	(2)	(3)	(3)	(3)	(2)
Very large	4	10	19	33	42	61	72	87	93	97	123	134	172
(%)	(1)	(2)	(3)	(2)	(2)	(2)	(1)	(1)	(1)	(1)	(1)	(1)	(1)
Total excluding microcomputers	506	578	667	986	1,258	1,700	2,083	2,214	2,663	3,209	4,122	5,493	6,637
Total	506	578	667	1,572	2,772	3,843	5,214	6,060	6,953	8,000	8,844	14,249	24,339

Source: SEI, Boletim Informativo 1 (August–October 1981), 9; 2 (July–September 1982), 4; and 3 (June–September 1983), 6.
* = Available information is unreliable.

of the total. By 1982 this latter figure had jumped to 87 percent. Large computers also grew at a high rate: 346 percent between 1977 and 1982, 51 percent between 1980 and 1981 alone.[14] Because by 1982 mini- and micro-computers were doing what small and medium-sized computers had done in the past, and since the power and speed of large and very large computers were unmatched, the market for medium-sized computers was compressed while the extremes grew significantly.

Before Brazil formulated a computer policy, the country's computer requirements were met by MNCs such as IBM, Burroughs, Hewlett-Packard, Honeywell Bull, Data General, Digital, and Olivetti. Brazil's computer imports increased from US$13.3 million in 1969 to US$99.8 million in 1974 and to US$111.9 million in 1975.[15] IBM, Burroughs, and Hewlett-Packard manufactured computers in Brazil to meet domestic as well as global requirements. By 1980, IBM do Brasil, the largest computer company in Brazil, held 53.8 percent of the total value of installed computers and was IBM's fastest-growing subsidiary, generating about 50 percent of the company's Latin American business with the medium-sized and large computers, tapedrives, terminals, printers, and data-entry equipment produced in its Sumaré plant.[16] Burroughs, the second-largest company with approximately 15 percent of the total value of installed computers in 1980, manufactured medium-sized, large, and very large computers.[17]

Once Brazil decided to enter the domestic computer market, the industry developed rapidly. Only two years after that decision, domestic companies were producing hardware and software, peripheral devices, terminals, modems, and special ('intelligent') terminals. The dollar value of installed domestic computers grew from 2 percent of the total value of installed computers in Brazil in 1978 to 19 percent by 1982, by which time 67 percent of installed computers had been produced by domestic companies. Figure 5.1 shows the growth of domestic installed computers between 1980 and 1982, by number and value.

By 1983, Brazil had about 100 domestic computer companies, which employed 18,000 individuals; gross sales amounted to US$687 million or 46 percent of total gross sales.[18] Most had been founded after 1976 under the guidance of the national computer policy. In 1982 they accounted for 67, 91, 13, and 1 percent of the value of installed micro-, mini-, small-, and medium-sized computers, respectively.[19] The largest company, Cobra SA (a state-owned company), ranked third in sales, with about 36.2 percent of the total value of installed minicomputers by June 1982. At that time the other large national companies important in this segment of the market were Labo (18.4 percent), SID (7.6 percent), Edisa (23.3 percent), and Sisco (5 percent). Cobra, Dismac, Edisa, and Prológica held approximately 72 percent of the value of installed microcomputers.[20]

Domestic computer companies invest a relatively high share of their sales in research and development. In 1980 domestic firms producing computers with indigenous technology spent an average of 14.4 percent of their sales on R&D, while national firms working under foreign licenses spent an

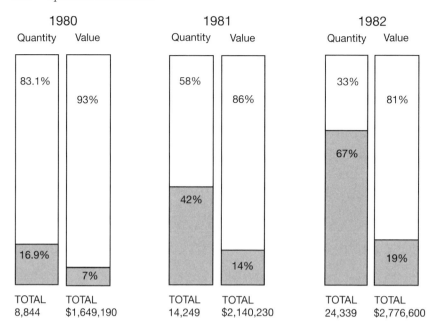

Figure 5.1: Number and value (in thousands) of installed domestic (shaded sections) and foreign computers, 1980–82 Source: SE1, *Boletim Informativo* 3 (June–September 1983), p.10

average of 7.9 percent. The total Brazilian domestic computer industry's R&D average was 8.7 percent, which was more than the 6.1 percent spent by the American computer industry during the same year.[21]

The reduction of domestic industry imports—they fell from US$81 million in 1981 (26.6 percent of total computer imports) to US$49 million in 1983 (21.4 percent of total computer imports)[22]—is one indicator of the success achieved by the pragmatic anti-dependency policy and its emphasis on R&D. Shares in sales of products based on local technology (technology not obtained under licensing agreements or for which such agreements had recently expired and only minor improvements made since) rose dramatically between 1979 and 1981, while those of imports declined during the same period (see Table 5.2). Domestic systems rose from 28 percent in 1979 to 60 percent in 1981, and imports fell from 29 to 7 percent. Although at the height of the reserve policy all terminals were manufactured domestically, peripheral devices still depended on foreign technology. Totaling the five categories shown in Table 5.2, we find domestic technology increased from 31 percent in 1979 to 53 percent in 1981, while imports decreased by a factor of almost four. During the same period the MNC import content of total sales rose from 28 to 40 percent.[23]

Finally, it should be pointed out that some domestic computer companies reached a level of technological sophistication and economic efficiency that allowed them to produce for export. Cobra, Microdigital, Prológica, and

Table 5.2 Dollar share of sales for equipment manufactured with local technology and of imports

	1979		1980		1981	
	Technology	*Imports*	*Technology*	*Imports*	*Technology*	*Imports*
Systems	28 %	29 %	41 %	18 %	60 %	7 %
Peripheral devices		111	4	48	6	36
Terminals	100	8	100	8	100	3
Modems	10	21	37	22	50	13
Special terminals	100	6	100	22	100	14
Total	31	29	39	20	53	8

Source: UNCTC, *Transborder Data Flows and Brazil* (New York: United Nations, 1983), 223–25.

Notes: Figures for sales include exports. Imports for a given year appear as percentages of sales during that year. Since corporations may import to increase inventories, percentages may be higher than 100.

Elebra were the domestic export leaders (Elebra even exported components to the United States).

Economic growth, technology, and the international computer industry

From 1968 to 1973—the period of Brazil's economic miracle—Brazil's GDP grew at an average yearly rate of 10.1 percent. Industrial production grew even faster, so that by 1975 the Brazilian manufactured added value was about 25 percent of the Brazilian GDP, representing almost 20 percent of the added value of all the developing countries combined. Even more remarkable was Brazil's real growth in capital-goods manufacturing output, which averaged 20.8 percent a year between 1968 and 1973.[24] This growth rate produced the capital necessary for Brazil's industrial and technological development and kindled expectations that Brazil had at last found the road to self-sustained growth.

Buttressing the economic progress was the relative stability and continuity of Brazil's political regime, which began with the coup in 1964 that overthrew João Goulart and continued until the 1984 elections. Economic leadership during this period was also remarkably stable: the minister of planning, João Paulo dos Reis Velloso, a key figure in the development of Brazil's computer industry, held this position (later changed to secretary of planning) from 1969 to 1979.

Emboldened by its economic growth, Brazil became involved in large infrastructure and industrial projects: during this period Brazil built Itaipú, the biggest hydroelectric plant in the world, implemented a policy to run cars on alcohol, and established a huge nuclear energy program.[25] The evolution of computer technology and of the international computer industry came at an opportune time for Brazil. Searching for new ways to develop domestic technology, Brazil took advantage of the rise of mini- and microcomputers and of the progress in semiconductor technology.

Semiconductor technology received a boost when the transistor, invented by Bell Laboratories in 1947, was integrated, along with other necessary components, into a single silicon base, or 'chip.' This integration reduced manufacturing costs, increased efficiency, and enlarged information storage capacities.[26] The price per bit of storage fell from about 1.000 cent per bit in 1970 to 0.050 cent per bit in 1979,[27] and was expected to fall to 0.001 cent per bit by 1989.[28]

The revolution in semiconductor technology was responsible for the development of minicomputers, which appeared for the first time in 1965 when Digital Equipment Corporation introduced its PDP-8 model. The minicomputer industry has since become fiercely competitive. At the beginning of the 1970s, approximately forty companies were created to manufacture minicomputers.[29] Since then minicomputers

> have experienced price declines of at least five while at the same time their main memory capacities have increased by factors of two to four times, and processing speeds have increased by perhaps a factor of 1,000. ... [B]y the middle of the 1970s technological innovations were leading minisystems to be so powerful as to challenge the lower range of the mainframe computer market.

By 1980, before the appearance of 32-bit superminicomputers or 'superminis,' the minicomputer market was estimated at US$15 billion—roughly a quarter of the world computer market.[30]

Probably the most important technological jump in semiconductor technology to date occurred in 1971, when Intel introduced a chip known as the microprocessor, which can be programmed to carry out information-processing and control functions[31]—in essence, a computer-on-a-chip. After several generations, processing power of the chip increased tremendously, while cost per function decreased.[32] The microprocessors were built into microcomputers almost as powerful as minicomputers, at a fraction of their cost, and found their way into homes as 'personal computers.'

When Brazilian technocrats first discussed developing a domestic computer industry in 1971, these advances in computer technology did not escape them. However, their ideas of the state of the art at that time were based on computer technology of the late 1960s; they were not aware of the advantages they would later receive from advances in the technology of microprocessors and microcomputers. By 1977, when the crucial political decisions were made, those responsible for domestic computer policy were fully aware of the importance of these developments. Timing was not irrelevant. That MNCs, in particular IBM, had not yet begun manufacturing mini- and microcomputers in Brazil when the national endeavor was first considered constituted an opportunity. For had the MNCs already established a niche in Brazil with these systems, the cost and difficulty of pushing them out of the market might have proved too high.

The new technological developments generated a very dynamic world semiconductor market characterized by the entry of companies from several nations with the capacity to supply millions of computers-on-a-chip every year. The worldwide worth of semiconductors increased from about US$400 million in 1959 to US$5.4 billion in 1974 and to approximately US$20 billion in 1983. The growth of this market spawned many additional firms in the United States as well as in Japan and Europe, which began to compete for the production market for integrated circuits. For example, Japan sold 70 percent of all the 64k chips in 1982 and became aggressively involved in the production and sale of 256k chips;[33] six out of the ten largest manufacturers of chips were Japanese. By 1982, Japan, Western Europe, and the United States controlled 30, 17, and 50 percent, respectively, of the production of integrated circuits.[34]

These technological and market changes have partially transformed the highly concentrated and oligopolized international computer industry. In the 1970s this industry grew at a rate of between 10 and 15 percent annually; correspondingly the number of computers in use worldwide doubled every few years.[35] One giant, IBM, overshadowed all other computer companies. In 1970, IBM controlled 60 percent of the computer market (valued at US$11.7 billion). By the end of the decade this lead had narrowed to a still impressive 40 percent of the US$53.5 billion market.[36] IBM's gross sales were worth US$46 billion in 1984.[37]

In the mid-1980s, US companies held 80 percent of the computer market. Seven of the industry's top ten companies were American: IBM, Burroughs, Texas Instruments, Motorola, Digital, NCR, and Control Data. But Japan, which had been making large inroads, held close to 10 percent, or about US$9 billion, of that market. In 1983, Japan's computer equipment exports amounted to US$3.9 billion, with Nippon, Fujitsu, and Hitachi listed among the ten largest computer companies worldwide.[38] Smaller Japanese companies were supplying computer hardware to US firms and, together with Taiwanese and Korean companies, selling components and personal computers on world markets. In all, 500 computer hardware manufacturers, 5,000 software companies, and about 430 producers of communication equipment sold US$268 billion worth of products. With a compound annual growth of 20 percent, data-processing revenues were expected to reach US$1 trillion by 1990.[39]

Development of a Brazilian computer industry

Encouraged by the changes that were taking place in the international computer industry, and anxious to promote industrialization and domestic technological development, as early as 1971 Brazil's technocrats decided to invest the capital made available by the economic miracle in a domestic computer industry. The availability of inexpensive chips, along with the possibility of obtaining technology under license, helped Brazil shift its technological dependence from the older computer hardware market dominated by market giants to the dynamic semiconductor market dominated by foreign components and software know-how available from small new companies. The domestic computer industry development was thus an ideological, institutional, and political outgrowth of the general science and technology policy that Brazil implemented at the end of the 1960s.

A group of economists working for the National Bank for Economic and Social Development (BNDES), headed by José Pelúcio, identified the source of Brazil's underdevelopment as technological dependency. Their diagnosis assumed that economic development was linked not only to growth rates but also to an increased capacity for understanding and perceiving the impact of forces of modernization. This diagnosis found partial support from the military; the diagnosis received strong support from planning institutions, which were staffed largely by economists trained by the Economic Commission for Latin America, and from the scientific and technological community, many of whom had been involved in setting up the National Research Council (CNPq) and the nuclear independence policy at the beginning of the 1950s. Adherents of the dependency diagnosis believed Brazil would achieve autonomy not by rejecting foreign technology but by attaining the ability to make technological decisions.

The dependency diagnosis may be considered pragmatic because it did not accept the structuralist view that the world capitalist system necessarily leads to stagnation and to eternal dependence. Instead, it attempted to identify Brazil's weaknesses in order to effect reforms. To achieve the objective of technological autonomy, Brazil developed an indigenous technological capacity guided by a national strategy of selective interdependence, possibilities of importing technology, local comparative advantage, and possibilities of exporting the resultant technology.[40]

The strong relationship that developed between Pelúcio, the guiding force behind the science and technology policy during the 1970s, and Velloso was crucial to the implementation of such a policy. Velloso was a powerful advocate for technological anti-dependency ideas and their realization. A strong supporter of a market economy and interdependence, he nonetheless believed that the key to an economically sound future lay in developing a domestic technological potential including strategic sectors such as computers.

The government established the Studies and Projects Financing Agency (FINEP) in order to support national technological development and to link the domestic technological infrastructure to national industry; Pelúcio headed FINEP for most of the 1970s. The National Science and Technology Development Fund, which operated under the jurisdiction of FINEP, became the main financial instrument for scientific and technological development. The National Research Council, later renamed the National Council of Science and Technology, became the central organism for planning, coordinating, and implementing scientific and technological policy. The Industrial Technology Secretariat was charged with promoting and developing domestic technology. Further, technological funds were made available within the framework of research institutes and banks; technology foundations and companies were attached to research institutes to work in priority areas; the university system was reformed and a graduate studies plan issued; and fellowships and grants for scientific and technological training increased significantly.

The share of the national budget earmarked for science and technology, which had been 0.84 percent in 1970, rose to 3.64 percent in 1982, R&D expenditures as a percentage of Gross National Product almost tripled between 1971 and 1979, from 0.24 to 0.65 percent, and the number of scientists and engineers engaged in R&D increased from 0.8 to 2.1 per 10,000 people between 1974 and 1978.[41] Brazil also promulgated a strong Industrial Property Code and related acts aimed at opening 'technological packages' so that indigenous technologies would be used when possible.

Pelúcio, the BNDES, and the other autonomy-oriented science and technology institutions and planners also provided the means to train computer-science professionals. The improvements in the scientific and technological infrastructure in the sector produced a critical mass of experts sufficient for 'the government to adopt an aggressive policy of technological independence in the sector.'[42]

FINEP supported development of hardware, software, and process-control uses in addition to financing several university projects and establishing computers at Brazilian universities. The CNPq provided fellowships and research support to institutions, assisted a microelectronics project, and organized a task force to coordinate the policy of future data-processing technology.

By the mid-1970s, when the computer policy began to take shape, those graduates sent abroad to study were beginning to return, strengthening their institutions and universities. Although prior to 1972 professional training depended heavily on MNCs and their 'free courses,' by 1977 forty undergraduate and graduate university courses were being offered.[43] Universities in São Paulo, Minas Gerais, and Rio Grande do Sul offered graduate programs in computer science. By 1982, Brazil had 19 universities, 450 research scientists organized into 74 groups, and 12 government research centers working on computer technology. Total human resources available in the data-processing equipment industry were 14,646 in 1981, 31.5 percent of whom were university graduates.[44]

Cobra: the early days

Early in 1971, when the Brazilian navy decided to equip its vessels with English Ferranti computers, it also initiated a project to plan, develop, and manufacture a domestic computer prototype suitable for naval operations, preferably one that could interface with Ferranti. [45] The navy's Communication and Electronics Directorate contacted Pelúcio at the BNDES Science and Technology Fund. The Guaranys Project (naval officer José Luis Guaranys became more involved in this project than anyone else) grew out of this relationship, as did a special working group (GTE/FUNTEC 111) established to formulate goals for the project. The Guaranys Project had two primary objectives: to establish a three-sided (*tripé*) partnership of Brazilian state and private enterprises with MNCs[46]—with the foreign partner agreeing to transfer its technology to the company; and to promote and finance the development of a domestic minicomputer prototype.

The selection in April 1973 of the private Brazilian company, E. E. Eletrônica, and the creation of a holding company called Brazilian Digital Electronics initiated the first course of action. One year later Brazilian Digital Electronics became Digibrás, in effect an industrial promotion agency set up to study the market, provide consulting services and support for national firms, identify R&D needs, and organize the necessary supporting companies.

Digibrás was originally supposed to create two computer companies, one in association with Ferranti mainly to meet military requirements, and the other in association with either the Japanese Fujitsu or the West German Nixdorf to produce computers for the civilian markets. The first company, founded in 1974, was Cobra, a joint venture between the state, E. E. Eletrônica, and Ferranti (which held only about 3 percent of the capital shares and acceded to Cobra's demand to transfer its technology). The venture resulted in the first Brazilian-assembled minicomputers, the 700 Series.

When the attempt to create a second company failed, Cobra began a search for the foreign technology that would allow Brazil to produce a minicomputer for commerce and industry by itself. Although Data General seemed the most likely candidate to transfer minicomputer technology to Cobra, the American company was not willing to accept Brazil's condition that patents, blueprints, and general know-how be transferred to Cobra at the end of the licensing period. A small American company, Sycor, Inc., did, however, accede to Cobra's terms; in 1976 Cobra and Sycor signed agreements to effect technology transfer, provide technical assistance and training, and purchase certain products. Sycor was exempted from import controls and thus gained almost exclusive access to a fast-growing market, while Cobra obtained the necessary technology to develop what became its 400 Series.[47]

Cobra relied on foreign technology while the development of the domestically designed minicomputer and peripheral devices were still in the making, but remained committed to absorbing this technology. The use of foreign technology was relatively successful because 'it substantially reduced the time required to begin local production of minicomputers and helped to avoid mistakes both in product and process designs that would probably have occurred had Cobra relied initially on local technological sources only.'[48] The 400 Series became Cobra's main product until its domestically designed minicomputer, the G-10, came of age.

The hardware for Brazil's first domestic computer was developed at the University of São Paulo, while the software was worked on at the Pontifical Catholic University of Rio de Janeiro. First planned as solely a scientific computer, the G-10 was then transferred to Cobra, which broadened its scope. Cobra received another boost when the Federal Data-Processing Service, the largest Brazilian data-processing enterprise, and the University of Rio de Janeiro transferred terminals they had developed to Cobra. With these additions the G-10 minicomputer became Cobra's 500, a computer designed in Brazil and using almost entirely locally developed components.

Cobra's financial situation in 1976 did not match its relative success in R&D and technology transfer. Lacking purchase requests from the private market, Cobra initially sold only to government institutions and the armed forces. Assistance for the failing enterprise came from two quarters. IBM's help was inadvertent: its plan to introduce its System 32 minicomputer, which would have killed Brazil's domestic minicomputer industry even before it was born, mobilized Cobra's allies. More positive help came from a consortium of eleven banks, including such giants as Bradesco and Itaú. Foreseeing the need for electronic automation in banking, these banks decided to purchase 39 percent of Cobra's shares.[49]

The government's determination to keep Cobra alive was based on the belief that only a state-owned company could lead the effort to absorb foreign technology, develop local technology, and satisfy Brazil's growing need for domestic computers. Cobra had thus become a means to achieve a national goal that was more significant than market efficiency and even import substitution. By setting up Cobra, Brazil was following in the foot-steps of India, which had established a 'national champion,' the Electronics Corporation of India Limited,[50] in order to develop its domestic computer industry. But equally influential to Brazil's ultimate success in reducing dependency in the computer field was CAPRE.

CAPRE and the guerrillas' autonomy model

The government created the Commission for the Coordination of Electronic Processing Activities (CAPRE) on April 5, 1972, to manage the development of a domestic computer. CAPRE undertook to gather available information about the computer market and human resources, as well as to provide incentives for scientific and technological development in this sector. CAPRE also endeavored to prevent unnecessary imports and to prevent government agencies from using data-processing equipment inefficiently.

CAPRE's subordination to the Planning Ministry, under Velloso, was crucial for its ultimate success. The ministry's transformation into a secretariat with direct links to the president and assumption of responsibility for

Brazil's scientific and technological network became a source of political power for CAPRE and a shelter for the guerrillas involved.

The pragmatic anti-dependency ideology unified the Planning Secretariat, the scientific and technological institutions, the universities and their scientists, and CAPRE. While Pelúcio set up the groundwork and Velloso provided cautious support, Ricardo Saur, CAPRE's executive secretary, engaged in direct action to turn this ideology into industrial reality.

CAPRE became more than the institution entrusted by presidential decree to develop a specific technology: it became the home of an ideologically assertive group—a 'guerrilla headquarters' of sorts—that set itself up to sell ideas, raise consciousness, and use political power to achieve its goals. While CAPRE took its first formal actions—creating national programs for data-processing centers and computer training, identifying the strengths and liabilities of the scientific and technological infrastructure[51]—the pragmatic anti-dependency guerrillas began their intellectual and political 'attacks.' Although most of the guerrillas came from CAPRE, some worked in institutions such as the Federal Data-Processing Service and Cobra. The core, known among themselves as the Group, included Saur, Ivan de Costa Marques, Mário Ripper, Arthur Pereira Nunes, and Claudio Zamitti Mammana. They began by formulating in their own minds a doctrine that became known as the National Model.

The Model had two key features: only national companies would participate in Brazil's computer industry; and each piece of foreign technology could be purchased only once. The Group infused the scientific and technological community and the political system with optimism, insisting that 'the thing could be done.' As teachers at universities and as technocrats at government agencies, they emphasized Brazil's few but significant technological successes in order to generate a positive feedback effect. Computers, industry, politics, and academia became interwoven with the creation of the Computation Seminars at the university, which became another forum for airing the guerrillas' ideas: market protection, national enterprises, and technological autonomy.[52] *Dados e Idéias*, a monthly data-processing magazine issued by the Federal Data-Processing Service, also provided pressure for instituting economic controls on the computer market. Besides publishing technical material, *Dados e Idéias* became a forum for commentary and criticism of the government's computer policy and on the dangers of technological dependency.

It is interesting to note that a similar phenomenon seems to have occurred in India. Grieco hinted at the existence of guerrillas and guerrilla 'attacks' when he discussed the political actions of the Atomic Energy Commission (referred to as a 'network'):

> This gave the atomic energy policy 'network' a strong incentive to break its stalemate with Defense and, building upon national dissatisfaction over the country's progress in electronics, this network waged a

campaign in 1969 and 1970 that led to a victory over Defense for control of national electronics policy. New policy units were created—the Electronics Commission and the Department of Electronics—which were supposed to be neutral but which were, in fact, heavily staffed by key members of the atomic energy network.[53]

As is widely known, India's Atomic Energy Commission has been one of the country's ideological leaders in the push for technological independence.

In December 1975 CAPRE acquired new power through Resolution 104, which held that all imports of computer parts, accessories, and components required CAPRE's prior authorization. CAPRE raised import duties, required deposits without interest for the value of imports, and set import quotas. In addition it established an import limit: US$110 million in 1976, US$100 million in 1977, and US$130 million in 1978. [54] Its formal power grew when it was charged with imposing further import control measures and with studying the state of the art and proposing a national informatics policy. CAPRE thereby became the 'guardian of the gate,' freeing the guerrillas to act as they chose.

Brazil's deteriorating balance-of-payments situation after 1974 played into the need for import controls, which gave CAPRE increasing authority over the computer market. But CAPRE's concerns were

> much broader than the simple objective of controlling imports so as to rectify the country's balance-of-payments problems. The Government was convinced that informatics was strategically important to the nation and that, therefore, Brazil needed a policy which would enable it to acquire the technical capability necessary to reduce its dependence.[55]

From the guerrillas' perspective, the balance-of-payments crisis was a blessing.

CAPRE's power stemmed from its ability to set guidelines and policies without much high-level interference. Despite CAPRE's position, however, Velloso and other high-level policymakers did not envision a totally domestic computer industry. The government still wanted to exploit the MNCs' technology, although 'the multinationals here,' according to Saur, 'including the biggest, IBM, declared their lack of interest in this effort.'[56]

CAPRE made two decisions in July 1976 which created the basis for reserving the mini- and microcomputer markets for Brazilian enterprises and reflected the government's pragmatic approach *vis-à-vis* the MNCs. Decision 01 divided the market and the industry into two sections. While it recommended that 'the national informatics policy for the medium and large computer market be based on investment rationalization and optimization of installed resources' (i.e., on the market, namely foreign industry), it also recommended that, when feasible, mini- and microcomputers and peripheral devices be reserved for the domestic industry.[57] Decision 02 gave CAPRE the power to control the purchase of software and data-processing services by government agencies and enterprises.

Decision 01 continued the policy initiated in the early 1970s but also represented a response to IBM's announcement, made in a blitz advertising campaign that attracted almost 400 potential buyers,[58] that its System 32 minicomputer would be assembled in Brazil from parts brought in under its import quota.

These two policy decisions reflected CAPRE's efforts to protect a weak national industry without giving the MNCs the impression that Brazil was enforcing a protectionist policy. Because high-level government officials continued to hope that IBM and other MNCs would enter into joint ventures with domestic companies, they would not agree to reserving the entire mini- and microcomputer market for domestic companies.

CAPRE's strategy was determined by its council; however, the decision to have two 'containment lines'—allowing only Brazilian companies to produce domestic computers and accepting joint ventures with the MNCs—was strictly a guerrilla strategy.

The Economic Development Council's Decision 05 (January 12, 1977) aided the CAPRE guerrillas by establishing the following criteria for fiscal incentives in the data-processing industry: extent of nationalization; export potential; extent of technology transfer; analysis of enterprises already in the market; and domestic-capital majority. CAPRE used these criteria to select 'winners' from among the domestic and foreign companies invited under Decision 01 of June 1977 to present proposals for the production of mini-computers in Brazil.[59] Among the sixteen companies that submitted proposals were seven MNCs, but only joint ventures.

As the time for a decision approached, Velloso was under heavy fire from two camps. Ministers and high-level government officials outside the Planning Secretariat and the science and technology institutional network, and industrial elites, mainly from São Paulo, pointing out Cobra's ailing condition, remained unconvinced that Brazil could successfully challenge IBM. Furthermore, IBM and other MNCs were pressuring the highest echelons of Brazil's political power structure to prevent a decision that would leave them outside the market. The media put CAPRE's case on the front pages, playing up the tough MNC line regarding joint ventures and IBM's attempt to use System 32 to undermine Cobra. The subject of MNCs, which had traditionally aroused nationalist feelings, generated outrage once the facts became public knowledge. The government found it increasingly difficult to do anything that indicated it was bending under pressure from the MNCs. That the powerful banking consortia which had invested money in Cobra were pressing for the domestic alternative and that key military actors in the armed forces high command favored domestic companies and market closure also worked in CAPRE's favor.

The critical decision was made in mid-April 1977, at an informal meeting of the CAPRE council and the ministers directly and indirectly involved in the data-processing sector. Although the ministers tended to prefer joint ventures because they feared that the movement toward a national computer industry was based on enthusiasm alone, they nevertheless decided that any interested company could present a bid and that final decisions would be based on the conditions specified by the Economic Development Council.

The ministers told CAPRE informally that nationals should be preferred only if their bids were as good as those of MNCs; if not, CAPRE should accept IBM's proposal. However, because, according to one of the Economic Development Council's criteria for investment in computers, MNCs had to be willing to engage in joint ventures, it would have been almost impossible for CAPRE to choose IBM. Thus, the CAPRE council decision of June 1977 calling for bids from domestic and foreign firms to produce minicomputers was in fact a cover-up: a decision had already been reached.

CAPRE's blow to the MNCs came at the end of 1977. It chose four companies, rather than the anticipated three: Cobra and three private domestic consortia that had just been or were still in the process of being created and that were developing minicomputers under foreign licenses: SID, Labo, and Edisa. CAPRE later approved a fifth company, Sisco, which developed minicomputers with its own technology.[60] Under the terms agreed to by the companies involved, technology transfer had to be completed by 1982, and payment for this technology was not to exceed 3 percent of net sales. Local firms could purchase foreign technology only once and had to develop further models locally.

This choice represented a strategic victory for CAPRE and Saur, as it allowed the market reserve policy to be implemented. In addition it permitted government policymakers to say: 'We played according to the rules, we asked for bids from everyone, and we let the best bid win.'

Velloso played his cards very diplomatically, assuring the MNCs that the joint-venture condition was not mandatory and that CAPRE would judge the proposals by additional criteria. The MNCs, taking Velloso's words as a genuine indication that the door was open to them, felt that, although Brazil would prefer to have local equity—even control—it was prepared to waive this condition if other factors proved more compelling.[61] However, while Velloso was telling the MNCs that everything was fine, CAPRE was telling IBM's vice-president the opposite. Although some domestic companies among the bidders had yet to begin operation, CAPRE decided to favor them anyway as a result of its strong determination to exclude MNCs from the minicomputer market and of the green light signaled by the ministers' decision.

After winning the minicomputer battle, CAPRE began to eye the medium-sized computer market. Fearing that the MNCs might scale down medium-sized computers and use them to compete with Brazilian minicomputers, and/or that the domestic industry once in operation might not be able to compete in this market, CAPRE in December 1978 issued new criteria for the manufacture of central processing units and peripheral devices beyond the minicomputer range. These criteria included assurances that such projects would not interfere with mini- and microcomputers and that there would be local decision-making, the possibility of technology transfer, a growing nationalization index, and export potential.[62] CAPRE thereby prohibited IBM and Burroughs from manufacturing medium-sized computers in Brazil.

SEI: the evolution of the Model and its struggle to survive

CAPRE's responsibilities increased as new domestic computer companies appeared on the scene. The military, which, except for the navy, had not shown any particular interest in the process, was impressed by the successful challenge to IBM. By the end of 1978, it realized that the data-processing sector was too strategically important to leave in the hands of a Planning Secretariat that, after the 1979 elections, might be led by 'internationalists' (as actually happened when first Mário Henrique Simonsen and then Antônio Delfim Netto became planning secretary) who might retreat from the anti-dependency policy and again fall prey to the MNCs.

Heading the military's interests was the National Intelligence Service (SNI), from whose ranks came João Batista Figueiredo, elected president of Brazil in March 1979. In January 1979 the SNI initiated an inquiry commission, headed by Ambassador Paulo Cotrim, whose findings criticized CAPRE. According to the commission, CAPRE lacked a policy aimed at reducing dependency on foreign sources of software and microelectronics. With the Figueiredo government poised to take office, and the SNI's mistrust of CAPRE's 'leftist' technocrats, CAPRE began to lose its power base, and the architects of the autonomy policy were edged out.

When the Cotrim commission was turned into a presidential committee, it decided to abolish CAPRE and to place data-processing policy under the jurisdiction of the National Security Council (CSN). Following the commission's guidelines, the committee recommended increasing incentives for domestic technological development and establishing a policy to nationalize development of semiconductors. The Special Secretariat of Informatics (SEI) replaced CAPRE in December 1979, and the cooperation between government technocrats and the scientific community that had characterized the mid-1970s was eroded. SEI was attached to the CSN and reported directly to the president.

SEI's main tasks were to advise the CSN on informatics and to formulate a national informatics plan and policy. It was also charged with stimulating and assisting the development of technology, components, equipment, programs, and services, and with protecting the technical and commercial viability of domestic companies producing systems and components.[63] In addition, SEI was to try and coordinate real-time control systems, microelectronics, and national software policies.

SEI marked a new stage in the politics associated with Brazil's domestic computer industry and policy. Economic elites and consumer associations opposed the protectionist policy on efficiency grounds and, encouraged by the prevailing atmosphere of *abertura*, or political openness, also objected to CSN's control over policy matters. Furthermore, some members of the new cabinet strongly opposed CAPRE's Model and explicitly wished to enter into joint ventures with MNCs.

Also opposed to the changes were the guerrillas, the scientific and technical communities, and a majority of the computer associations created after CAPRE began to implement its policy—essentially the Model's watchdogs. Institutions such as the Brazilian Association of Computer and Peripheral Equipment Industries, the Association of Data-Processing Professionals, the Association of Data-Processing Service Enterprises, and the Brazilian Computation Society feared that SEI would, in time, ally itself to the MNCs, approve joint ventures, and eventually erode the Model.

Thus, SEI had to begin by rowing against not one but two streams. It had succeeded, and even prospered, by operating under the CSN's shield. But it had also strengthened its position by promising opponents of the Model that the market reserve would soon be watered down or even eliminated and promising watchdogs of the Model that the reserve would be not only maintained but strengthened.

SEI's first actions evidenced a determination to keep the market reserve, to control the data-processing sector, and to deal with the MNCs firmly yet pragmatically. Its first Normative Act (March 1980) set guidelines for data-processing imports, stipulating that preference be given to 'the national alternative' and that software be developed domestically. Later that year, SEI ordered that all data-processing equipment be registered, that both domestic and foreign federal government purchases receive prior permission, and that the government favor domestic data-processing services.[64] It also stated that approval for new projects aimed at manufacturing data-processing equipment and parts and the import of components would depend on the extent to which they used locally developed technology and were directed by Brazilians.

The first major test for the new policy came in August 1980, when SEI gave IBM permission to manufacture limited quantities of its medium-sized Model 4331 computers in Brazil. At that time the market for medium-sized computers was growing by 10 percent a year and SEI preferred locally made equipment over imports.[65] Domestic producers, scientists, and guerrillas feared that this decision would prevent the domestic development of medium-sized and large computers and would suffocate local industry. A permanent commission was therefore set up to oversee and protect the national computer industry's actions. The commission also decided to regard SEI's permission to IBM as inconclusive.[66]

SEI was slightly restructured in 1981: the Advisory Council consisting of private- and public-sector representatives was created, SEI's scope was broadened, and incentives were established for Brazilian firms only. The Advisory Council represented a major gain for supporters of the market reserve because it provided them with an additional forum in which to advance their ideology. For example, when SEI's secretary general, Octavio Gennari Netto, announced that the market reserve for computers would be maintained for only another three years,[67] supporters of the Model protested so strongly that the idea was never mentioned again; the SEI eventually passed Normative Act 016 of July 1981, which made permission to manufacture reserved products increasingly difficult to obtain. SEI grew even stronger in 1982 when it took over some of Digibrás' functions. (This take-over led subsequently to Digibrás' demise in 1983.)

Later SEI announced that it would have to approve all R&D performed in the informatics sector and that the federal government could contract informatics services from foreign firms only when no national company was qualified to render that service. SEI also broadened the market reserve to include digital machinery used in measurements and in biomedical work and created a section to register all domestic and foreign software programs marketed in Brazil. Although the registry was not obligatory, SEI did not approve any unregistered imports or manufacturing projects.

Aiming to correct a major bottleneck that had prevented Brazil from producing genuine domestic systems and to promote development of domestic 16-bit software, Normative Act 027 of November 1983 stated that SEI would approve only those microcomputer manufacturing projects with locally developed software. In 1984, the Special Software Commission was set up to establish the juridical basis for a Software Law.

SEI leaders also confronted the problem of developing their own chips; at the time, Brazil purchased these from abroad or from foreign companies located in Brazil. In the 1970s, the Ministries of Industry and Commerce and of Communications tried to get a foothold in the semiconductor industry; FINEP and the CNPq helped by training appropriate personnel and promoting relevant R&D. But these efforts did not bear fruit; a semiconductor company set up by the state was shut down in 1980 because of financial difficulties.

When SEI began dictating Brazilian microelectronics policy in 1981, it established a component import-control policy and began to coordinate the R&D activities of various institutions. In order to carry out these activities, SEI created a microelectronics research institute. The Informatics Technological Center (CTI) opened in May 1984 in Campinas, near São Paulo; two private domestic firms, Itaú and Doças de Santos, were chosen to locate near CTI and to open plants to manufacture microelectronic products.

The development abroad of the superminicomputer reopened the technological gap between the Brazilian data-processing industry and foreign competitors. This new development, which fueled consumer and political opposition to domestic computer policy, sent both SEI and domestic manufacturers back to the drawing board. In an effort to close the gap, SEI decided to encourage the development of the superminicomputer in Brazil. Its call was answered by eight domestic companies: three committed themselves to developing the superminicomputer with local technology; another five requested permission to manufacture them with imported technology. These companies committed themselves to effect technology transfer and a high nationalization index.

SEI had to choose among several alternatives: local production of superminicomputers with foreign technology; local production with local technology; joint ventures with MNCs. Some prominent senators, members of Congress, and industrialists, including Minister of Industry and Commerce João Camilo Penna,[68] called for joint ventures. SEI policymakers were in favor of acquiring foreign technology but rejected joint ventures. But supporters of the Model held out for total local control over the industry.

Initially SEI decided to allow Cobra, SID, Labo, and Edisa to manufacture 'supermicros'—16- or 32-bit microcomputers with increased memory capacity—with local technology. At the same time, SEI was hoping that some of the companies involved would merge. When they had not done so by June 1984, SEI approved all five superminicomputer projects using foreign technology.

The Model's supporters responded swiftly. The Brazilian Association of Computer and Peripheral Equipment Industries, the Association of Data-Processing Professionals, and the Brazilian Computation Society, together with the Brazilian Society for the Progress of Science (counterpart to the American Association for the Advancement of Science), issued a communiqué stating that SEI's decision represented a retreat from the quest for technological autonomy in the computer area and calling upon SEI to reconsider.[69] Assuming that they would not be able to compete with foreign technology, the three local companies involved in developing the superminicomputer with indigenous technology put a halt to their projects and decided that they, too, would purchase technology abroad. Failure to develop a system for that market eventually forced Cobra to sign a technology transfer contract with Data General.

In retrospect, SEI took a tough yet pragmatic position: tough because it ruled out joint ventures, and pragmatic because it understood domestic industry's need for foreign technology to allow it to stay abreast of developments abroad. Although some foreign technology proved useful, the industry adhered to the Model because only domestic companies were chosen to develop the superminicomputer, and the foreign technology was supposed to be transferred eventually.

Supporters of the Model fought additional battles during 1983 and 1984. More crucial in their eyes than the superminicomputer struggle was the battle to transform the Model (also known as the National Informatics Policy—PNI) into national law.

PNI supporters had to contend with bills calling for its extinction. The most threatening bill, proposed by Senator Roberto Campos of the then-ruling Social Democratic party, would have abolished the market reserve, dismantled SEI and substituted a tariff system and joint ventures, and placed informatics policy under the Ministry of Industry and Commerce. This proposal had the blessing of internationally oriented business circles, MNCs, and the US government, which has always been openly critical of Brazil's computer market reserve and used Brazil's financial dependence to pressure its government into changing its policy.

On the other side of the political spectrum was an array of bills aimed at retaining the market reserve and import controls and nurturing domestic computer companies. On September 20, 1984, the military government introduced a bill that would protect the Brazilian computer industry from foreign competition for eight years, provide fiscal incentives to stimulate local firms, and establish the National Council on Informatics and Automation (CONIN). The eighteen-member council would be attached to the presidency; on an equal footing with the CSN, it would control SEI's policies. This would mean that SEI would no longer belong to the CSN and that MNCs already producing computers in Brazil would be allowed to continue their operations; but foreign companies would be allowed to make new investments only if the resultant products were to be exported.[70]

The guerrillas, the computer associations that favored the market reserve, the scientific community, and others organized a propaganda campaign to ensure that Congress would pass a law favorable to the market reserve. The Brazilian Association of Computer and Peripheral Equipment Industries and the Brazilian Computation Society issued a document signed by 200 institutions, which was entitled 'The Defense of Brazilian Technology.' This document, which accused the US Commerce Department of interfering with Brazil's computer policy, called on Brazilian business circles to reject proposals to allow joint ventures with MNCs.[71] The campaign held public meetings at universities, published a new journal called *Brazil Informatics*, and sponsored an annual 'National Informatics Day.' The campaign succeeded: on October 3, 1984, Congress voted in favor of the government motion. Saur's reaction to the vote was that CONIN represented a refinement of the CAPRE informatics model; and, he added, 'we have returned to what it was.'[72]

The empires strike back

Data General was one of the first foreign companies to fight the market reserve and associated policies. In June 1977, after its minicomputer deal with Cobra fell through, Data General tried to strengthen its position by applying pressure through the US president's special representative for trade negotiations and Congress. But despite Data General's claim that other countries might follow Brazil's lead if Brazil's computer industry succeeded, the United States refused to involve itself in the negotiations. Data General thus ended up with no share of the Brazilian minicomputer market.[73]

Convinced that the Brazilian government would not exclude it from the minicomputer market, IBM do Brasil decided to play tough. The company initially held fast to its official policy of avoiding joint manufacturing ventures. Then it refused to comply with the technology transfer policy and complained about Brazil's new low import level. IBM's lobbying efforts emphasized the 'obscurity' of Sycor's minicomputer technology and its lack of software. IBM also thought that the System 32 computers they had placed on the market in 1976 would generate demand for continued production. As a final argument, IBM pointed out that in view of its balance-of-payments difficulties, Brazil could not afford to pass up an IBM manufacturing venture that involved a strong export potential.

IBM do Brasil's president, José Bonifacio de Abreu Amorim, expressed his surprise at the government's policy: 'We don't need to ask the government in advance for permission to build System 32. Does Ford ask the government for permission every time it wants to introduce a new model automobile? ... The government, after all, wants us to export.'[74] Amorim's attitude reflected IBM's failure to see that the Brazilians sought much more than exports or even jobs and control of the majority of shares; the government's ultimate aim was domestic technological development.

The pressure exerted by IBM in fact generated nationalist sentiments that supported CAPRE's objectives. Had IBM been more flexible and accepted some of the government's conditions, the Group's second containment line might have been able to accommodate it. But, despite Amorim's worry that the pressure might backfire, IBM World Trade argued that compliance with Brazilian regulations would eventually involve IBM in joint manufacturing ventures, a policy it specifically avoided. In light of IBM's investment in countries such as France, that policy was very important.

Other MNCs such as Burroughs and Hewlett-Packard watched the gathering storm. Though less influential than IBM, they put additional pressure on the Brazilian government. For example, Burroughs' marketing manager remarked that if Brazil protected the market, the MNCs would have to set up factories somewhere else, in 'neighboring countries in Latin America.'[75]

As time went by, and Brazil showed the MNCs that its domestic minicomputer industry was there to stay, foreign companies adapted to the new reality. Burroughs stated that it would continue to market products other than micro- and minicomputers in Brazil and (along with other companies) also indicated that it was considering association with Brazilian enterprises. Although they were left out of the lucrative micro- and minicomputer markets,

> IBM and Burroughs seem to have made the best of the situation, manufacturing large systems in Brazil since the mid-1970s. Both corporations

have gained advantages from the informatics policy because the products produced locally by them benefit from the preference rules regarding imported goods and services.[76]

IBM, Burroughs, and Hewlett-Packard did get some of their projects approved through intensive lobbying, and IBM found ways to circumvent domestic manufacturing restrictions; in the end, however, they all had to accept the Brazilian computer industry's development and work with rather than against it. IBM signed an agreement with the Association of Data-Processing Service Enterprises involving nine joint software projects and promised to provide technological help to the CTI.[77] Burroughs also signed a technical and commercial agreement with the association to develop and market programs for Burroughs systems together with Brazilian software enterprises.

Moreover, some MNCs established sales agreements with their Brazilian counterparts; and their attitudes toward licensing also changed. Whereas in the mid-1970s Cobra had difficulty finding a foreign company willing to transfer its technology, six years later '18 agreements had been signed involving 16 foreign and 14 local firms.'[78]

There is a lesson here for MNCs in developing countries: successful MNCs will demonstrate sensitivity to the host country's prevailing set of beliefs, expectations, and objectives, and recognize that it is to their advantage to accommodate any differences. MNCs can yield or remain inflexible. IBM tried it both ways before learning the value of flexibility *vis-à-vis* a developing country that was determined to achieve its goals.

Conclusion

By mobilizing its material and ideological resources against IBM and other MNCs, Brazil successfully demonstrated that it could determine its own computer policy. In establishing its domestic computer industry, Brazil started out with one 'national champion'; only then did it call upon domestic private enterprises to enter the field. It developed assertive institutions to create computer policy, initiated import controls to allow the domestic industry to develop, and carefully established pragmatic guidelines that avoided radical conceptions of autarky. The guerrillas, whose ideology infused their technical know-how with norms and policy directions, supported the domestic computer model unfailingly. Despite, or maybe even because of, the removal or circumvention of some individuals and institutions that originally determined the industry's policies and technology, the computer industry maintained its momentum.

Institutions such as CAPRE, Cobra, the Federal Data-Processing Service, and even *Dados e Idéias* were crucial not only because of what they did but also because they gave the guerrillas a base. Institutions were able to achieve outcomes because of their political power, but the definition of their goals, means, and policy agendas stemmed from the collective understanding that united individuals within and often among these institutions.

SEI's replacement of CAPRE severed SEI's dependency on its founders— Pelúcio, the BNDES, FINEP, and the Group. The Model that CAPRE had developed remained vigorous after CAPRE's extinction because it was able to generate its own institutions, domestic companies, and pressure groups, and thus prove its viability to the nationalists within the CSN.

Crucial to the understanding of how the pragmatic anti-dependency guerrillas succeeded in making the Model operational is the fact that technological and political factors reinforced each other as much as ideological and institutional actions did. For example, in the 1970s computer technology became increasingly accessible and inexpensive; capital was available both to buy such technology and to (re)produce it locally; and earlier programs (such as that initiated by Cobra) to improve Brazilian computer technology were flourishing. Market, technology, political, and international forces combined with purposive actions, *ad hoc* choices and coalitions, and reactions by the MNCs to shape Brazil's domestic computer industry.

Brazil's actions may be compared with those of India, one of the few developing countries other than Brazil to successfully challenge the MNCs in the computer market. It is no coincidence that India and Brazil decided to reduce their dependency in the same field. For both countries recognized early on the importance of technological autonomy. In both countries a national ideology acted on forces of change and modernization to bring about independence from the MNCs in the computer field. Moreover, outcomes in both cases seem to have been strongly affected by the actions of ideologically motivated intellectual guerrillas acting within state institutions.[79]

To consider Brazil's computer policy and industry a roaring success would be more than premature. Some companies may still fail, and the government's commitment to the domestic computer industry may falter in the face of political and economic changes. As long as Brazil continues to rely on foreign production of semiconductors, it will remain somewhat technologically dependent. Furthermore, SEI's actions with regard to the superminicomputers show that overcoming dependency is not an overnight affair. A developing country can close the technological gap with foreign technology; yet if the gap widens again, a developing country may have to take political, industrial, and technological action both to close the gap and to calm the resulting consumer and political unrest.[80]

But, if we take Brazil's technological development as the main indicator of the success of its computer policy, we can say that Brazil came to enjoy a more developed electronics and computer R&D base, with a critical mass of scientists and technologists in the computer field, and gained know-how in the areas of technological management, production, and engineering. Furthermore, in some cases Brazil's computer policy forced MNCs to accede to joint ventures, a policy many MNCs had previously avoided. In this regard, Brazil's computer policy created an example for other sectors and other nations.

The Brazilian computer case thus strengthens the claims by advocates of bargaining theory—as reformulated to include high-technology sectors—that developing countries that skillfully mobilize their resources *vis-à-vis* MNCs can reduce industrial and technological dependence. It also strikes a blow to theorists of structural dependency by demonstrating that, as important as the political and economic domestic and international constraints on a country are, ideological resources can outweigh them.

Furthermore, though the motivation to achieve autonomy is important, this case shows that elites in developing countries are not united in favor of taking nationalist pro-autonomy measures at the expense of MNCs. Thus, those who wish to understand motives should start at the level of elites (and their ideologies) rather than at the state level. Only by taking a close look at Brazilian elites and their ideologies could we identify the pragmatic anti-dependency guerrillas and their crucial role in Brazil's computer policy.

The guerrillas, in turn, suggest the existence of a 'subversive elite,'[81] one whose members share beliefs about the nature of politics and economics which differ from those usually defined as belonging to the elite. Members of this elite have a resource that makes them very valuable: knowledge. This subversive elite succeeds in transferring its ideas to the individuals and institutions in power. It is an elite by virtue of its ability—sometimes overt, explicit, and direct, and at other times indirect—to affect the predisposition of policymakers. 'Rather than dictating specific policy moves, these predispositions influence behavior by shaping and coloring the way new information is processed.'[82]

Brazil's pragmatic anti-dependency guerrillas fully qualify as a subversive elite. And because of the authority they acquired in their own country, and in the regional and international forums in which they represented their country, 'the process that in the realm of science and technology is known as the protracted sequence from invention to innovation often takes remarkably little time in Latin America with respect to economic, social and political ideas.'[83] Ideological elites such as Brazil's pragmatic anti-dependency guerrillas have the ability to mobilize the collective beliefs, expectations, and concepts that are ultimately responsible for institutional action.[84]

6 The emergence of cooperation

National epistemic communities and the international evolution of the idea of nuclear arms control

This article documents how an American epistemic community played a key role in creating the international shared understanding and practice of nuclear arms control. It emphasizes the roles played by epistemic communities in policy innovation and in the diffusion of understandings across nations and communities, analyzes how the theoretical and practical ideas of the arms control epistemic community became political expectations, were diffused to the Soviet Union, and were ultimately embodied in the 1972 antiballistic missile (ABM) arms control treaty. The article provides a striking example not only of how communities of practice organize themselves and expand—in this case, the American arms control epistemic community 'cloned' itself in the Soviet Union—but, also, and primarily, of the intellectual origins of arms control and of why certain strategic ideas made it to the top and others did not.

They were also instrumental in diffusing this understanding to the Soviet Union. Indeed, after a time the Soviets agreed to negotiate with the Americans on the basis of this understanding, and it has formed the foundation of US–Soviet cooperation over the last thirty years.

The relevance of my study of the arms control epistemic community for understanding international cooperation lies in the notion that *domestically* developed theoretical expectations which were created by a *national* group of experts and were selected by the US government as the basis for negotiations with the Soviets became the seed of the ABM partial security regime.[4] Although many of these original expectations were later 'renegotiated' at the bargaining table and the Americans came to follow a more political approach to arms control, it was the set selected by the US government that became the regime's conceptual basis.[5]

Thus, the Americans and Soviets signed the 1972 ABM treaty and created a regime, not only because the balance of power and technology had changed, nor simply because of any deep sharing of strategic cultural or political goals, but because they were able to converge on an American intellectual innovation as the key to advancing both their irreconcilable interests and their shared interest of avoiding nuclear war. Once nuclear arms control became conventional and was routinized in government practices, however, the superpowers saw it as in their interest to conform with arms control agreements.

The political selection, retention, and diffusion at national and international levels of *new* conceptual understandings suggest an evolutionary approach. The mutually reinforcing national and international arms control games—two-level games, as it were—were structured not only by fixed interests and power but also by common understandings and practices. Such an evolutionary approach is at odds with explanations of international change advanced by structural realism and approaches based on it.[6]

For example, Steve Weber has used a modified structural realist analysis to shed light on superpower cooperation during the Cold War. He argues that 'the condition of nuclear deterrence constitutes a structural change in the international political system' and that, beginning in the early 1960s, the superpowers became 'socialized' to structural change and constraints in different ways.[7] Thus, in the ABM case, a lack of shared interests or compatible visions of the long-term goals to be achieved through agreement led the superpowers to learn different lessons, hence dooming the détente episode of the 1970s. Beginning in the mid-1980s, however, for reasons that Weber does not fully specify, expectations began to converge.

Weber's approach differs from mine in many conceptual and practical ways. Weber uses a conventional structural analysis to show how a new structural organizing principle, mediated by ideas, influences concepts of state interests.[8] In contrast, I use a structurationist approach to show how epistemic communities play a role in establishing interpretations of interests as practices that help organize, structure, and coordinate international behavior.[9] In Weber's theoretical world, structural reality constrains behavior and then challenges agents to coordinate their behavior. In my theoretical world, agents coordinate their behavior according to common practices that structure and give meaning to changing international reality.

The epistemic community approach has some clear 'comparative advantages.' First, it allows us to understand why superpower cooperation was conceptualized via arms control in the first place. Second, it increases our sensitivity to domestic political factors, especially to the notion that within each national actor different interpretations of the national interest compete for the shaping of international agendas as well as international practices. Third, in ways that allow for empirical research, focusing on an epistemic community draws our attention to the impact of scientific knowledge on international cooperation processes. Fourth, the approach shows that states become socialized not only to structural constraints but also to each other's understanding of the world. Fifth, it helps us see that, in spite of or even because of superpower disagreement over political interests and visions, the fact that the 'Soviets also seem to have understood and shared to some degree the American concerns about arms-race and crisis instabilities that might be engendered by ABM deployments'[10] was not inconsequential for peaceful change. The outcome of a lack of such shared understanding might have been nuclear war, rather than the temporary demise of détente. Sixth, common epistemic understandings proved to be more lasting than disagreements over long-term goals. With the end of the Cold War, most of the divergent long-term goals are gone; what still remain, however, are an abundance of weapons and the practice of arms control.

On the basis of my theoretical approach, I have devised an evolutionary research framework to describe how arms control ideas were selected from the lot, carried into the power stratum, and survived to become reality in 1972. This framework consists of five variables: (1) *units of variation* (the 'genetic stuff,' as it were), consisting of tentative new conceptual variants, interpretations, and meanings based on expectations, which circulate within the academic and political communities; (2) *innovation*, or the processes by which intellectual communities package such units of variation and thereby create a collective understanding—as, in our case, about the nuclear predicament; (3) *selection*, or the political processes that determine which policies are effectively adopted by the government; (4) *diffusion*, or the spread of expectations, values, and other types of ideas to other nations; and (5) *units of effective modification*, or the patterned normative behavior of two or more states that results in part from innovation, selection, and diffusion of expectations.[11] In the following sections of my article, I relate the concept of an epistemic community to the issue of nuclear strategy and offer an empirical description of the variables. First, however, let me state the working hypotheses that inform my approach:

1   In a strategic relationship, expectations are not derived in some auto-
    matic and deterministic fashion from a structural condition but emerge
    from meanings and understandings or 'theories' that show a relation
    between causes and effects and create interpretations of structure.
2   When there is no prior experience with the phenomenon at hand, such
    as nuclear war, these theories are based on generalizable and abstract
    propositions and models.
3   Because of the 'scientific' and technical nature of these theories, they are
    most likely to be developed in academic circles, given validation there,
    and taken to the political system by academic communities.
4   Through direct and indirect means, nations transmit to each other the
    content of their theories.
5   This transfer of meanings and concepts from nation to nation allows
    decision-makers of different nationalities and cultures to share historical
    experience, epistemic criteria, and expectations of proper action and to
    rationally calculate their choices according to an intersubjective under-
    standing of the structural situation and of each other's payoffs.
6   The sharing of strategic epistemic criteria induces decision-makers to
    behave according to these criteria, thus helping to fulfill them in prac-
    tice.
7   International cooperation emerges, changes, and decays along with
    shared meanings and expectations and thus depends on whether or not
    decision-makers make the rational choice to learn.

Knowledge, power, and nuclear strategy

Epistemic communities

Both national and international epistemic communities may play roles in
the evolution of international cooperation in fields characterized by technical
uncertainty and complexity. But the political influence of transnational epistemic communities, such as the Pugwash group in the security field,[12] is
most likely to rest on the transfer from the international to the domestic
scene of the ideas that *national* scientists and experts raise at their transnational meetings. Pugwash, for example, can best be described as what John
Ruggie calls a 'switchboard' through which connections are 'established and
maintained, rather than being a depository of activity and authority.'[13] The
decisive 'customers,' then, from both domestic and international political
perspectives, are, first, national experts, and ultimately, national governments.

That is why we need to pay more attention to the international influence
of national epistemic communities in various fields, including arms control.
They may be able to affect international political processes and outcomes by
binding present and future decision-makers to a set of concepts and meanings that amount to a new interpretation of reality and also by becoming

actors in the process of political selection of their own ideas. As international negotiation agendas are formulated on the basis of these ideas and as negotiation and diplomatic processes start to take place, diplomats act to advance not only a set of policies but also a set of ideas. They 'communicate,' as Michael Brenner puts it,

> to the leaders of other states their 'theoretical' understanding about the military–political characteristics of nuclear weapons in addition to signaling their intent on the particular issue at hand. ... This exchange of beliefs and images is especially significant in the area of nuclear weapons where the issues of perception and deterrent psychology bulk so large.[14]

The success of epistemic communities is historically contingent. Historical contingency is afforded by the state of technology, the distribution of power in the international system, domestic political and administrative structures and procedures, and political, economic, and military events. As the historical context changes, theories or policy proposals that previously did not make much sense to politicians may suddenly acquire a political (perhaps even urgent) meaning, thus becoming politically viable.

The field of military strategy is propitious for the emergence of an epistemic community because, as Wesley Posvar has argued, strategy is 'formulated by the cumulative action of subordinate and outlying elements. Individual, piecemeal decisions add together and build upon one another, and the aggregate comprises the strategic posture of the nation.'[15] Thus, although the government or state agencies are directly in charge of developing national strategies, institutions outside the structure of government may also be able to perform this function.[16]

The 'imaginary' science of nuclear strategy

To prescribe an effective course of action, a community of strategists requires a theory that, as Charles Reynolds suggests, 'show[s] a causal relationship between conditions, a governing principle, and a result. The [political] actor then has the choice, should he so wish, to procure the result by fulfilling the conditions.'[17] For the most part, strategists arrive at their theories by inductive processes, as they look to the past for information, understanding, and inspiration. But when there is no prior experience, as in the case of nuclear war, strategic thinking must depend principally on theories that seek to explain human behavior on the basis of some generalizable propositions, such as rationality, and on the basis of abstract models, simulations, and games. Thus, because the science of nuclear strategy has no empirical reference points and data banks, it cannot be falsified and is, in this sense, 'imaginary.'[18]

This is especially true of nuclear arms control, since theory on this subject was developed in the absence of experience with nuclear war and at a time when there was little or no meaningful experience with nuclear disarmament and arms control. Theorizing about nuclear arms control requires assumptions about how weapons would operate in various hypothetical nuclear war scenarios and what might or might not deter conflicting powers from launching a surprise nuclear attack. These assumptions must rest partly on a theory of international behavior, arrived at mainly on the basis of conjectures, assumptions, and nonscientific expectations.

Arms control theory, therefore, cannot be *a priori* valid or true. Its validity and power as a conceptual basis for international cooperation will depend on the following: the temporary existence among the members of an epistemic community of shared expectations and of intersubjective and consensual meanings, arrived at via verbal communication; the domestic political selection of shared expectations as practices of governments, based on the fact that expectations meet the decision-makers' criteria for advancing national interests; and the fulfillment of these expectations in practice, once they are diffused to other nations and become the epistemic criteria on which a strategic relationship between two or more nations is based. On all three levels—epistemic community, domestic political system, and international system—the sharing of premises and expectations, or 'theories,' creates the 'evidence' that confirms the validity of norms.

Because the superpowers are engaged in a strategic situation characterized by the interdependence of expectations, the sharing of deterrence, stability, and arms control expectations induces policymakers to behave *as if* they are true, thus fulfilling the theories' conditions in practice. Progress in arms control and the absence of war over time may then help reinforce the belief in stable deterrence and arms control expectations. In this manner, the science of nuclear strategy has an input in creating the reality it is supposed to explain and predict.

It also follows that the power of expectations as an explanatory variable is independent of the 'instillation' of the expectations in any subjective mind. If arms control ideas succeeded in transforming the practice of deterrence and cooperation with the adversary, what mattered was not that the personal expectations of the people involved changed in the course of their careers, nor was it how preferences were first proposed. Instead, what mattered was how the preferences were ultimately disposed through the presence or absence of social validation.[19] Furthermore, the realization of communicable expectations and theories depends on whether their practical applications are readily perceived by policymakers. For example, Thomas Schelling's theory of interdependent decision seems to lead to important and striking political proposals and actions. And these proposals are striking and important not merely because of their content but also because they seem to be based on his theories.[20] Reality thus results from a collective redefinition of problems that carries first the clout of 'scientific knowledge' and then the clout of political and institutional power.

Knowledge relating to arms control cannot be separated from values, for while values are backward-looking in their frequent appeal to past conduct for justification, they also guide anticipatory and goal-directed behavior and thus affect expectations. Human values affect action by influencing our definition of a particular situation and by directing our choice of relevant 'facts' or 'interests.' The interdependence of facts and values implies a constant shifting between empirical and normative elements in decision-making.[21] Thus, arms control expectations became a political practice, both within the United States and between the super-powers, only after arms control had acquired: (1) domestic political value; (2) foreign policy value (as a means of achieving foreign policy goals); (3) instrumental international value (as a means of preventing nuclear war); (4) intrinsic value (arising from the reasoned assumptions behind the theory); and (5) moral value (the consequentialist ethical standard wherein stable deterrence and arms control are temporarily good for avoiding nuclear war).

Units of variation: arms control expectations

Since the dawn of the nuclear age, two intellectual communities and two sets of collective understandings, values, and visions have had the crucial impact on national security policymaking.[22] Embedded in these two world-views are different expectations about war, cooperation with the adversary, and technology, the most important of which is probably the expectation of nuclear war and of its outcome.

Those who favored arms control shared a loose cause-and-effect mode of reasoning which was sufficient to qualify them as believers in a body of 'knowledge' that was distinctively 'theirs.' Because they expected war in the nuclear age to break out as a result of crisis instability and misperception, as it had in 1914, and predicted that nuclear war could never be won yet would be likely without measures to avoid it, they placed the greatest rela-tive value on forces and tactics designed to prevent a first strike (rather than on an American war-fighting capability); put a premium on coopera-tion with the adversary; and promoted the development of a high threshold of nuclear weapons use. They also predicted that technology would not be able to create the 'magic bullet' with which to achieve superiority, but they valued technological changes that might help stabilize the nuclear balance.[23]

On the basis of this particular interpretation of war, cooperation, and technology, the arms controllers developed a distinctive set of assump-tions about the reciprocal fear of surprise attack and crisis stability that became the backbone of arms control. Interpreting the state of the world in 1960 as being extremely dangerous because of the Cold War, they doubted that the political and ideological divide between the super-powers would be bridged in the near future, but they nevertheless expressed confidence in the Soviet ability to learn the secrets of deterrence and arms control and stressed that conflicting powers have common interests, which provide a basis for cooperation. The members of this community expected general disarmament to fail, although they reached no consensus about whether disarmament might be an option in the long run. They perceived arms control to be an integral part of national security policy, believed that arms control could include a variety of unilateral measures, and expected that in time arms control might help create a psychology of peace.

This set of views was challenged by an intellectual and political community that expected war to break out because of a premeditated attack by an aspiring world hegemonic power, as it had in 1939. The main cause-and-effect mode of reasoning of this community was, according to Robert Jervis, that wars 'are caused by states failing to develop the military strength and credible threats necessary to dissuade others from challenging the status quo. Furthermore, threats are most likely to be believed when the state can carry them out at reasonable cost.'[24] Thus, the community members regarded the use of nuclear weapons as quite possible and expected that, if the right measures were taken, a nuclear war could be won. Expressing a preference for counterforce strategies, they emphasized a less restricted type of deterrence and maintained that cooperation with the adversary would lead to instability and was dangerous. While they were optimistic that military superiority and even victory could be achieved through technological fixes, they shared the view that their strategy would make nuclear war less likely over the long run.[25] Albert Wohlstetter, Herman Kahn, Richard Pipes, Eugene Rostow, Colin Gray, Fred Ikle, Keith Payne, Edward Teller, Richard Perle, and Kenneth Adelman, to mention just a few, have, more or less, held the above set of views, which was also prevalent in the military establishment.

Jervis is right in pointing out that the views which identify the two communities overlap and are partly compatible. The overlap over deterrence is more apparent than real, however, because the two outlooks are based on different theories of war and therefore, in practice, their policy prescriptions contradict each other. 'Arms control,' suggests Jervis, 'stresses the dangers that arise when reassurances and promises—especially the promise not to strike—are either not made or are not believed; deterrence stresses the dangers that arise when threats are absent or dismissed.'[26] It is therefore not surprising that the arms control ideas met with challenge from those advocating nuclear superiority and that their challenge was as manifest in the 1960s, when they largely opposed a partial test-ban treaty (PTBT) and supported ABM deployment, as it was in the 1980s, when they placed their prestige on the line in favor of the strategic defense initiative (SDI). Only recently, with the revolutionary events in Eastern Europe and the end of the Cold War, has this challenge begun to weaken and the conceptualization of the strategic debate to change.

Intellectual innovation

The arms control epistemic community

The arms control epistemic community was an informal association of scientists and civilian strategists who for intellectual, ideological, and political reasons adopted the arms control approach, in spite of all their differences over national security issues, including arms control itself.

Two subgroups constituted this community. One group of experts, whom Robert Levine characterized as 'analytical middle marginalists,' considered the underlying cause of international conflict to be the clash between the interests of nations as they pursue their separate goals. They stressed the futility of disarmament and the dangers of misperception and crises that get out of hand, and they expected that for the foreseeable future the world would have to depend for stability on the possession of nuclear weapons. The other group, whom Levine called 'moderate antiwar marginalists,' believed that armaments were indeed a serious cause of international tension and that reducing weapons would therefore reduce tensions. But they also believed that the intensity of mutual grievances as manifested in the Cold War made a transitional period, wherein peace was guaranteed by nuclear deterrence, unavoidable.[27] While they preferred disarmament to limited arms control measures, the latter were seen as much better than an unlimited and dangerous nuclear arms race.

These two groups converged into an epistemic community because, surprising as it may seem, they were in agreement about the short-term advantages and necessity of arms control and there was scarcely a member of either group who did not concede the validity of the recommendations of the other. As Posvar wrote at the time, 'One might even question whether the term "schools" as applied to these groups should be abandoned in favor of something like converging points of view.'[28]

Certainly some of the epistemic community's members did not get along well, and sometimes there were personal, career, and institutional conflicts.[29] Many of the arms controllers, having made original intellectual contributions in their own fields of expertise and in nuclear strategy, guarded their own ideas and interpretations. But their discussions, arguments, and mutual criticisms actually helped them in shaping a consensus over concepts, surmounting interdisciplinary barriers, and creating a common vocabulary.

Members of this community knew each other well; they frequently encountered each other on television and in round-table and debate performances, were often colleagues at the same or nearby universities, and regularly made use of each other's written and oral presentations. Thus, they learned from one another and together generated the standards by which they verified the validity of their ideas. In this way, they came to share expectations that set them apart from the experts and policymakers who had a strong faith in technological fixes, military superiority, and 'victory' in nuclear war. Yet 'admission' to the arms control epistemic community was based not only on the sharing of epistemic criteria but also on an active dedication to 'the cause,' collectively recognized expertise, and 'the ability to come up with new proposals and arguments.'[30] The result, as one member of this community put it, was a group of people who had experiences in common and were supremely confident in their ability to deal rationally and analytically with almost any problem.[31]

Several factors explain the ability of these people to prevail in many instances. To begin with, confident in their ability to use their scientific knowledge to solve problems,[32] arms controllers used their scientific prestige to gain legitimacy and authority within the political system. They were one community, yet they were everywhere dispersed among government bureaus, research organizations and laboratories, profit and nonprofit organizations, university research centers, and think tanks. Such dispersion was important because their effectiveness depended on their relative autonomy from political power, their ability to keep separate from current critical pressures,[33] to retain their scientific integrity and authority, and to continue to innovate. At the same time, they were public figures who required a certain power legitimation, and this was achieved through personal links with policymakers or with individuals such as Paul Nitze, who linked the community with government institutions,[34] and through the fact that their arms control ideas, after being diffused to the political system, were in demand by Presidents Eisenhower and Kennedy and their advisers. In other words, power legitimation arose from the creation by the arms control epistemic community of a *politically viable* alternative both to disarmament and to military superiority.

A small but key group of civilian strategists within the epistemic community had been affiliated with the RAND Corporation, which helped turn civilian strategy into a profession.[35] From RAND, the strategists absorbed an engineering approach and the methodologies, models, and assumptions that helped them articulate their ideas on arms control. By 1957 or 1958, noted Fred Kaplan,

> a definitive strategic community had formed within RAND. It had reached—by dint of small numbers, a common outlook, a [mostly] common academic background in mathematics and economics, and the forcefulness of a few strong personalities—a fairly tight consensus on the major issues, the most solidly held of which was the not unlikely prospect of a Soviet surprise attack against the increasingly vulnerable Strategic Air Command.[36]

While to some prominent RAND strategists the prospect of a Soviet surprise attack meant a redoubling of efforts to achieve military superiority through technological fixes, to others, such as Thomas Schelling, Lewis

Bohn, and Amrom Katz, it meant the necessity of stabilizing mutual deterrence by means of arms control technical measures.

Schelling spent parts of 1957 and 1958 at RAND, where his work influenced and was influenced by theorists such as Bernard Brodie, Daniel Ellsberg, Malcolm Hoag, Herman Kahn, William Kaufmann, and Albert Wohlstetter.[37] Later, Morton Halperin, a Yale graduate student, attracted the attention of Schelling, and they decided to collaborate. Donald Brennan, another key member of the community in its early years, had worked for nine years at the MIT Lincoln Laboratory, had come into direct contact with the RAND strategists, and had developed a close relationship with Kahn, with whom he went to work at the Hudson Institute. (By 1964, however, Brennan had become disenchanted with the idea of basing strategic stability on controlling defensive weapons and crossed over to the 'other' community. The sense of betrayal that was felt by arms controllers suggests the strength of their feelings of communal cohesion.)

Schelling, Brennan, and other economists and mathematicians used game theory—at that time a relatively new methodology invented by John von Neumann and Oscar Morgenstern[38]—to make deductions and predictions about deterrence and arms control. Aided by the rapid advance in computers, game theory allowed the strategists to make all kinds of assumptions, construct imaginary situations and worlds, and deduce from their models the answers to the problems posed by Soviet nuclear weapons.[39] 'What I got out of game theory,' said Schelling, 'was more of a conceptual framework, a way of organizing problems. ... It helps one to see ... whether some outcomes are better than others for both parties.'[40] This formal approach certainly reflected the ascendance of behaviorism within academia during the 1950s.

The rationality assumption, the realist assumptions about the nature and resolution of conflicts, and the fear of Communism, which was almost equal to the fear of nuclear war itself, were transmitted from RAND to the political structures that later formulated arms control policies. Strategists who worked in institutions other than RAND and were trained in a more classical and less behaviorist approach also made a contribution. Furthermore, intellectuals from various traditions had become acquainted with arms control ideas and methods in the universities, in think tanks, and in governmental institutions, and they played an active role, helping to train—through teaching and publication—security analysts who joined the community later on.[41]

The role of the scientists who joined the ranks was as important as that of the strategists. They were trained mainly in physics and engineering and had been involved since the 1940s in the making of weapons and other technological systems, such as air defenses. They had participated in government-sponsored projects[42] and had become disenchanted about the failure of disarmament negotiations as well as pessimistic about technological solutions to the nuclear weapons predicament.

The scientists were the first to participate in active discussions with policymakers on arms control. As members of the Presidential Science Advisory

Committee (PSAC), they had access to President Eisenhower, who gave support to 'his' scientists. They also had firsthand experience with arms control, as active participants in the test-ban treaty talks, which were used as a testing ground for their ideas—a paradigmatic case, so to speak, that could be applied to other cases later on.[43]

Among the most prominent of these scientists were Jerome Wiesner, Herbert York, Isador Rabi, Jerrold Zacharias, James Fisk, Bernard Feld, Paul Doty, George Kistiakowsky, Hans Bethe, Eugene Rabinowitch, Jack Ruina, George Rathjens, Spurgeon Keeny, Wolfgang Panofsky, Harvey Brooks, and James Killian, president of MIT. That many of the scientists and a majority of the strategists were from either Harvard or MIT (and thus referred to as the 'Charles River gang') was doubly significant. First, it was easier for them to interact on a daily basis, formally or informally exchanging ideas. Second, the institution with which a thinker was connected helped determine whether his ideas got a hearing where it mattered most—at the White House, the Pentagon, or the State Department.[44] And the fact that many members of this community had access to government secrets—whether through RAND, PSAC, or Pentagon research agencies—was important because it made them feel like 'insiders' and provided them with information they thought reliable.

The scientists regarded their experience in handling major security projects as a model for organizing arms control. For instance, Wiesner, seeing no incentive for the development of special seismic detectors because they were not needed in the development of nuclear weapons and because no bureaucracy or organization existed to create a political stake in them, spoke of a need 'to create a vested interest in arms control, to develop a cadre of people whose full-time occupation is research and development on means of arms control and on the analysis of the political and military problems of arms control.'[45]

Peace research and conflict resolution were attaining academic legitimacy and were being fueled by a score of interdisciplinary programs, and many academicians, strategists, and scientists found the *Bulletin of the Atomic Scientists* to be a perfect medium for disseminating the emerging ideas of nuclear arms control.[46]

We should be careful not to confuse the arms control epistemic community with a profession.[47] The community cut across professions; its members were involved in arms control only some of the time; they shared responsibility for their decisions with political actors; and their ethical standards did not arise from a professional code.[48] Indeed, this community can be described as a functional, politically driven, ideologically self-contained, and distinct cross-section of the 'scientific estate.'[49]

The innovation process

Between 1955 and 1960, a group of civilian nuclear strategists, some of whom were associated with the RAND Corporation,[50] gave a new meaning to the concept of war, based on the assumption that nuclear deterrence had become unstable and that a catastrophe could now occur against the wishes of the adversary states. These notions were fueled by a string of events, including Wohlstetter's investigation of the vulnerability of US strategic forces,[51] the Killian Committee's presentation of a report on 'Meeting the Threat of Surprise Attack' in 1955,[52] the Soviet tests of an intercontinental ballistic missile (ICBM) in August 1957, the launching of the first Soviet satellite (Sputnik I) into space two months later, and President Eisenhower's establishment of the Gaither Committee, which, by recommending an across-the-board military buildup,[53] alarmed Eisenhower and made him more receptive to arms control ideas.

James Killian argued that Sputnik I created a

> crisis of confidence that swept the country like a windblown forest fire. Overnight there developed a widespread fear [unfounded, as it turned out] that the country lay at the mercy of the Russian military machine and that our own government and its military arm had abruptly lost the power to defend the homeland itself.[54]

Indeed, after Sputnik, Wohlstetter's studies on the vulnerability of ICBMs caught the attention of some strategists from RAND and elsewhere, most notably Schelling, who opposed an indiscriminate quest for military superiority and the belief in the possibility of winning a nuclear war on the ground that this orientation might, in fact, lead to such a war. So instead of planning how to regain—by means of a massive technological and rearmament leap—the invulnerability that had suddenly been lost, the strategists started to concentrate on ideas about how to regain invulnerability by means of unilateral stabilizing force deployments, as well as diplomacy. Thus, as noted by Strobe Talbott, 'they began laying the conceptual foundations for negotiations that might limit the number of weapons with which the Soviet Union could carry out a preemptive attack. This was the enterprise of nuclear arms control.'[55]

Some of the scientists who had helped draft the Gaither Committee report also became disenchanted with its recommendations and with the trend in US–Soviet relations. Having become members of PSAC, [56] they made their ideas known to Eisenhower, who was receptive and supportive. [57] Spurgeon Keeny, a member of the arms control community, remarked in retrospect that the Gaither report represented 'the high watermark of the belief that a technological solution could be found,' a position the PSAC scientists increasingly came to see as unrealistic.[58]

Thus, as the PSAC scientists started to offer Eisenhower reliable technical information with which he could counter those opposing a test-ban treaty with the Soviets, they also began to transmit to him and other government officials a set of arms control assumptions, expectations, and values. They also proposed the creation of a 'peace agency' to embody and empower them.

President Kennedy later created this institution and called it the Arms Control and Disarmament Agency (ACDA). According to Saville Davis,

> It is an oversimplification, but a useful one, to say that the President [Eisenhower] now listened primarily to men whose information and judgment of fact indicated that a safeguarded arms-control agreement would be to the advantage of the national interest and security of the United States, whereas before that time he had listened chiefly to men who said such an agreement would gravely damage national security. ... Like most shifts in policy, this one will not be found in documents. Policy is determined by political momentums operating on the existing balance of forces in Washington. The arrival of the new group of presidential advisers set up such a fresh momentum.[59]

Many of the strategists and scientists who were drawn to arms control ideas met in 1958 at two conferences in Geneva—one dealing with surprise attack and the other with a nuclear test ban—to exchange ideas and try to reach an agreement with their Soviet counterparts over cooperative technical measures to avoid nuclear war. Neither conference produced any such agreement. But the Surprise Attack Conference, which was by far the more relevant one from a strategic arms control perspective, together with a preparatory conference held by Americans in Washington to formulate an American position for Geneva, became a watershed in the consolidation of an emergent nuclear arms control approach.[60]

The Surprise Attack Conference and its preparatory conference, which brought together the PSAC scientists and the RAND strategists to discuss stable deterrence and arms control, consolidated the ranks of the emerging epistemic community. It can even be suggested that at the Surprise Attack Conference the arms control epistemic community was born.[61] In any case, at that conference an arms control seed was planted in the minds of many reluctant Soviet scientists and political officials. True, the Soviets reacted with dismay to the American technical approach that was presented, arguing that deterrence would only fuel the arms race. But the papers written for the conference suggested to the American and Soviet experts how a surprise attack could be prevented and how deterrence could be stabilized and managed by means of arms control. After a week, according to Johan Holst, deliberation changed into ' 'cognitive negotiations' aimed at exploring the position of the adversary ... and at conveying the Western thoughts and concerns.'[62] Thus, in retrospect, one can agree with Bernard Bechhoefer that the talks served as a 'catalyst for much of the serious rethinking of arms control and stabilized deterrence which took place in the US between 1959 and 1961.'[63]

The ideas that the strategists and scientists took to the Surprise Attack Conference were a response to changes in technology and weapons systems, the balance of power between the superpowers, and American domestic politics.[64] Yet they were also rigorous theories which had been deduced from a set of hypotheses about technology and stability and which had evolved together with theories about strategic war, limited war, and escalation, and whose reference point was not past experience but only expectations of the future. Being a disciplined creation deriving from artificial worlds and speculations in the strategists' minds, these theories could not have been built-in or determined only by structure.[65]

It would be naïve to suggest, however, that the arms control epistemic community created nuclear arms control from scratch.[66] Indeed, a great deal of thinking on arms control was produced in the United States, starting immediately after World War II. (Leaving aside Hedley Bull's contribution to arms control ideas,[67] it can be argued that arms control was an American invention, as political economy was an invention of British and Scottish economists in the eighteenth century.)

Very few people were as influential in the intellectual development of the arms control approach as Leo Szilard, whom Norman Cousins described as 'an idea factory.'[68] Although Szilard remained an outsider to RAND and to the halls of government, his indirect influence was considerable because he affected those who had an impact on political decisions. About a decade before arms control ideas had gained prominence, Szilard anticipated the nuclear stalemate and the use of mobile ICBMs, called for intermediate steps of force reduction with different totals for different systems, considered that an overwhelming counterforce capability would cause instability, was one of the first people to oppose an ABM system, and pleaded for a no-first-use policy on nuclear weapons. Some of Szilard's proposals were unorthodox and visionary and thus made people think hard about unorthodox solutions. For example, he proposed the relocation of populations to eliminate large urban targets, suggested that the superpowers should hold each other's cities hostage while forgoing war, and advanced the idea of a nuclear-free zone in Europe. He also envisioned an international corps of scientists and engineers to report and investigate nuclear violations, pioneered the idea of meetings between US and Soviet scientists, and pushed the still largely undefined concept of nuclear deterrence to the limit by suggesting to Herman Kahn the idea of a 'doomsday machine.'[69]

Edward Shils and William Fox, although to a lesser degree than Szilard, also anticipated the nuclear arms control approach by a decade. Shils made a strong case for integrating bilateral arms control negotiations and defense planning. Fox linked arms reduction to the decrease of vulnerability to nuclear attack. Concurrently, the Acheson–Lilienthal report (1946) stressed the need for unobtrusive inspection, improving continental air defense, and, most importantly, reducing incentives for surprise attack. While Hans Bethe called for superpower bilateral negotiations, a panel of consultants on disarmament, set up in 1952 by Dean Acheson, called for new ways of communicating with the leaders of the Soviet Union to discuss the arms race.[70] At about the same time, an emerging 'realist' school of International

Relations challenged the rationalist approach of the postwar scientists—who placed their faith in scientific method, reason, and international organization and who expected world disarmament to occur once a world government had been created[71]—and argued instead that the nuclear predicament had no moral solution and could be mitigated only with the help of prudential behavior and diplomacy.[72]

Early work on arms control intensified in the 1950s with the advent of behaviorism and mathematical techniques and the rise of the civilian strategists. For example, in 1951, David Inglis and Donald Flanders suggested limiting the nuclear capabilities of the adversary to a particular stable level. Three years later, James Newman suggested that inspection need not be comprehensive, only practical. And soon after, assuming an expected vulnerability to surprise attack and arguing that arms control verification could be undertaken by national technical means, Inglis proposed a test ban. In turn, Hornell Hart showed that expected increases in Soviet offensive capability could counter any expected improvement in passive and active defenses.[73]

By 1956, some of the most important distinctions between arms control and disarmament had been suggested. For example, Richard Meier had used game theory to deduce several propositions about arms control, including the principle of a high nuclear threshold. In addition, a ballistic-missile builder for Convair had introduced the idea of achieving invulnerability by means of second-strike forces, an idea that was further developed by Warren Amster, who suggested the viability of mutual assured destruction. As Jennifer Sims points out, Amster's suggestion was subsequently noted in an article by C W. Sherwin, which was in turn quoted by Schelling.[74]

Beginning in 1957, the Pugwash meetings that brought together Western and East European scientists to discuss disarmament also played an intellectual role in the 'invention' of the nuclear arms control approach.[75] The dominant paradigm at the first Pugwash meetings was disarmament; arms control ideas were received with skepticism. Said Schelling: 'I was almost expelled from a Pugwash Conference [1960] because of the belief by the Soviets and some Americans that anyone who thought about arms control wasn't interested in disarmament.'[76] But discussions between Western and Eastern scientists had some impact on arms control ideas and policies. According to J. Rotblat,

> in many instances the scientists from the West received, for the first time, reasoned objections to their views from scientists in the East and vice-versa. This confrontation of ideas, of prejudices, and of causes of mistrust, was in itself very valuable, as it gave an opportunity for better understanding of the motivation of others and, in some cases, removed misunderstandings and dispelled fears.[77]

The main value of these discussions, however, lay in the fact that the lessons they generated were taken by American scientists back to the US political system, where they became part of a collective understanding about what should be done to control the nuclear arms race. For example, Walt Rostow and Jerome Wiesner, who played key roles in the Kennedy administration, discussed matters of international security with the Soviets at a Moscow meeting of Pugwash in December 1960; and they came back from the disarmament meeting with the feeling that the Soviet Union might be ready for action in arms control.[78] Pugwash meetings that dealt with a test-ban treaty played a similar, if not more important, role in developing some of the technical bases for arms control.

Several developments closer to the halls of government during the formative years of nuclear arms control ideas also had some influence on their evolution. First, the Baruch plan of 1946 left a legacy that was not overlooked by arms controllers.[79] Second, as Sims notes, the inconclusive disarmament negotiations of the 1950s

> had a great impact on the evolution of ideas about weapons control. The ups and downs of the negotiations themselves inspired controversy and commentary: the Open Skies proposal [1955] stimulated thinking about limited agreements and bilateral negotiations; preparation for the Surprise Attack Conference generated studies—particularly at RAND—of the technical requirements of strategic stability; 'Atoms for Peace' [1953] inspired consideration of controlled information-sharing as a stabilizing instrument.[80]

Third, the center of interest in new ideas of arms control shifted from the State Department, where John Foster Dulles was no enthusiast of arms control,[81] to the White House; and President Eisenhower, with the aid of his arms control assistant Harold Stassen and of Nelson Rockefeller, 'discovered' nuclear arms control before the academic strategists did.[82] And, fourth, the idea of a test-ban treaty continued to evolve throughout the 1950s; negotiations with the Soviets on such a ban were in fact initiated before the crucial events of 1958–60. Most of the policy proposals, however, were still in the disarmament mode, with the possible exception of Open Skies.

Creativity or innovation does not involve new ideas but new combinations of ideas—for example, that surprise attack and preventing nuclear accidents must be considered together or that arms control should not be separated from military and defense policy. For the first time, arms control theory was articulating the strategically crucial idea of the interdependence of expectations. Schelling's notion— 'he thinks we think ... he'll attack; so he thinks we shall, so he will, so we must'[83]—was in the air at the Surprise Attack Conference. Thus, as academicians and policymakers gradually began to reach a common understanding about war and peace, weapons and negotiations, and conflict and cooperation, their approach to international negotiations shifted from measures designed to remove nuclear weapons from world affairs to measures designed to make their presence more tolerable.[84]

Gerald Holton, editor of *Daedalus*, the journal of the American Academy of Arts and Sciences, argued that by 1959 an 'enormously refined art and science of controlling war' had become 'critical.' The academy thus convened a summer session to deal with arms control, and this session resulted in the participation of more than fifty individuals and the publication of several books that became landmarks in the intellectual history of arms control.[85] In 1960, the academy also initiated two projects to study and formulate the ideas of arms control, thereby creating an opportunity for academicians, public officials, and journalists—many of whom had come to the arms control worldview—to strengthen their shared understanding about arms control.

In the fall of 1960, *Daedalus* published a special issue that distilled the main insights and currents of thought on arms control and soon became known as 'the Bible of arms control.' With this publication, nuclear arms control came of age.[86] Intellectual consolidation and refinement of the arms control approach continued, however, within the framework of a Harvard–MIT seminar on arms control that met more or less continuously throughout the 1960s. Reflecting on the entire period, Schelling wrote:

> That 15-year period from 1957 to 1972 is a remarkable story of intellectual achievement transformed into policy. ... Three books appeared in 1961 that epitomized an emerging consensus on what strategic arms control should be about. Each was a group effort, and each stimulated discussion even while being written. ... A number of participants in the Harvard–MIT seminar took positions in the Kennedy White House, Department of State and Department of Defense; others from RAND and elsewhere, who had been part of this intellectual movement, moved into the government as well. So it is not completely surprising that those ideas became the basis for U.S. policy and were ultimately implemented in the ABM treaty.[87]

Political selection

A political selection process determined the epistemic community's success in translating its theories into policies. The policymaker, in principle at least, served as judge, jury, and, if necessary, executioner for the professional output of strategic theories. Many, though not all, of the community's aspirations were satisfied only through policy decisions.[88] It was not necessarily the best-fitted ideas that were selected and turned into policies, however, but those which best fit the interests of policymakers and which passed the test of domestic politics. This is why the epistemic community had to persuade other actors in the system of the validity of its ideas. The key was not only inventing new concepts but also raising them to new heights of public awareness.[89]

The selection process started under Eisenhower, and by the time Kennedy entered office certain significant trends were underway. First, because the United States was actively engaged in test-ban negotiations with the Soviet Union, Kennedy inherited a framework for negotiations and a policy on which to build. Second, because Eisenhower had been listening since 1958 mainly to his PSAC scientists, he helped legitimize the emerging arms control concepts as the focus of the policy debate. Kennedy, then, was aware of the positions of the various government agencies with an interest in arms control and inherited personnel and organizational structures to deal with it, including the scientific adviser, PSAC, and an interagency group called the Committee of Principals.[90]

The Eisenhower legacy is insufficient, however, to explain why ideas of stable deterrence and arms control were accepted so rapidly by the Kennedy administration. 'Indeed,' quipped E. Licklider, 'the ideas no sooner became public than they seemed to become governmental policy.'[91] Kennedy, who enjoyed close connections to many security intellectuals and had an innovative orientation,[92] played an important role. Certainly, presidential leadership was crucial in this area because arms control ideas were relatively new and seemed counterintuitive. They were rejected by some prominent strategists, such as Wohlstetter, and some prominent scientists, such as Teller; had little support in the military; and received only a mixed review in Congress. Moreover, because the concepts of disarmament and arms control had been used interchangeably, the latter was bound to be misrepresented and misunderstood as idealistic, pacifist, and disarmament-driven. And since arms control ideas lacked provisions for complete and effective verification, they were not likely to be accepted readily by parts of the bureaucracy, Congress, and the American public.[93]

Yet the content and quality of the ideas gave them broad political appeal and helped Kennedy build a political coalition on their behalf. Indeed, disarmament proponents, if they so wished, could regard arms control ideas as a first step toward disarmament. And conservatives could be reassured that arms control could mean more, rather than fewer, weapons. Thus, in every important aspect, as Colin Gray observed, the arms control community 'found that the Kennedy administration and its brief era offered a permissive environment in which it could exercise influence.'[94]

The creation of the ACDA provided a home for the arms control community, a political voice for its theoretical ideas, and a laboratory where policy ideas were first designed and developed. From 1961 onward, the ACDA members took part in most of the political deliberations on national security and arms control policy; still, the agency remained a weak bureaucratic player.[95] Being entrusted with the mission of controlling the arms race without undermining the military balance, the agency's power depended on the level of external threat, which was usually high, and on the force that the

President personally put behind the arms control process, which was not consistently high.[96]

More significant, however, was the fact that many of the most prominent members of the arms control community had taken key positions in the Kennedy administration. At the White House, McGeorge Bundy (formerly of Harvard) became the adviser of the National Security Council (NSC) and brought along Carl Kaysen and Walt Rostow. Jerome Wiesner became scientific adviser, and James Killian, George Kistiakowsky, Paul Doty, and Harvey Brooks became members of the PSAC. Abram Chayes went to the State Department, while Herbert York, Jack Ruina, and George Rathjens worked at the Pentagon in research and weapons development (with Rathjens also working for ACDA). Key positions in the Pentagon were filled by Defense Secretary Robert McNamara's 'whiz kids': Roswell Gilpatrick, Henry Rowen, and Charles Hitch. The office of assistant secretary of defense for international security affairs (ISA) was entrusted to Paul Nitze, who was then only at the beginning of a long career as the 'master of the arms control game.' These institutional and recruitment developments helped create a network of relations between political elites and the arms controllers. The arms controllers also affected political elites indirectly through op-ed articles in the *New York Times* and *Washington Post* and articles in *Foreign Affairs*.

While many of the community scientists affected the policymaking process through the PSAC and ACDA, the strategists had effectively taken over the ISA office. Nitze offered Schelling a job as his arms control deputy; Schelling declined but recommended the appointment of his Harvard colleague John McNaughton, who was a professor of law. According to Fred Kaplan, McNaughton told Schelling that he knew nothing about arms control, to which Schelling replied that he would teach him all there was to know.[97] Apparently he did: McNaughton was appointed assistant secretary of defense for ISA in 1963, became McNamara's 'general counselor and chief aide on arms control,' and had a hand in persuading the Pentagon of the merits of the PTBT.[98]

The ability of the epistemic community members to persuade and forge alliances with policymakers was crucial for their ultimate success. As soon as Kennedy became president, Wiesner 'started to educate Kennedy on the limitations of the ABM,' and Ruina and York were influential in persuading Kennedy to bag the Nike-Zeus antiballistic missile.[99] A committee on the level of forces that ACDA had appointed that included Wiesner, Bethe, Doty, and Henry Kissinger apparently participated in preparing the 1965 defense budget and helped McNamara place a limit on Minuteman forces.[100] On the other hand, some policymakers used the arms control experts to rationalize and explain their actions, especially after the Cuban missile crisis of October 1962 demonstrated the need for arms control.

The hotline agreement of June 1963—the agreement to install a teletype line between Washington and Moscow to serve as an emergency communication link in case of crisis and to prevent unintended nuclear war—illustrates how various persons, institutions, and factors mentioned above played a role in determining arms control outcomes. The idea of a hotline had first been suggested by Schelling in the late 1950s; he told Henry Owen of the State Department about it, and Owen in turn passed the idea along to Gerard Smith, head of the State Department's policy-planning staff. Journalist Jess Gorkin, who edited *Parade*, the *Boston Globe*'s Sunday magazine, picked up Schelling's idea, wrote articles about it, and sent open letters to Eisenhower and Soviet Premier Nikita Khrushchev outlining his proposals. He was later able to talk briefly with Khrushchev about the matter and tried to sell the idea to presidential candidates Kennedy and Nixon. He therefore created public awareness that led other individuals, periodicals, and experts to begin advocating the approach.

But it was Owen, working within government circles, who led the American government to finally accept the idea in April 1962. The Soviets reacted favorably to the American proposal but tied their agreement to other general disarmament proposals. The idea might have died of 'linkage disease' had it not been for the Cuban missile crisis, in a vivid and practical way, showing the superpower leaders what Schelling had in mind. Several months later, the idea had turned into reality.

With characteristic modesty, Schelling later remarked that 'it was not a question of inventing the hotline, but simply of realizing that such an elementary means of communication did not already exist.' The hotline idea arose from Schelling's interpretation of a structural condition, an interpretation that differed markedly from the 'hard-liner' view that 'Washington is ideologically close enough to Moscow without making the White House a branch office of the Kremlin.'[101]

The transition from disarmament to arms control meant that the bureaucracy had to go through a process of adjustment and conceptual evolution. In 1961, Americans and Soviets were still formally negotiating 'total and universal disarmament' within the framework of the Eighteen-Nation Disarmament Committee in Geneva. In practice, however, they had already started to negotiate arms control but chose to refer to it as 'first-stage disarmament.'[102] Also during this transition period, Kennedy and the arms control community began to frame PTBT negotiations around the concept of nuclear deterrence stability and around expectations that a technical agreement over tests could amount to a first step in the thawing of the Cold War.

By the end of the Kennedy years, arms control had become an irreversible factor in the domestic political game and a key consideration as agreements were negotiated and even as new weapons systems were contemplated. Indeed, the bureaucracy and the arms controllers who participated in the bureaucratic process were constantly involved in preparing a position for negotiation, defending an existing agreement, or carrying out bureaucratic guerrilla warfare against military programs.[103] Thus, the institutionalization of arms control ideas guaranteed that, as bureaucratic battles flared up, institutions and individuals who carried the arms control ideas would throw their weight in favor of their selection by the President and his closest advisers. Domestic politics then became the arena where national security and world order ideas were raised, legitimated, and selected as policy choices and where they were tested once they became national policies and had international effects.

'Educating' and persuading McNamara were vital steps in the movement of arms control ideas from innovation to political action. Like Kennedy, McNamara was well suited for arms control expectations and values. With his analytic command of the nuclear weapons problem and his managerial and engineering instinct to do something about an irrational situation,[104] McNamara came to see in arms control the rational alternative to nuclear war. He trusted the RAND strategists, whose techniques and analytic style he shared, and was instrumental in protecting the community's members from the wrath of the Joint Chiefs of Staff.

Once McNamara was persuaded that there was 'no technical solution to the arms race'[105] and that it had to be limited, he became a powerhouse for arms control ideas—an epistemic community's dream. He worked hard every year at budget time to prevent ABM deployment and helped persuade Lyndon Johnson to try arms control with the Soviets before deploying ABMs. To make sure Johnson would not change his mind on ABMs, McNamara assembled in the Oval Office all past and present PSAC chairmen, who made clear their opposition to it. And in a speech in San Francisco in 1967, he told the American people about the 'mad momentum of the arms race.' Indeed, Johnson's election in 1964 proved a victory for those who opposed ABM systems, if only because it ensured that McNamara would continue as defense secretary for almost four more years.[106] At the 1967 Glassboro summit meeting, McNamara lectured Soviet Premier Aleksei Kosygin about 'the action-reaction phenomenon,' explaining that, should the Soviets proceed with the deployment of their own ABM system (nicknamed Galosh), all the United States had to do, really, was to increase its offensive forces, thus neutralizing Soviet defenses but fueling the arms race even more.[107]

Ideas about controlling ABMs had started in the late 1950s, roughly at the same time Defense Secretary Neil McElroy, under the influence of Sputnik and the Gaither Committee report, authorized the army to develop an operational ABM system called Nike-Zeus.[108] Also at that time, McElroy created within the Pentagon the Advanced Research Projects Agency (ARPA) and the Directorate of Defense Research and Engineering (DDR&E). The scientists at these institutions played an important role in the development of an American ABM technical capability, but some of them were among the first to raise doubts about the technical capability of ballistic-missile defenses (BMDs) to fulfill their mission and therefore were among the first to promote their control.[109] York reports that Ruina was the first member of the community to seriously study an ABM moratorium and to get the Pentagon interested in the idea.[110] In 1962, Schelling, Charles Hertzfeld, Thomas Wolfe, and Daniel Fink participated in task force discussions about controlling ABMs.

During 1964, as Americans learned about Galosh, the battle positions for and against ABMs were drawn and the epistemic community was called to defend its turf. One of the first shots in the ideological and political battle was fired by Wiesner and York in 1964 in the pages of *Scientific American*, where they argued that it was their 'professional judgment' that the nuclear dilemma had 'no technical solution,' a clear reference to the ABM system.[111] Other arms controllers started to work more quietly within ACDA to formulate practical arms control ideas about banning ABMs. Five years of intense involvement by members of the epistemic community followed. This had less to do with intellectual innovation and scientific analysis than with politics, political alliance formation, and lobbying and rallying the support of bureaucrats, Congress, and public opinion against BMDs. By 1967, a new 'thin defense' system, called Sentinel, which was aimed at protecting American cities against a Chinese attack and against an accidental Soviet attack, was being approved for deployment by the Johnson administration.[112] Nevertheless, in 1968 the Soviets were persuaded to negotiate a strategic arms control agreement, and ISA's Morton Halperin (who was co-author with Schelling of *Strategy and Arms Control*) succeeded in producing an agenda for the ABM and strategic arms limitation talks (SALT) and in getting the Joint Chiefs of Staff to give their reluctant approval to it.

Halperin's success was due partly to ISA, which provided an institutional home to arms control ideas and their carriers. ISA's power came from the fact that policymakers such as Defense Secretary Clark Clifford were willing to listen to its people. And because Halperin was the first to generate a strategic arms control negotiating agenda, he could benefit from the bureaucracy's uncertainty and lack of experience. Knowing that the Chiefs would never accept an agenda developed at ACDA, Halperin took the action to the Pentagon, where he involved military personnel in the agenda-making process in a skillful manner that allowed him to retain his political alliance with the State Department and ACDA but at the same time enabled him to put pressure on the Chiefs to reach a quick decision.[113]

Congress was another battlefront where the epistemic community did well. During the Eisenhower and Kennedy years, arms controllers managed to engage Senator Hubert Humphrey and his Disarmament Subcommittee in the business of arms control. Hearings held by this subcommittee diffused arms control ideas to the public; Humphrey himself made a contribution to the special 1960 *Daedalus* issue. But relations between the epistemic community and Congress were cemented mainly during the 1968–69 congressional ABM debate.

This debate was aided and even fueled by the intervention of arms controllers. In a June 1968 letter to the *New York Times*, Wiesner argued that the ABM system was a waste of resources. One month later, Senator Eugene McCarthy released a position paper that was written by Wiesner and Kistiakowsky and recommended a unilateral freeze on Sentinel and on offensive nuclear weapons deployment.[114] Indeed, at that time an alliance between the arms control epistemic community and powerful senators began to take shape.

When reporters picked up the story about the technical controversy in Congress regarding the deployment of BMDs in the vicinity of major American cities, their media coverage helped close the ranks between scientific associations and a variety of peace and grassroots groups that had formed around the ABM issue. Some of these groups were directly mobilized by the scientists, who also organized popular committees and public rallies in major US cities.[115] In fact, the political environment—the Vietnam War, campus unrest, the exceptionally low prestige of the American military— was very conducive to the creation of an anti-ABM coalition.

During the ABM debate, Senator J. William Fulbright was alerted to the fact that government-based scientists who opposed Sentinel were the only scientists called to testify before the Armed Services Committee. As Sentinel's fate was being decided by Nixon's new Republican administration, Fulbright's Foreign Relations Committee decided that Senator Albert Gore's Disarmament Subcommittee would begin holding educational hearings on ABMs and, breaking with an old tradition, would invite nongovernmental scientists to testify. 'The real purpose,' wrote Benson Adams, 'was to provide a means to counter the influence of the Armed Services Committee and to oppose BMD.'[116] Arms controllers such as Wiesner, Ruina, York, Kistiakowsky, Bethe, Rathjens, and Panofsky were summoned to these hearings and, using the ABM system as their showcase, diffused the arms control paradigm to the senators, the media, and the American public. So impressive was the epistemic community's anti-ABM pressure that prominent scientists such as Wohlstetter and Kahn, who favored ABMs, became involved in the debate only to counter it.[117]

Arms controllers lost the ABM battle in Congress by one vote, and a new system called Safeguard, aimed at defending American land-based ICBMs against a Soviet attack, was approved by Congress.[118] Nevertheless, the epistemic community had won the war, because, by educating both Congress and the public on deterrence and arms control, it had managed to put the Nixon administration, as well as the ABM supporters in Congress and in the scientific community, on the defensive.[119] Furthermore, the community created a more or less permanent, broad political constituency in favor of arms control by instilling concern about the issue among a much wider public than before—grassroots, labor, and religious groups, professional associations, and peace organizations.

It is true that the success of arms control ideas was directly related to the public insistence that military self-restraint accompany policies of nuclear rearmament,[120] but the meaning, direction, and content of self-restraint were provided by the epistemic community, which helped make the public aware that ABM policy was one example in which self-restraint was required. By the end of the 1960s, arms control had become one of the dominant interpretations of national security—so dominant, in fact, that decision-makers and negotiators in the Nixon administration, who had long believed in American military superiority, were now endorsing nuclear parity and taking stable deterrence and arms control for granted.[121] National Security Adviser Kissinger, however, was no stranger to arms control ideas; he had been one of the contributors to the 1960 *Daedalus* issue and had kept close links to arms controllers in Cambridge all along.

The Nixon administration appears to have signed the SALT and ABM treaties because of a diminished fear of surprise attack following the attainment of invulnerability, as well as the awareness that a ceiling on offensive weapons would constrain the Soviets more than it would the Americans (the United States was not then building any new ICBMs, Polaris submarines, or bombers) and would limit the Soviet SS-9s, which the Americans feared the most. Soviet insistence on a treaty was also instrumental, and certainly the public uproar over ABMs that the epistemic community and its allies helped bring about put the Nixon administration on notice that the American people did not want ABMs in their backyards. Questions of linkage and détente also played a role.

All of these factors would not have had any meaning—indeed, would not have been rationally considered or even relevant—had not the ideas of stable deterrence and arms control become a salient paradigm of national security and been diffused to government institutions, where they were instrumental in shaping an arms control agenda and a political coalition to carry it out. During the ABM debate process, the arms control epistemic community and its allies convinced the American people that the superpowers had a mutual interest in avoiding nuclear war and that this interest should be symbolically, politically, and practically manifested in an ABM arms control treaty.

Intellectual diffusion to the Soviet Union

The diffusion of American arms control ideas to the Soviet Union was necessary for the creation of the ABM regime. Helping to create an international negotiation agenda and to provide the epistemic framework for negotiation and agreement, these ideas structured not only the American domestic but also the international political game. According to Marshall Shulman, the transfer of ideas had 'a residual educational effect that you cannot always measure but which may be terribly important. There is a kind of diffusion of conceptions that goes on, there is an educational process ... because we are just ... beginning to have insights into what makes for stability.'[122]

The international diffusion of nuclear arms control ideas began in the 1950s and continued throughout the 1960s. Direct means were negotiation proposals, bargaining and negotiation positions, summit meetings, technical conferences (such as the Surprise Attack Conference), and scientific forums (such as Pugwash and the 'Doty,' 'Dartmouth,' and 'Panofsky' groups).[123] Indirect means included Western statements and strategic debates, congressional hearings and debates, press reports, and academic books and articles.

When ideas of strategic nuclear arms control were first raised by Americans in the 1950s, they were interpreted by the Soviets to mean inspection without disarmament, and evoked suspicions of espionage and a capitalist plot. (In Russian, *kontrol* means to 'count, audit, or inspect' and does not share with the English concept of control the meaning of 'regulation and management.'[124]) At the Surprise Attack Conference, the Soviets insisted that they could not envisage a technical solution to the nuclear predicament.[125] They argued instead that 'any technical device may fail, but a technical failure may lead to disaster only in a climate of artificially heightened tensions.'[126] But the conference was nevertheless a turning point because even this formal and ostensibly 'unsuccessful' discussion had a constructive effect on the superpowers' continuous dialogue over strategic issues.[127]

By the early 1960s, the Soviets had begun to move unilaterally to make their strategic weapons invulnerable and to recognize the value of reconnaissance satellites. Moreover, their military writings started to mention that accidents could be a *casus belli* in times of international tension,[128] and eventually they adopted an American device to prevent accidental war, the permissive action links (PALs).[129] They went along with the idea of the hotline and were finally persuaded to sign the PTBT. 'Thus, by 1963,' wrote Robin Ranger, 'the Soviet Union's adaptation of the concepts of arms control to meet its political objectives had produced an implicit theory of political arms control.'[130] Aware that the American perception of strategic problems was primarily technical and that, to engage Americans, they would have to discuss political problems within the American technical framework, the Soviets also recognized the benefits of negotiating political agreements without appearing to do so. According to Ranger, one of the unintended consequences of this process was that as 'the bilateral Soviet-American relationship became more clearly defined through agreements that were couched in terms of the explicit theoretical framework of technical arms control ... the Soviet leadership became increasingly explicit about its approach to strategic stability.'[131] Americans, conversely, increasingly became involved in political arms control.

The PTBT and hotline agreements reached in the early 1960s, the space and nonproliferation treaties signed in the late 1960s, and three agreements negotiated and concluded concurrently with SALT/ABM negotiations in the early 1970s—the seabed treaty of February 1971, the nuclear-accidents measures and direct-communications-link agreement of September 1971, and the biological weapons convention of April 1972—were important steps toward strategic agreements because they indicated to Soviets and Americans alike that cooperation by means of arms control agreements was indeed possible. Moreover, these treaties became a testing ground for some of the provisions of the SALT agreements, such as the use of 'national technical means of verification,' post-agreement evaluation conferences, and provisions for withdrawal from agreements. [132] Both sides saw that some intermediate goals were being achieved and some progress was being made. The Soviets came to realize that, as Arthur Schlesinger put it, 'arms control might be a means of approaching rather than avoiding general and complete disarmament.'[133]

The ABM treaty was the culmination of a decade-long process of diffusion of American arms control ideas to the Soviets. The pattern usually began with an American proposal, followed by a Soviet response, a new set of American suggestions based on that response, and engagement in a new round of negotiations.[134] Much of the official discussion of strategic doctrine and force position consisted of such 'talking to Moscow at a distance,' including the education of the Soviets in the requirements of a safe and secure second-strike force during the Kennedy and Johnson years.

Part of this education took place by means of direct contacts between American and Soviet scientists, for example in Pugwash meetings or in the meetings of a committee organized by Doty and the American Academy of Arts and Sciences. These meetings, argued Frank von Hippel, 'often provided an opportunity to investigate new experimental ideas that government agencies have been loath to explore for fear of reducing political maneuvering room.'[135] For example, during the twelfth Pugwash meeting, in 1964, Jack Ruina told his Soviet counterparts about the idea of controlling ABMs. Herbert York recalls that 'after Jack's presentation the head of the Soviet delegation approached him and said there must have been something wrong with the translation. He explained that he actually heard the interpreter say Jack proposed to limit defensive weapons.' Ruina and Murray Gell-Mann then drafted a paper on the subject and submitted it to the conference. The Soviets 'still considered it a strange notion but agreed to think more about it.' In later years, some of the Soviet scientists who had participated in the meetings with American arms controllers helped persuade Soviet policymakers. Von Hippel reports that

> Lev Artsimovich (who was head of the Soviet fusion program) and Mikhail Millionshchikov (who was vice-president for applied physics and mathematics of the Soviet Academy of Sciences) subsequently helped bring their government around ... thereby contributing to the achievement in 1972 of the ABM Treaty.

In turn, Doty adds that 'it is widely thought that the willingness of the USSR to negotiate an ABM Treaty arose from the seminars that this group held.'[136]

Before 1968, the Soviet leaders gave every indication that they could not or did not want to understand why defenses were 'bad.' At the Glassboro meeting, Kosygin rejected McNamara's initiative to ban defenses. Beneath the surface, however, not only the Soviet perceptions but also the Soviet political–strategic game had started to change. Referring to the relatively long time it took the Soviets to react to McNamara's proposals, a Soviet diplomat said, 'don't think we weren't studying the problem. It was just too soon. We didn't think we were ready.'[137] In fact, as David Holloway pointed out, both

> the ambition to attain superiority and the recognition of mutual vulnerability were present in Soviet thinking in the 1960s. But a choice became necessary only with the attainment of parity [and was] forced by the practical consideration that the pursuit of superiority might prove extremely costly, and ultimately unsuccessful.[138]

Two important new premises that the Soviets had already adopted made the acceptance of strategic arms control possible. According to Michael MccGwire,

> one was that a war in Europe would not inevitably lead to massive strikes on Russia, except in retaliation for an attack on North America. The other was that the size and diversity of the U.S. strategic arsenal meant that a preemptive strike on the United States would do little to limit the devastation of Russia.[139]

In any event, Samuel Payne argues, in 1968 'an era ended for Soviet arms control policy and a new era began. Before 1968 strategic arms limitation was simply not on the agenda for discussion in the Soviet Union.'[140]

By 1968 a faction of the Soviet political and academic establishments had already started to oppose the view of the Soviet military. Payne suggests that those who first raised ideas of strategic arms control were mainly 'academic specialists and commentators on foreign affairs who wrote for the scholarly journals in the field and also for the central press.'[141] These Soviets were well aware of what the members of the American arms control epistemic community were writing and saying and shared some of their expectations.[142] Andrei Kokoshin remarked that 'at the beginning, the Americans had a larger pool of ideas of arms control and we borrowed some of them.'[143] In fact, Payne noted, the majority of the Soviet arms controllers' attacks on ABMs 'were direct or indirect quotations from statements made by American opponents of ABMs': Iu. Arbatov, for example, quoted George Rathjens as someone who believed that 'with the present relationship of forces the strategic position of the USA basically would not change if the Soviet Union had twice as large or half as large a strategic force.'[144] V. V. Larionov, echoing an American statement, argued that 'from the point of view of national security the effort to have quantitative superiority in rockets and bombers has lost its significance, because at any realizable level the other side, spending sufficient energy and resources, can also reach that level.'[145]

Although Soviet arms controllers were well aware of the ideological divisions on nuclear issues in the United States, they drew confidence from the fact that a strong group of arms control lobbyists existed in the United States and used this fact to persuade reluctant Soviet actors.[146] According to Payne, the Soviet leadership

> apparently accepted the SALT I agreements for some of the same reasons that the [Soviet] arms controllers had advanced for strategic arms limitation over the previous several years. As the negotiations gathered momentum and, even more, after the agreements were signed, members of and spokesmen for the supreme leadership increasingly echoed arms controller arguments. Ideas that had previously been aired in *SShA* and *Mirovaia ekonomika i mezhdunarodnye otnosheniia* now appeared in Brezhnev's speeches and in authoritative editorials in *Pravda*, *Izvestia*, and *Kommunist*.[147]

For example, in the summary report of the Central Committee to the Twenty-Fourth Party Congress, arms control strategic negotiations were portrayed as aiming to prevent a new round in the arms race while protecting Soviet security and releasing significant resources for creative objectives.[148] Schelling and Halperin could not have explained the purposes of arms control better. Thus, even if the Soviet leadership started the negotiations without a clear picture of their end result or without a definition of the political battle between arms control supporters and opponents, the fact that it eventually chose arms control shows that the bureaucrats who opposed it suffered a temporary defeat.[149] By placing the ABM agenda at the highest levels of the Soviet government—thus circumventing the bureaucracy—American policymakers helped Soviet arms control supporters prevail in the Soviet policy game. At the same time, once the top Soviet leaders threw their weight in favor of arms control, they put pressure on the American policy game, helping to break the political impasse between American ABM supporters and opponents.[150]

One cannot avoid noticing the hegemonic quality of the process involving the diffusion of US arms control ideas to the Soviets. Some light is shed on this phenomenon by Scott James and David Lake's notion of the 'three faces of hegemony.'[151] The first and second 'faces' are only tangentially related to the diffusion process. According to the first face or process, the hegemon uses positive and negative sanctions as a means of directly influencing the policy choices of other states. Thus, the United States was able to affect Soviet behavior by means of 'linkage politics' and the 'China card,' but only after the superpowers had already been negotiating arms control for some time on the basis of an American agenda. According to the second face, the hegemon pursues a sort of rational-choice Trojan-horse strategy in order to alter the incentives and the political influence of societal actors in foreign countries. In the case of strategic arms, the United States used its superior technological power to persuade Soviet actors that a defensive weapons race would not be in the Soviet interest. Later, these actors did have some influence on the Soviet political game. But this face of hegemony only explains how the United States was able, in the bargaining process, to raise the cost for the Soviets of not controlling defenses; it does not explain the 'sudden' Soviet interest in controlling ABMs.

The third face of hegemony is directly linked to diffusion processes and may help us understand why certain ideas 'diffuse' better than others. In this face, the hegemon 'uses ideas and ideology to structure public opinion and the political agenda in other countries so as to determine what are legitimate and illegitimate policies and forms of political behavior.'[152] On a closer look, however, this face too provides only a limited explanation. For obvious reasons, affecting public opinion was almost irrelevant in the Soviet case. Moreover, James and Lake's description of the third face gives us few clues as to how US ideas managed to control the Soviet agenda and helped to structure policy preferences in the Soviet Union.

There seems to be a fourth face of hegemony that goes a long way to clarify what the other three faces fail to explain. The United States was able to diffuse its ideas to the Soviets and 'gently' impose its agenda on them because the US arms control epistemic community had undergone the process of ramification, thereby gaining adherents in the Soviet Union. This expansion of the community's base allowed arms control understanding to flow to the Soviet polity, thus becoming an integral part of the Soviet domestic political game. It also endowed Soviet arms controllers with a legitimate claim to a new interpretation of the Soviet national interest, which became the basis upon which political coalitions were created and, ultimately, policies made. In the fourth face of hegemony, then, hegemonic ideas structure not only the political agendas but also the political games of other countries. They also play a reflexive role by increasing the propensity of other countries to learn.

Once strategic negotiations were underway, the United States expressed its willingness to scrap ABMs entirely if the Soviets would limit their SS-9s and eliminate their ABM system poised around Moscow. Eventually, in 1972, both sides settled for limiting ABMs to two sites, and a few years later they agreed on a one-site limit. 'The signing at Moscow in May 1972 of the SALT treaties,' wrote Gregg Herken,

> seemed an occasion of barely restrained joy for those who had come to identify themselves collectively and sometimes self-consciously as 'the arms control community.' ... The treaties seemed to represent, therefore, a substantial—if not yet final—acceptance of the idea that there could be no victor in a nuclear arms race.[153]

In the long run, the diffusion of arms control ideas to the Soviet Union had profound effects. Since the late 1960s, the Soviet political system has carried an understanding embodied in political and academic institutions—and perhaps even, recently, in military institutions—wherein defenses are seen as detrimental to, and arms control as beneficial for, national security. This understanding, similar to the US case, helped balance and moderate pressures arising from an opposing and also very powerful understanding, carried mainly by military elites, that a protracted nuclear war could be fought and won and that arms control might prevent a victory on the battlefield.

When Mikhail Gorbachev came to power, he not only adopted some of the classic arms control assumptions, which by then some American elites had forgotten about or did not want to remember, but also pushed them further. And he managed to affect American and international political games by creating favorable conditions and opportunities for arms control. Helping this trend was a group of Soviet civilian strategists who had acquired their defense expertise in the West with Western strategists and were now enjoying direct access to power. Even high-ranking Soviet military officers admitted that their new ideas of unacceptable damage could be traced back to McNamara.[154] Thus, once arms control ideas became embodied in domestic and international procedures and institutions, the domestic and international games were irrevocably changed. Each new generation of leaders now had to make its (rational) decisions on the basis of an inherited intellectual code of arms control ideas which, with the passage of time, was enlarged, refined, and taken for granted.

The political road for arms control ideas was, however, full of obstacles, arising in part from the international game but in even larger part from the domestic game. Setbacks included the SALT II treaty and the lack of support for arms control during the first years of the Reagan administration. President Reagan, aided by Edward Teller, Richard Perle, and other members of the 'deterrence' community, devised the SDI not as a complement but as an alternative to arms control. Nevertheless, the practice of and national interest in arms control not only survived and kept the superpowers busy talking rather than fighting, but with Gorbachev's coming to power became, once more, a key factor in superpower relations. And since the revolutions of 1989 in Eastern Europe, arms control has also become a means for enabling the transition to a new European order.

Conclusions: the arms control epistemic community and the emergence of prudential regimes

The role played by the arms control epistemic community in the emergence of nuclear arms control cooperation between the superpowers was significant and multifaceted.

First, the community created an intellectual climate favorable to arms control. Decision-makers need not have read Schelling to understand arms control; the ideas were in the air as part of the vague but historically important 'spirit of the times.'[155]

Second, the members produced the technical knowledge required to deal with nuclear arms control. This knowledge, in turn, was used by the arms controllers to gain political legitimation and authority.

Third, the community focused attention on cooperative phenomena and helped provide the superpowers with reasons why—despite all their ideological and political differences and despite the fact that in the past disarmament negotiations had never been taken very seriously—it was important that they cooperate.[156]

Fourth, it paved the way for the creation of vested interests in arms control, including government agencies such as ACDA and a large number of nongovernmental interest and pressure groups. ACDA, even if leading what Paul Walker described as 'a rather precarious existence with a history of very mixed success,'[157] was important because it institutionalized arms control ideas and procedures and provided the bureaucracy with an institutional counterweight to the Joint Chiefs of Staff. Because arms control ideas were also institutionalized in the Pentagon and the White House, they could more easily find their way into policy agendas. The epistemic community also helped foster new areas of research and development and other arms control activities, with the result that additional communities sprang up around these activities at universities, think tanks, arms control associations, academies of science, and the meetings of the American Association for the Advancement of Science.

Fifth, the epistemic community helped generate an awareness about arms control that eventually led to public support for it. Acting to influence the media because of the opposition encountered in some inner policymaking circles, the community was able to convey to people the national security quality and value of arms control ideas. By suggesting how arms control ideas might be related to US–Soviet relations and by creating in people's minds an almost instinctive analogy between arms control and avoiding nuclear war, arms controllers were able to shape public attitudes well into the future.

Sixth, arms controllers helped persuade Congress about the value of specific arms control agreements. Thus, during the ABM debate, they acted as a counterweight to government scientists who advocated the deployment of defenses.

Seventh, members were able to propose a logically coherent arms control negotiation agenda and helped think through the bargaining positions to be taken in the ABM negotiations. Armed with arms control theory, they suggested the winning bargaining tactics and called the negotiators' attention to focal points of cooperation such as BMDs, space, the bottom of the sea, and so on. They also pointed to the need for confidence-building measures to prevent accidental wars. And they explained the political consequences that would follow from technological changes and from various alternative bargaining positions.

Eighth, the community helped formulate specific norms and rules, researched and proposed verification means, and suggested post-treaty reviews and conditions for withdrawal from agreements,

Ninth, arms controllers in many cases became what Robert Gilpin called 'full partners with politicians, administration, and military officers in the formulation of policy.'[158]

Finally, the community was instrumental in transmitting arms control ideas to the Soviet Union.

The fact that many members of the arms control epistemic community were brought into the halls of government, where they persuaded and worked together with policymakers to institutionalize the arms control paradigm, explains in part why arms control expectations were politically selected by the American government. The pluralistic nature of the American political system and the relatively decentralized process by which policy agendas are determined actually helped the epistemic community create an arms control agenda within the government. By providing community members with several alternative sources of political power, the political system helped protect them against political, ideological, and personnel changes at the top. When they were not able to count on the direct support of the president and his immediate advisers, they could turn to other government institutions, including Congress. In addition, government institutions such as ACDA, ISA, and, at times, the NSC protected arms controllers from opposing interests and points of view.

The ideological affinity between the arms controllers and the Kennedy cadre smoothed the transition of arms control ideas from the intellectual to the political realm. These ideas also had some inherent advantages. In one stroke, they addressed the two most important concerns of the time— enhancing national security and avoiding nuclear war—and they expressed a middle-of-the-road position, appealing to both pro-disarmament and conservative political groups who were nondogmatic. Thus, they produced a balance, indeed a temporary consensus, between competing trends within the government and society.

President Kennedy's backing of early arms control measures played an important role in the political selection process. Even more important, however, was the fact that he gave the arms controllers a chance to get established within government institutions, where they could spread their influence throughout the political system.

The education of McNamara by arms controllers also played a critical role; indeed, he was the national security 'czar' for most of this crucial period. Convinced that there was a mad momentum in the arms race that could be mitigated only by arms control, McNamara fiercely opposed ABM deployment and persuaded Johnson to engage the Soviets with an arms control agenda before the momentum could take another turn for the worse. After McNamara resigned early in 1968, the task of 'selling' an ABM treaty to the government was continued by the arms controllers.

By that time, however, public consciousness had changed and strategic arms control had gained wide support among the American people. This was not only because at the beginning of the 1960s a group of experts within the government had championed arms control ideas, which McNamara then helped to institutionalize, but also because these ideas were validated in later years by structural changes, such as the attainment of strategic parity by the Soviet Union. As the two superpowers started to act both independently and in coordination on the basis of arms control ideas, they generated domestic and international tendencies that would induce future generations of leaders to continue with the arms control process.

The Soviet political elites, for their part, had been affected by the diffusion of arms control ideas for over a decade and, for their own reasons, agreed to leave aside rhetorical demands for total disarmament and negotiate arms control on the basis of an American agenda. We should be careful, however, not to conclude from this that the Soviet leadership simply saw the light, dropped classic Soviet military doctrine—best exemplified by V. D. Sokolovskiy's writings[159]—and adopted American strategic doctrines and political beliefs and goals. But after the Soviets had achieved strategic parity with the United States and after the American arms control movement had grown in size and power, the idea of stabilizing the arms race through technical arms control began to make more sense to the Soviets, if only because arms control negotiations and treaties could be used to achieve Soviet political and strategic objectives.

Sharing with the United States the desire to avoid nuclear war and encouraged to turn the achievement of parity into political power, Soviet leaders—not unlike their American counterparts—saw arms control ideas as an obvious focal point for pursuing both shared and divergent interests. Indeed, all the Soviets had to be persuaded about was that arms control would help deter the West and limit its weapons, that, having achieved parity with the United States and having built an invulnerable nuclear force, it was in the Soviet interest to keep the situation stable, and that arms control could be used to further Soviet political interests.[160] But the ABM regime depended also on Soviet willingness to negotiate on the basis of the American arms control paradigm and on the sharing of some meanings and concepts about stability, deterrence, the use of force, and cooperation with adversaries.

Terry Nardin's distinction between 'purposive' and 'practical' association is useful for illustrating why, contrary to what Steve Weber suggests,[161] security regimes need not necessarily depend on the parties learning the same lessons, adopting similar military doctrines, and sharing political beliefs and goals. According to Nardin, purposive association is 'a relationship among those who cooperate for the purpose of securing certain shared beliefs, values, and interests, who adopt certain practices as a means to that end, and who regard such practices as worthy of respect only to the extent that they are useful instruments of the common purpose.'[162] An international regime based on purposive association—or what can be called instrumental association—assumes that two or more nation-states have indeed learned the same lessons and developed common political beliefs and goals and are acting together to achieve those goals. The further we get from power politics, the higher the likelihood for the emergence of instrumental regimes.[163] The ABM regime, however, was clearly not instrumental: power politics was essential, and the parties shared neither political beliefs and goals nor objective or scientific knowledge about how to avoid war.

Practical association, on the other hand, is 'a relationship among those who are engaged in the pursuit of different and possibly incompatible purposes, and who are associated with one another ... only in respecting certain restrictions on how each may pursue his own purposes.'[164] An international regime based on practical association—or what can be called prudential association—may result from the recognition by two or more states that it is in their separate interests to cooperate. In other words, the parties converge on a recognition of what has to be prevented rather than of what has to be mutually achieved; each side constrains itself in order to constrain the other. A prudential regime emerges, however, only after governments share some epistemic criteria about why and how they should cooperate, how to start negotiations, what to include on the agenda, and how to conceptualize norms and rules for particular tasks.

Because this type of 'knowledge' will most likely be developed by national institutions and politically legitimized by national governments, an international regime will emerge only after meanings and understandings are diffused and, based on them, a negotiation agenda is created, agreed upon, and acted upon. Writ large, then, arms control practice became an institutionalized way to 'know'; that is, it became a means for generating and diffusing 'information' about a common interest in avoiding nuclear war. Thus an overlapping set of epistemic criteria, together with convergence on a common practice, enabled the superpowers to develop a coordination game and to discover the extent to which its symbolic contents suggested compromises, limits, and regulations. I cannot improve on Schelling's pertinent observations:

> The players must bargain their way to an outcome. ... They must find ways of ... communicating their intentions. ... The fundamental psychic and intellectual process is that of participating in the creation of traditions, and the ingredients out of which traditions can be created, or the materials in which potential traditions can be perceived and jointly recognized, are not at all coincident with the mathematical content of the game.[165]

The countries at the receiving end of ideas, which become the target for strategic persuasion during the prenegotiation and negotiation processes, will allow themselves to be constrained by mutual injunctions only to the extent that three conditions are met. First, the policy proposals and the normative and epistemic understandings being diffused must be interpreted as advancing a shared interest in avoiding a particular outcome, such as a nuclear war or an environmental disaster.[166] Second, the proposals must create opportunities for advancing other national, political, military–strategic, and economic interests. The positive expectation of furthering all these interests will tend to increase the value of cooperation, affect the calculation of risk, and, overall, induce cooperation. Third, the parties must become conscious of their interdependence and its implications. An awareness of limits on independent behavior stems naturally from changes in technology, the balance of power, and political and economic conditions. But it also results from the interpretations that people give to these changes.

Those, then, who develop the original expectations, who really 'create' the political interests that spur motivation toward the forging of a regime, are creating a regime potential. The expectations created by the arms control epistemic community were thus a necessary condition, though certainly not the only condition, for the forging of the ABM regime, and they preceded rather than followed the units of effective modification—namely, the creation of normative behavior patterns and the formal creation of the regime. [167] Indeed, international norms, rules, and decision-making procedures express only tacit or explicit collective understandings and the theoretical expectations that are transformed into practices of government and externalized to other nation-states.

Part IV

Security communities

7 Imagined (security) communities

Cognitive regions in International Relations

In this article, I argue that the concept of security communities, coupled with a constructivist approach, offers a way to reorder our thinking about international security in the post-Cold War period, shifting the focus of security studies away from states and toward transnational social, political, economic, ecological, and moral forces. However, this concept cuts deeper, because a security community suggests not merely a group of states that, thanks to increased communication, have abandoned war as a means of social intercourse. It also implies the evolution of a community that practices peace, i.e., a security community of practice. Hence the concept of security communities suggests a social theory of IR in which shared identities play a crucial role in the construction of national interests, international practices, and regions. The Organization for Security and Cooperation in Europe (OSCE), as I demonstrate, exhibits attributes that are conducive to the building of a pluralistic security community.

Originally published in *Millennium* 26(2) (1997): 249–77

> Marco Polo describes a bridge, stone by stone.
> 'But which is the stone that supports the bridge?' Kublai Khan asks.
> 'The bridge is not supported by one stone or another,' Marco answers,
> 'but by the line of the arch that they form.'
> Kublai Khan remains silent, reflecting. Then he adds: 'Why do you
> speak to me of stones? It is only the arch that matters to me.'
> Polo answers: 'Without stones there is no arch.'
> Italo Calvino, *Invisible Cities*[1]

A renewed interest in the study of security communities calls for a careful examination of the relationship between changes in what John Ruggie labels 'social epistemes'—what people collectively know about themselves and others, or intersubjective images of reality—and the places and regions that people feel comfortable calling 'home.'[2] During the last few centuries, 'home'—as far as political organization, authority, and allegiance are concerned—has come to mean the nation-state. Benedict Anderson portrays national 'homes' as 'imagined communities,' because 'the members of even the smallest nation will never know most of their fellow members, meet them, or even hear of them, yet in the minds of each lives the image of the communion.'[3]

As has been confirmed since the end of the Cold War, national 'imagined communities' are not about to disappear as the basic reality of international life any time soon. Nevertheless, momentous changes in technology, economic relations, social epistemes, and institutions are causing globalizing and localizing pressures that are squeezing the nation-state from both above and below.[4] As a consequence, people have begun to imagine new communities, or 'homes.' When it comes to their security and well-being, in some parts of the world, growing numbers of people have begun imagining that they share their destiny with people of other nations who share their values and expectations of proper behavior in domestic and international political affairs.

Forty years ago, Karl Deutsch developed the concept of 'pluralistic security communities.' In this chapter, I extend this concept by arguing that such communities are socially constructed 'cognitive regions' or 'community-regions' whose people imagine that, with respect to their own security and economic well-being, borders run, more or less, where shared understandings and common identities end. People who are territorially and politically organized into states, owe their allegiance to states, and act on their behalf, will also take their identity cues from the community-region as these communities become more tightly integrated. Further, *liberal* community-regions, in particular, are more prone to turn into security communities because of shared practical knowledge of peaceful conflict resolution and a propensity to develop strong civil societies and a transnational civic culture. Nevertheless, nonliberal community-regions may also become security communities, because, as this chapter will argue: (1) the conditions for a community to develop are socially constructed—by the individuals and, more generally, by the states that eventually form the community, as well as by international organizations; and (2) international institutions can diffuse 'selected' liberal practices to nonliberal regions. Finally, I argue that what binds pluralistic security communities into a unit is not principally 'feeling' (subjective emotion), but intersubjective knowledge and shared identity. Accordingly, since international and transnational institutions can help diffuse and internalize norms and knowledge about how to peacefully resolve conflicts—the norms and knowledge which form the basis of security communities—they can play a critical role in the social construction of these communities.

The first section introduces the notions of 'cognitive region' and 'community-region.' The next section discusses and redefines Deutsch's concept of a security community as a special instance of a 'cognitive region.' The third section suggests a constructivist explanation for the relationship between pluralistic security communities and liberal ideas. The fourth section discusses the relationship between knowledge, power, and community to elucidate how material and sociocognitive factors combine to set in motion the construction of security communities. Section five examines the role that shared identities play in the evolution of pluralistic security communities; it suggests that sovereign states, in the process of becoming representatives of a security community, may ultimately redefine their interests and the meaning of sovereignty. Subsequently, I argue that the social construction of pluralistic security communities may depend on pre-existing security community-building institutions. By way of illustration, I show that the Organization for Security and Cooperation in Europe (OSCE),[5] although a creature of the Cold War, exhibits the attributes of an institution conducive to building a pluralistic security community. I end this chapter with some thoughts about the relevance of security communities for International Relations theory.

Cognitive regions

'Dirt, as Mary Douglas ... has noted, is matter out of place.'[6] For traditional realist and neorealist accounts of international relations, everything that is outside the realm of territorially based states and their 'co-actions' or relations is, in the sociological sense, 'dirt.' Hence, the conventional view in the International Relations (IR) discipline is that 'a state is a fixed territorial entity ... operating much the same over time and irrespective of its place within the global geopolitical order.'[7] This view lies at the root of the classic understanding of international relations.

To begin with, the modern territorial sovereign state has rested on the principle of spatial exclusion, which entailed that 'identification of citizenship with residence in a particular territorial space became the central facet of political identity'—or, in Alexander Wendt's terms, of the corporate identity of the state.[8] This principle meant that states became the primary vehicles for individual citizens to form societies and achieve human progress—that is, security, economic welfare, and justice. Politics, 'in the sense of the pursuit of justice and virtue, could exist only within territorial boundaries.'[9]

By taking the state as an abstract individual unitary actor, endowed only with a corporate identity, and by artificially separating the domestic and international realms, realism lost sight of the social identities of states.[10] I argue instead, from a constructivist perspective, that state social identities and interests are not fixed but evolve from the diffusion and convergence of causal and normative understandings across national boundaries, high levels of communication, economic interdependence, and cooperative practices. Furthermore, not only do identities and interests evolve; they also have the potential to converge.[11]

Moreover, as several authors point out, and as John Ruggie articulates, territoriality 'has become unbundled.'[12] For example, international regimes and common markets occupy a 'nonterritorial functional space.'[13] Epistemic communities, social movements, and issue-networks not only inhabit this space; they are also actively involved in determining its boundaries. More importantly, state authority in the realms of security, economic welfare, and human justice (human rights) is increasingly being distributed across these international functional cognitive spaces.[14]

Ruggie is right to say that international society is anchored in this nonterritorial space;[15] societal relations regarding global issues, such as the environment, do take place in what Ronnie Lipschutz perceives as a primitive 'global civil society.'[16] However, what some people are tenuously starting to perceive as 'home' and 'insideness'[17] is not the whole 'Planet Earth,' but a transnational region where they imagine sharing a common destiny and *identity*.[18] People who share ethnic or national identities and organize themselves into states imagine boundaries that separate 'us' from 'them'; as citizens occupying the space within state boundaries, they give expression to community life. When, however, for reasons referred to above, their self-identification and loyalties begin to change, their identities will be directed to (and boundaries will be imagined to run between): (a) territorial regions or locales within states; (b) newly formed territorially based (super)states; or (c) transnational nonterritorial regions constituted by peoples' shared values, norms, and practices.

It is this last kind of imagined human community that has trailblazing potential for international and transnational relations. It suggests an evolution towards socially constructed and spatially differentiated transnational *community-regions*, which national, transnational, and international elites and institutions, sometimes under the leadership of outstanding individuals, help to constitute. Community-regions are regional systems of meanings (an interdependent group of meanings among individuals or collectivities) and are not limited to a specific geographic place.[19] They are made up of people whose common identities and interests are constituted by shared understandings and normative principles other than territorial sovereignty and who: (a) actively communicate and interact across state borders; (b) are actively involved in the political life of an (international and transnational) region and engaged in the pursuit of regional purposes; and (c) impel, as citizens of states, the constituent states of the community-region to act as agents of regional good, on the basis of regional systems of governance.[20]

Within community-regions, people give their cultural allegiance to nations (here broadly referring to cultural community) and their political allegiance to states as political entities. At the same time, people institutionalize commonalities running through the whole region, including shared perceptions of external threats, and promote reciprocally nonthreatening practices. Postwar Europe is the most advanced community-region so far. People of the fifteen [twenty-five since 2004] European states have started to organize themselves into, and to join in the practice of, a supranational system of rule, which Ruggie calls a 'multiperspectival polity.'[21] However, only in a formal political union would people give political allegiance to a centralized regional government. For example, this would be the case were people in the countries of the European Union to give political allegiance primarily to Brussels.

While community-regions possess a territorial dimension, they are not merely a physical place. Instead, we may view them as *cognitive regions* or cognitive structures that help constitute the interests and practices of their members, whose meanings, understandings, and identities help keep the region 'in place.'[22] The social construction of a cognitive region out of inter-subjective understandings, values, and norms enables people to achieve a community life that transcends the nation-state and indeed any territorial base. According to this interpretation, the United States and the European Union inhabit the same cognitive space.[23] Australia and Canada are also part of this space. Tel Aviv is 'closer' to London and New York than it is to Riyadh or Amman, and closer to Warsaw than it is to Jericho (now under the Palestinian Authority).

In special circumstances, and within the cognitive boundaries of the community-region, the people of these communities may acquire mutual responsiveness; that is, they may gain the ability to more or less predict one another's behavior and come to *know* each other as trustworthy.[24] Within some community-regions, then, people, while organized into states, may nevertheless be able to exploit this mutual trust to develop pluralistic systems of intraregional governance that minimize or even eliminate the threat of war in that community-region. We may refer to such fortunate community-regions as 'security communities.'

Security communities

In a pioneering 1957 study, Deutsch and his associates introduced the concept of *security community*, that is, a group of people who have become integrated to the point where there is a 'real assurance that the members of that community will not fight each other physically, but will settle their disputes in some other way.'[25] According to Deutsch, security communities may be either 'amalgamated' or 'pluralistic.' In an amalgamated community, two or more (sovereign) states formally merge into an expanded state. On the other hand, a pluralistic security community retains the legal independence of separate states but integrates them to the point that the units entertain 'dependable expectations of peaceful change.'[26] A pluralistic security community develops when its members possess a compatibility of core values derived from common institutions and mutual responsiveness—a matter of mutual identity and loyalty, a sense of 'we-ness,' or a 'we-feeling' among states.[27]

More recently, Michael Barnett and I have redefined the concept of pluralistic security communities as those 'transnational regions comprised of sovereign states whose people maintain dependable expectations of peaceful change.'[28] Furthermore, we used the following criteria for distinguishing between loosely and tightly coupled pluralistic security communities: the depth of trust between states; the nature and degree of institutionalization of the governance system of the region; and whether states reside in formal anarchy or are on the verge of transforming it. A 'loosely coupled' pluralistic security community maintains the minimal definitional properties just mentioned. 'Tightly coupled' pluralistic security communities, on the other hand, possess a system of rule that lies somewhere between a sovereign state and a centralized regional government. This system is something of a post-sovereign system, composed of common supranational, transnational, and national institutions, and some form of collective security system.[29]

Deutsch, Barnett, and I agree that the existence of security communities does not mean that interest-based behavior by states will end, that material factors will cease to shape interstate practices, and that security dilemmas will end. Nor do we argue that security communities transcend the mutual dependence between regional orderly security arrangements and stable economic transactions.

To date, according to these criteria, there are only a few pluralistic security communities. These include the European Union, which is tightly coupled, and the Atlantic community, which is partly tightly coupled. Scandinavia as well as the United States and Canada also form security communities. In the future, perhaps, the states that compose the North American Free Trade Agreement (NAFTA) and the incipient regional communities in South America and in Southeast Asia (revolving around the Association of Southeast Asian Nations (ASEAN)) may become such communities. Given that we are discussing collective cognitive phenomena, there may be controversy about boundaries and membership. These controversies arise because states may be members of more than one community-region as a result either of their 'liminal' status (e.g., Turkey) or of concentric circles of identity.[30] For example, citizens in the states of the European Free Trade Association (EFTA) 'inhabit' a shared cognitive space with citizens of the European Union, who, in turn, share some core constitutive norms with citizens of Canada and the United States. All of these states together constitute the North Atlantic security community.

Since the end of the Cold War, the states of Eastern Europe, including Russia, have been knocking at the doors of the institutions that symbolically and materially represent this North Atlantic community—the European Union, the North Atlantic Treaty Organization (NATO), the Council of Europe, and even the Western European Union (WEU). These countries are seeking an avenue through which they can exert an influence on politics in the 'West,' as well as reap the benefits of Western markets by becoming full members of a political community 'where the very fact of such membership empowers those included in it to contribute to the shaping of a shared collective destiny.'[31] From the perspective of the states already organized in this North Atlantic security community, however, new members can be admitted only after the 'applicants' have learned and internalized their norms. For the original members, 'it's not enough to behave like us; you have to be one of us.' The status of 'partnership,' invented by the European Union, the Council of Europe, and NATO intends to provide a probationary status to states that wish to join the North Atlantic security community. Besides testing the intentions and institutions of applicant states, this probationary status is intended to enable members of the security community to distinguish whether applicants are making instrumental choices or are adopting the shared identity.[32] In addition, their partnership in common economic and security enterprises is meant to play a major role in changing the identities of the applicants to make them 'more like us.'

The OSCE has taken a different approach. Rather than waiting for 'the other' to change its identity and interests before it can be admitted to the security community-building institution, the OSCE has incorporated, from the outset, all states that express a political will to live up to the standards and norms of the security community, hoping to transform their identities and interests. Thus, the OSCE is building security by means of inclusion rather than exclusion or conditional future inclusion. According to Paul Schroeder, since the end of World War II, international order increasingly depends on 'associations' based on a normative consensus that 'certain kinds of international conduct ... ha[ve] to be ruled out as incompatible with [states'] general security and welfare' and on the power of these associations to offer and deny 'membership.'[33]

Liberal pluralistic security communities

In principle, we could conceive of community-regions that might be constituted around (to give an extreme example) fascist or Nazi ideologies. However, such communities are never likely to become security communities. In communities where ideologies consecrate state goals and condone every possible means that can lead to the achievement of these goals, individuals and states know that one day their fellow community members might stab them in the back, just as they themselves, given the chance, would do. Thus the mere fact that people in different territorial spaces share knowledge does not lead them to feel safe from organized violence. In other words, while people within totalitarian communities may achieve shared understandings, they are most unlikely to develop mutual trust.[34] The quality of the relationship between people is crucial. Accordingly, security communities are *socially constructed* and rest on *shared practical knowledge* of the peaceful resolution of conflicts.[35] Moreover, security communities are socially constructed because shared meanings, constituted by interaction, engender collective identities.[36] They are dependent on communication, discourse, and interpretation, as well as on material environments.

Practical shared knowledge of the peaceful resolution of conflicts goes a long way in explaining why the majority of existing security communities developed out of *liberal* community-regions. This knowledge, however, characterizes only parts of the world, is associated with collective historical experiences, and is related to British hegemony in the nineteenth century and American hegemony in the twentieth century, which helped diffuse and institutionalize liberal values.[37]

Practical liberal knowledge of the peaceful resolution of disputes is not only institutionalized in the memories of elites; it is also being continually reconstituted through the dense networks of relationships among civil societies and their members. This knowledge becomes an identity marker that helps create the boundaries between 'us' and 'them.' In other words, liberal community-regions become security communities because of intersubjective understandings among people, their shared sense of identity, and their common notion that they inhabit a nonterritorial region or space where, being *at home*, they can feel safe.[38] Accordingly, in theory, it is possible to identify a liberal community-region which is not a security community, but is very likely to become a security community.

However, since security communities are socially constructed, nonliberal community-regions may develop into security communities. First, liberal international institutions may socialize nonliberal states into adopting and institutionalizing 'selected' liberal practices. Second, nonliberal ideologies— for example, a shared ideology of development perhaps similar to that pursued by Southeast Asian states—may promote a joint project characterized by increasing interdependence and the development of common institutions. Such a project might conceivably promote collective purposes around which emerge a shared identity and, thereafter, dependable expectations of peaceful change.[39] However, liberal and nonliberal community-regions cannot become security communities unless their shared knowledge of the peaceful settlement of disputes is institutionalized in some kind of rule of law or regulation structure that generates trust— 'the expectation that another's behavior will be predictably friendly.'[40]

In liberal democracies, for example, this practical intersubjective knowledge is part of a 'civic culture,'[41] whose concepts of the role of government, legitimacy, duties of citizenship, and the rule of law constitute the identities of individuals.[42] The behavior of member states in a pluralistic security community reproduces this civic culture, which, in turn, constructs a community-region civic culture. This culture further helps constitute the identities and interests of the individuals, elites, and organizations whose interactions form the community. Unstable democracies and nondemocracies are characterized by an absence of these shared understandings.[43] In a *liberal* community-region, people learn the practices and behaviors that differentiate aggressive states from peaceful states. In other words, each side develops a common knowledge of 'the other's dovishness.'[44] In this sense, the democratic nature of a state becomes an indicator of its 'dovishness.'[45] It follows that the process of socialization and social integration that enters into the building of a security community provides policymakers, in Harvey Starr's words,

> with overwhelming information which allows them to have full confidence in how they separate states. Those states with whom they form a security community [with whom they begin to share a common identity] *are* doves, averse to the use of force. All the members of the security community have learned this.[46]

Furthermore, liberal democracies and their civic cultures encourage the creation of strong civil societies—and of transnational networks and processes—that promote community bonds and a common identity through the relatively free interpenetration of societies, particularly with regard to the movement and exchange of people, goods, and ideas.[47] For example, strong civil societies greatly facilitate the spread and strengthening of practices that promote human rights and environmental protection.[48] These, in turn, help produce and reinforce community bonds and common identity.[49] Moreover, social networks constituted around liberal norms facilitate the transfer of democratic norms and practices to societies that lack them.[50] I believe that a socially constructed civic culture may help to explain, more than anything else, the findings of studies that deal with the last two centuries of warfare, which have more or less conclusively shown that democracies do not fight each other and create among themselves a 'separate peace.'[51]

Flows of private transactions in conjunction with transnational institutions (such as epistemic communities and nongovernmental organizations (NGOs)) and community law (such as European Union law) can play important roles in transmitting and diffusing shared normative and causal beliefs of a civic culture (beliefs or knowledge that, for example, CFCs cause depletion of the ozone layer and, therefore, that their use should be regulated). International institutions—which provide a forum in which state and nonstate representatives debate and bargain about their understandings and interests and in which ideas flow back and forth between the domestic and international arenas—can play similar, if not, indeed, more important roles than civic cultures.[52]

Knowledge, power, and community

Power plays a crucial role in the development and institutionalization of security communities, a fact that Deutsch did not overlook. According to Deutsch, 'larger, stronger, more politically, administratively, economically, and educationally advanced political units [are] the *'cores of strength'* around which in most cases the integrative process developed.'[53] For decades, realist scholars have defined power exclusively in terms of material capabilities.[54] Steve Lukes' analysis, which divided power into three dimensions—sheer power, power to set agendas, and ideological, Gramscian-type power—went a long way to problematize power and make the concept more amenable to a constructivist project.[55] However, we have neglected the power of norms and rules to frame and redefine reality and thereby determine the range and value of political choices.[56]

While I do not entirely disregard the presence of Lukes' three dimensions of power in the social construction of cognitive regions, power can also be understood as the authority to determine the shared meanings that embody the identities, interests, and practices of states, as well as the conditions that confer, defer, or deny access to 'goods' and benefits. Since social reality is a result of imposing meanings and functions on physical objects that do not already have those meanings and functions,[57] the ability to create the underlying rules of the game, to define what constitutes acceptable play, and to get other players to commit themselves to those rules, because those rules are now part of the players' self-understandings, is, perhaps, the most subtle and most effective form of power.[58] This means that there is a very strong relationship between knowledge and power. Knowledge is rarely value-neutral, but frequently enters into the creation and reproduction of a particular social order that benefits some at the expense of others. In this reading, power is primarily the institutional power to include and exclude, to legitimize and authorize.[59] Also, in this sense, international organizations are related to power, because they can be sites of identity and interest formation, and because states and sometimes individuals and other social actors can draw on their material and symbolic resources.[60]

It is important to keep in mind, however, that if (as I argue) social reality is a result of imposing meanings and functions on physical reality, then material and technological (economic and strategic) resources are also needed to get some actors to accept or internalize the sets of meanings and rules of other actors. Not only do material resources facilitate the reproduction of institutional activities;[61] they may also provide incentives for outside members to choose an identity. As David Laitin holds, the choice of an identity 'is often guided by instrumental reasoning, based on the potential resources available for identifying yourself.'[62]

Furthermore, recent technological developments actually contribute to the construction of security communities, making possible interactions between agents 'who are not physically co-present' and turning national communities into transnational 'imagined security communities.'[63] Technology (e.g., the Internet) and economic interdependence (e.g., trade, finance, and aid) may also contribute to the thickening of social relations between domestic civil societies. For instance, they facilitate the work of environmental and human-rights movements and NGOs that diffuse understandings from country to country and help in the creation of a regional civil society.

Material structures, such as economic well-being and technological advances, also empower communities, because they elicit the formulation of images of political, economic, and social domestic organization that come to be associated with the material progress of the community. These images of, for example, democracy and a market economy are coupled with normative understandings that define legitimate regional behavior and create the basis for the development of the shared civic culture on which a pluralistic security community is based. Economically and technologically weak states thus associate positive images of material progress with 'successful' or powerful states or regions, such as the European Union.[64]

In fact,

> power can be a magnet; in a community formed around a group of strong powers, weaker members will expect to share the security and

(potentially) other benefits associated with the stronger ones. Thus, those states that belong to the core of strength do not create security, *per se*; rather, because of their positive image, security communities develop around them. This is clearly the case of Europe, where the former Communist states, rather than being invited to form part of the security community, issued their own invitations.[65]

Thus, provided that domestic political resistance against the idea of community is overcome, successful or strong states may empower this idea with the material and normative resources that are necessary to realize shared purposes and interests. In this way, power provides practical meaning to regional governance systems, that is, to the shared values, expectations, and practices of member states.[66]

Although the above interpretation of power may be amenable to a Gramscian explanation, there is, nevertheless, a subtle but still significant difference between the concept of Gramscian hegemony and that of security communities.[67] First, although cultural hegemony may be exerted without the existence of a shared identity, the latter is a necessary condition for a pluralistic security community. When Eastern European states attempt to become part of the institutions and organizations of Western Europe, not only are they not being coerced or lured by Western states, but they are also expressing their identity-affinities with them.

Second, whereas Gramscian hegemony is based on a thin concept of society, class domination, and on the language of cultural dominance, and does not require direct interaction for its existence, pluralistic security communities are endowed with a thick concept of society, shared identifications, many-sided and direct or indirect interactions, and the language of community ('we' and 'they'). In the case of Gramscian hegemony, the disregard of norms may result in material or political sanctions. In the case of pluralistic security communities, however, states that disregard norms may undermine their self-identity and sense of belonging to the community.[68]

The social construction of pluralistic security communities

Common identity and the construction of cognitive structures

Communities exist on the basis of commitments, duties, and obligations, and, more generally, on expectations held collectively by the group.[69] To grasp the process by which mutual responsiveness develops in pluralistic security communities, we must understand community not as a matter of feelings, emotions, and affection, but as a cognitive process through which common identities are created.[70]

In other words, the sense of 'we-ness,' of belongingness, which indicates that we are dealing with a community, does not arise from 'social cohesion' or mutual attraction.[71] On the contrary, the 'first question determining group-belongingness is not 'Do I like these other individuals?' but 'Who am I?' What matters is how we perceive and define ourselves and not how we feel about others.'[72] In this sense, a social category, such as being a democrat, defines persons 'by systematically including them with some, and excluding them from other related categories. They state at the same time what a person is and is not.'[73]

Following this line of thought, when a state assumes a particular social identity—for example, democratic, law-abiding, respectful of human rights—people in this state will be able not only to answer, in part, the question 'Who am I?' but also to guess or *know* the identities of individuals from other similar states. This knowledge does not merely constrain the state. In a positive sense, it empowers it to act in the world and contributes to the development of mutual responsiveness. In this case, mutual responsiveness develops more from knowing 'who I am' and 'who the other is' than from some mutual 'feeling' that people in 'Western-style' democracies may have towards one other.

There is much evidence in the social psychology literature that cooperative behavior between individuals is mediated by the perception of membership in a common category.[74] Additionally, within communities we

> help others, apparently selflessly, because we perceive their needs and goals as those of our social category and hence as our very own. Social categorizations which extend self-definition beyond the individual person provide a simple and elegant mechanism for bypassing the supposed 'egotism' of human beings.[75]

To sum up this discussion about common identity, when people define their state as belonging to a group of states— 'the democracies,' for example—they internalize certain norms that go with that self-definition. Certain behaviors—such as concern for human rights—become appropriate, while others—such as torture—become inappropriate or illegitimate. Henceforth, the state follows democratic norms not simply because its people believe in democracy, but because the category 'democratic state' now defines, in part, their identity. The key point to remember, when we seek to explain peaceful change, is that the identity factor allows peoples from different states to know each other. This reduces the uncertainty spawned by the anarchic nature of the international system and increases mutual responsiveness. The corollary to this argument is that when it comes to democratic norms, not only can states know each other better, they *can also know each other as states that tend to solve their internal and external problems by peaceful means.*

Is there something in the national identities of peoples that hinders the evolution from states to security communities? Social psychology and studies of nationalism do not deny this possibility. Indeed, the notion of concentric circles of allegiance stands on firm empirical ground.[76] '[H]owever dominant the nation and its national identification, human beings retain a multiplicity of allegiances in the contemporary world. ... Under normal circumstances, most human beings can live happily with multiple identifications and enjoy moving between them as the situation requires.'[77]

The notion of concentric circles of identity fits well with the argument that while 'nations are not "transient phenomena,"'[78] other and broader regional communities of common identity may develop. For example, events in Western Europe show that, notwithstanding the fact that new and more encompassing identities are developing (such as a European identity), national identities remain strong.

Barry Buzan underscores this point when, borrowing from Ferdinand Tönnies, he describes two processes for the development of international societies—*Gemeinschaft*, in which international society develops from a common culture, and *Gesellschaft*, which takes international society as created by a contractual act of volition.[79] Buzan rightly points out that while *Gemeinschaft* is too 'civilizational' to act in the short run, *Gesellschaft* omits the notion of common identity. 'The development of common norms, rules, and institutions,' Buzan notes, 'must eventually generate, as well as be generated by, a common identity.'[80] He adds, however, that people are quite capable of holding several identities in parallel. 'One can, for example, be English, British, European, and Western all at the same time.'[81]

Pluralistic security communities and the 'agent-state'

When pluralistic security communities, such as the European Union, become tightly coupled, can sovereignty still remain the constituting and legitimating principle that 'differentiates units in terms of juridically mutually exclusive and morally self-entailed domains?'[82] Do states still have the same authority over their own territory?

Outside the European Union, the intersubjective understanding on which sovereignty is based gives countries almost unlimited authority to treat their own citizens as they deem necessary and to act in the international system as independent units, waging war or making peace when required.[83] Within the European Union, too, political authority remains essentially in the hands of the state. States are still free to act in the world—but as *agents* rather than solely as sovereign *states*. In other words, states also act as the local agents of a regional good.[84]

Thus, within *tightly coupled* security communities, authority and legitimacy—the conditions under which states view each other as part of the community and give each other certain rights, obligations, and duties—are contingent on their ability to abide by the cognitive normative structure of the cognitive region. My reasoning here is structurationist: cognitive structures—like games whose constitutive rules give meaning to the moves—constitute identities, interests, and behavior, but are, in turn, also constituted by them. Thus, agents (states, or more accurately individuals acting on behalf of states) and structures (pluralistic security communities) socially co-construct one another.[85] This means that states can express their agency insofar as they meet and reproduce the epistemic and normative expectations of the community. States remain 'free agents,' acting on the basis of their own preferences, as long as these preferences are cognitively framed by the shared understandings of the community.

In the European Union, the thirteen judges of the European Court of Justice (ECJ), 'quietly working in Luxembourg, managed to transform the Treaty of Rome ... into a constitution. They thereby laid the legal foundation for an integrated European economy and polity.'[86] In less developed or even incipient pluralistic security communities, however, liberal democratic norms need not necessarily be converted into a formal legal framework of obligations. Instead, they may bind their members politically when, in the wake of the concerted or coordinated political decisions of the agent-states, these norms become a matter of practice and public policy in each member state and thus, *de facto*, a system of regional governance.[87]

This conceptual framework makes it easier to understand why people acting on behalf of their states can nevertheless decide to identify their security with that of other states. According to the classical intersubjective understanding of sovereignty, states defend their 'local' points of view, interpretations, and norms.[88] In pluralistic security communities, however, states come to defend a regional point of view—where 'regional' is defined in cognitive terms.[89] People may still be able to imagine themselves as belonging to cultural–national communities, organized as states endowed with agency. However, people, as members of security communities, also imagine that, with regard to their security and economic well-being, borders run more or less where shared understandings and common identities end.

Within tightly coupled security communities, then, states perceive insecurity not only when their authority is challenged or their existence is endangered, but also when the basic understandings that constitute the community are threatened.[90] (In turn, this may threaten the shared knowledge of the peaceful resolution of conflict.) Again, the European Union clearly exemplifies this notion. The 'constitutive processes whereby each of the twelve [now twenty-five] defines its own identity ... increasingly endogenize the existence of the other eleven. Within this framework, European leaders may be thought of as entrepreneurs of alternative political identities.'[91]

Ruggie's claim, however, raises an ontological problem in addition to a theoretical one. If, in tightly coupled security communities, the community is the structure and its twenty-five members are agent-states, why do we say that leaders or institutions, too, may be agents in the community region? The answer is that, although leaders and institutions rely on a territorial base and are empowered by states, their identity, roles, and interests are increasingly being shaped by the cognitive community rather than by the particular states.[92] Thus, in principle, state agency (which people and their political elites reproduce) represents the interests, not just of states, but also, and at the same time, of the community of agent-states.

A crucial question arises now: Can the concept of citizen be carried over from the agent-state to the pluralistic security community? Can people fall within the jurisdiction of several authorities, have multiple identities, and possess rights of participation in supranational structures, and, thus, be citizens both of their own state and the security community?[93] In principle, if people are engaged in the political life of their state and their security community, the answer is 'yes.' 'Citizenship,' as Dennis F. Thompson writes,

> is not meant to suggest merely those rights possessed by a passive subject by virtue of residing under a particular territorial jurisdiction. Nor is it meant mainly to connote patriotism or loyalty to a nation-state. 'Citizenship' … refers to the present and future capacity for influencing politics. It implies active involvement in political life.[94]

Institutions, legitimacy, and identity: the pluralistic security community-building mission of the OSCE

In the last fifty years, a new type of institution—a security community-building institution—made its appearance on the world scene.[95] Security community-building institutions are *innovators*, in the sense that they create the evaluative, normative, and sometimes even causal frames of reference. This type of institution may also play a critical role in the *diffusion* and *institutionalization* of values, norms, and shared understandings. Finally, by establishing norms of behavior, monitoring mechanisms, and sanctions to enforce those norms, all of which encourage, and also depend on, mutual responsiveness and trust, security community-building institutions may help shape the practices of states that make possible the emergence of security communities.

The OSCE provides a clear illustration of a security community-building institution. Being a pan-European security organization that spans three continents, from Vancouver to Vladivostok, the OSCE encourages the elites and peoples of its fifty-five member states to imagine that they inhabit a shared cognitive region, increasingly being referred to as 'the OSCE region.' Thus, regardless of its accomplishments, or lack thereof, we cannot understand what the OSCE is or is trying to do unless we embed this understanding in the concept of pluralistic security communities. The CSCE, also known as the 'Helsinki Process,' was constituted in August 1975 by the Helsinki Final Act, which was signed by thirty-five countries, including Canada, the United States, and all European states (as well as the Soviet Union) except Albania. This act—supplemented over the years by a series of follow-up conferences, such as Belgrade (1977–79), Madrid (1980–83), and Vienna (1986–89), as well as by expert seminars and conferences—establishes ten basic principles of behavior as well as three broad areas (or 'baskets') of activity (security, economics, and the human dimension). As such, the Helsinki Final Act provides a normative framework for its member states, based on adherence to multiparty democracy, the rule of law, human rights, and liberal economic systems. The effectiveness of the CSCE depended on the way in which the three baskets were tied together in political dialogue and processes of negotiation, which became the foundation of the 'cooperative security' of the CSCE system. Until 1990, the CSCE operated as an institutionalized diplomatic conference with no permanent organizational structures. With the end of the Cold War, however, the CSCE began a rapid transition to a full international organization. In 1992, with the dissolution of the Soviet Union and Yugoslavia, the membership of the CSCE rose to fifty-three states and later to fifty-five.[96]

The Charter of Paris for a New Europe marked a turning point in the history of the CSCE. With the addition of important injunctions on democracy, the rule of law, and human rights, what had been a regional code of conduct turned into the normative structure for a security community that OSCE leaders expected to evolve in the CSCE region. In addition, the new CSCE institutions created in Paris actively encouraged the normative structures to develop in the region. These institutions include the Secretariat and the Council of Foreign Ministers, the Conflict Prevention Center, and the Office of Free Elections, which later became the Office for Democratic Institutions and Human Rights (ODIHR), along with other institutions that were added in the following years, such as the Forum on Security Cooperation and the High Commissioner on National Minorities (HCNM). They improved the decision-making and enhanced the monitoring capabilities of the future OSCE. The CSCE institutions also extended the reach of democratic pluralism, the rule of law, human rights, and market systems eastward, and they promoted the peaceful settlement of disputes. In addition, the CSCE became a regional arrangement, in the sense of chapter VIII of the UN Charter. It established early-warning, conflict-prevention, and crisis-management practices and expanded peacekeeping activities, especially in Nagorno-Karabakh and Bosnia.

At the Budapest follow-up meeting, the newly renamed OSCE settled for its present institutional structure, consisting mainly of the Summit of Heads of Government (meeting every two years), the Ministerial Council, the Senior Council, the Permanent Council, the Forum for Security and Cooperation, the Court of Conciliation and Arbitration, and the OSCE Parliamentary Assembly. In addition, the OSCE is administered by a Chairman-in-Office (CIO), a Troika (made up of the immediate past, present, and future CIOs), and a Secretary General (and Secretariat). Particularly noteworthy is the role the OSCE has been playing in the management of the post-conflict situation in Bosnia-Herzegovina; the approval of a Code of Conduct on Politico-Military Aspects of Security (1994); and the Lisbon Declaration on a 'Common and Comprehensive Security Model for Europe for the Twenty-First Century' (1996)—a politically binding document that outlines the future of the OSCE.[97]

The OSCE fulfills seven community-building functions: (1) it promotes political consultation and bilateral and multilateral agreements among its members; (2) it sets liberal standards—applicable both within each state and throughout the community—that are used to judge democratic and human-rights performance, and monitors compliance with them; (3) it attempts to prevent violent conflict before it occurs; (4) it helps to develop the practices of peaceful settlement of disputes within the OSCE space; (5) it builds mutual trust by promoting military transparency and cooperation; (6) it supports the building of democratic institutions and the transformation to market-based economies; and (7) it assists in reestablishing state institutions and the rule of law after conflicts. More generally, the OSCE aims to shape new transnational identities based on liberal values and serves as a conduit for the transmission of liberal values, norms, and practices to Eastern Europe, thereby helping to create new vested interests in a pan-European cognitive space.[98]

Three notions are crucial for understanding how the community-building practices of the OSCE work. First, the same practices that offer a means of dealing with specific problems, such as early warning, conflict prevention, and the protection of human rights and minorities, also fulfill the role of 'building a secure and stable CSCE [now OSCE] community, whole and free.'[99] For example, when the OSCE performs tasks—such as sending a mission to Tajikistan or to Estonia, organizing a seminar on military doctrines or confidence-building measures (CBMs), or, as part of its CBMs regime, requiring states to open up their military activities for inspection—what matters most is not the short-range success of the project, but the construction of a foundation for community practices and behavior.

These practices, together with the normative structure embodied in OSCE documents, institutionalize a new way of cognitively framing regional problems and solutions around liberal ideas. These documents include the 1975 Helsinki Final Act; the 1990 Copenhagen Declaration on democracy, the rule of law, and human rights; and the 1990 Charter of Paris, with its blueprint for a democratic Europe, whole and free. They also help to constitute new vested interests in, and generate the material and institutional resources for, reducing human-rights violations, helping minorities, preventing conflicts that can endanger newly created and feeble democratic institutions in Eastern Europe, and facilitating the resolution of secessionist conflicts by peaceful means.

Second, to create shared values and mutual responsiveness, the OSCE has cleverly exploited expectations of international legitimacy and fundamen-tally transformed the constitutive norms of the OSCE region.[100] In other words, changing the identities and interests of former Communist countries entails setting, promoting, and diffusing two ideas. The first is the *expectation* that international legitimacy depends on the democratic nature of domestic regimes. This implies that peaceful change is predicated on the knowledge that member states and societies have of one another as liberal democracies, that is, as 'doves.' The second is the *accountability norm*, according to which OSCE states are accountable to one another and to the OSCE community for what they do to their own citizens. This means that trust and peaceful change are predicated on replacing the non-intervention norm with the mutual accountability norm.[101]

Third, developing a 'we-feeling' (based on cognition rather than affection) within a region requires institutional resources, incentives, and encouragement. This is why the OSCE has adopted the view that it must first let the largest possible number of states believe that they are part of a cognitive region. Only then, when member states have formally and instrumentally accepted the shared institutional normative structures and practices, does the OSCE socialize state elites by means of continuous diplomatic interaction and a wide range of community-building practices. Thus, the rationale for the crucial 1992 decision to bring all the successor states of the Soviet Union into the OSCE could be phrased as follows: 'We know you are not "us." Let us pretend, however, that you are, so we may teach you to be "us." The far worse alternative—to leave you "outside" and not let you become one of us—is most likely to turn you into "them," and against us.'[102]

We cannot understand the role the OSCE plays in security community-building without taking a closer look at 'cooperative security.' This is the OSCE 'demilitarized' security concept that

> has resulted in imbuing security with political and human dimensions, and in basing security on confidence and cooperation, the elaboration of peaceful means of dispute settlement between states, the consolidation of justice and democracy in civil society, and the advancement of human freedom and rights, including national minority rights.[103]

According to the classic notion of security, no weapon or political intention of an adversary may be beyond the reach or concern of another state.[104] According to the OSCE's original notion of cooperative security, however, '*no domestic institution or norm is beyond the jurisdictional reach of the CSCE*.'[105] Indeed, the constitutive norms, associated institutions, and practices of the OSCE may be conceived as a crude governance system, relying for compliance on a shared identity that creates and maintains public order within the cognitive region. Thomas Buergenthal caught the subtle but crucial essence of the OSCE when he asserted that its 'instruments can be compared ... to those domestic constitutions which are not legally enforceable in national courts.'[106]

A plethora of new practices, institutions, and mechanisms give the OSCE 'governance system' its practical meaning. For example, the Human Dimension Conference (all Basket III issues, such as human rights, human contacts, and other humanitarian issues, grouped together since 1989), together with the High Commissioner on National Minorities (HCNM) (which tries to investigate, mediate, and prevent minority conflict), are superficially intended only to prevent ethnic conflict and to monitor the implementation of minority-rights provisions.[107] *In practice*, however, they also aim at reconstructing the identities of OSCE members and, thus, their preferences. Moreover, the Office for Democratic Institutions and Human

Rights (ODIHR) provides support for free elections and civil society-related programs. Additionally, it reviews the implementation of Human Dimension provisions and the results of expert missions, and it also organizes expert seminars on a variety of issues. Equally important for community-building are the innovative practices of the OSCE in arms control and the peaceful settlement of disputes. In the early 1970s, the CSCE created *ex nihilo* the practice of CBMs, now diffused around the world.[108] Originally thought (in political and academic circles) to be merely a variant of arms control measures aimed at enhancing transparency so as to reduce the danger of surprise attack, CBMs have become a community-building mechanism based on the social construction of mutual trust.

Because trust is closely related to the legitimacy of a government 'and the way it treats its people,'[109] military cooperation and trust, and, more generally, peaceful change in the OSCE region depend on member states' compliance with OSCE norms. Thus, the right to request information and to make representations on human rights is the other side of the coin of CBMs. As part of this mutual trust-building instrument, 'mechanisms,' as they are called, allow for: (1) the exchange of information and convening of bilateral and multilateral meetings on human-rights violations (the Human Dimension Mechanism); (2) the querying of other states about their military activities (Unusual Military Activities); (3) the facilitation of peaceful resolution of disputes by a group of third-party experts (the Valetta Dispute Settlement Mechanism, followed by the 1993 Convention on Conciliation and Arbitration); (4) the holding of emergency meetings at a high political level (the Emergency Meeting Mechanism); and (5) fact-finding, rapporteur, long-term, and sanctions-assistance missions. The Forum for Security Cooperation coordinates CBMs and other arms control activities with security enhancement and conflict prevention activities. The Code of Conduct on security matters sets standards of behavior for the democratic control of armed forces and the activities of internal security forces of member states.[110]

The institutional processes and attributes of the OSCE,[111] frequently criticized for their lack of coherence and teeth, are, in fact, compatible with the task of community-building. First, the fact that most OSCE injunctions are politically rather than legally binding makes adherence to stated intentions a test 'of political credibility rather than an invitation to search for legal loopholes,' which promotes mutual trust.[112] Furthermore, politically binding instruments lead to changes in practices, political interests, and public policies, rather than in legal instruments. In other words, politically binding instruments can sometimes be as effective at producing change as legal instruments. OSCE processes work less by constraining political behavior through law than by promoting public policies that are congruent with regional norms.

Second, the accountability norm is particularly important for a system of governance that works through legitimation and delegitimation. Third, the informality of the Helsinki process, especially in its first stages, prevented the development of huge bureaucracies. Instead, it has empowered individuals,

NGOs, social movements, and other civil-society actors to act on behalf of their rights.[113] In other words, informality helped generate the dense web of transnational relations throughout the region that is essential for the development of a transnational community.[114] Fourth, the consensus rule, only recently modified to consensus-minus-one, in the event of gross violations of OSCE norms, means that once consensus is achieved, 'it has higher moral credibility and greater political weight.'[115] It also generates the need to persuade other members by peaceful means, thus structurally promoting socialization and learning processes.

Fifth, institutionalized learning also results from OSCE follow-up conferences, which review the effectiveness of previous documents, decisions, and measures. 'This review of practices,' Alexis Heraclides maintains, 'was novel not only in the Helsinki process, but also in the history of diplomacy.'[116] Moreover, the follow-up practice breeds the need to define the notion of success and failure, promoting both self-correcting and goal-oriented behavior.[117]

Sixth, the Helsinki process promotes and makes prevalent a new type of diplomacy that integrates academic and diplomatic discourse and practice. For lack of a better word, I call it 'seminar diplomacy.' The practice, now widespread in other security organizations, such as the North Atlantic Cooperation Council of NATO and the Partnership for Peace,[118] institutionalizes the diplomatic practice of teaching norms and legitimizes expertise as the basis for common agreement. [119] More importantly, however, seminar diplomacy, as in the case of the 1990 and 1991 CSCE seminars on military doctrine, helps generate not only causal understandings about specific technical issues, but also a measure of 'we-feeling' and mutual trust among seminar members.[120]

Conclusion

Merely to imagine security communities does not make them all-pervasive. Balances of power, alliances, hegemonies, and deterrence still are—and probably will continue to be—part of the international political landscape, not only in areas riven by interstate or interethnic conflict, such as the Middle East, but also in areas where security communities exist, such as Western Europe, or are in the process of developing, such as Southeast Asia. The architects of security communities must still compete with and fight against power–political practices and conflicting identities.

Moreover, as we look at the institutional map of International Relations, it becomes apparent that many contemporary multilateral institutional activities—for example, the international trade, monetary, and nuclear nonproliferation regimes—although themselves the result of processes of social construction, are only indirectly linked to community-building. Instead, to a large extent, they respond to the instrumental logic of self-interested states that coordinate their policies—and thus construct a thin version of society—on the basis of consensual principles of conduct.[121]

Regardless of power politics, strong conflicting identities, and the above 'weak' version of multilateralism, a 'strong' kind of multilateralism has evolved in the postwar international system. This strong multilateralism refers to the social construction and institutionalization of security communities by means of multilateral dialogue and community-building practices, on the basis of collective normative knowledge forged through new and/or pre-existing institutions. Strong multilateralism—which is partially replacing power politics in parts of the world—and, more generally, the workings of security community-building institutions—are, nevertheless, indicators that international security is increasingly associated with the establishment of a security community. They are evidence 'that regions themselves are socially constructed and susceptible to redefinition.'[122] A constructivist approach is helpful in identifying this phenomenon, as well as in discerning the many 'strong' multilateral institutional attributes, processes, and consequences that could otherwise escape our attention. Importantly, constructivism sheds light on the way in which norms constitute identities and, concomitantly, the effect that these socially constructed identities have on the places that people are comfortable calling 'home.'

This is why the concept of pluralistic security communities, coupled with a constructivist approach, offers a way to reorder our thinking about international security in the post-Cold War period, shifting the focus of security studies away from states and towards transnational social, political, economic, ecological, and moral forces. However, this concept cuts much deeper, because a pluralistic security community suggests not merely a group of states that, thanks to increased communication, have abandoned war as a means of social intercourse. It also implies the social evolution of a community-region in which people have mastered the practice of peaceful change. Hence, pluralistic security communities suggest a social theory of International Relations according to which shared international and transnational understandings, identities, and norms play a crucial role in the social construction of national interests, international practices, and regions.

According to this theory, security communities are transnational cognitive regions whose people possess collective identities and share other normative and regulatory structures. Shared cognitive structures, such as liberal civic cultures, provide purpose, meaning, and direction to material structures and power resources and help constitute and reproduce common interests. Powerful states, or cores of strength, are necessary for the development of security communities because, like a magnet, they attract weaker states that expect to share the security and welfare associated with them. Economic and social transactions also play a role by encouraging increased communication. Communication helps to thicken the social environment of cognitive regions and thus promotes the development of shared identification. In addition, security community-building institutions, such as the OSCE, nurture the development of shared normative structures, facilitate the channeling of material resources in the direction of shared transnational goals, promote political, economic, and social transactions, and play a role in fostering the development of transnational identities and 'we-feeling.' Indeed, the positive and dynamic interaction between these variables under-girds the process of collective identity formation and trust, which, in turn, drives dependable expectations of peaceful change.

This constructivist theory explains how intersubjective understandings, through socialization and learning processes, help 'frame' international social reality and lead to the development of shared practices and institutions. At the same time, it also explains how the purposeful and sometimes innovative actions of individual and institutional agents constitute intersubjective structures. The theory may also be of help in explaining why and how states establish shared political purposes or interests only after their elites and, more generally, their people articulate a common identity within cognitively and spatially defined regional communities.

8 Condition(s) of peace

Based on an analysis of the views of three leading IR scholars—E. H. Carr, Karl Deutsch, and Ernst Haas—about the meaning of peace, in this chapter I argue that peace is neither the antithesis of war nor some idealist future state of affairs, such as world government, but something very much like a security community. In other words, because collective identities (and other collective understandings that are the marks of a security community) are manifested in and through practice, peace, I maintain, is first and foremost a practice. This chapter also suggests a series of contextual variables, such as a civic culture and the development of what Dorothy Jones referred to as 'codes of peace,' as conducive to the development of a practice of peace. Moreover, it takes a brief look at European efforts to 'construct' a Mediterranean region, efforts that borrow heavily from security community-building practices. The importance of analyzing regional peace as the enlargement of a security community of practice is emphasized. According to this analysis, an increasing number of people across national borders and institutional divides learn to entertain dependable expectations of peaceful change and also—with the purpose of institutionalizing peace—to use security community practices.

Originally published in *Review of International Studies*
24(5) (1998): 165–91

Ladies and gentlemen, the time for peace has come.
The late Yitzhak Rabin, prime minister of Israel

Introduction

The conditions in which peace can exist are now only what they have always been (even if time and place make them appear different): a higher expected utility from peace than from war; a 'civic culture'; a commitment to the peaceful resolution of disputes; strong institutions; an ethical code; mutual legitimization; peacemakers (because peace is socially constructed); a social communicative process; material and normative resources; social learning (to take us from here to there); shared trust; and, most important, a collective purpose and social identity. As I will explain below, these are not 'necessary' conditions in any formal sense. Nor are there really sufficient conditions of peace, other, perhaps, than lobotomy and the total elimination of weapons, including fingernails.

Like war, peace is a moving target. People in the Middle Ages probably understood peace very differently than did their descendants in the seventeenth century. Our understanding of peace, too, seems to be changing: if war may soon become the mutual infliction of disease, would peace mean a state of 'mutual inoculation'? And if, as I believe, future wars will be fought in and by computers, will peace exist only in cyberspace?

Again, is it not the case that peace has always been 'virtual' or nonexistent, from an epistemological or an ontological point of view? The notions of peace that realists of all colors and denominations have advanced since classical antiquity, under the rubric of 'the absence of war,'[1] amount to nothing at all. The concept of 'negative peace'[2] may indeed represent a situation in the real world where organized violence between political units does not occur for a number of years. Epistemologically speaking, however, peace merely as the absence of war is an oxymoron; we cannot positively define something as the opposite of something else.[3] In other words, peace may exist but we cannot know it.

'Positive peace,'[4] on the other hand, has no ontological existence at all; it is a goal that can never be achieved in our times.[5] Idealists of all stripes have portrayed peace as a utopia, incorporating the improvement of politics and human nature, social justice, morality, international organization and law, and human progress.[6] Seen this way, peace never existed, does not exist now, and probably never will. In other words, although we may be able to imagine peace and understand what is required to achieve it, peace really does not exist.

This is why, while inspired people, such as Immanuel Kant, may have been able to *imagine* the necessary conditions for 'perpetual peace' among republics,[7] all that contemporary scholars have been able to say about the 'democratic peace' (to stick to Kant's theory) is that 'democracies *do not make war* on each other.'[8] Even Kenneth Boulding, who was keenly aware of the ontological and epistemological traps of characterizing peace in 'negative' and 'positive' ways, defined 'stable peace' merely as 'a situation in which the *probability of war* [my emphasis] is so small that it does not really enter into the calculations of any of the people involved.'[9]

And yet, at the end of the second millennium, peace, though still uncommon, does exist. It has a positive meaning, is ontologically real and epistemologically significant, and can be empirically described. The state of peace, as envisaged by E. H. Carr more than fifty years ago, given specific meaning by Karl Deutsch and Richard Van Wagenen more than forty years ago, and recently redefined by Emanuel Adler and Michael Barnett, is neither the antithesis of something else nor something that exists only in the future; rather, it is something very much like a *security community*.[10]

Deutsch and his associates defined a security community as 'a group of people which has become integrated.' This means 'the attainment, within a [transnational] territory, of a sense of community and of institutions and practices strong enough and widespread enough to assure, for a 'long' time, dependable expectations of peaceful change.'[11] Thus peace is not some temporary absence of war or a phantom to be achieved in the future. The nature and quality of the relationships among states that share collective identities and trust one another have created transnational regions of people who maintain dependable expectations of peaceful change.

Because collective identities (and other collective understandings that are the marks of a security community) manifest themselves in and through practice, peace is, first and foremost, itself a *practice*.[12] Practices are real, not only because their physical and material manifestations can be empirically described, but also in the socio-ontological sense that they embody the collective meaning that people give to material reality. In other words, peace as it exists today can be traced back to the cognitive structures or collective understandings—mainly collective identities—that constitute the practices characteristic of security communities.[13]

Defining peace as a practice also endows the concept with a dynamic character. In this view, 'it is not possible to tame or freeze history for long';[14] that is, neither war nor peace is permanent and absolute or evolves according to some philosophically based teleology. Rather, they exist in time and space; which of the two dominates depends on whether, in dealing with their ever-changing reality, societies (not only of the anarchical type[15]) resolve their conflicts by violent means[16] or have learned to expect and implement peaceful change.

Defining peace as a practice also entails agency.[17] 'Peacemakers' (active or passive, individual or institutional) play a social and political role in endowing physical objects (including people and physical resources) with collective meanings, identities, and myths. Furthermore, the equation of peace with the practice of the security community means that, like all practices, it can be arrived at through *learning*. Rather than existing as an a-historical fact, it owes its existence to the attachment of meaning to physical reality in particular historical, cultural and political contexts.[18] In other words, peace is socially constructed.

Finally, because meanings are not direct representations but interpretations of physical reality, which, in turn, depend on other meanings (for example, sovereignty and state), the social construction of shared meanings, and thus of security communities, depends on the sharing of experiences, narratives, symbols, and, more generally, historical, political, and cultural contexts. Whether states that enjoy an absence of war become a security community, then, depends not only on time (be it twenty, thirty, or fifty years), but also on the particular contexts within which the social construction of shared meanings and identities takes place.

This means that, although we should look to constitutive conditions—such as collective identity, mutual trust, social processes of communication, and social learning—to explain the social construction of security communities, we should take account of facilitative conditions—including a higher expected utility from peace than from war or Great Power commitment to the peaceful resolution of disputes—to explain the historical, political, and cultural contexts that permit the constitution of security communities. For example, a higher expected utility from peace than from war, in addition to bringing about the temporary absence of war, may also, and more importantly, help warring societies see each other with greater empathy and thereby promote the development of collective meanings and identities.

The state or *condition* of peace[19] is the practice of security community sustained by the attachment of collective meanings and purposes to physical reality. It can be concisely represented by the formula (borrowed from philosopher John Searle): 'X counts as Y in C.'[20] The paradigmatic case is: 'This paper counts as money in a given context.' In our case, X is the material aspect of living in peace in a security community (demilitarized borders, extensive trade, etc.); Y is the collective meanings and purposes attached to physical reality, which are manifested in the practice of peaceful change ('we' democracies, 'we' who follow the 'Asian way,' etc.); and C is the historical, cultural, and political contexts through and within which social reality acquires a particular meaning (the nuclear era, a global economy, American hegemony, etc.)

As used here, the *conditions* for peace—what Carr, in the title of his often overlooked book, called the 'conditions of peace'—does not refer to its determinants in a positivist (if A then B) or a realist–scientific (A causes B) sense. Rather, I have in mind the material and ideological attributes that *enable* X to be constituted as Y in C—the propensities that, when actualized by the practices of peoples of states, enable them to de-emphasize national borders, stop imagining war among themselves as a real possibility, and feel instead that they can be safe within the cognitive borders of their community.

In this chapter, I will define, describe, and explain the *condition* and the *conditions* for peace in the context of what, evoking E. H. Carr's *The Twenty Years' Crisis*,[21] the special issue of the *Review of International Studies* in which this chapter was originally published referred to as the 'eighty years' crisis.' I find it appropriate, therefore, to begin by pointing out that, more than fifty years ago, Carr believed that peace would take hold in the European continent only if and when the peoples of Europe came to understand that 'the national unit[s] ha[d] become visibly too small' for controlling military and economic policy and were consequently 'induced to determine themselves into different units for different purposes' and build up 'a wider form of international community.'[22] Moreover, according to Carr, Europeans might then discover that they had 'constructed something which mankind will come gradually to recognize as indispensable to its future well-being and which can some day be given both wider geographical extension and appropriate constitutional forms.'[23]

From the perspective of what Carr thought to be the resolution of the 'twenty years' crisis,' the way out of the 'eighty years' crisis' becomes much more intelligible: the development of security communities and the diffusion of security community practices and institutions around the world. Although, at the end of the second millennium, the crisis is far from being over (in fact, there is room to argue that it has gotten worse since the end of the Cold War), in some (overlapping) parts of the world—such as Scandinavia, Western Europe, the Euro-Atlantic space, the US and Canada, the US and Mexico, the southern cone of Latin America, and, increasingly, the region encompassed by the Association of Southeast Asian States (ASEAN)—people who have learned to organize themselves into security communities now practice and experience peaceful change.

My arguments may sound profoundly idealistic; indeed they are, in the sense that ideational structures are both ontologically *real* and also help constitute reality. They are not idealistic (in the 'pie in the sky' sense), however, because they view power and sociocognitive processes as two sides of the same coin. Otherwise, how can we explain that Carr, generally regarded as the 'father of realism,' linked the development of a European international community to a collective transnational identity that arises from a shared moral purpose?[24] In fact, Carr believed (as I do) that the material world and power affect the world through the medium of purposeful and meaningful action;[25] consequently, history need not repeat itself endlessly and can evolve in directions made socially possible both by power relations and by the collective ideas of an age.

In the next section I shall continue to explore what Carr considered to be the reasons for the crisis of the twentieth century and its solutions and compare his ideas about the development of shared purpose and loyalty with those of more recent scholars, especially Deutsch, Ernst Haas, and Charles Taylor. The third section explains the concept of security communities and reflects on the processes by which domestic societies adopt new and broader transnational identities. Section four analyses the conditions for peace and briefly describes some recently created war-prevention practices that enhance the propensity to develop security communities. In the fifth section, by way of example, I describe contemporary attempts to construct a 'Mediterranean region' by imbuing leaders and civil societies with the practice of peaceful change. In the last section, I look around the corner of the year 2000, including the conditions of interstate, intrastate, and transnational violence, and reflect on courses of action that can protect and further promote the *state* of and *conditions* for peace.

Common purpose, collective identity, and security community

Evoking the linkage between identity and understanding, Charles Taylor wittingly wrote that, in the human sciences, the valid response to 'I don't understand' is 'change yourself!'[26] In this section, after a short review of Deutsch's notion of security community, I will draw on the work of Carr,

Deutsch, Haas, and Taylor to advance the argument that peaceful change involves a change of identity, such that 'I' becomes 'we.'[27] In other words, a new and more encompassing social identity is developed, one that instills an enhanced sense of mutual trust and security in people's minds.

As already mentioned, Deutsch and his associates defined a *security community* as 'a group of people which has become integrated.' This means 'the attainment, within a [transnational] territory, of a sense of community and of institutions and practices strong enough and widespread enough to assure, for a "long" time, dependable expectations of peaceful change.'[28] Security communities may be either 'amalgamated' or 'pluralistic.' In an amalgamated community, two or more (sovereign) states formally merge into an expanded state. Deutsch cites the United States as an instance. A pluralistic security community preserves the legal independence of its component states but integrates them to the point that the units entertain 'dependable expectations of peaceful change.' A pluralistic security community develops when its members possess a compatibility of core values derived from common institutions and mutual responsiveness—a matter of mutual identity and loyalty, a sense of 'we-ness,' or a 'we-feeling' among states.[29]

Security communities, according to Deutsch, are different from more limited 'no-war communities.' Whereas the former are characterized by a communicative process that leads to integration at the level of 'we-feeling' or identity, thus making war 'unimaginable' among its members, the latter, which can best be exemplified by a successful balance-of-power system, is a community of nations enjoying a stable truce, where war is always possible and preparations for war among its members are always a distinct possibility.[30]

At first glance, associating Carr, 'the father of realism,' and Deutsch, one of the main exponents of postwar 'idealism,' as part of a common tradition may seem an aberration.[31] When it comes to the conditions for peace, however, it is not. According to Carr, peace is to be found only as a by-product of the search for something else.[32] Building peace, therefore, means creating positive conditions for an orderly and progressive development of human society;[33] these conditions in turn depend chiefly on the identification of a common moral purpose. Because modern military technology and economic life and organization demand the construction of transnational units that are larger than the modern state, however, a common moral purpose depends on the construction of new and broader transnational social identities.

When Carr applied these thoughts to the construction of a European transnational unit (the 'New Europe') at the end of World War II, he realized that several conditions would have to be met: (1) There would have to be enlightened power, because 'no durable peace can be made unless those who have the power have also the will ... to take and enforce with vigor and impartiality the decisions which they think right.' Yet 'those who have the power should recognize the moral obligation which alone makes its exercise tolerable to others.'[34] (2) There would have to be a recognition that the right of nation-states to self-determination 'must carry with it a recognized responsibility to subordinate military and economic policy and resources to the needs of a wider community, not as a hypothetical engagement to meet some future contingency, but as a matter of the everyday conduct of affairs.'[35] (3) New institutions would be required that could 'be made effective only on the basis of new loyalties arising out of newly felt needs: yet to create the new loyalties new institutions are required.' [36] Finally, there would have to be (4) leadership and, above all, (5) a common moral purpose.[37]

Carr's analysis of the twentieth century's crises made perfectly clear that a common moral purpose was the most important condition. Beyond the crises of *liberal democracy* (which excluded the masses and thus failed to generate a feeling of mutual obligation),[38] *self-determination* (which equated self-determination with nationalism and led to the emergence of a large number of small states, whose survival was rendered problematic by advances in military technique),[39] and *laissez-faire economics* (which created unemployment and left war as the only way to generate employment),[40] there loomed the moral crisis of the breakdown of the ethical system that prevailed during the last part of the nineteenth century and the first half of the twentieth century: the 'harmony of interests' doctrine. The other three crises were only specific particular manifestations of the larger moral crisis.[41]

Solving the liberal-democratic, self-determination, and economic crises meant, therefore, that postwar Europe (C) would be compelled to develop a new common ethical purpose (Y) that would give meaning and direction to people's actions and their use of resources (X). This common moral purpose, however, was also needed in a more practical sense, that is, to enable the

> establishment of a procedure of peaceful negotiation in disputes [which] presupposes, not merely an acute perception on both sides of the strength and weaknesses of their respective positions at any given time, but also a certain measure of *common feeling* as to what is just and reasonable in their mutual relations, a spirit of give-and-take and even of potential self-sacrifice, so that a basis, however imperfect, exists for discussing demands on grounds of justice recognized by both. It is this *common feeling* between nations, not the lack of a world legislature, and not the insistence of states on being judges in their own cause, which is the real obstacle in the way of an international procedure of peaceful change.[42]

Conceptually, then, Carr linked peaceful change to an effective bargaining mechanism that owes its existence to a collective identity. Historically, peaceful change was predicated on a resolution of the crises that dominated the twentieth century by means of the development of a European collective identity and a transnational unit that, while satisfying the needs of modern military and economic organization, would at the same time respect 'the urge of human beings to form groups based on common tradition, language, and usage.'[43] This meant first creating the framework of international order and only then encouraging national independence to develop and maintain itself within the limitations of that framework.[44] Were Carr alive today, he would probably argue that it is a common moral purpose, on which a collective identity is based, that permits the emergence of a 'security community.'

Carr, echoing contemporary studies of security communities, also realized that a European collective identity would not evolve by itself but would have to be constructed by supranational institutions. This was the main rationale for his proposals to create a European Planning Authority (and Bank), a European Relief Commission, a European Transport Corporation, a European Reconstruction and Public Works Corporation, and an international military unit to keep the peace.[45] Fifty years later, Carr's vision was realized: Europe had become a highly institutionalized pluralistic security community.[46]

Although Carr found what he thought was the solution to the twentieth century's crises in the development of multiple identities and loyalties and the construction of something resembling a European security community, he nonetheless thought that to forecast the moral foundations and assumptions of the coming age would be ineffectual and presumptuous. He nevertheless insinuated that 'popular authority as much as popular liberty will be the keynote of the new faith.'[47]

Of the four theorists considered here, Carr was the only one who made a linkage between *moral* purpose, collective identity, and peace. Deutsch, Haas, and Taylor all saw community-building as chiefly a social–epistemological process that results from common meanings. Common meanings enable people to live in the same normative reference world. Deutsch argued that international community results mainly from communication, mutual responsiveness, and shared identity. Haas, on the other hand, linked the development of international community to a process of 'rationalization' that accompanies the acceptance of liberal decision-making procedures, coupled with a growing inability of the classic state to satisfy people's economic and security aspirations.[48] All four agreed that common meanings and political community in general are socially constructed. In Taylor's words:

> Common meanings are the basis of community. Intersubjective meaning gives a people a common language to talk about social reality and a common understanding of certain norms, but only with common meanings does this common reference world contain significant common actions, celebrations, and feelings. These are objects in the world everybody shares. This is what makes community.[49]

Although Deutsch gave too little attention to the concept of collective identity, and his behaviorist methodology made it difficult for him to distinguish the growth of collective identity from mere instrumentally led interdependence, he nevertheless thought that the key constitutive factor of community was a 'we-feeling' or collective identity. By 'we-feeling,' however, Deutsch did not mean a psychological, largely affective matter of feelings, emotions, and trust, but a socially constructed social–cognitive process.

The core of Deutsch's security community approach was the assumption that communication binds social groups in general and political communities in particular. 'Communication alone enables a group to think together, to see together, and to act together.'[50] Moreover, communication processes and transaction flows between peoples are not only 'facilities for attention' but also factories of shared identification. Through transactions such as trade, migration, tourism, cultural and educational exchanges, and the proliferation of communication facilities, a social fabric is woven among both the elites and the masses, instilling in them a sense of community, which becomes

> a matter of mutual sympathy and loyalties; of 'we feeling,' trust and mutual consideration; of partial identification in terms of self-images and interests; of mutually successful predictions of behavior; ... in short, a matter of perpetual dynamic process of mutual attention, communication, perception of needs, and responsiveness in the process of decision making.[51]

Communication, according to this view, is the social glue that enables peoples to share common meanings across national borders and, therefore, a common normative environment. Security communities can count on compliance with collective norms because some of them are not only regulative, designed to overcome the problems associated with interdependent choice, but also constitutive (Deutsch referred to them as 'main values,' which 'can be determined from the internal politics of the participating units'),[52] a direct reflection of the actor's identity and self-understandings.[53]

Sense of community also requires particular habits of political behavior, which are acquired through processes of social learning and socialization. People learn the new habits slowly, as background conditions change; they diffuse their 'lessons' and expectations to one another through various processes of communication. Security communities are thus communities with deeply entrenched habits for conflict resolution; they are a representation in the material world (X) of a collective identity (constituted by shared meanings through the medium of communication) (Y) in the context (C) of what Deutsch thought of as 'background conditions'—'main values,' mutual responsiveness, and predictability of behavior (so that people can 'perceive one another's sensitive spots or 'vital interests,' and ... make prompt and adequate responses to each other's critical needs').[54]

Deutsch's notion that collective identities have a *history*, i.e., are *socially constructed*, is evident from the fact that he thought that security communities may have humble and self-interested beginnings. All that is required initially, he thought, is a 'complementarity' of needs and resources.[55] With: (a) increased communication; (b) a large number of transactions; (c) learning and socialization processes, which lead to the generation of a common normative framework and common behavior patterns; (d) a 'core of power' that attracts weaker states; and under the guidance of (e) security community-building institutions; and (f) elites that use material and symbolic resources to empower a particular set of identity traits, to the detriment of others, the cultural affinities ('a way of life')[56] needed for a collective identity to exist would develop and become institutionalized.[57]

Like Deutsch, Haas rejects the idea that moral ideas are necessary for the construction of international community. Associating liberalism 'with a certain procedure for the making of collective decisions, not with a distinct moral substance' that has universal connotations, he believes that attachment to a particular moral doctrine that must necessarily be less than universal would contradict the very notion of shared meanings that he advances.[58] Haas' mostly epistemic view of liberalism, however, is partly at odds with that of Deutsch, who made the development of security communities contingent not only on expectations but also on (*de facto* liberal) values.

To be sure, Haas' analysis has much more to do with the rationalization of the nation-state and with progress—the improvement of every person's lot with respect to health, wealth, and peace[59]—than with the development of international community. Security communities have become important and a real possibility, however, because in some parts of the developed world rationalization processes are beginning to lead to the development of confederation-like transnational communities. The whole process is fuelled by common meanings.[60]

In short, Haas argues that states can effect outcomes that are first imagined by political actors and then projected onto the stage of history. Social visions, however, must have some coherence; in Haas' terms, they must be rationalized and consistent with a set of institutions. Nationalism, he claims, has provided this sense of rationalization to modernizing societies. But there are different types of nationalism, each offering its own vision of coherence. Haas claims that liberal nationalism has been relatively successful in producing coherence in the North and in parts of the South because 'the overwhelming majority of the world's political elites wants to have the trappings of material–industrial civilization of the secular civilization of the West.'[61] Liberal nationalism, he continues, will eventually prevail in much of the Third World.

But, just as the Third World is beginning to enjoy the fruits of the 'rationalization' process, post-industrial states appear to be increasingly unable to govern and produce these same gains for their peoples. In response to these fundamental changes, and in an attempt to avoid jettisoning centuries of experience and progress, Western Europe is *learning*—questioning original shared meanings and replacing them with others—to create international community; in other words, it is inventing a new type of rationalization that, though depending less on an already ailing national myth, does not necessarily demand a pan-European national identity.[62] 'Only the kind of nationalism we call "liberal,"' says Haas, 'is consistent with the progressive transnational sharing of meanings.'[63]

To sum up, Carr, Deutsch, and Haas agree that common meanings are the building blocks of the collective identities on which international or transnational communities are based. But, whereas Carr believed that European states would have to develop a new common *moral* vision in order to overcome the twentieth century's crises and transform themselves into a peaceful transnational community, Deutsch and Haas understood the process of community formation as a social–cognitive rather than a moral process and as involving the social construction of shared understandings (Deutsch also introduced a normative dimension). Essentially, the three advanced a positive (temporally and spatially contextual) concept of peace, one that involves the progressive metamorphosis of nation-states into pluralistic security communities.

The state of peace: security communities

Peace, according to the positive definition put forward in the previous section, refers to *pluralistic* rather than to amalgamated communities. States that have integrated to the point where they constitute a new enlarged nation-state do not fulfil the ontological and epistemological conditions for peace *among* sovereign states. Adler and Barnett have recently redefined pluralistic security communities as 'transnational regions comprised of sovereign states whose people maintain dependable expectations of peaceful change'; they distinguish 'loosely coupled' from 'tightly coupled' pluralistic security communities. Loosely coupled communities maintain the minimum properties of the foregoing definition. Tightly coupled communities, on the other hand, possess a political regime that lies somewhere between the sovereign state and centralized regional government. The latter kind of community is something of a post-sovereign system, comprising common supranational, transnational, and national institutions, and some form of collective security system.[64]

Empirical data indicate that pluralistic security communities can develop without a tightly coupled institutionalized environment; for example, in Scandinavia, the southern cone of Latin America, the Euro-Atlantic Community, and ASEAN (the last-mentioned is only in the process of becoming a pluralistic security community). Nor, as the cases of the United States and Canada and the United States and Mexico demonstrate, is such an environment required for security communities to remain stable over time.

A tight institutional environment, therefore, is not a necessary condition for regional peace.[65] On the other hand, post-World War II conditions have increased the role of multilateral institutions in the social construction of pluralistic security communities; Western Europe has become a clear case of a tightly coupled pluralistic security community.

A tightly coupled security community lies between the anarchical arrangement of sovereign states and a system of rule characterized by either hierarchy (as within states) or heteronomy (as in the Middle Ages, when multiple layers of authority coexisted in the same territorial space). In these communities, mutual aid becomes a matter of habit, the institutional context for the exercise of power changes, and the right to use force is transferred from the units to the ensemble of states, which deems it legitimate only against external threats or against community members that revert to un-community ways.[66]

From the perspective of either loosely or tightly coupled pluralistic security communities, then, real positive peace does not require the transcendence of the nation-state or the elimination of existing cultural and ethnic loyalties and identities or full integration into a single state. It merely requires sovereign states to adopt a novel form of regional governance that, relying on collective identity and mutual trust for coordination and compliance with norms, sustains dependable expectations of peaceful change.

Dependable expectations of peaceful change are consequently driven by the development of trust and the formation of a collective identity. 'Trust and identity are reciprocal and reinforcing: the development of trust can strengthen mutual identification, and there is a general tendency to trust on the basis of mutual identification.'[67] Trust and collective identities are themselves prompted by the dynamic and positive relationship between structural variables—power and knowledge—and process variables—transactions, international institutions and organizations, and social learning.[68]

Structural variables make security communities possible. In this context, material and ideological resources are power, as is the authority to determine shared meaning and the 'magnetic' attraction that strong, secure, and materially successful states ('core of strength'[69]) exert over relatively weaker states. This attraction arises from weaker states' expectations of the security and economic benefits that can arise from belonging to a community that includes stronger states. Collective knowledge, mainly normative rules about proper behavior in international and domestic affairs, makes possible the development of a regional governance system based on collective identity. Both—power and knowledge—may be considered to be collective resources that create the propensities for the development of security community practices.

Processes, on the other hand, translate material and social structural propensities into practice. To begin with, economic and social transactions are part of the interaction through which broader social identities are created and re-created. International institutions, on the other hand, not only provide monitoring capabilities and help states discover new areas of common interest; by helping establish, articulate, and transmit norms of acceptable and legitimate behavior, they also encourage elites and people in general to consider themselves to be part of a region, thereby building a sense of community and shaping state practices. Finally,

> by promoting the development of shared definitions of security, proper domestic and international action, and regional boundaries, social learning encourages political leaders to see each other as trustworthy. And it also leads people to identify with those who were once on the other side of cognitive divides.[70]

The idea that communication (even communication that is motivated by previous interests), such as debate and persuasion, can be the basis for new bonds and understandings is consistent not only with Deutsch's views of social communication but also with Jürgen Habermas' theory of 'communicative action.'[71] The main idea behind this theory is that social actors, rather than bargaining to achieve the utilities they expect, as in rational choice theory, engage in debate or discourse that helps demonstrate the validity of their arguments and thereby promote collective understanding.[72]

More specifically, according to Thomas Risse,

> communicative behavior oriented toward argumentation, persuasion, and mutual understanding enables and changes social relations among actors. Such discursive processes can also establish a joint definition of the situation and, thus, define in the first place the situational structure and the nature of the collective action problem. Moreover, international negotiators may engage in a moral discourse challenging the validity claims entailed in each other's interests and preferences. Thus, the theory of communicative action abandons the assumptions of 'common knowledge' and of fixed preferences in game theoretical approaches by showing that both are social constructs which can be established in the discursive process.[73]

Communicating and acting, in short, are two sides of the same coin. The key insight for the subject of security communities is that common meanings are necessary for communicative action and, when unavailable, must be socially constructed by institutional and individual agents.

Having identified the main variables that explain the development of security communities, I next turn to two questions that cut to the heart of the security community approach. First, how do people in domestic societies change their identities and preferences?[74] Second, do security communities, once constituted, re-create anarchy in their mutual relations?

With regard to the first question, a change in structural variables may bring domestic societies to learn new 'rules of the game,' dealing mainly with how they should redefine themselves in order to achieve security and economic progress. Moreover, a structural change is likely to empower one set of domestic institutions and elites to the detriment of others. The empowered elites will be in a better position to persuade policymakers that security and economic progress henceforth depend on the adoption of a new social identity and a set of related practices.

For example, Mikhail Gorbachev's decision to implement the momentous changes that led to the end of the Soviet empire and the Cold War was related to his understanding of the Soviet Union's domestic economic constraints as well as to his realization that the country could only gain from linking its fate to a transnational European identity and participating in the activities of multilateral institutions and practices. What prompted this understanding, however, was the continual strengthening of the Western alliance, not only from the military but also from the economic and techno-logical perspective (to the point where the alliance became an indisputable 'core of strength'), and new ideas about international reality (e.g., interde-pendence and 'cooperative security') that Soviet technocrats adopted and which Gorbachev expressed as part of his 'New Thinking.'[75]

Second, as the above example shows, even closed domestic societies need individual and organizational agents to drive home the implications of structural change. Through social–communicative processes, agents concep-tually connect structural causes to what they consider to be desirable effects. Communicative processes involving debate and persuasion are the chief vehicle for constructing a collective transnational shared identity around material and cultural attributes. Moreover, collective understandings are diffused to domestic and societal settings around a would-be region through a dense web of economic and social exchange and international and transna-tional organizations. Initially, domestic elites and societies in general may adopt collective meanings for instrumental reasons only. With the passage of time, however, and, especially with the rise to political power of individuals and groups that have internalized the new ideas (in fact, they probably came to power *because* they adopted these ideas), a new collective identity may become firmly established.

Third, with the intensification of exchange and under the prompting of security community-building institutions, transnational subcommunities—of diplomats, businesspeople, soldiers, academics, etc.—may form and add their input to the communicative processes referred to above. Representing a variety of societal sectors and often intensely involved in state policymaking and implementation, these transnational subcommunities may become the carriers of a collective transnational identity. They may also play a major role in the internalization of new meanings by individuals and institutional routines and may thereby help frame the alternatives entertained by policy-makers and the choices they make.[76]

Finally, when they interact, domestic institutions and elites from different countries come into direct sustained contact and may learn to 'know' each other as trustworthy and as belonging to the same region. As part of the process, they become involved in conceptual bargaining; that is, they bargain not only over the issues on the table but also about the concepts and norms that constitute their social reality. Sometimes they may learn to frame issues in totally new ways and make choices about the material and cultural attributes around which a collective transnational identity might be built.

I now return to the second question, namely, whether security communities can re-create anarchy in their mutual relations. To answer this question, it is essential to bear in mind that, when it comes to security communities, a state-centric logic is limited at best. It is true that: (a) pluralistic security communities are composed of mostly sovereign states; (b) within security communities, (non-military) security dilemmas may still be common and the use of coercive power (other than war) may still occur; and (c) state elites are still the most important agents of security community-building.

On the other hand, security communities are neither military alliances nor collective security systems; nor are they state-like units, only larger. Rather, they are transnational nonterritorial 'cognitive regions' where peaceful change is practiced. Consequently, security communities cannot threaten one another, any more than peaceful interstate relations can be mutually threatening. Moreover, because security communities often have overlapping membership—for example, the Scandinavian countries constitute a security community that is in turn part of the wider Western European security community—it is hard to imagine that their relations could be similar to those of states in an anarchical system. It may help, then, to think of security communities, not as transnational aggregations of state power that are differentiated on spatial or functional lines and can therefore engender anarchy between security communities, but as transnational domains of peaceful practices differentiated by their community meanings and consequently unlikely to engender intercommunity anarchy.

It follows, therefore, that whether security communities are also military alliances is less a function of intercommunity anarchy than of the 'neighborhood' (the strategic environment) where the states organized into security communities happen to 'live.' It would be hard to imagine a Latin American security community—e.g., Argentina, Brazil, Paraguay, and Uruguay—forming a military alliance against the United States and Mexico, another security community.[77] Moreover, there is a military alliance in the Euro-Atlantic space today, not because a security community of Western European and North American states created NATO, but because, in response to the Soviet threat, these states created NATO and then gradually—and in part because of NATO—became a security community.[78]

The conditions for peace: contextual variables that promote the development of security communities

In the last section, I identified material and normative power, knowledge, communicative processes, institutions, and social learning as variables that contribute to the development of collective identities and mutual trust—which in turn drive dependable expectations of peaceful change. In this section, I will start by analyzing conditions that, while not necessary for the development of security communities, may nevertheless play a facilitating role: (1) a higher expected utility from peace than from war; (2) a 'civic culture'; (3) Great Power commitment to the peaceful resolution of disputes; (4) an ethical code; (5) mutual legitimization; and (6) peacemakers. Then I will consider multilateral war-preventing practices that may help avert war and create favorable conditions for the development of dependable expectations of peaceful change.

(1) The development of security communities may be favored where the expected utility of peace exceeds that of war, including victorious war. Technological change, economic development, and a perception of war as inefficient, unnecessary, and normatively unacceptable [79] may lead to what I have elsewhere called 'a peace trap,' in which states, taking everything into consideration, choose peaceful rather than violent means of achieving their goals.[80] For example, nuclear weapons have had a strong influence on expectations of the outcome and efficacy of war and have produced a recognition of the need to cooperate with adversaries (mainly through nuclear arms control).[81] To a large extent, these expectations help explain why the Cold War remained and ended cold.

Also, consistent with liberal theory, since the end of World War II expectations of economic progress have done much to increase the disparity between the expected utilities of peace and war. Ole Waever, for example, has persuasively shown that one of the factors that encouraged Western Europe to become a tightly coupled security community was the evolution of a practice and discourse of international politics that gave greater prominence to economic than to security and defense issues.[82] Moreover, according to John Mueller, F. H. Hinsley, and Michael Howard, people attach a smaller social value to war than they did, for example, before World War I, when war was 'almost universally considered an acceptable, perhaps an inevitable, and for many people a desirable way of settling international differences.'[83]

The point is not that the ascription of a higher expected utility to peace than to war is a necessary or sufficient condition for the development of security communities. It may only explain the development of a 'non-war community.' But if people come to expect war only as an unwanted event that is caused by the predatory practices of a surviving minority of predatory states or breaks out only when all efforts to avert hostilities have failed, the higher expected utility of peace may be conducive to the promotion of social, economic, and cultural transactions, the legitimization and strengthening of multilateral institutional means of conflict prevention and resolution, and the development of a climate in which states redefine their understanding of international reality and their social identities and interests.

(2) Peace among democratic states has become almost axiomatic, even though, as I argued above, when scholars refer to the 'democratic peace' they do not mean a state of peace, but only the absence of war among democracies.[84] Liberal democracy, however, may help create a favorable context for the evolution of security communities. To see this, we must take the liberal system of values that sustains democratic practices and institutions not as a deterministic variable, as 'democratic peace' scholars usually do, but as primarily the historical development and diffusion of a transnational *'civic culture'*[85] that, cutting across national borders, becomes an identity marker and indicator of reciprocal peaceful intentions.

A democratic civic culture encourages the creation of strong civil societies—and of transnational networks and processes—which promote community bonds and a common identity through the relatively free interpenetration of societies, particularly the movement and exchange of people, goods, and ideas. For example, strong civil societies greatly facilitate the spread of practices that promote human rights and environmental protection. These, in turn, help produce and reinforce a collective social identity and security community bonds. Moreover, social networks constituted around liberal norms facilitate the transfer of democratic norms and practices to societies that lack them.[86]

(3) Security communities are more likely to develop and remain stable when 'outside' Great Powers (we have already seen that security communities tend to develop around 'cores of strength,' which may include Great Powers) are committed to the peaceful resolution of conflicts.[87] Otherwise, their predatory practices may interfere with the proliferation of regional economic exchanges, the work of regional international institutions, and regional social learning processes; in the long run this can only endanger the development and stability of security communities. While it is possible that real or perceived outside military threats from Great Powers may trigger the development of security communities—for example, the Soviet Union *vis-à-vis* Western Europe and China *vis-à-vis* ASEAN—over the long term the threat and use of organized violence against some or all of the members of a security community may actually undermine its survival. To assess the future of ASEAN as a security community, therefore, we should keep an eye on China's behavior toward its members and on whether they manage to bind China to multilateral security practices and institutions.[88]

(4) Despite all the horror stories of the twentieth century, Dorothy Jones maintains that what she calls the 'world of the warlord states' has increasingly been challenged by the development of a 'Code of Peace' or set of international standards of peaceful behavior.[89] She claims (and I agree) that the August 1975 Helsinki Final Act—which spawned the continuing Conference on Security and Cooperation in Europe (CSCE)—did much to

strengthen the 'Code of Peace.'[90] Although history has repeatedly shown that 'codes of peace' may prove insufficient to prevent war, they can nevertheless create favorable conditions for the development of security communities. Moreover, as in the case of the CSCE (which in 1995 became the Organization for Security and Cooperation in Europe (OSCE)), a 'code' may be merely a legal or political representation of the constitutive rules that make up a collective identity.

The Helsinki Final Act, which was signed by all European countries (except for Albania), the Soviet Union, the United States, and Canada, comprised ten principles of legitimate international behavior (e.g., respect for territorial integrity and the political independence of states) and domestic political conduct (e.g., respect for human rights and fundamental freedoms). With the addition by the Charter of Paris (1990) and subsequent documents of important stipulations about democracy, the rule of law, and human rights, what began as a regional code of conduct turned into a constitutive normative structure for a security community expected to develop in the area between Vancouver and Vladivostok.[91]

The 'OSCE region' has not yet become a security community; I doubt that it will any time soon. In spite of the ethnic conflicts now raging in its domain, however, and despite the fact that two steps forward have sometimes been followed by one step backward, OSCE injunctions have helped increase the interdependence of East and West and transactions between them, thereby laying the foundation for a liberal transnational collective understanding in the OSCE region. To a large extent, whether Eastern European states are accepted as members of the European Union (EU) and the North Atlantic Treaty Organization (NATO) will depend on the extent to which they internalize the OSCE 'code of peace,' which now includes, for example, the innovative 'accountability norm' whereby OSCE states are accountable to one another and to the OSCE community for what they do to their own citizens.[92] Thomas Buergenthal captured the subtle but crucial essence of the OSCE 'Code of Peace' when he asserted that it can be compared to those national constitutions that, without being legally binding or enforceable in the courts, serve as the normative source of a country's public order.[93]

(5) The development of a security community also requires states wishing to become part of it to see one another—and the future community—as legitimate. It is the community's legitimacy in the eyes of its members that, more than anything else, explains the workings of a regional governance system based on collective identity. At the same time, the conditions in which members of a security community view each other as part of a community and are given certain rights, obligations, and duties are contingent on their ability to abide by the community's constitutive principles.[94]

This explains why the EU and the Euro-Atlantic security community, as represented by NATO, have extended 'probationary' status to Eastern European states that wish to join them. The behavior of the probationers is constantly scrutinized for indications that they can be legitimate members of these communities. The main purpose, for example, of NATO's Partnership for Peace is to transform (teach and socialize) some of the former Communist states of Eastern Europe into legitimate members of the Euro-Atlantic security community. As far as I know, nothing in realist theory says that states wishing to enter an alliance with other states must transform the prospective partners' domestic institutions and practices. NATO's enlargement, therefore, is not only the strengthening of an already strong military alliance, but also the expansion eastward of a veteran and generally stable security community.

(6) Although particular individuals cannot be conceived as a necessary, let alone a sufficient, condition for the development of security communities, I nevertheless include peacemakers in my list of the conditions for peace, because resourceful, powerful, and sometimes courageous and visionary leaders can create propitious circumstances for the development of security communities. In other words, it takes agency to create common purpose, collective identity, and mutual trust.[95] Moreover, it takes leaders who know they can be trusted to trust others as well.[96] More importantly, it takes peacemakers—whence my epigraph from Yitzhak Rabin—to start communicative processes in conditions of mistrust and adversity; in the long run, trust may spill over to the elites and the masses and thus be conducive to the construction of security communities.

Before ending this section, I would like to refer to war-preventing practices that help generate a propitious setting for the development of security communities. Nuclear arms control practices, for example, now widespread around the world, may help states and societies in conflict initiate communicative processes that create a common ground for evaluation and action. Elsewhere I have argued that the practice of nuclear arms control was beneficial not so much in limiting weapons, in a formal technical sense, but primarily because it engendered international cooperative processes that helped the superpowers develop a coordination game and discover the extent to which its symbolic contents suggested compromises, limits, and regulations.[97] To some extent, and beyond their specific functions—such as conflict prevention and resolution—multilateral diplomacy and UN global peacekeeping activities engage contending states in social communicative and exchange processes that augment the future possibility of peace.[98] Particularly noteworthy are the practices of 'cooperative security,' such as confidence-building measures, which are increasingly being adopted in Europe, Southeast Asia, and Latin America. This demilitarized concept of security

> has resulted in imbuing security with political and human dimensions, and in basing security on confidence and cooperation, the elaboration of peaceful means of dispute settlement between states, the consolidation

of justice and democracy in civil society, and the advancement of human freedom and rights, including national minority rights.[99]

Thus, while arms control and cooperative security practices cannot, in and of themselves, help constitute a state of peace, they can do three things. First, they can promote communicative processes that help states discover their affinities and common interests. Second, they can help keep regional conflicts at bay and facilitate the development of transactions, institutions, and learning processes that are conducive to the development of security communities. Third, they can impede the spread of instability and predatory practices to regions that already enjoy a measure of dependable expectations of peaceful change. Thus, for example, in the absence of urgent and effective arms control and confidence-building measures, the nuclear tests by India and Pakistan may not only bring disaster to these countries but may also unleash a proliferation chain reaction that would negatively affect existing security communities (such as the EU) and prevent the formation of new ones (in Asia and the Middle East, for example).

By way of example: constructing a Mediterranean region

There is no inevitable trend in world affairs toward security communities; as we have seen, people are enjoying a state of peace in only a few regions. In less 'fortunate' parts of the world, such as Africa, South Asia, Central Asia, and North Asia, security communities are less likely to develop any time soon. And although Israel, the Palestinians, and Arab countries have flirted with ending their protracted conflict, the conditions for peace in the Middle East are weak or nonexistent and a state of peace may still be decades away.

On the other hand, the Euro-Atlantic community is expanding eastward, while the North and South American security communities may yet become a single Western Hemisphere security community. Moreover, in spite (or because) of internal and external sources of instability, the ASEAN countries have been keeping on course toward becoming a security community. A weak but noticeable effort is under way to socially construct a Mediterranean regional identity that may in the long run be critical for what happens in the Middle East. Owing to the present and future importance of the Mediterranean area, I will focus on this case.

It is not implausible to suggest that the Mediterranean basin (Southern Europe, North Africa, and the Middle East) may soon become one of the world's most strategically important and contentious regions. Straddling two of the deepest divides of our era—that between the West and the Muslim world, and that between the (prosperous) North and the (destitute) South—the Mediterranean basin harbors some of the most dangerous threats to contemporary international security, including the proliferation of weapons of mass destruction, international terrorism, internal and external low-level warfare, interstate military conflict, and—no less serious—the drug trade, uncontrolled migration, and unsustainable development. As one of Samuel Huntington's critical areas, where the 'fault lines' of the 'Clash of Civilizations' are located,[100] the Mediterranean region provides a 'hard case' for assessing the conditions for and state of peace on the eve of the new millennium.

Thus it may be a sign of the times that, when Western states, especially the members of the EU, felt threatened by instability in the South, they chose, not to send in (or threaten to send in) the tanks, build a new system of alliances, or create a collective security system, but to attempt to extend the European area of stability southward by creating a Mediterranean region and identity. To jump-start this process, European governments, EU institutions, the OSCE, the Western European Union (WEU), the Council of Europe (C of E), NATO (to some extent), and a large number of private nongovernmental organizations began to promote: (a) increased economic and social interactions around the Mediterranean (for example, by means of free-trade zones); (b) multilateral institutional dialogues, 'track-two diplomacy,' and confidence-building measures; (c) a plethora of relations across civil societies between business, professional, and cultural groups; and (d) a long but nevertheless necessary social learning process.[101]

So far, however, this attempt has been impeded not only by violent conflict in the Middle East and Algeria, but also by Muslim states' suspicions that lurking behind the Mediterranean initiative are Western attempts to impose a hegemonic regional identity. Moreover, owing to the cleavages referred to above, the process of building a Mediterranean regional identity is likely to be much more difficult than any previous attempts at pluralistic regional integration such as the EU and ASEAN.[102] Thus, while the process of building a Mediterranean region is still in its infancy, the odds may already favor a 'clash of civilizations.' For this reason it is interesting to analyze the conditions for and state of peace in this area.

Past efforts to create a Mediterranean 'region' were severely limited or failed altogether. The first multilateral effort was launched in 1972 by the foreign ministers of Italy, Libya, Malta, and Tunisia.[103] They held a series of meetings aimed at establishing cooperative programs in communications, tourism, fishing, and trade. The failure to attract other participants, however, kept such cooperation from materializing. In 1975, the predecessor to the OSCE, the CSCE, identified a Mediterranean component of its program; throughout the 1970s and 1980s it convened regional experts in economics, science, culture, and the environment to explore cooperative efforts that would build mutual trust and contribute to regional stability.[104] The meetings accomplished little, however, and did not attract the attention of the United States, who focused primarily on the East–West conflict. The Euro-Arab Dialogue began in 1974, in the wake of the oil crisis, in order to institute cooperation between members of the European Community and members of the Arab League. These efforts, too, remained unproductive because of the Cold War, Iraq's invasion of Kuwait in 1990, and the Arab League's condition, rejected by the Europeans, that the Palestinian issue be included on the agenda. The Mediterranean Action Plan, formulated within the framework of the 1976 Barcelona Convention to combat pollution of the Mediterranean Sea, was indeed successful. But the focus of cooperation has remained limited to technical environmental issues, with no 'spillover' effects on other areas of concern.

In a postwar world dominated by East–West confrontation, the creation of a Mediterranean region of cooperation and stability was a low priority for the Great Powers. The end of the Cold War however, promised to eliminate the obstacles to regional cooperation. Accordingly, the notion of a Conference on Security and Cooperation in the Mediterranean (CSCM) became popular. Like earlier efforts, the aim was to boost regional economic development and social conditions through cooperation and to increase regional trust and transparency.[105] The end of the Cold War created fertile ground for the OSCE, WEU, and C of E to become involved in regional activities to promote trust. In 1990–91, several southern European countries proposed a plan for a Western Mediterranean CSCM; in 1994, NATO formulated a Mediterranean policy and promised to work with nonmembers to strengthen regional stability.

Encouraged by progress in the Arab–Israeli peace process, the EU became formally involved in the project to create regional stability with the establishment of the Euro-Mediterranean Partnership in 1994. In 1995, a Euro-Mediterranean Conference was convened in Barcelona to establish a framework for the region, with its population of 700 million people in twenty-seven countries along the shores of the Mediterranean Sea. In addition to the fifteen EU states, the Euro-Mediterranean Partnership (EMP) includes Algeria, Cyprus, Egypt, Israel, Jordan, Lebanon, Malta, Morocco, Syria, Tunisia, Turkey, and the Palestinian Authority. The political element of the Barcelona declaration includes a list of principles concerning respect for democracy and the rule of law, human rights, the right of self-determination, non-interference in the internal affairs of other states, and the peaceful resolution of disputes. It also stipulates cooperation to combat terrorism. On the economic front, the Barcelona document provides for a regional partnership to promote economic development by means of a free-trade zone to be created by the year 2010.[106] The objectives of the Barcelona Declaration were supposed to be confirmed by twenty-seven Mediterranean countries in Malta in 1997. But the stalled Middle East peace process overshadowed that meeting and cast grave doubts on the success of the EMP.

The EMP and related efforts have in large part been about helping Mediterranean basin countries adapt to economic globalization and protecting European states from potential sources of regional instability and insecurity arising from the South.[107] Culture, nonetheless, permeates the entire initiative.[108] By culture, I mean neither what Huntington meant in 'The Clash of Civilizations' nor a romantic view of Mediterranean cultural attributes—olives, wine, sunshine, and gorgeous beaches. Rather, I have in mind the development of a relatively new type of preventive diplomatic practice that depends for its success on the political and social engineering of a Mediterranean 'we-feeling' or collective social identity. Thus, while it is true that the EMP is mainly driven by short-term incentives, such as material interests and a perceived mutual threat, the long-term interest behind the initiative is to catalyze conditions that may help bring about a future state of peace in the region.

Because few if any of the conditions mentioned in the previous section exist in the Mediterranean area, the challenge of the ongoing Mediterranean 'dialogue' is to socially *engineer them*. To do this successfully, however, greater efforts must be devoted to: (a) providing economic incentives so that peace will have a higher expected utility than war; (b) seeking the support of the US (which seldom buys into the type of diplomacy associated with the EMP) and a commitment from that country and Russia to the peaceful resolution of disputes in the area; (c) developing transnational and international social networks[109] to promote the emergence of a Mediterranean civic culture based on values that both Northern and Southern countries can live with, such as sustainable development and the rule of law (which allows for differences in political regimes); (d) investing resources and building strong multilateral institutions, in order to raise the regional political stakes to the point that it becomes imperative for political actors in the Middle East and North Africa to settle their differences; (e) instituting confidence-building measures to promote the development of mutual legitimacy and a consensual Mediterranean identity; and (f) agreeing on the basic normative or 'constitutional' principles—such as sovereignty, nonintervention, the rule of law, and sustainable development—around which shared practices can be constituted.

To sum up, behind the EMP and related efforts lies the haunting (some would say discouraging) idea that the most promising—perhaps the only— way to achieve long-term security, economic welfare, political stability, and peace in the Mediterranean area is neither an elaborate system of alliances or collective security system, nor a functional scheme of economic integration, but the socio-cultural process of constructing a region. The challenges are immense; it will probably take decades to construct a Mediterranean region. Nevertheless, as long as other security practices are unavailable or impracticable there, the only alternative left for socially constructing the conditions for peace is Huntington's 'clash of civilizations.'

Beyond the eighty years' crisis

Since Carr referred to the twenty years' crisis, immense changes have occurred in International Relations, notably the victory of liberal democracies over fascism and Communism, economic globalization, multilateralism, the widening gap between North and South, the development of nuclear weapons and other weapons of mass destruction, and the emergence of international human-rights and environmental regimes. These changes, however, have done little to overcome what Carr called the crisis of democracy, the crisis of self-determination, and the moral crisis. Many states have yet to become (liberal) democracies. The contradictions between self-determination and the sovereign integrity of states have worsened since the end of the Cold War. And, at the global level, we are very far from having found a common moral purpose around which to build 'the state of peace.' The 'twenty years' crisis' became 'the eighty years' crisis.' Moreover, the eighty years' crisis has probably become more intractable, because of: (a) primordial primitivism; (b) technological and integration imperatives; (c) remnants of 'warlord' organization and doctrine; (d) economic inequality; and (e) unsustainable development.

It would go beyond the scope of this chapter to analyze these threats to peace in depth; hence I will conclude with a few words about how they are endangering the state of and conditions for peace, supplemented by remarks about positive conditions that may help international society overcome these threats.

By *primordial primitivism* I mean the return, mainly since the Cold War, of nationalist ideologies that glorify the restoration of an ostensible 'golden age,' the triumph of the ethnic 'tribe' over other 'tribes,' and the use of religion as a 'rationalizing' alternative to secular and modern nationalism. In some parts of the world, including Europe, primordial primitivism and the ethnic conflicts fueled by it are threatening the state of and conditions for peace. Bosnia, Chechnya, Kosovo, and Hebron—all raise doubts about the ability of peacemakers and international institutions to promote the conditions for and state of peace and constitute warning signs for existing security communities.

Another dangerous threat to peace comes from what I call a *technological and integration imperative*, which is not unrelated to primordial primitivism. I mean the peril posed by the ultramodern technologies in the hands of the leaders of some states that lack domestic integration and evince an inability and/or unwillingness to integrate into international society and a concomitant pattern of uninhibited bellicose behavior.

Yet another threat to the state of and conditions for peace comes from the fact that practices of peaceful change, such as arms control and cooperative security, have not replaced what Dorothy Jones called 'warlord' organization practices and doctrines.[110] Even in the most stable security communities, military establishments and doctrines are changing much more slowly than regional economic and political behavior and constitute a latent threat to dependable expectations of peaceful change.

The gravest threat of all, however, one that requires global cooperation to find adequate and equitable solutions, stems from the economic inequality between the North and South. In other words, the growing poverty, misery, hunger, and, most importantly, frustration of the less-developed countries that are home to a large fraction of the world's population interfere with social communicative processes and prevent the development of mutual trust both within underdeveloped regions and across the North–South divide. Moreover, unsustainable development, still prevalent in most of the world, coupled with unsustainable population growth, are ticking bombs that threaten to set off the wars of the next century.

To help overcome or at least manage some of these threats and facilitate the development of new security communities and strengthening of existing ones, we need to encourage: (a) the practice of establishing the rights and obligations of states and peoples by means of *politically* binding regional codes of conduct; (b) the principle of multiculturalism; and (c) managed globalization and sustainable development.

The promotion, negotiation, and establishment of *politically* binding codes of conduct, such as the Helsinki Final Act and related injunctions, may be crucial for alleviating the ongoing eighty years' crisis and creating favorable conditions for the development of security communities. These regional 'constitutions' or 'codes of peace' should not be seen as coming at the expense of the global constitutive norms, especially sovereignty, which constitute the identities of states *qua* states, but as complementary to them. Regional codes of conduct are constitutive only of privileged regional communities (privileged because they have developed a system of regional governance) and of the social identities of people living in them.

To encourage the development of security communities, regional codes of conduct should include the 'accountability norm,' make the rule of law a *sine qua non* principle of regional sociability, and—following Carr's suggestion of more than sixty years ago—consecrate not only the mutual *rights* of states (e.g., territorial integrity) and of peoples (e.g., human rights), but also the mutual *obligations* of states (e.g., protecting national minorities and preventing transboundary pollution) and peoples (e.g., respecting other peoples' right to self-determination).

The state of peace will also be enhanced by the promotion—through domestic (education) and international (multilateral diplomacy) means—of multicultural principles that encourage people to view nations not as 'real' but as 'imagined communities.'[111] 'One hundred and fifty years of civil peace in multicultural Switzerland make my point.'[112] In other words, taking national identities in a more plastic, if not socially constructed, sense should promote the idea that peoples of several cultures can self-determine and aspire to build up their shared state. Ernst Haas has shown that, while liberal decision-making procedures are better equipped than other types to accommodate multiculturalism, in practice liberal nation-states have still not learned to cope with it.[113]

Finally, to deal adequately with the pressures caused by economic globalization and unsustainable development, international society must develop a practice of preventing and managing global and regional economic crises. By managing economic crises, I do not necessarily mean interference with global and regional markets, but the development of improved routines of international cooperation that are better suited to foresee, prevent, and manage the undesirable effects of globalization on individual states and security communities. Concomitantly, the strengthening of the practice of sustainable development may not only help states and societies coordinate their development and environmental policies, but may also, and more importantly, become an important resource for the social construction of transnational collective identities and thus of security communities.[114]

As we approach the new millennium, and in light of my analysis of the state of and conditions for peace, I find no better way to conclude this article than by referring to Carr's final statement in *The Conditions of Peace*, which is still relevant today, both morally and practically: 'The future lies with those who can resolutely turn their back on [the old world] and face the new world with understanding, courage and imagination.'[115]

Part V

Identity and peace in the Middle East

9 A Mediterranean canon and an Israeli prelude to long-term peace

This short essay argues that the construction of a Mediterranean region—which will require Mediterranean countries, including Israel, to change how they identify both themselves and their place—can help institutionalize security community practices in the region. Although it cannot do much to achieve a short-term solution of the Israeli–Palestinian conflict, the development of a Mediterranean regional identity is essential for laying the long-term foundations of stable peace in the region. The discouraging events that have taken place in the Middle East in the last few years appear to render this argument utterly idealistic. I contend, however, that, not despite, but because of these events, developing a Mediterranean identity is imperative, especially if the alternative is a 'clash of civilizations.' The linkage between identity and peace hypothesized here reaffirms the book's contention that the key to understanding international practice—here regional practice—lies neither at the individual level nor at the systemic level, but at the level of communities of practice.

Unpublished manuscript, 2001. Appeared as a Jean Monnet Working Paper in Comparative and International Politics at the University of Catania, Italy

A canon is a piece of music in which a single theme is played repeatedly. The repeated theme that I will weave into this essay is 'pluralistic security communities,' that is, 'transnational regions composed of sovereign states whose people are integrated to the point that they maintain dependable expectations of peaceful change.'[1] Some examples of pluralistic security communities include Scandinavia, the North American Free Trade Association (NAFTA) region, the European Union (EU), the Euro-Atlantic community, and, to a lesser extent, the southern cone of Latin America and the Association of Southeast Asian Nations (ASEAN). There is no chance whatsoever that a pluralistic security community, based on shared culture and identity, will develop in the Middle East in the near future. Because this is where most of the remaining realists in the world live and act, liberal ideas about the construction of regional communities will have a hard time penetrating and succeeding. In this neck of the woods, political actors will continue for the foreseeable future to rely on military deterrence and, if all else fails, on force.

Yet culture and identity are at the heart of the Middle East conflict and must consequently be part of its long-term solution. By culture, I mean neither Samuel Huntington's reified view of culture[2] nor a romantic view of cultural attributes. Rather, I have in mind collective understandings, including those of self and others. The security community solution, which is viable only in the long term, when warring parties have more or less begun to resolve their most acute grievances, associates regional security and peace with regional integration and the accompanying development of regional identities and a common political culture. It thus requires the development of a relatively new type of diplomatic practice whose success depends on the political and social engineering of regional identities.

I contend that the construction of a Mediterranean region—which would require Mediterranean nations, including Israel, to change their identification not only of self, but also of place—serves the goal of institutionalizing security community practices in the region and thus, ultimately, achieving long-term peace. But it cannot do much to achieve a short-term solution to the Israeli–Palestinian conflict, let alone to stabilize the current situation. If you wish to apply European experience to today's Middle East, do not think EU; think, rather, July 1914. If, however, out of the rubble, or, let us hope, out of renewed common sense, we would like to turn a truce into peace, a *sulha* into *salaam*, then constructing a Mediterranean regional identity is the key. Why start now, if I am referring only to a long-term solution? Because, if not now, when? And if not us, who?

If the effort to construct a Mediterranean region did not exist, we would probably have to invent it. It exists, however, not only in the minds of academics, but also out there, as part of the Barcelona Process, mainly in the growing efforts of voluntary civil-society networks. This solution involves creating new Mediterranean narratives and myths, but also using the existing Mediterranean 'surplus of identity,'[3] which goes back many centuries. Of course, this surplus of identity is partly a myth and the Mediterranean Sea plays the role of 'imaginary link.' But isn't this the whole point about how identities develop?

Why should Israel, the Palestinians, and Arab states be interested in the development of a Mediterranean identity? The answer is peace; peace requires not only common trust, but also the development of a shared identity of place. A Mediterranean identity will help Israelis, Palestinians, and at least moderate Arab states jointly imagine that, as members of the same regional group, they inhabit a common space, share interests, and have much to lose from war.

First movement: *adagio*

The Barcelona Process, or Euro-Mediterranean Partnership (EMP), is a multilateral framework of political, economic, and social relations. Launched in 1995, it involves 700 million people in twenty-seven countries around the Mediterranean. In addition to the fifteen EU states, the EMP includes Algeria, Cyprus, Egypt, Israel, Jordan, Lebanon, Malta, Morocco, Syria, Tunisia, Turkey, and the Palestinian Authority. Like the 1975 Helsinki Final Act, which set in motion the Conference on Security and Cooperation in Europe, on which the Barcelona Process was modeled, the EMP established three baskets. These deal with: (a) security on the basis of mutual confidence and partnership; (b) a zone of shared prosperity through economic integration; and (c) a rapprochement between peoples through social and cultural links and the creation of a Mediterranean civil society.

Realist observers will argue that the Barcelona Process refers primarily to one of the EU's leading foreign policy projects and one of its main Middle East policy mechanisms. The EU was moved to start the Barcelona Process for purely instrumental reasons: (a) fear of immigration from the South and of xenophobia in the North; (b) perceived security threats arising from the South, such as terrorism and weapons of mass destruction; and (c) anxiety about the growth of militant Islamic fundamentalism. The EU also regards the Barcelona Process as a strategy to compete with other trade blocs without having to invite non-European Mediterranean countries to join the EU. The EU is saying, in effect 'take this money, the norms, and the practices, go create your own region, and give us your stability.' To the South, however, the Barcelona Process has so far meant at best euros and at worst a neocolonialist plot. More liberally oriented observers would add that the Barcelona Process is a liberal attempt to bring about regional security through partnership and mutual confidence.

I would like to add another point of view; namely, that the Barcelona Process is also a laboratory where one of the outstanding experiments in International Relations may be taking place. I am referring to *the invention of a region that does not yet exist and to the social engineering of a regional identity that rests neither on blood nor on religion, but on voluntary civil-society networks and civic beliefs.* The very long-term aims of this experiment are to construct in the Mediterranean region a security community whose practices are synonyms for peace. Thus, the Mediterranean concept is about building future peace by building present community links. By peace I mean neither 'cold peace' (an oxymoron) nor 'warm peace' (it does not exist), but a collective cognitive inability to imagine war as a real alternative in the settlement of political conflicts.

It is no wonder that the Barcelona Process looks so idealistic to most Israelis, especially since the start of the al-Aqsa Intifada (September 2000), and that tough-minded security people dismiss it as the counterpart of chat forums on the Internet. The Barcelona Process is idealistic, however, not in the pie-in-the-sky, 'new Middle East,' everything-is-possible kind of way, but in the philosophical sense that ideas help construct social reality. By way of reinventing who we are, who is 'we,' and where we are, I am referring to an experiment—which no doubt will take decades—in redefining security interests, political power, and rational courses of action. In fact, its chances of success are so low that, if forced to make a bet, I would lay my money on Huntington's 'clash of civilizations.' Yet precisely because of this, I nonetheless pledge my intellect and my commitment to its alternative, a convergence of civilizations, by means of security community-building processes and practices.

Second movement: *andante*—more on security communities

The concept of security community goes back to Karl Deutsch, who distinguished between 'amalgamated' and 'pluralistic' security communities.[4] In an amalgamated security community, such as the United States, two or more states formally merge into an expanded state. A pluralistic security community retains the legal independence of separate states but integrates them to the point that the units entertain 'dependable expectations of peaceful change.' A pluralistic security community develops when its members possess a compatibility of core values derived from common institutions and mutual responsiveness—a matter of mutual identity and loyalty—and a 'we-feeling' among states.

Although security communities first develop due to factors that encourage states to orient themselves in each other's direction, security communities are not spontaneous creations. Rather, it is the dynamic and positive relationship among power, ideas, increased interactions, international organization, and social learning that is the wellspring of both mutual trust and collective identity—which, in turn, are the proximate necessary conditions for the development of dependable expectations of peaceful change.

To grasp what security communities are about, it is important to understand, first, that community 'we-feeling' is not only in people's heads, but is also institutionalized in community practices. Second, security communities are not just a geographic place, but also a representation in the material world of peaceful expectations. In other words, peace is an ongoing condition in which the peoples and states that constitute pluralistic security communities find themselves.

Third, security communities are a mechanism of international security that is different from and in some ways antithetical to the balance-of-power mechanism. Achieving security by means of the balance of power justifies the use of force and deterrence; but a security community mechanism enables states, thanks to shared norms and identities, to become secure in relation to one another. They can thus rely on a different and more benign set of practices, such as dialogue and persuasion. Within security communities, then, security seems to be related not only to how many tanks and missiles a state has in relation to other states, but also to whether the states inhabit a common space characterized by common values and norms. Because the shared meanings around which identities become fixed are usually those of materially powerful states, power plays a major role in security communities. This role may be understood as a magnetic attraction of periphery states to the core.

Shared identities that produce 'we-feeling,' however, must be learned. In other words, only those states that learn how to achieve and maintain a 'we-feeling' develop into security communities. Thus learning, not balancing, becomes part of the mechanism of change; in other words, 'a change of change.' By learning I do not mean exclusively the internalizing of some idea or belief by individuals. I also mean an active process of collective redefinition and interpretation of reality, which, based on new causal and normative knowledge, becomes institutionalized and thus has practical effects.

Third movement: *crescendo*—incentives

The experiment in long-term security community-building around the Mediterranean will be facilitated, first, by the region's geo-strategic and economic importance. Straddling two of the deepest divides of our era—that between the West and the Muslim world and that between the prosperous North and the destitute South—the Mediterranean harbors some of the greatest dangers for regional and global security. This is why, in order to deal with these dangers, and realizing that sending in the tanks (against whom?), building a new system of alliances (with whom?), or creating a collective security system (for what?) would not do, the EU chose to extend its area of stability southward and promote Mediterranean pluralistic integration. The emergence of the EU as a major player in world politics is another facilitating factor. As the EU consolidates its common foreign and security policy and institutions, it is likely to redouble its efforts to engage Mediterranean partner states in cooperative measures. This may help exert pressure on the United States to cooperate with Europe over the Mediterranean, without, of course, neglecting NATO and its own 'Mediterranean Dialogue.'

In the long term, however, there are other and more fundamental changes that might facilitate Mediterranean pluralistic integration. For example, despite the fact that the state is here to stay, state practices and identities are nonetheless changing; for example, human rights, environmentalism, and multilateral diplomacy. Becoming part of 'who we are,' as opposed to 'who they are,' these practices are beginning to shape new state identities. Moreover, changes in the scope and depth of interaction and interdependencies, along with new technologies such as the Internet, facilitate the creation of transnational society, networks, and communities, which, in turn, help produce changes in state practices and identity. This is also true with the increasing globalization of trade, finance, and labor markets, despite its corrosive and disintegrating effects. Collective identities are also on the move; for example, a change in collective identities in Europe and Southeast Asia is engendering new security practices based on inclusion rather than on exclusion, on persuasion rather than on deterrence. And regions are also changing. ASEAN and the Asia-Pacific? These regions did not exist forty years ago. Where is Mexico? It moved a decade ago from Central to North

America. And where is Europe or Australia? Regional borders seem to be characterized not only by geography but also by shared identity.

Fourth movement: *largo*—constraints

The Barcelona Process is a 'hard case' of regional integration for many reasons. First, conventional wisdom suggests that the fate of the Barcelona Process is tied to the fate of the Middle East conflict. With the end of the Oslo peace process, after only seven years, the 'spirit of Barcelona' is almost gone. Second, there are numerous other conflicts in the Mediterranean, such as the Algerian conflict, Greek–Turkish relations, North–South economic gaps, and stereotypical reciprocal images of the West and the Muslim states. In addition, international terrorism increasingly threatens European and Middle Eastern states and their citizens. Thus, because cultural and political differences and economic inequalities in the Mediterranean are so explosive, a Mediterranean integration process will be much more difficult than the integration of Europe or even that in the Asia-Pacific region, where national cultural differences are smaller and less explosive. Third, the poor and predominantly Muslim states in Northern Africa and the Middle East are deeply suspicious of Western attempts to impose 'a regional identity' on them. Many in these states believe that Western security concerns are unjustified and view the attempt at 'region-building' as a threatening neocolonial machination. Fourth, many of these states are also torn by internal schisms and by blurred territorial definitions. Their very existence is tenuous and their own national identities are uncertain. It is questionable whether, without a secure national identity, these states can assume the regional identity believed to be necessary for regional security.[5]

Fifth, since September 11, 2001, when Al Qaeda struck at the heart of the United States, fighting terrorism has become the main focus of international security; it is doubtful whether cooperative security processes, such as the Barcelona Process, will be able to withstand the pressure exerted by the global war on terrorism. Sixth, in recent years Europe has reacted to increased immigration from Mediterranean Arab states with heightened xenophobia and a shift toward the right. This trend runs counter to attempts to build a partnership with Mediterranean Arab states. Finally, the Barcelona Process has focused much more on form and procedure than on content.

To become energized again, therefore, the Barcelona Process will require at least the renewal of the peace process in the Middle East. The Barcelona Process will also have to be endowed with new shared content and meaning, which can result only from a fundamental change in the attitudes and behavior, not only of non-European partner states, including Israel, but also of the EU. In other words, the Euro-Mediterranean partnership must give a new meaning to the concept of partnership and endeavor to avoid being mistaken for either a Western (and Northern) hegemonic design or a Southern initiative to impose a new economic order on the North. In

Southeast Asia, for example, where ASEAN political elites have begun to change the way they understand security and their concept of 'home,' they are discovering that it is imperative to their security and welfare to 'co-bind' their destinies into larger political entities that do not come at the expense of their cultural identities and allegiances.

Fifth movement: *pianissimo*—Israel and the Mediterranean region

What can Israel gain from a change of identities of self and place around the Mediterranean Sea?

(1) A Euro-Mediterranean region may be one solution for Israel's identity conflicts between Arabs and Jews and between Ashkenazi and Sephardi Jews. A Mediterranean identity links East and West and offers an alternative to Israel's troubled belonging to the 'Middle East.' Sephardi Jews would be able to feel at home with this identity, but so would Ashkenazim. Mediterranean culture and identity can also serve as a bridge between Israeli and Arab cultures and societies.[6] In other words, this identity provides Israelis (including Israeli Arabs) and Arabs the chance to belong to the same cognitive region, where, for many centuries, Arabs and Jews cooperated.

(2) The Barcelona Process may also offer the Arabs a partnership with Europe, which traditionally has been closer to the Arab position. It may also allow Europe to ease Arab fears of Israel's alleged attempts to achieve regional economic hegemony.

(3) Mediterranean integration may also be instrumental in promoting agreement on a legitimate post-peace settlement regional order. This means dealing not only with issues of material power stratification, but also with the principles on which a regional peace should rest, which are critical for Arab states, in general, and for Egypt (which has regional hegemonic pretensions), in particular. Thus, for example, the (currently frozen) Barcelona Process initiative to institute a Charter for Peace and Stability in the Mediterranean, even if not legally binding, could affect the partner states' public policies and thus become a basis for starting a dialogue on a postwar Middle East order.

(4) The Barcelona Process could also provide Israel and Arab countries with a useful venue for getting involved in multilateral practices, such as human rights, arms control, confidence-building measures, and the environment.

(5) The Barcelona Process has already started to promote the creation of civil-society networks of businesspeople, academics, artists, and the media, which are beginning to set in motion the wheels of learning in the Mediterranean. These transnational communities are encouraging the development of regional practices as well as the long-term transformation of Mediterranean identities.

(6) The Barcelona Process also creates an opportunity for building bridges between Islam and the West.

(7) The Barcelona Process is a vehicle for Israel to become economically integrated with Europe in ways that may be less threatening to Arab countries.

(8) Finally, the Barcelona Process may be able to socialize non-democratic states to democratic institutions and promote a shared understanding of the rule of law and of the rules that promote peaceful change.

Epilogue: hopefully, not a *requiem*

If, in the midst of a war between Israelis and Palestinians, all this sounds idealistic, that is because we seldom look beyond the social structures that constitute our identities and practices. We are so much prisoners of our own classifications that we do not realize that the hard material realities of our conflict only partly determine our needs, practices, and public policies. Collective knowledge, especially identities, does the rest. This is why I have not considered whether to employ rubber bullets or one-ton bombs in the Intifada, or discussed ways to secure a cease-fire or beef up Israel's deterrence. Rather, because of, and not despite, current events, I have referred to learning—learning how to construe social reality, including collective identities, differently, and learning how to act on a new social reality. To the pundits who remain skeptical I say, following philosopher Charles Taylor: 'If you do not understand something, change yourself.'[7]

10 Changing identities

The road to peace

This essay develops the theme, raised only briefly in chapter 9, that the road to peace between Israelis and Palestinians depends on identity change. Starting with a powerful speech by an imaginary Israeli prime minister, who uses it to set forth an agenda for mutual and reciprocal identity changes, the essay moves on to analyze the deep roots of the failure of the Oslo peace process. These lie at the epistemic, normative, and identity levels and include the misguided effort to change 'the other' in one's image—when, in fact, the key to peace in the Middle East lies in self-change. Israelis must undertake three identity changes: a reformed Jewish state; the adoption of a Mediterranean identity; and a reformulation of Zionist ideology so that peacemaking is viewed as a Zionist imperative.

Unpublished manuscript based on a slightly revised version of the first Andrea and Charles Bronfman Lecture on Israeli Studies, University of Toronto, March 21, 2002

A speech that was never delivered

Mr. President, Speaker of the Knesset, Members of Knesset, leaders of the Palestinian people, UN Secretary General, world leaders, people of Israel, Palestinian people, ladies and gentlemen:

I stand before you today to speak on behalf of the Israeli people about the historical tragedy of Israelis and Palestinians, who, so far, have not been able to settle their disputes, learn to live in peace, and treat each other with dignity and respect. The reason we are still caught in a horrible cycle of violence is that, in spite of the suffering and death, and in spite of the Oslo process—some say because of it—the two peoples have not yet reconciled themselves to each other's existence. The Oslo process was supposed to lead to reconciliation and mutual respect. Instead, it caused both sides to feel cheated, and thus led to mutual recrimination and expectations that the problem would be solved by military victory rather than by compromise.

Many Palestinians may have mistakenly interpreted regional events as proof that violence and intimidation, coupled with international intervention, would force Israelis to give in to Palestinian demands. Indeed, once Palestinian refugees returned to their lands in Israel, the road to 'two states for one people' (I mean, of course, the Palestinians) would be open; and then, as have all other colonial peoples in the past, Jews, too, would leave the country.

A majority of my people, on the other hand, took the recent Intifada as proof that Palestinians have never accepted the existence of a Jewish state and never will. Recent global events may even have nurtured the hope in some Israeli hearts that the Palestinian movement could now be defeated and that finally we would be able to keep in perpetuity the territories that we have occupied since 1967. Slowly but surely, our peoples became so entrenched in our own narratives, our feelings of self-righteousness, and our expectations of ultimate success that we did not realize that we were building a Tower of Babel of sorts.

To the Palestinian people I say: You have cared more about seeing that the Jews do not have their own state than you have cared about achieving a state of your own. You have asked us for 'justice,' but a justice that did not, and still does not, include a Jewish state. We Israelis, in turn, wanted 'life.' We asked you—indeed demanded from you—'peace,' but seldom treated you as equals so as to engender in you trust and a thirst for peace. Thus the Tower of Babel grew higher and higher.

I stand before you today to say that all this has to stop! It is time for the two peoples to recognize that this is a conflict between two rights, that one people will not be able to defeat the other, and that we must therefore divide this land so that both peoples can live and feel that justice has been done. It is also time for both peoples to know that we will have to make painful compromises, giving up not only real estate and assets, but also dreams, myths, and symbols of identity. Leaders must tell their peoples the truth: that in the absence of compromise there will be no life and no justice here, and that in the end both peoples will bleed to death. Most important, we must erase from our hearts the expectation that one national movement will be able to overcome the other. The injustice that Palestinians suffered when Israel was created cannot be erased by causing an equal injustice, that is, the dismantling of a Jewish state that is 81 percent Jewish. This is why justice will not be served by the return of Palestinian refugees to Israel, in its pre-1967 borders. It is equally impractical and immoral to demand peace from you when we not only occupy the West Bank and Gaza, but have also been unable to reconcile ourselves to the concept of your national rights. It is absolutely absurd that you demand the right to flood our state with Palestinians and that we flood the land of your future state with Jews. Thus the only just and viable solution is for you to have your state and for us to have ours.

Your sense of justice must include the secure existence of a Jewish state, and our demand for peace must include recognition of your national rights. That is why, in the name of my people, I offer the Palestinians a historic compromise: the occupied territories for Palestinian abandonment of the right of return. I do not mean territories for peace, as the tired formula says; rather, I mean to abandon, albeit painfully, our right to settle your future

Palestinian state in return for your equally painful abandonment of the right to settle within the Israeli state. If both peoples accept this compromise and the idea of 'two states for two peoples,' peace will be at hand, including with moderate Arab states, and justice will be served. This will happen, however, only if we pledge to ban the use of violence against each other and only if Israel and the future Palestinian state treat their minorities justly, so that minorities, too, can call their state 'home.'

As proof of our good intentions and commitment to our proposal, it is high time for us to tell you, the Palestinians, that we regret all the suffering that the Palestinian people have had to endure over the last century. We are aware that our independence caused suffering and material duress to hundreds of thousands of Palestinians. We came to the land of our ancestors not as colonizers, but as a people who finally returned 'home,' but we were insensitive to the notion that this was also your 'home' and that, therefore, the 'apartment' would have to be divided fairly. Many times our people treated your people badly, denying them both respect and dignity. The opposite is also true. Thus it is time for us not only to recognize your rights to part of this land, but also to treat you as equals.

We cannot and need not look at each other with contempt and disrespect; rather, from now on we should talk to one another 'at eye level,' as we say in Hebrew. The hand that I am extending to you, therefore, means no more humiliation and no more checkpoints; but your hand, in turn, must relinquish violence for peace.

We do not take responsibility for your suffering, if only because what we did, war after war and Intifada after Intifada, was in self-defense. But we recognize that whether Palestinians fled or were expelled in the heat of battle—or both—Israel's existence became your 'Nakba' or tragedy. However, you must understand that your unwillingness to accept the Jewish state became our Nakba—slow and sometimes non-dramatic, but a Nakba as well. Too many young Israelis' dreams and expectations were shattered and will never be fulfilled. We may have dispossessed you from part of your past, but you keep threatening to dispossess us of our entire future. This is our tragedy. We deplore your tragedy, but we are nevertheless troubled that your hate for us became so deep, and that your incitement against us became so normal, that you send your children against us as suicide bombers. As a first step to mutual reconciliation, therefore, we must agree on mutual respect for life. Your community may be worth dying for and our community may be worth dying for, but nothing—including victory—is worth a peace of the cemeteries, where both people lie dead in the end.

It is very important that you not interpret our offer as a sign of weakness. The hand that we extend to you is firm and strong. We will know no compromise if, in return, we receive a knife in our back. If that happens, do not expect us to leave, for we will become even more determined and more adamant about defending our legitimate rights. Our offer is an honest attempt to make peace, not only between leaders, but also between peoples.

How do we translate these idealistic words into deeds? We first call upon you to accept the historic compromise I have just suggested. If you do, we are willing to contemplate the acceptance into Israel of a small number of Palestinian refugees on a humanitarian basis. We can then discuss other issues, such as border arrangements and exchanges of territory, reparations to your refugees and to ours, security arrangements, and Jerusalem, the Palestinian parts of which will become your capital, while the other parts will remain our eternal capital. We will see to it, however, that Jerusalem will be an open city, which people from all over the world will be able to visit and revere. Furthermore, for the sake of reconciliation, we must agree that you will not question our religious beliefs and our legitimate historical connection to the holy places, and we will not question yours. But for the sake of the future, we must seek a compromise on the holy sites: without a compromise, there will be no people to remember the past.

Ladies and gentlemen, on behalf of the Israeli people I am offering not only our recognition of the Palestinians' legitimate right to a viable state in Palestine, alongside our state, but also that which the Palestinians have seldom received from their own Arab brothers—namely, dignity and respect. We expect and demand the same. We extend our hand in peace to the Palestinians, but we will not lower our shield until both peoples have learned to practice peace. We also call upon the Arab world and the international community, including the UN, the US, Europe, and other Great Powers, to help our two peoples reach the shores of a just Mediterranean peace.

The foregoing is the speech that Ariel Sharon should have given, but did not and never will. My lecture will explain why a prime minister of Israel should make this speech. If you understand my talk as saying that part of the blame for the historic failure to achieve peace in the Land of Israel lies with past and current Israeli and Palestinian leaders, I will not try to correct you. In short, I contend that making peace comes from identity and from the way people construct not only 'the other,' but also the reality in which both 'self' and 'other' live. I will try to show that the roots of the failure of the Oslo process go deeper than the way they are generally portrayed in academia and the media. I will also explain what is wrong with the Oslo paradigm and offer an alternative paradigm that, stemming from identity, does not build on changing 'the other' in one's own image, but rather on changing (as opposed to blaming) oneself. This paradigm, among other things, includes a post-post-Zionist statement: Zionism must be redefined from an ethos of perpetual settlement to an ethos of peacemaking; only peace can guarantee the perpetuation of the Zionist dream and reality.

Why Oslo failed

After decades of violent conflict, Yitzhak Rabin and Yasser Arafat signed the Oslo peace agreement between Israel and the Palestinian people in

September 1993. Oslo's grand bargain included mutual recognition, Palestinian renunciation of violence, the incremental withdrawal of Israel from occupied territories, and the establishment of a Palestinian Authority in the Palestinian territories. The end of the process was to have been a final agreement for a permanent end to the conflict, dealing with final borders, security, Jerusalem, and refugees. The Palestinian Authority, however, did not control terrorism against Israel; Israel did not remove old settlements and continued to promote new ones. At Camp David, in July 2000, Prime Minister Ehud Barak offered the Palestinians 'the deal of their lives.' It included 91 percent of the occupied territories, parts of East Jerusalem, a token agreement about the refugees, security guarantees, and, for security reasons, a long-term Israeli lease of the Jordan River valley—all in exchange for the termination of the conflict. Arafat did not think that this was the Palestinians' dream come true and refused to accept the deal. That September, the Intifada began; a few months later, at Taba, in a heroic attempt to save the peace process, the two sides came closer than ever to an agreement, which included, among other things, an Israeli withdrawal from 97 percent of the territories. By then, however, propelled by Israeli anger and suffering, Ariel Sharon was already on his way to becoming prime minister. What happened next will be told in the annals of the history of Israel and the world. There are many explanations for why the Oslo process failed. For the sake of clarity, I will summarize the most important of them.

Some say the Oslo process was alive and well until Sharon entered the Temple Mount, the site of the al-Aqsa Mosque. Had he not committed this act of provocation, the Intifada would not have started and the Oslo process would have proceeded to its ultimate goal: peace.

Many pundits blame Arafat, maintaining that he never made the transition from terrorist to statesman. Others say that Arafat made a calculated, rational decision to return to violence, so as to increase the price Israel pays for the occupation and attain a better deal than he was offered at Camp David. Moreover, Palestinians in general, and Arafat in particular, thought that provoking Israel to use violence against them (on CNN cameras) would induce the international community to intervene and impose a deal more favorable to the Palestinians. Martin Indyk, former US ambassador to Israel, says that Arafat was not sincere when he claimed that he was renouncing violence. Former Israeli foreign minister Shlomo Ben-Ami says that Arafat is incapable of compromising. The embittered Ben-Ami echoed what had previously been the argument of Israel's right: 'Oslo will never work because the Arabs will never give up their intention of destroying Israel.'

From the perspective of the Israeli left, it is always Israel's fault. Oslo failed because of the settlements, the checkpoints, and the humiliation of Palestinians. Israel never really relinquished full control of Palestinian life, borders, and economic infrastructure. Former prime minister Binyamin Netanyahu and the Israeli right did everything possible to undermine the letter and the spirit of Oslo. When Barak finally decided to make himself available for a settlement of the Palestinian problem, it was too little too late.

Another set of arguments emphasizes the Oslo process, including the Camp David meeting itself. According to Terje Larsen, the unrelenting Norwegian mediator, Oslo was a failure of psychology and process rather than of substance. Oslo was an opportunity for peace, says Ron Pundak, head of the Peres Center for Peace, but it was squandered through miscalculations and mismanagement. He refers to Netanyahu's efforts to kill Oslo gently, Barak's mismanagement of the negotiations, his failure to implement the third redeployment of Israeli forces, his failure to gain the trust of the Palestinian leadership, and his all-or-nothing approach. Palestinians, on the other hand, were foolish to stick to the maximalist position on the right of return; and, as Ben-Ami notes, they did not offer a plan of their own. Others have argued that at Camp David Arafat was not ready for a final settlement and that he felt cornered by Clinton and Barak. Had he agreed to the Barak plan, he would have met the same fate as previous Arab leaders, such as King Abdullah of Jordan and President Anwar Sadat of Egypt, who were assassinated for daring to compromise with the Jews.

Many have said, openly or quietly, that the Oslo process was killed by the bullets that also killed Yitzhak Rabin. Once Rabin—the only prime minister who ever came close to a real reconciliation with the Palestinians and whom Arafat called 'my friend'—was murdered by his own people, the process was doomed. The assassin, Yigal Amir, achieved his purpose too well: following the murder, mutual trust between Israelis and Palestinians eroded rapidly and domestic politics in Israel effectively vetoed the agreement.

There are more explanations of Oslo's failure, however. According to Daniel Kurtzer, the current US ambassador to Israel, the absence of more forceful American involvement is to blame. Some people have focused on the psychological dimension of the conflict, saying that Palestinians did not understand the devastating effects of terrorism on the Israeli psyche, or, alternately, that they understood them only too well. Or similarly, that Israelis did not understand the devastating effect of occupation on the Palestinian psyche, or that they did but did not really care. Some political scientists have blamed the failure on the large gap in power between the two sides.

But the argument that has probably most caught the Israeli imagination is the 'Hizbullah effect.' Impressed by the way Hizbullah had ended the Israeli occupation of southern Lebanon and the disorganized manner of the IDF withdrawal, the Palestinians concluded that they had found the key for ending the occupation, and perhaps for ending Israel's existence altogether. It has also been said that Israelis and Palestinians are caught inside their own narratives, which Oslo did little to bridge. As Uzi Benziman wrote in *Ha'aretz*:

with hindsight, it seems that Oslo failed because neither side really regarded it as an agreement to end the dispute. Instead, both attempted to maneuver within the Oslo framework to squeeze out maximum benefit. Palestinians never relinquished their dream of erasing the Zionist State from the map of the Middle East; Israelis never abandoned their dream of keeping the West Bank and the Gaza Strip. [1]

There is some truth, perhaps a great deal of truth, in the various arguments I have outlined, which means that Oslo's failure was over-determined. At the same time, not all the arguments are valid, let alone consensual and proven beyond doubt. For example, Sharon's pilgrimage to the Temple Mount was to the end of the Oslo process what the murder of Archduke Franz Ferdinand was to World War I—a catalyst, not a prime cause of the violence that followed. In fact, one of the main reasons for Sharon's media show was to stop Netanyahu from challenging him as leader of the Likud Party. Again, it is difficult to know what was and is in Arafat's mind—many wonder whether he himself knows what is in his mind; but he cannot have been both rationally calculating and irrational, wary of the price he was asked to pay for peace yet adamantly opposed to peace, a leader and a follower of the mob, etc.

The problem with the argument that the Arabs have not reconciled themselves to the existence of Israel and never will is one of disentangling cause from effect. The onus is on the proponents of this thesis to show conclusively that Arab intransigence is not partly a self-fulfilling prophecy. The Israeli left's argument that all the blame for what happened lies with Israeli behavior toward the Palestinians disregards the insidious influence of terrorism on Israeli society. As to the argument that Oslo fell prey to mismanagement, it may be partly true; but had the structural conditions for an agreement existed, I doubt that mismanagement would have had such a devastating effect. The same applies to Rabin's assassination and the US role in the Oslo process. I believe that there is much to the 'Hizbullah effect,' but we should ask why, even at the height of the Oslo process, the Palestinians were still seeking a way to eliminate Israel. Furthermore, while it may be true that many Palestinians and Israelis never abandoned their maximalist goals of destroying Israel and retaining the occupied territories in perpetuity, some Palestinians and some Israelis did. The question, then, is why the extremists came to call the shots?

We must also distinguish between the Oslo process and what happened after the Intifada flared up. After Sharon came to power in Israel and the action–reaction between Israelis and Palestinians intensified, the entire situation began to be characterized by a self-reinforcing escalatory mechanism that feeds on each side's domestic politics and on emotional factors. It also feeds on the respective leadership's concept of time. Palestinians believe that time is on their side. Although today the Palestinians are weak and embattled, they believe that years from now life will become so miserable for the

Westernized Israelis that they will be unable to cope with the situation and, like the Crusaders centuries ago, they will ultimately leave. Sharon, however, thinks that time is in Israel's favor, for in contrast to the past, when the Arabs dominated the world oil supply and oil meant hard currency, today it is high technology that counts, and Israel is one of its largest producers. In addition, September 11 and the US campaign against 'evil' created a situation favorable to Israel's interests. According to this line, Israel will eventually defeat the Palestinians and keep the occupied territories in perpetuity. Add to this Sharon's belief that most Israeli settlements should not be dismantled and that Israel will remain embattled forever, the current strength of Palestinians who deny Israel's right to exist, Arafat's emotional distress, and the chaos in the Palestinian Authority, and the conclusion is clear: as long as Israelis and Palestinians continue to construe reality in incompatible and mutually exclusive ways, and unless a profound change of identities takes place, then, to paraphrase Nietzsche, they will look at the abyss and it will look back at them. This brings us to the deep sources of why Oslo failed.

Why Oslo really failed

The Israeli–Palestinian conflict can be characterized in geological terms. The deeper we penetrate the layers of rock, the closer we are to the moment of birth, to the original sins, and to the constitutive factors of the conflict. Thus far I have spoken about layers that lie close to the surface. I now invite you on a journey to the center of the earth. The Israeli–Palestinian conflict comes from the way that people construe their reality (let's call it 'the bubble'), their basic normative beliefs, and their identity—the understanding of self in terms of others.

Regarding the bubble, Palestinians view Israeli Jews as colonizers who came from afar and regard themselves as the native inhabitants of the land. This reality, in fact, does not allow for any alternative other than the Israelis' eventual departure from Palestine: after all, all other colonial powers left, and there is no reason why Israel should be any different in the end. And the more that Israelis settle what Palestinians consider their native sacred land, the more Israelis help prove them right and reconstitute the framework that Palestinians use to understand reality. If Israeli leaders say that Israel's War of Independence has not ended, this means that the Palestinians are still experiencing their 'Nakba' or tragedy.

Israeli Jewish reality, however, draws from the hatred of Jews across the ages, including the Holocaust. Thus, the more Palestinians use terrorism against Jews, the more they reproduce the Jewish beliefs that there can be no compromise with antisemitism. On the liberal left, there is a belief in the ability to change humanity for the better. On the right, however, there is no such illusion; and the right is in power today. This view of Israeli reality is compounded by the notion, advanced by sociologist Baruch Kimmerling, that the bubble includes ideas about Jewish exclusivity and the equation of nation-building with settling a territorial frontier. [2] It is a pity that neither Palestinians nor Israelis can get outside their own bubble and see the world from the perspective of the other; for they would then see that Israelis are today colonizing the lands of tomorrow's Palestinian state, while the Palestinians want to colonize, tomorrow, the lands of today's Israel. Either Israelis and Palestinians have an interest in building the other's state, or they are embarked on a 'March of Folly.'

At the normative level, Israelis most of all want life and thus ask for peace from the Palestinians. So far, however, Israel has been unable and unwilling to make peace *with* the Palestinians. Israel has never really attempted to reconcile itself to the Palestinians' existence as holders of equal national rights to the land. Israel offered almost everything at Camp David, says a choir of voices; but it did not offer the one thing that might have made a difference: dignity and respect. Palestinians, on the other hand, are less interested in peace than in justice, but because their sense of justice aims to erase the wrong that Israel inflicted on them in its War of Independence, that justice has no room for a Jewish state, so the peace that Israel seeks is tantamount to capitulation.

Because of their bubble and their norms, Palestinians have developed an identity that is partly based on the Jewish other, who came from abroad to uproot them from their native land. On the other hand, Israelis have adopted an identity that is partly based on Palestinian others, who, unwilling to recognize the Jews' legitimate right to the Land of Israel, would like to send Jews back to from whence they came. In both cases, each side needs the other to know itself and therefore demonizes the other. Once the bubble, constitutive norms, and identities were established, they fed the basic fears, lack of trust, thirst for revenge, and desires to eliminate the other. The resulting wars and Intifadas thus became constitutive of Israeli and Palestinian understanding of self and other. To change the situation from the root, moderates on both sides must begin to see both Israeli and Palestinian extremists as the other. This requires a change of self.

With the exception, perhaps, of the secret meetings held in Stockholm in May 2000, the Oslo process never came close to addressing the deep issues that have turned this conflict into a self-fulfilling prophecy. Oslo stayed on the surface of things and did not address the bubbles or the required balancing act between peace and justice. For example, Palestinians failed to understand the connection between the Israeli bubble and the terror they inflicted on Israel. Israelis reacted with surprise when Palestinians raised the issue of the right of return. Oslo was an attempt to change the other in ways that served each side's interests; but neither side tried to change itself and adopt a different and more benign image of reality, compatible normative goals, or identities that might serve their common rather than their separate interests. Oslo also failed because the paradigm on which it was based was partly flawed.

The Oslo paradigm

The Oslo process rested on five main conceptual premises. First of all, the process was incremental. The architects of the process understood that the Israeli–Palestinian conflict was too deep and complex to be solved in one or two rounds of negotiations. More importantly, an incremental approach was intended to build mutual trust and change beliefs, goals, and interests on both sides, from conflict and war to cooperation and peace.

Second, the Oslo process was based on what political scientists call 'neofunctionalist' premises: through functional cooperation on, for example, water, health, and economic issues, psychological barriers between the two peoples would be broken. Thus functional cooperation would be institutionalized. Ultimately, the common bonds achieved through functional cooperation would spill over to the political realm and help bring peace.

Third, the Oslo process was based on the development of a 'community of the committed'—a small elite of Israelis, Palestinians, and members of the international community whose commitment to the process and political assets would serve as a lever for institutionalizing the process, enlarging the constituency that supports it and, eventually, implementing the agreements.

Fourth, the Oslo process built on conceptual premises, then prevalent in the academic community, that persuasion and socialization are more efficient means to bring about conflict resolution than deterrence and power politics.

Finally, and most importantly for my argument, Oslo was based on the premise that conflict resolution rested on the ability of one side to change 'the other' in its own image. As Israel was a country with nation- and state-building experience, it was supposed to 'coach' the Palestinians in building their institutions and political and economic systems. The international community—mainly Europeans, Americans, and Canadians, some of them academics—would also lend its experience and expertise in these matters.

What was the problem with the Oslo concept? First, the incremental nature of the process came to haunt its architects, because, since it is always easier to destroy than to build, extremists on both sides had more time and opportunities to derail the process—as was done by Baruch Goldstein, Yigal Amir, and Hamas and Jihad terrorists. In other words, extremists had no problem in killing off the minimum amount of trust and shared identity without which a sustainable peace process is impossible. Also, the fact that the Oslo agreements were opaque and left plenty of room for interpretation meant that the longer it took to reach an agreement, the more momentum was lost and the harder it became to arrive at shared meanings.

Second, the neo-functionalist premises and the belief in socialization and persuasion were fine as long as the deep identity issues were directly addressed. However, because of the incremental nature of the process, people chose not to address them. Thus, when Barak placed his plan on the table and the parties finally began to address identity issues, the boat had already begun to sink.

Third, the premise that one can change the other without first changing oneself proved fallacious. Because ethnic conflicts stem from identity, which has to do with the relation of self and other, it is very difficult to change the structural conditions that lead the other to change without a willingness to get out of one's bubble and change oneself as well.

Finally, Oslo failed because you cannot make peace with 'the other' when you do not know or have a deep conflict about who you are yourself. Oslo was undermined by Israel's deep identity divide and, I would say, by the deep divide among Palestinians between modernist and anti-modernist factions as well. Before, during, and to a lesser extent after the Oslo process, Israel was torn between two identities. One 'Israel' (let's call it 'Tel Aviv') is liberal, individualist, rationalist, and modernized, draws its self-identification from humanist and liberal values, is future-oriented, and is plugged into the global community. The other 'Israel' (let's call it 'Jerusalem') is nationalist, collectivist, partly messianic, draws its self-identification from ethnic nationalist beliefs and religion, looks to the past for self-understanding, and sees the whole world as 'against us.' 'Tel Aviv,' to paraphrase Yaron Ezrahi, believes that the earth belongs to the living; 'Jerusalem,' that the living belong to the earth.[3] The identity divide in Israel created a political stalemate and confused the Palestinians, who did not know with whom they were bargaining. Even more important, it froze Israel's capacity to make peace with the other. Being unable to make peace with itself, Israel was also unable to make peace with the Palestinians. Barak's plan was a last heroic attempt by 'Tel Aviv' to make a Rabin-like peace. Once Camp David failed, it was 'Jerusalem's' turn to call the shots. 'Tel Aviv' and 'Jerusalem' failed in their respective attempts to bring peace and security because, unable to decide who they are, who is 'we,' what is 'we,' and who should 'we' become, Israelis have not been strong and secure enough in their identity to change for the sake of peace. This brings me to the alternative paradigm: change yourself!

The new paradigm: change yourself

To change interests, we must first change identities. No interest can be articulated until a 'we' is established.[4] Are settlers in the occupied territories part of the 'we'? Are Neturei Karta—Ultraorthodox Jews who still do not accept Israel's existence—part of the 'we'? Do Israeli Arabs belong to the 'we'? Do they wish to? To change the other—in this case, to bring about trust and the conditions necessary to build a stable peace with the Palestinians—requires changing ourselves, which is a sign and source of strength. Identity change entails a deep learning process, not in the sense of adding more information, but in that of transforming the basic assumptions of our long-term existence as a nation and state. Not just any identity will do, however. The shared identity that Israelis need to adopt must draw from the past while also being future-oriented. It must be based on the premise that Zionism's dream will not be complete until we make peace; in fact, without peace there will be no dream and no dreamers. This requires facing what Oslo did not face: the justice issue, the deep psychological roots of the conflict, and the basic premises of social life in this region, such as sanctity of life, respect for each other's property, security, and self-interest, which is satisfied through cooperation rather than violence.

One may well ask why Israel has to take the initiative. Did not the Palestinians start the violence and still refuse to accept Israel's legitimate right to its own state? One reason that Israel has to take the initiative is that it is the stronger side: it has a state and the Palestinians do not. As such, it is practically and morally right that Israel should start first. Second, taking the initiative is in Israel's short- and long-term interest. Plainly speaking, without changes of self there will be no stable peace; without stable and durable peace, in the long run, there will be no Israel. Third, Israel should take the initiative because, in any case, this is the 'we' that Israel should become.

I will now focus on what I believe are three of the most important changes Israel needs to consider: first, a reformed Jewish state; second, the adoption of a Mediterranean identity; and third, understanding peace-making as the practical essence of Zionism, or post-post-Zionism, today. First, however, I would like to point to the measures that are required to initiate the process of change: first, Israel must find ways to signal its will-ingness to change (as in the hypothetical speech with which I began). Second, Israel should signal its willingness to withdraw from the occupied territories, with minor border changes, in exchange for something so dear to the Palestinians that they would be unable to represent Israel's retreat as capitulation to them. I refer, of course, to their right of return. Third, leaders on both sides must show courage and start preparing their peoples for the historic compromise: Israeli leaders must tell the Jewish settlers that most of the settlements will have to be removed; Palestinian leaders must tell the Palestinian refugees that they will not be able to return *en masse* to Israel proper. Fourth, it is in Israel's interest to stop the current violence at all costs, not only because of the damage the Palestinians inflict upon Israel, but also because of the damage that Israel inflicts upon itself when it uses violence against them. Quiet is also needed, because the very violence that is supposed to drive Israel from the territories contributes to Israel's intransi-gence and unwillingness to retreat from them. Fifth, the historic agreement I have suggested must be sponsored by the UN Security Council and backed by the US, the European Union, and other powers. Finally, because of the strategic dangers Israel may continue to face, even after a historic compro-mise with the Palestinians, and in order to overcome Israeli domestic political opposition to this compromise, the US will be required to formalize its commitment to defend Israel in its post-settlement borders against orga-nized Arab aggression.

A reformed Jewish state

To live in peace, Israel must be both Jewish and democratic, not because Israel's neighbors are democratic—they are not—but because Israel has a sizable Arab population that defines itself not only as Israeli but also as Palestinian. The morality of Jewish self-determination in the Land of Israel depends upon building a Jewish state, without dispossessing others, and on maintaining a Jewish majority.[5] To maintain a Jewish majority, Israel must withdraw from the occupied territories. Further, to make sure that it does not dispossess its Arab minority, Israel must provide full rights, equality, and security to its Arab citizens, recognize Israel's Arab population as a national minority with rights of power-sharing, and accept Israeli Arabs as full partners of the Jewish majority. A reformed Jewish state will thus entail changing some Basic Laws, so as to emphasize Israel's democratic nature, and drafting a constitution that combines Jewish and democratic values. It will also entail amending the Law of Return, and adding a few Arab symbols to the Israeli state. A reformed Israeli state, while maintaining Jewish religious symbols as constitutive of the Jews' right to the State of Israel, will require separating state and religion as much as possible. Although religion will continue to be a fundamental part of the identity of the Jewish majority in Israel in a reformed Jewish state, Israeli Jews and Israeli Arabs will face each other not as religious groups, but as national groups that consociate to create a Jewish yet pluralistic state. A reformed Jewish state will be conducive to peace, because, by addressing the justice issue, it will be legitimate not only in the eyes of Israeli Jews, but also in the eyes of many Palestinians inside and outside Israel. In fact, a Palestinian state will be the other side of the coin of a reformed Jewish state, thus serving the interests not only of the Palestinian people, but also of Israelis. Once a Palestinian state is created, it will help sharpen the identity choice of Israeli Arabs. Those who want to leave should be able to do so freely, but those who decide to stay in Israel will then have to become full partners with Israeli Jews in rights and in duties. This proposal is a far cry from a post-Zionist call to dismantle the Jewish state; rather, it is a call to reform the Jewish state so it can continue to be Jewish and moral, and thereby live and prosper.

A Mediterranean identity

The goal of achieving long-term peace necessitates not only common trust, but also the development of a shared identity of place. If we think of Israel as part of the West, Israel is out of place. If we think of Israel as part of the Middle East, then the Arabs think of it as being theirs and Israel has no place in it. This is why I suggest that Israelis and Palestinians work separately and jointly to promote the development of a Mediterranean identity, so that they can jointly imagine that, as members of the same regional group, they share interests and have much to lose from a return to war. This change involves using the existent Mediterranean 'surplus of identity,'[6] which goes back many centuries, to create new collective narratives and myths. Mediterranean culture and identity will not only unite Sephardim and Ashkenazim within Israel, but will also serve as a bridge between Israeli and Arab cultures and societies. In other words, a Mediterranean identity will provide Israelis (including Israeli Arabs) and Palestinians and Arabs in general the chance to belong to the same cultural region, where, for many centuries, Arabs and Jews held reciprocal influences and cultural exchanges.[7] A Mediterranean identity will also help build bridges between Islam and the West—a *sine qua non* condition for Israel's long-term survival. Even if this 'experiment' takes decades to bear fruit, Israel has to start now; tomorrow may be too late.

Post-post-Zionism

Post-Zionism is a stereotypical brand name given primarily by defenders of classical Zionism to a variety of positions critical of Zionism. These range from mild interpretations about the end of Zionist ideology (because the goals have already been achieved) to calls, based on revisionist history, for dismantling the Jewish state and replacing it with a democratic or bi-national state. Although I share some of the criticisms of Zionism, I still believe in a reformed Jewish state and do not think that Zionism's goals have been achieved. First, there is the goal of making peace. Zionism needs to redefine itself, away from being an ideology that mobilizes Jews to come to Israel on the basis of a settlement ethos and on the assumption that the relationship with the Arabs who inhabit the land will somehow solve itself. Rather, Zionism should be given new meaning: the post-post-Zionist message should be 'Come to Israel to make peace,' so the Zionist legacy will endure over time. Inasmuch as I side with 'Tel Aviv,' I prefer to see a land serving people and life, rather than people and life serving a land. Second, Zionism has yet to find an equal and just compromise between a Jewish and a democratic state. A third goal of post-post-Zionism is to renew the vitality of human and social goals in Israel, such as the redistribution of wealth and the eradication of poverty. Finally, post-post-Zionism must bring Israel to the Jewish Diaspora. The meaning of coming to Israel to help make peace should be emphasized, however: 'Give us your ideas, your emotions, and your hands for the sake of peacemaking, and in helping us guarantee Israel's future, you also will help preserve Jewish past and identity.'

Permit me to conclude with lyrics by Shmuel Hasfari about 'the children of the winter of seventy-three' (the time of the Yom Kippur war); my daughter Shirli is one of them.

> *The winter of seventy-three*
>
> We are the children
> Of the winter of seventy three.
> The first time you dreamed of us

Was at dawn, when the battle was over.
You, the bone-weary men,
Grateful for having survived.
You, the anxious young women,
So eager for love and for life.
And so you conceived us with love
In the winter of seventy-three,
To replenish with your bodies
What war had taken away.

We were born into a country
That was wounded and sorrowful.
You gazed at us, held us close,
Seeking consolation.
When we were born, the old men
Gave blessing with tearful eyes.
They said, 'Please God,
These children won't go to war.'
Your faces in the old photograph
Prove that you meant it sincerely
When you promised to do your utmost for us
To transform enemies into friends.
We are the children
Of the winter of seventy-three.

Now we too have grown up to be soldiers
With rifles and helmeted heads.
We too know how to make love,
To laugh and to cry.
We too are men,
We too are women,
We too dream of babies.
So we will not urge you,
So we will not demand,
And we will not utter threats.

When we were little,
You told us promises must be kept!
If you need our strength,
We will give it unstintingly.
We just wanted to whisper:
We are the children
Of that winter—the winter of seventy-three.

You promised a dove and an olive branch,
You promised us peace at home.
You promised us spring and blossoming
You promised to keep promises!
You promised a dove.[8]

Post-post-Zionism means fulfilling this promise.

Notes

1 Communities of practice in International Relations

1 Thomas R. Rochon, *Culture Moves: Ideas, Activism, and Changing Values* (Princeton: Princeton University Press, 1998).

2 Global governance 'is conceived to include systems of rule at all levels of human activity—from the family to the international organization—in which the pursuit of goals through the exercise of control has transnational repercussions' (James Rosenau, 'Governance in the Twenty-First Century,' *Global Governance* 1(1) (1995): 13).

3 Etienne Wenger, *Communities of Practice: Learning, Meaning and Identity* (Cambridge: Cambridge University Press, 1998).

4 See, for example, Charles R. Beitz, *Political Theory and International Relations* (Princeton: Princeton University Press, 1999), who followed John Rawls (*A Theory of Justice* (Oxford: Oxford University Press, 1972)); see also Robert Nozick, *Anarchy, State, and Utopia* (Oxford: Basil Blackwell, 1974); Ronald Dworkin, *The Philosophy of Law* (Oxford: Oxford University Press, 1977).

5 See, for example, Michael Walzer, *Spheres of Justice* (Oxford: Basil Blackwell, 1983); see also Michael Sandel, *Liberalism and the Limits of Justice* (Cambridge: Cambridge University Press, 1982); Charles Taylor, *Philosophy and the Human Sciences* (Cambridge: Cambridge University Press, 1985).

6 See, for example, Bruce Cronin, *Community Under Anarchy: Transnational Identity and the Evolution of Cooperation* (New York: Columbia University Press, 1999). Whereas normative IR approaches raise questions primarily about the 'good and just' international life and about the possibilities of moral communities evolving beyond the state toward universality, analytic IR approaches focus mainly on the explanation or hermeneutic understanding of social reality (including norms) and on its ontological, epistemological, and methodological implications. Normative theory and analytic theory are not incompatible, however, and have been successfully combined, primarily by critical theory (Andrew Linklater, 'The Problem of Community in International Relations,' *Alternatives* 15 (1990): 135–53; *The Transformation of Political Community: Ethical Foundations of the Post-Westphalian Era* (Columbia: University of South Carolina Press, 1998)). This is an important though not mainstream constructivist IR approach (Emanuel Adler, 'Constructivism and International Relations,' in Walter Carlsnaes, Thomas Risse, and Beth A. Simmons, eds, *Handbook of International Relations* (London: Sage, 2002), 95–118) that uses analytic theory not only to create knowledge but also to move away from the current state of affairs toward a more moral human condition.

7 *Ibid.*; Stefano Guzzini, 'A Reconstruction of Constructivism in International Relations,' *European Journal of International Relations* 6(2) (2000): 147–82.

8 Richard K. Ashley, 'The Geopolitics of Geopolitical Space: Toward a Critical Theory of International Politics,' *Alternatives* 12 (1987): 403.

9 Mervyn Frost, *Ethics in International Relations: A Constitutive Theory* (Cambridge: Cambridge University Press, 1996); Linklater, *The Transformation of Political Community*;

Mark Neufeld, *The Restructuring of International Relations Theory* (Cambridge: Cambridge University Press, 1995); Richard Shapcott, *Justice, Community, and Dialogue in International Relations* (Cambridge: Cambridge University Press, 2001).

10 A person is 'the agent of an act if what he [she] does can be described under an aspect that makes it intentional. ... To describe an action as one that had a certain purpose or intended outcome is to describe it as an effect; to describe it as an action that had a certain outcome is to describe it as a cause' (Donald Davidson, 'Agency,' in Robert Binkley, Richard Bronaugh, and Ausonia Marras, eds, *Agent, Action and Reason* (Toronto: University of Toronto Press, 1971), 7, 9). See also Anthony Giddens, *The Constitution of Society* (Berkeley: University of California Press, 1984); Alexander Wendt, 'The Agent–Structure Problem in International Relations Theory,' *International Organization* 41(3) (1987): 335–70.

11 Giddens, *The Constitution of Society*.

12 James Fearon and Alexander Wendt, 'Rationalism and Constructivism: A Skeptical View,' in Carlsnaes, Risse, and Simmons, *Handbook of International Relations*, 57.

13 Emanuel Adler and Michael Barnett, eds, *Security Communities* (Cambridge: Cambridge University Press, 1998).

14 Peter Haas, 'Introduction: Epistemic Communities and International Policy Coordination,' *International Organization* 46(1) (1992): 1–35; Emanuel Adler and Peter Haas, 'Conclusion: Epistemic Communities, World Order, and the Creation of a Reflective Research Program,' *ibid.*, 367–90.

15 Margaret Keck and Kathryn Sikkink, *Activists beyond Borders* (Ithaca: Cornell University Press, 1998).

16 Frost, *Ethics in International Relations*.

17 Giddens, *The Constitution of Society*.

18 Emanuel Adler, 'Cognitive Evolution: A Dynamic Approach for the Study of International Relations and Their Progress,' in Emanuel Adler and Beverly Crawford, eds, *Progress in Postwar International Relations* (New York: Columbia University Press, 1991), 43–88 (chapter 3 in this volume); Emanuel Adler, 'Seizing the Middle Ground: Constructivism in World Politics,' *European Journal of International Relations* 3(3) (1997): 319–63 (chapter 4 in this volume).

19 Shapcott, *Justice, Community, and Dialogue*, 3.

20 David Morrice, 'The Liberal–Communitarian Debate in Contemporary Political Philosophy and Its Significance for International Relations,' *Review of International Studies* 26 (2000): 233–51.

21 *Ibid.*

22 Frost, *Ethics in International Relations*.

23 Max Weber, *Economy and Society*, ed. G. Roth and C. Wittich (Berkeley: University of California Press, 1978).

24 Rawls, *A Theory of Justice*; Nozick, *Anarchy, State, and Utopia*; Dworkin, *Philosophy of Law*.

25 Adler, 'Seizing the Middle Ground'; Alexander Wendt, *Social Theory of International Politics* (Cambridge: Cambridge University Press, 1999).

26 *Ibid.*

27 Linklater, *The Transformation of Political Community*.

28 Jürgen Habermas, *The Theory of Communicative Action*, vol. 1., trans. Thomas McCarthy (Boston: Beacon Press, 1984); Thomas Risse, "Let's Argue!": Communicative Action in World Politics,' *International Organization* 54(1) (2000): 1–40.

29 Ashley, 'Geopolitics.'

30 Iver B. Neumann, 'Returning Practice to the Linguistic Turn: The Case of Diplomacy,' *Millennium* 31(3) (2002): 627–51.

31 Shapcott, *Justice, Community, and Dialogue*, 6.

32 For Chris Brown, the problem is not epistemological but whether the boundaries of human communities lie in the state or in the human species (Chris Brown, *International Relations Theory: New Normative Approaches* (New York and London: Harvester Wheatsheaf, 1992)).

33 See, for example, Rawls, *A Theory of Justice*.
34 See, for example, Michael Walzer, 'The Communitarian Critique of Liberalism,' *Political Theory* 18 (1990): 6–23.
35 Morrice, 'The Liberal–Communitarian Debate,' 236.
36 *Ibid.*, 235.
37 Ferdinand Tönnies, *Community and Society*, trans. and ed. Charles P. Loomis (East Lansing: Michigan State University Press, 1957); see also Barry Buzan, 'From International System to International Society: Structural Realism and Regime Theory Meet the English School,' *International Organization* 47(3) (1993): 327–52.
38 Fearon and Wendt, 'Rationalism and Constructivism,' 52–72.
39 See, for example, Beitz, *Political Theory*.
40 *Ibid.*
41 Morrice, 'The Liberal–Communitarian Debate,' 237.
42 *Ibid.*, 235.
43 Tönnies, *Community and Society*; see also Buzan, 'From International System to International Society.'
44 In constructivist analytic parlance we would say that subjectivity is endogenous to social structure; i.e., the belief of a single individual cannot exist without the beliefs of the other members of the group or community.
45 Walzer, 'The Communitarian Critique of Liberalism.'
46 *Ibid.*
47 Linklater, *The Transformation of Political Community*; Shapcott, *Justice, Community, and Dialogue*.
48 Morrice, 'The Liberal–Communitarian Debate,' 239.
49 Linklater, *The Transformation of Political Community*; Shapcott, *Justice, Community, and Dialogue*.
50 Frost, *Ethics in International Relations*.
51 Richard Rorty, *Objectivity, Relativism and Truth* (Philosophical Papers, vol. 1) (Cambridge: Cambridge University Press, 1991).
52 See, for eaxample, Hedley Bull, *The Anarchical Society: A Study of Order in World Politics* (New York: Columbia University Press, 1977); Buzan, 'From International System to International Society.'
53 *Ibid.*
54 Morrice, 'The Liberal–Communitarian Debate,' 246.
55 Shapcott, *Justice, Community, and Dialogue*, 60.
56 Frost, *Ethics in International Relations*, 158.
57 Shapcott, *Justice, Community, and Dialogue*, 57.
58 Frost, *Ethics in International Relations*, 158.
59 Shapcott, *Justice, Community, and Dialogue*, 50.
60 *Ibid.*, 51.
61 H. G. Gadamer, *Philosophical Hermeneutics*, trans. D. E. Linge (Berkeley: University of California Press, 1977).
62 See, for example, Beitz, *Political Theory*.
63 Shapcott, *Justice, Community, and Dialogue*, 202.
64 Neufeld, *The Restructuring of International Relations Theory*.
65 Linklater, 'The Problem of Community in International Relations'; *The Transformation of Political Community*.
66 *Ibid.*
67 *Ibid.*, 218.
68 *Ibid.*, 8, 218.
69 'Participation within a post-Westphalian international society,' says Linklater, 'rests upon the commitment to widen the boundaries of the political community so that insiders and outsiders can be associated as the equal members of a transnational citizenry' (*ibid.*, 175).
70 Habermas, *The Theory of Communicative Action*.

71 Shapcott, *Justice, Community, and Dialogue*, 86.

72 Linklater, *The Transformation of Political Community*, 167.

73 Ashley, 'Geopolitics,' 421.

74 *Positivism* is a metaphysical theory that holds: (a) 'a belief in the unity of science' (it applies to the social as well as to the natural sciences); (b) 'the view that there is a distinction between facts and values'; (c) 'a powerful belief in the existence of regularities in the social as well as the natural world'; and (d) 'a tremendous reliance on the belief that it is empirical validation or falsification that is the hallmark of "real" enquiry' (Steve Smith, 'Positivism and Beyond,' in Steve Smith, Ken Booth, and Marysia Zalewski, eds, *International Theory: Positivism and Beyond* (Cambridge: Cambridge University Press, 1996)), 16.

75 *Materialism* is the view that material reality exists, regardless of perception or interpretation, and that what we know is a faithful representation of the reality 'out there.' Materialism informs functionalist and rational choice social theories, which are the basis, respectively, of neorealism and neoliberalism in IR.

76 *Idealism* holds that the physical is just a collection of ideas and that, therefore, the foundation of all knowledge is the mind.

77 As a radicalized version of idealist philosophy, *post-structuralism* aims to deconstruct the dominant readings of reality; *post-modernism* aims to uncover the discourse and power structures that control practice. Both approaches agree that subjects are ontologically unimportant, reason is a chimera, there is no foundational point, and science is just power disguised as knowledge. Unless a distinction is necessary, I will refer to both approaches as post-modernism.

78 *Nominalism* is the philosophical view that the world does not come already classified and that it is human beings who classify it (Ian Hacking, *The Social Construction of What?* (Cambridge, MA: Harvard University Press, 1999)).

79 Thomas Kuhn, *The Structure of Scientific Revolutions* (Chicago: University of Chicago Press, 1970).

80 Alexander Wendt, 'Constructing International Politics,' *International Security* 20(1) (1995): 73.

81 John R. Searle, *The Construction of Social Reality* (New York: Free Press, 1995).

82 Patrick Baert, *Social Theory in the Twentieth Century* (New York: New York University Press, 1998), 104; see also Giddens, *The Constitution of Society*.

83 *Ibid.*

84 Fearon and Wendt, 'Rationalism and Constructivism,' 52–72.

85 *Ibid.*, 58.

86 John G. Ruggie, *Constructing the World Polity: Essays on International Institutionalization* (London: Routledge, 1998).

87 Rey Koslowski and Friedrich Kratochwil, 'Understanding Change in International Politics: The Soviet Empire's Demise and the International System,' in Richard N. Lebow and Thomas Risse-Kappen, eds, *International Relations Theory and the End of the Cold War* (New York: Columbia University Press, 1995), 127–66; David Dessler, 'What's at Stake with the Agent–Structure Debate,' *International Organization* 43(3) (1989): 441–73.

88 Richard Price and Christian Reus-Smit, 'Dangerous Liaisons? Critical International Theory and Constructivism,' *European Journal of International Relations* 4(3) (1998): 259–94.

89 Adler and Crawford, *Progress in Postwar International Relations*.

90 *Instrumental rationality* is 'the efficient pursuit of exogenously determined interests within the constraints of available information, the interests and strategies of other actors, and the distribution of power' (Christian Reus-Smit, *The Moral Purpose of the State: Culture, Social Identity, and Institutional Rationality in International Relations* (Princeton: Princeton University Press, 1999), 159–60).

91 Robert Wuthnow, *Communities of Discourse* (Cambridge, MA: Harvard University Press, 1989), 16.

92 Neumann, 'Returning Practice to the Linguistic Turn.'

93 Morrice, 'The Liberal–Communitarian Debate,' 237.

94 Bull, *The Anarchical Society*.

95 Beitz, *Political Theory*.

96 Ruggie, *Constructing the World Polity*.

97 Jutta Weldes, *Constructing National Interests: The United States and the Cuban Missile Crisis* (Minneapolis: University of Minnesota Press, 1999).

98 Neumann, 'Returning Practice to the Linguistic Turn.'

99 Nicholas Onuf, 'Constructivism: A User's Manual,' in Vendulka Kubalkova, Nicholas Onuf, and Paul Kowert, eds, *International Relations in a Constructed World* (London: M. E. Sharpe, 1998), 58–78.

100 Robert W. Cox, 'Social Forces, States and World Orders: Beyond International Relations Theory,' in Robert O. Keohane, ed., *Neorealism and Its Critics* (New York: Columbia University Press, 1986), 204–54.

101 Jeffrey T. Checkel, 'Why Comply? Social Learning and European Identity Change,' *International Organization* 55(3) (2001): 553–88.

102 Rodney B. Hall, *National Collective Identity: Social Constructs and International Systems* (New York: Columbia University Press, 1999).

103 Adler and Barnett, *Security Communities*.

104 Karl Deutsch, Sidney A. Burrell, Robert A. Kann, Maurice Lee, Jr., Martin Lichterman, Raymond E. Lindgren, Francis L. Loewenheim, and Richard W. Van Wagenen, *Political Community and the North Atlantic Area* (Princeton: Princeton University Press, 1957).

105 James G. March and Johan P. Olsen, 'The Institutional Dynamics of International Political Orders,' *International Organization* 52(4) (1998): 943–69.

106 'An epistemic community is a network of professionals with recognized expertise and competence in a particular domain and an authoritative claim to policy-relevant knowledge within that domain or issue area' (Haas, 'Introduction,' 3; see also Adler, 'Cognitive Evolution').

107 Michael Barnett and I have defined the concept of security community, first developed by Deutsch *et al.* in *Political Community*, as a 'transnational region comprised of sovereign states whose people maintain dependable expectations of peaceful change' (Adler and Barnett, *Security Communities*, 30).

108 'A transnational advocacy network includes those relevant actors working internationally on an issue, who are bound together by shared values, a common discourse, and dense exchanges of information and services' (Keck and Sikkink, *Activists*, 2).

109 Networks of knowledge and practice are 'channels for the transfer of the bodies of technological knowledge and associated systems of hardware, practice, and values' (Ronnie D. Lipschutz and Judith Mayer, *Global Civil Society and Global Environmental Governance* (Albany: State University of New York Press, 1996), 74).

110

> The creation of new ideas occurs initially within a relatively small community of critical thinkers who have developed a sensitivity to some problem, an analysis of the sources of the problem, and a prescription for what should be done about the problem. ... These critical thinkers do not necessarily belong to a formally constituted organization, but they are part of a self-aware, mutually interacting group.
>
> (Rochon, *Culture Moves*, 22)

111 See above, p. 14 and n. 91.

112 'The members of even the smallest nation will never know most of their fellow members, meet them, or even hear of them, yet in the minds of each lives the image of the communion' (Benedict Anderson, *Imagined Communities: Reflections on the Origin and Spread of Nationalism* (London: Verso, 1991), 15).

113 Members of reading clubs in the eighteenth century were linked 'in invisible communities whose aptitude could only be imagined and could easily be exaggerated as their publishers had ample reason to do' (Sidney Tarrow, *Power in Movement: Social Movements and Contentious Politics* (Cambridge: Cambridge University Press, 1994), 58).

114 The concept of practice accounts for the authoritative interpretation of texts in the context of 'interpretive communities' (Stanley Fish, *Is There a Text on This Class? The Authority of Interpretive Communities* (Cambridge, MA: Harvard University Press, 1980).

115 An interpretive community is

> composed of the participants in a field of practice who set the parameters of what constitutes reasoned argumentation for that enterprise ... [and] is best understood as a way of speaking about the power of institutional settings, within which assumptions and beliefs become matters of common sense.
> (Ian Johnstone, 'Security Council Deliberations: The Power of the Better Argument,' *European Journal of International Law* 14(3) (2003): 439–44)

116 William M. Snyder, 'Communities of Practice: Combining Organizational Learning and Strategy Insights to Create a Bridge to the 21st Century' (http://www.co-i-l.com/coil/knowledge-garden/cop/cols.shtml; accessed May 5, 1999). The concept of community of practice, pioneered by Jean Lave and Etienne Wenger (*Situated Learning: Legitimate Peripheral Participation* (Cambridge: Cambridge University Press, 1991)), plays an important role in the recent development of the field of 'knowledge management' in business administration, which has nurtured an entire cottage industry of knowledge-management theories and studies. See, for example: Etienne Wenger, *Communities of Practice: Learning, Meaning and Identity* (Cambridge: Cambridge University Press, 1998); Etienne Wenger, Richard McDermott, and William M. Snyder, *A Guide to Making Knowledge: Cultivating Communities of Practice* (Boston: Harvard Business School Press, 2002); Eric L. Lesser, Michael A. Fontaine, and Jason A. Slusher, eds, *Knowledge and Communities* (Boston: Butterworth-Heinemann, 2000). Knowledge management (KM) refers to a 'broad collection of practices and approaches related to generating, capturing, disseminating know-how and other content relevant to the organization's business' (Stephen Denning, 'What is Knowledge Management?' A Background Document to the World Development Report White Paper, World Bank, http://www.unssc.org/unssc1/programme/km/WorldBankKM.pdf (1998); see also K. M. Wiig, 'Knowledge Management: Where Did It Come from and Where Will It Go,' *Expert Systems with Applications* 13(1) (1997): 1–14). So far, the concept of community of practice has been applied mainly in domestic and transnational corporate environments (e.g., IBM, Xerox). Recently, however, the World Bank adopted the concept and went on to create 200 communities of practice (Denning, 'What is Knowledge Management?').

117 Wenger *et al.*, *A Guide to Making Knowledge*.

118 Wenger, *Communities of Practice*, 83.

119 Etienne Wenger, 'Communities of Practice: Learning as a Social System,' www.co-i-l.com/coil/knowledge-garden/cop/lss.shtml (accessed May 5, 1999); also published in *Systems Thinker* 9(5) (1998).

120 Wenger, *Communities of Practice*, 99.

121 Lave and Wenger, *Situated Learning*.

122 Deutsch *et al.*, *Political Community*; Adler and Barnett, *Security Communities*.

123 Thus I take a broader view of communities of practice than does Wenger, who emphasizes mainly knowledge exchange.

124 Richard Price, 'Reversing the Gun Sights: Transnational Civil Society Targets Land Mines,' *International Organization* 52(3) (1998): 613–44.

125 Peter Haas, *Saving the Mediterranean: The Politics of International Environmental Protection* (New York: Columbia University Press, 1990).

126 See n. 110.

127 Rochon, *Culture Moves*, 25.

128 Social communication is integral to how communities of practice work. First, in the process of communication, practitioners bargain about and fix meanings. Second, communication flows more rapidly within a community of practice and facilitates its interactions with other communities. Third, through social communication, practitioners develop their distinctive identity and learn their practice.

129 Wenger, *Communities of Practice*.

130 Global public policy networks are 'alliances of government agencies, international corporations, and elements of civil society that join together to achieve what none can accomplish alone' (Wolfgang Reinicke, 'The Other World Wide Web: Global Public Policy Networks,' *Foreign Policy* 117 (1999/2000): 44–57). See also Diane Stone, 'Introduction: Global Knowledge and Advocacy Networks,' *Global Networks* 2(1) (2002): 1–11; 'The "Knowledge Bank" and the Global Development Network,' *Global Governance* 9 (2003): 43–61 and, Anne-Marie Slaughter, *A New World Order* (Princeton: Princeton University Press, 2004).

131 Keck and Sikkink, *Activists*.

132 William D. Coleman and Anthony Perl, 'Internationalized Policy Environments and Policy Network Analysis,' *Policy Studies* 47 (1999): 691–709.

133 Stone, 'Introduction.'

134 Keck and Sikkink, *Activists*.

135 'Episteme' is the term used by Emanuel Adler and Steven Bernstein ('Knowledge in Power: The Epistemic Construction of Global Governance,' in Michael Barnett and Raymond Duvall, eds, *Power and Global Governance* (Cambridge: Cambridge University Press, 2004) to denote structural social dispositions (ordering collective understandings and discourse) that make the world meaningful. See also John G. Ruggie, 'International Responses to Technology: Concepts and Trends,' *International Organization* 29(3) (1975): 557–83.

136 Keck and Sikkink, *Activists*, 3.

137 Richard McDermott, 'Why Information Technology Inspired but Cannot Deliver Knowledge Management,' in Eric L. Lesser, Michael A. Fontaine, and Jason Slusher, eds, *Knowledge and Communities* (Boston: Butterworth-Heinemann, 2000), 26.

138 Practices are the material expression of authoritatively selected and institutionalized collective meanings and understandings, including rules, roles, and identities, which members of communities of practice draw upon in order to know their bearings.

139 Wenger, *Communities of Practice*, 49.

140 *Ibid.*, 96.

141 I owe much of the next few paragraphs to Wenger, *Communities of Practice*, 280.

142 Karl R. Popper, *The Open Universe: An Argument for Indeterminism*, ed. W. W. Bartley, III (Totowa: Rowman and Littlefield, 1982).

143 John Mearsheimer, 'The False Promise of International Institutions,' *International Security* 19(3) (1994–95): 5–49.

144 Samuel Sitkin, 'Learning through Failure: The Strategy of Small Losses,' *Research in Organizational Behavior* 14 (1992): 231–66.

145 D. Kahneman, P. Slovic, and A. Tversky, *Judgment under Uncertainty: Heuristics and Biases* (Cambridge: Cambridge University Press, 1982).

146 Albert Bandura, *Social Learning Theory* (Englewood Cliffs: Prentice Hall, 1977).

147 Jack Levy, 'Learning and Foreign Policy: Sweeping a Conceptual Minefield,' *International Organization* 48(2) (1994): 279–312.

148 Philip E. Tetlock, 'Learning in U.S. and Soviet Foreign Policy: In Search of an Elusive Concept,' in George Breslauer and Philip E. Tetlock, eds, *Learning in U.S. and Soviet Foreign Policy* (Berkeley: University of California Press, 1992), 20–61; Deborah W.

Larson, *Origins of Containment: A Psychological Explanation* (Princeton: Princeton University Press, 1985).

149 Jean Piaget, *The Moral Judgment of the Child* (New York: Harcourt Brace, 1932).

150 J. C. Turner, *Rediscovering the Social Group* (Oxford: Basil Blackwell, 1987).

151 Checkel, 'Why Comply?'; Risse,' '"Let's Argue!"'; Wendt, *Social Theory*.

152 Wenger, *Communities of Practice*, 280.

153 *Ibid*.

154 James March, *Decisions and Organizations* (New York: Basil Blackwell, 1988); Ernst B. Haas, *When Knowledge Is Power* (Berkeley: University of California Press, 1990).

155 Participation describes the 'social experience of living in the world in terms of membership in social communities and active involvement in social enterprises' (Wenger, *Communities of Practice*, 55).

156 *Ibid*., 4.

157 *Ibid*., 95–96.

158 *Ibid*. 7–8.

159 Searle, *The Construction of Social Reality*.

160 Michel Foucault, *The Order of Things: An Archeology of Human Sciences* (New York: Pantheon, 1970); Ruggie, 'International Responses'; Adler and Haas, 'Conclusion'; Adler and Bernstein, 'Knowledge in Power.'

161 Rochon, *Culture Moves*, 15.

162 Wenger, *Communities of Practice*.

163 *Ibid*., 78.

164 *Ibid*., 77.

165 Adler and Bernstein, 'Knowledge in Power.'

166 See www.worldbank.org/devforum/communities.html.

167 Based on concepts of pluralistic integration and inclusion, cooperative security is *comprehensive*, because it links classic security elements to economic, environmental, cultural, and human-rights factors. It is also *indivisible*, in the sense that the security of one state is inseparable from that of other states. Most important, it is *cooperative*; security is based on confidence and cooperation, the peaceful resolution of disputes, and the work of mutually reinforcing multilateral institutions. See Richard Cohen and Michael Mihalka, 'Cooperative Security: New Horizons for International Order,' The Marshall Center Papers, No. 3 (Garmisch-Partenkirchen, Germany: The George Marshall Center, 2001).

168 Wenger, *Communities of Practice*, 73.

169 *Engagement* is active involvement in the process of negotiating meanings (*ibid*., 173).

170 *Imagination* refers to the creation of images of the world and perception of connections through time and space based on extrapolation from our own experience (*ibid*.).

171 *Alignment* means the coordination of our energy and activities so they fit into broader structures and contribute to broader enterprises (*ibid*., 174).

172 *Ibid*., 182.

173 *Ibid*., 118–19.

174 Mathias Albert, David Jacobson, and Yosef Lapid, *Identities, Borders, Orders: Rethinking International Relations Theory* (Minneapolis: University of Minnesota Press, 2001).

175 Wenger, *Communities of Practice*, 129.

176 Adler, 'Cognitive Evolution'; Matthew Evangelista, *Unarmed Forces: The Transnational Movement to End the Cold War* (Ithaca: Cornell University Press, 1998).

177 William Drake and Kalypso Nicolaidis ('Ideas, Interests, and Institutionalization: "Trade in Services" and the Uruguay Round,' *International Organization* 46(1) (1992): 37–100) thought of epistemic communities as being composed of two concentric circles; Johnstone ('Security Council Deliberations') had a similar conception of interpretive communities.

178 Daniel C. Thomas, *The Helsinki Effect: International Norms, Human Rights, and the Demise of Communism* (Princeton: Princeton University Press, 2001).

179 Searle, *The Construction of Social Reality*. We must, however, allow for a gap between the causes of a decision and the actual decision and 'another gap between the decision and the performance of the action. The reason for these gaps is that the intentionalistic causes of behavior are not sufficient to determine the behavior' (John R. Searle, *Mind, Language, and Society: Philosophy in the Real World* (New York: Basic Books, 1998), 107). Because reasons are sensitive to interpretation, reflexivity, learning, and the outside world, the expression of an intention is a process of temporal unfolding, in which contingency and indeterminacy are the rule.

180 Paul Muller, 'The Role of Authority in the Governance of Knowledge Communities,' paper presented at the DRUID winter 2003 Conference, January 16–18, 2003, Aalborg, Denmark. http://www.druid.dk/conferences/winter2003/Paper/Muller.pdf (accessed May 1, 2003).

181 *Ibid.*

182 Rochon, *Culture Moves*, 23.

183 John Maresca, *To Helsinki: The Conference on Security and Cooperation in Europe, 1973–1975* (Durham, NC: Duke University Press, 1985).

184 Amitav Acharya, *Constructing a Security Community in Southeast Asia* (London: Routledge, 2001).

185 E. H. Carr, *The Twenty Years' Crisis 1919–1939* (London: Macmillan, 1939); Bull, *The Anarchical Society*; Barry Buzan, 'The English School: An Underexploited Resource in IR,' *Review of International Studies* 27(3) (2001): 471–88; Barry Buzan, Charles Jones, and Richard Little, *The Logic of Anarchy: Neorealism to Structural Realism* (New York: Columbia University Press, 1993).

186 Fearon and Wendt, 'Rationalism and Constructivism,' 52–72.

2 From being to becoming

1 Ludwik Fleck, *Genesis and Development of a Scientific Fact* (Chicago and London: University of Chicago Press, 1979), 39.

2 Thomas S. Kuhn, *The Structure of Scientific Revolutions*, 2nd edn (Chicago: University of Chicago Press, 1970). I subscribe to Toulmin's understanding of paradigms: they 'are not "true" or "false" in any naïve sense. Rather they take us farther (or less far) and are theoretically more or less fruitful' (Stephen Toulmin, *Foresight and Understanding* (New York: Harper, 1961), 57). For a while, perhaps for a long time, old and new paradigms overlap until the new one finally manages to gain supremacy.

3 James E. Dougherty and Robert L. Pfaltzgraff, Jr., *Contending Theories of International Relations* (Philadelphia: J. B. Lippincott, 1971).

4 Kenneth N. Waltz, 'Theory of International Relations,' in Fred I. Greenstein and Nelson W. Polsby, eds, *Handbook of Political Science*, vol. 8 (Reading, MA: Addison-Wesley, 1975), 1–85.

5 Kenneth N. Waltz, *Theory of International Politics* (Reading, MA: Addison-Wesley, 1979).

6 Ole R. Holsti, Randolph M. Siverson, and Alexander L. George, eds, *Change in the International System* (Boulder: Westview, 1980).

7 Morton A. Kaplan, *System and Process in International Politics* (New York: Wiley, 1962).

8 George Modelski, 'Agraria and Industria: Two Models of the International System,' in Klaus Knorr and Sydney Verba, eds, *The International System* (Princeton: Princeton University Press, 1961).

9 Charles A. McClelland, 'The Acute International Crisis,' in Knorr and Verba, *The International System*.

10 Richard N. Rosecrance, *Action and Reaction in World Politics* (Boston: Little, Brown, 1963).

11 Waltz, *Theory of International Politics*.

12 Kaplan, *System and Process*, 4.

13 McClelland, 'The Acute International Crisis.'

14 Modelski, 'Agraria and Industria.'

15 Rosecrance, *Action and Reaction.*

16 Waltz, *Theory of International Politics.*

17 Kaplan, *System and Process.*

18 McClelland, 'The Acute International Crisis.'

19 Waltz, *Theory of International Politics.*

20 For a critical assessment of these theories and their concept of structure, see Gary R. Waxmonsky and Jeffrey A. Hart, 'Content in Search of Form: Systems, Structures and Regimes in International Relations Theory' (mimeo, 1976).

21 System theorists were concerned in varying degrees with several categories of subjects:

> (1) the internal organization and interaction patterns of complexes of elements hypothesized or observed to exist as a system; (2) the relationship and boundaries between a system and its environment and, in particular, the nature and impact of inputs from and outputs to the environment; (3) the functions performed by systems, the structures for the performance of such functions, and their effect upon the stability of the system; (4) the homeostatic mechanism available to the system for the maintenance of steady-state or equilibrium; (5) the classification of systems as open or closed, or as organismic or nonorganismic systems; and (6) the structuring of hierarchical levels of systems, the location of subsystems within systems, the patterns of interactions among subsystems themselves, and between subsystems and the system itself.
>
> (Dougherty and Pfaltzgraff, *Contending Theories,* 118)

22 Stanley Hoffmann, 'Theory as a Set of Questions,' in Stanley Hoffman, ed., *Contemporary Theory in International Relations* (Englewood Cliffs: Prentice Hall, 1960).

23 Klaus Knorr and James Rosenau, eds, *Contending Approaches to International Politics* (Princeton: Princeton University Press, 1969).

24 Karl Deutsch, *The Nerves of Government* (New York: Free Press, 1966).

25 Ernst B. Haas, *Beyond the Nation-State: Functionalism and International Organization* (Stanford: Stanford University Press, 1964).

26 Deutsch, *The Nerves of Government.*

27 Haas, *Beyond the Nation-State,* 77.

28 Robert O. Keohane and Joseph S. Nye, Jr., 'International Interdependence and Integration,' in Greenstein and Polsby, *Handbook of Political Science,* 363–414.

29 Robert O. Keohane and Joseph S. Nye, *Power and Interdependence* (Boston: Little, Brown, 1977).

30 Ernst B. Haas, 'Is There a Hole in the Whole? Knowledge, Technology, Interdependence and the Construction of International Regimes,' *International Organization* 29 (1975).

31 Waltz, *Theory of International Politics,* 138–60.

32 Edward L. Morse, *Modernization and the Transformation of International Relations* (New York: Free Press, 1976), 118.

33 James A. Caporaso, ed., special issue of *International Organization* 32 (1978) on dependency.

34 Waltz, *Theory of International Politics,* especially ch. 6. A classic critical review of the notion of balance of power is Ernst B. Haas, 'The Balance of Power: Prescription, Concept or Propaganda?' *World Politics* 5 (1953).

35 Morton A. Kaplan, *Variants on Six Models of the International System,* in James N. Rosenau, ed., *International Politics and Foreign Policy* (New York: Free Press, 1969), 292–93.

36 Waltz, *Theory of International Politics*; Rosecrance, *Action and Reaction.*

37 George Liska, *Quest for Equilibrium* (Baltimore and London: Johns Hopkins University Press, 1977).

38 Henry Kissinger, *A World Restored: Metternich, Castlereagh and the Problems of Peace, 1812–1822* (London: Weidenfeld & Nicolson, 1957).

39 Leon N. Lindberg and Stuart A. Scheingold, *Europe's Would-Be Polity: Patterns of Change in the European Community* (Englewood Cliffs: Prentice Hall, 1970), 137.

40 Charles P. Kindleberger, *The World in Depression, 1929–1939* (Berkeley: University of California Press, 1974).

41 Robert Gilpin, *U.S. Power and the Multinational Corporation* (New York: Basic Books, 1975).

42 Stephen D. Krasner, 'State Power and the Structure of International Trade,' *World Politics* 28 (1976).

43 Robert O. Keohane, 'The Theory of Hegemonic Stability and Changes in International Economic Regimes, 1967–1977,' in Holsti, Siverson, and George, *Change in the International System*, 136.

44 See Haas' description and explanation of 'ecoholism' in Ernst B. Haas, 'Sticks and Stones Can Break My Bones, but Words Can Never Hurt Me' (mimeo, 1981); published as 'Words Can Hurt You; or, Who Said What to Whom about Regimes,' in Stephen D. Krasner, ed., *International Regimes* (Ithaca: Cornell University Press, 1983).

45 Herman E. Daly, ed., *Economics, Ecology, Ethics: Essays toward a Steady-State Economy* (San Francisco: W. H. Freeman, 1980).

46 Cynthia Eagle Russett, *The Concept of Equilibrium in American Social Thought* (New Haven: Yale University Press, 1966), 84.

47 Robert C. North, *The World That Could Be* (New York: Norton, 1976), 55.

48 Post-industrial corrections refer to the problems that arise because of industrialization and indiscriminate growth and the means conceived to alleviate and correct them.

49 Ernst B. Haas, 'Why Collaborate?' *World Politics* 32 (1980).

50 *Ibid.*

51 According to Herbert A. Simon (*The Sciences of the Artificial* (Cambridge, MA: MIT Press, 1969), 100), in a 'nearly decomposable system, the short-run behavior of each of the component subsystems is approximately independent of the short-run behavior of the other components. … In the long run, the behavior of any of the components depends only in an aggregate way on the behavior of the other components.'

52 Ilya Prigogine, 'Order through Fluctuation: Self-Organization and Social System,' in Erich Jantsch and Conrad H. Waddington, eds, *Evolution and Consciousness* (Reading, MA: Addison-Wesley, 1976); *From Being to Becoming: Time and Complexity in the Physical Sciences* (San Francisco: W. H. Freeman, 1980); Ilya Prigogine, Gregoire Nicolis, and Agnes Babloyantz, 'Thermodynamics of Evolution,' *Physics Today* (November–December 1972); Ilya Prigogine, Peter M. Allen, and Robert Herman, 'Long-Term Trends and the Evolution of Complexity,' in Ervin Laszlo and Judah Bierman, eds, *Goals in a Global Community* (New York: Pergamon, 1977); P. Glansdorff and Ilya Prigogine, *Structure, Stability and Fluctuations* (London: Wiley, 1971).

53 Erich Jantsch, *The Self-Organizing Universe* (Oxford: Pergamon Press, 1980), 28.

54 *Ibid.*, 33; Milan Zeleny, *Autopoiesis, Dissipative Structures, and Spontaneous Social Orders* (Boulder: Westview, 1980).

55 Entropy refers to the process indicated by the Second Law of Thermodynamics, by which the universe and everything in it tend toward exhaustion, decay, disorder, and chaos.

56 Prigogine, *From Being to Becoming*, 5.

57 Prigogine, Nicolis, and Babloyantz, 'Thermodynamics of Evolution,' 24.

58 Prigogine, 'Order through Fluctuation,' 93.

59 Erich Jantsch, *Design for Evolution* (New York: Braziller, 1975), 37.

60 Malcolm W. Browne, 'Scientists See a Loophole in the Fatal Law of Physics,' *New York Times*, May 21, 1979, C3.

61 Prigogine, *From Being to Becoming*, 132.

62 Jantsch, *The Self-Organizing Universe*, 44–47.

63 In this case, the 'law of large numbers'—stating that an adequate description of a hetero-geneous system is possible by means of average values—is rendered invalid (*ibid.*, 46).

64 Jacques Monod, *Chance and Necessity* (New York: Vintage Books, 1971).

65 C. H. Waddington, *Tools for Thought* (New York: Basic Books, 1977), 105, 115–16.

66 Jantsch, *Design for Evolution*, 92.

67 Power is not only the ability to control events in the international system by preventing processes and events from taking place and/or by affecting the way they happen, but also the ability to make some processes and events happen, according to someone's wishes.

68 For the use of this concept applied to other types of systemic thinking, see C. S. Holling, 'Resilience and Stability of Ecosystems,' in Jantsch and Waddington, *Evolution and Consciousness*, 73–92.

69 Holsti, Siverson, and George, *Change in the International System*.

70 Waltz (*Theory of International Politics*) has called those who devise IR theories focusing on the individual or the national level 'reductionists.'

71 A theory of system transformation can be stated in a stochastic manner, i.e., in terms of probabilities, and is a handy tool for describing some of these probabilities. Decision trees and Markov Functions can analyze the sequence of fluctuations and the choices they generate, with special emphasis on the choices at bifurcations (thresholds).

72 The examples I chose to illustrate system transformation (2 and 4), based on World Wars I and II, do not imply that only a major war can drive the system to a change. I have chosen these illustrations because they are more salient and self-evident.

73 Canada, Israel, Japan, and West Germany have the capability to become nuclear powers almost instantly. Argentina, Brazil, Pakistan, South Africa, and Taiwan are close to becoming nuclear.

74 Joseph Nye, 'Nonproliferation: A Long-Term Strategy,' *Foreign Affairs* (April 1978); Thomas L. Neff and Henry D. Jacoby, 'Nonproliferation Strategy in a Changing Nuclear Fuel Market,' *Foreign Affairs* (summer 1979); Ronald Bettauer, 'The Nuclear Non-Proliferation Act of 1978,' *Law and Policy in International Business* (1978): 1105–80; Gerald Smith and George Rathjens, 'Reassessing Nuclear Nonproliferation Policy,' *Foreign Affairs* (1981).

75 *New York Times*, June 10, 1981, 6.

76 Shai Feldman, 'Peacemaking in the Middle East: The Next Step,' *Foreign Affairs* (1981).

77 C. Fred Bergsten, 'The Evolution and Management of the Multiple Reserve Currency System: A Very Preliminary Analysis' (mimeo, 1981).

78 *Ibid.*, 1.

79 *Ibid.*, 18–20.

80 *Ibid.*, 30–31.

81 The title of a book by Albert O. Hirschman (New York: Norton, 1973).

82 Gabriel Palma, 'Dependency: A Formal Theory of Underdevelopment or a Methodology for the Analysis of Concrete Situations of Underdevelopment?, *World Development* 6 (1978).

83 Julian S. Huxley, *Evolution: The Modern Synthesis* (New York: Harper, 1943); Talcott Parsons, *The Evolution of Societies* (Englewood Cliffs: Prentice Hall, 1977); Marshall D. Sahlins and Elman R. Service, *Cultural Evolution* (Ann Arbor: University of Michigan Press, 1973).

84 Pierre Teilhard de Chardin, *The Phenomenon of Man* (New York: Harper, 1959).

85 Kenneth E. Boulding, *Ecodynamics* (Beverly Hills: Sage, 1978).

86 Jantsch, *The Self-Organizing Universe*.

87 Donella Meadows, Dennis L. Meadows, Jorgen Randers, and William W. Behrens III, *Limits to Growth* (Washington, DC: Potomac Associates, 1972); Mihajlo Mesarovic and Eduard Pestel, *Mankind at the Turning Point* (New York: E. P. Dutton/Reader's Digest Press, 1974); Garrett Hardin, 'Living on a Lifeboat,' *Bioscience* 24 (1974); Nicholas Georgescu Roegen, *The Entropy Law and the Economic Process* (Cambridge, MA: Harvard University Press, 1971).

88 Peter A. Corning, 'The Biological Bases of Behavior and Some Implications for Political Science,' *World Politics* 23 (1971).

89 A metaphor has been defined as a 'way of proceeding from the known to the unknown. It is a way of cognition in which the identifying qualities of one thing are transferred in an instantaneous, almost unconscious, flash of insight to some other thing that is, by remoteness or complexity, unknown to us.' It is thus a way of converging complex units into a commanding image that allows for the sudden perception of relationship (Robert A. Nisbet, *Social Change and History* (London: Oxford University Press, 1969), 4).

90 Haas, 'Sticks and Stones'; Emanuel Adler, 'Evolution and Catalytic Interdependence: A Theory of Change in International Relations with Special Reference to Science and Technology Policies in Latin America' (Ph.D. dissertation, University of California at Berkeley, 1982).

91 June Goodfield, *An Imagined World: A Story of Scientific Discovery* (New York: Harper & Row, 1981).

92 Richard Schlegel, *Superposition and Interaction: Coherence in Physics* (Chicago: University of Chicago Press, 1980).

93 Jantsch, *The Self-Organizing Universe*, 257.

94 With regard to the ideas of the 'image of the future,' I was influenced by a very imaginative study by Fred L. Polak, *The Image of the Future* (Leyden: A. W. Sythoff, 1961). Polak, a sociologist, wrote this large philosophical study to describe how, from ancient times to the present, human beings, their societies, and their cultures have been pulled toward a future fulfillment of their own preceding and prevailing idealistic images of the future, as well as being pushed from behind by their own realistic past:

> The spirit of the times is both nourished by and operates on the basis of currently dominating ideas concerning past and future. Past and future come together with a mighty clash in the present, and out of the reverberations of this clash, the images of the future emerge. These in turn determine the shape both of the present and the future, in an endless chain of action, reaction and interaction.
>
> (*Ibid.*, 51)

95 Thomas C. Schelling, *Micromotives and Macrobehavior* (New York: Norton, 1978).

96 John Rader Platt, *The Step to Man* (New York: John Wiley & Sons, 1966), 71–86. Adler ('Evolution and Catalytic Interdependence') suggested a field of inquiry dealing with ideas, ideologies, and intellectuals and how these in turn influence policy and action. This field's appeal is that it enables researchers to get as close as possible to the original sources of political action and policy change.

97 Todd R. La Porte, ed., *Organized Social Complexity* (Princeton: Princeton University Press, 1975), 6.

98 Harlan G. Wilson, 'Complexity as a Theoretical Problem' (Ph.D. dissertation, University of California at Berkeley, 1978), 69–90.

99 *Ibid.*, 88.

100 According to F. E. Emery and E. K. Trist, turbulent environments or turbulent fields are the most complexly textured environments. 'These are environments in which there are dynamic processes arising from the field itself which create significant variances for the component systems' (F. E. Emery and E. K. Trist, *Towards a Social Ecology* (London and New York: Plenum Press, 1972), 52). See also Haas, 'Sticks and Stones.'

101 Franklin L. Baumer, *Modern European Thought: Continuity and Change in Ideas, 1600–1950* (New York: Macmillan, 1977), 421.

102 *Ibid.*

103 Mannheim's 'sociology of knowledge' (Karl Mannheim, *Ideology and Utopia* (New York: Harcourt, Brace, 1936)) suggested relativistic ideas that generated more criticism than intellectual continuity. Critics of Marxist theory also placed it in the

historicist category. Some of the harshest critics of historicism were Popper (Karl Popper, *The Poverty of Historicism*, 2d edn (London: Routledge, 1960); *The Open Society and Its Enemies*, 4th edn (London: Routledge, 1962)) and positivists such as Weber (Max Weber, *The Theory of Social and Economic Organization*, trans. A. M. Henderson and Talcott Parsons (New York: Free Press, 1964)), who believed in an empirical science based on rational concepts.

104 David Park, *The Image of Eternity: Roots of Time in the Physical World* (Amherst: University of Massachusetts Press, 1980), 64–65.

3 Cognitive evolution

1 Franklin L. Baumer, *Modern European Thought: Continuity and Change in Ideas, 1600–1950* (New York: Macmillan, 1977), 59.

2 Karl R. Popper, *Quantum Theory and the Schism in Physics*, ed. W. W. Bartley III (Totowa: Rowman and Littlefield, 1982).

3 Robert O. Keohane, 'Theory of World Politics: Structural Realism and Beyond,' in Robert O. Keohane, ed., *Neorealism and Its Critics* (New York: Columbia University Press, 1986), 164–65; *Neorealism and Its Critics* is a comprehensive collection of essays on neorealism. The best critique of neorealism is Richard K. Ashley, 'The Poverty of Neorealism,' in *ibid.*, 255–300.

4 Kenneth N. Waltz, *Theory of International Politics* (Reading, MA: Addison-Wesley, 1979); Robert Gilpin, *War and Change in World Politics* (New York: Cambridge University Press, 1981).

5 R. B. J. Walker, 'Realism, Change, and International Political Theory,' *International Studies Quarterly* 31(1) (1987): 77.

6 Waltz, *Theory of International Politics*, 70.

7 Such a system is neatly described by Herbert Butterfield ('The Balance of Power,' in Herbert Butterfield and Martin Wight, eds, *Diplomatic Investigations: Essays in the Theory of International Politics* (Cambridge, MA: Harvard University Press, 1966), 132):

> All the various bodies, the greater and the lesser powers, were poised against one another, each exercising a kind of gravitational pull on all the rest—and the pull of each would be proportionate to its mass, though its effect would be greatly reduced as it acted at a greater distance. When one of these bodies increased its mass, therefore … the rest could recover an equilibrium only by regrouping themselves … making a necessary rectification in the distances and producing new combinations.

8 John G. Ruggie, 'Continuity and Transformation in the World Polity: Toward a Neorealist Synthesis,' *World Politics* 35(2) (1983): 285. See also Stanley Hoffmann, *Janus and Minerva: Essays in the Theory and Practice of International Politics* (Boulder: Westview Press, 1987), 123.

9 Gabriel A. Almond and Stephen J. Genco, 'Clouds, Clocks, and the Study of Politics,' *World Politics* 29(4) (1977): 492.

10 Gilpin, *War and Change*, 13–14.

11 *Ibid.*, 15.

12 *Ibid.*, 210.

13 The term reflectivist was coined by Robert O. Keohane (*International Institutions and State Power* (Boulder: Westview, 1989), ch. 7) in his presidential address to the International Studies Association.

14 Walker, 'Realism, Change, and International Political Theory,' 81.

15 Karl R. Popper, *Objective Knowledge: An Evolutionary Approach* (Oxford: Clarendon Press, 1972), 228.

16 Friedrich Kratochwil and John G. Ruggie, 'International Organization: A State of the Art in an Art of the State,' *International Organization* 40(4) (1986): 764–66.

17 Donald T. Campbell, 'Evolutionary Epistemology,' in Gerard Radnitsky and W. W. Bartley III, eds, *Evolutionary Epistemology, Theory of Rationality and the Sociology of Knowledge* (La Salle: Open Court, 1987).

> The logical and methodological arguments are due chiefly to Popper, as are those that are drawn from physics. The biological and physiological support and interpretation come in part from Popper, but also from Lorenz and from such biologists as Sir John Eccles, Sir Peter Medawar, Ernst Mayr, and Jacques Monod. The psychological work can be traced back to Küple and Bühler, and is continued in the work of F. A. von Hayek ... as well as by Campbell. Campbell has made a fuller, more consistent, and more adequate statement of the position than any other person.
>
> (W. W. Bartley III, 'Philosophy of Biology versus Philosophy of Physics,' in Radnitsky and Bartley, *Evolutionary Epistemology*, 21–22)

See also Werner Callebout and Rik Pinxten, eds, *Evolutionary Epistemology* (Dordrecht: Reidel, 1987). The last-named has a comprehensive bibliography on evolutionary epistemology.

18 The new physics works on the assumption of complementarity between physical and perceptual events; biology has history and emergent conditions built in. See Victor F. Weisskopf, 'The Frontiers and Limits of Science,' *Daedalus* 113(3) (1984): 191–95.

19 For as 'cousin to the amoeba that we are, how could we know for certain?' (Donald T. Campbell, 'On the Conflicts between Biological and Social Evolution and between Psychology and Moral Tradition,' *American Psychologist* 30 (1975): 1120.

20 Ernst B. Haas, 'Words Can Hurt You; or Who Said What to Whom about Regimes,' in Stephen D. Krasner, ed., *International Regimes* (Ithaca: Cornell University Press, 1983), 24.

21

> Learning in the perspective of an evolutionary epistemology must be open, unspecifiable ahead of events in terms of substance, and as unpredictable as evolutionary adaptation. ... [Thus there] is no fixed 'national interest' and no 'optimal regime.' Different perceptions of national interest, changeable in response to new information or altered values, will result in different processes and in a variety of regimes that will be considered rational by the actors—at least for a while. Collaboration among states ... expresses no more than the convergence of such interests.
>
> (*Ibid.*, 25–26, 57)

22 Bartley, 'Philosophy of Biology,' 21.

23 Campbell, 'Evolutionary Epistemology'; Thomas S. Kuhn, *The Structure of Scientific Revolutions* (Chicago: University of Chicago Press, 1962); Stephen Toulmin, *Foresight and Understanding: An Inquiry into the Aims of Science* (New York: Harper & Row, 1961); *Human Understanding* (Princeton: Princeton University Press, 1972).

24 Karl R. Popper, *Conjectures and Refutations* (London: Routledge and Kegan Paul, 1963).

25 Bartley, 'Philosophy of Biology,' 24.

26 Karl R. Popper, 'The Place of Mind in Nature,' in Richard O. Elvee, ed., *Mind in Nature* (New York: Harper & Row, 1982), 54. One can, for example, investigate the structure and function of a theory, or whether it solves a problem, without having to get inside the mind and beliefs of the individual who conceived the theory.

27 Popper's philosophical basis for accepting the real existence of World 3 comes from Alfred Landé: something is real if it can be kicked and can, in principle, kick back. See

Karl R. Popper, *The Open Universe: An Argument for Indeterminism*, ed. W. W. Bartley III (Totowa: Rowman and Littlefield, 1982), 116.

28 Almond and Genco, 'Clouds,' 491; see also Popper, *Objective Knowledge*.

29 Popper, *Objective Knowledge*, 229.

30 Robert Jervis, 'Consistency in Foreign Policy View,' in Richard L. Merritt, ed., *Communication in International Politics* (Urbana: University of Illinois Press, 1972), 287.

31 David J. Depew and Bruce H. Weber, 'Innovation and Tradition in Evolutionary Theory: An Interpretative Afterword,' in David J. Depew and Bruce H. Weber, eds, *Evolution at a Crossroads: The New Biology and the New Philosophy of Science* (Cambridge, MA: MIT Press, 1985), 240.

32 Toulmin, *Foresight and Understanding*, 81.

33 Toulmin, *Human Understanding*.

34 Campbell, *Evolutionary Epistemology*. See also Colin Martindale, *Cognition and Consciousness* (Homewood: Dorsey Press, 1981), 411.

35 James N. Rosenau, 'Mudding, Meddling and Modeling: Alternative Approaches to the Study of World Politics in an Era of Rapid Change,' *Millennium* 8(2) (1979): 135.

36 Robert D. Putnam, 'Diplomacy and Domestic Politics: the Logic of Two-Level Games,' *International Organization* 42(3) (1988): 434. Rosenau has also developed an approach to study change in International Relations on the basis of 'micro–macro' interaction, wherein

> the macro and micro phenomena that make up any large-scale structure, process, institution, or collectivity are linked together in endlessly reinforcing interactions. ... Macro structures and collectivities may have a life of their own, but they draw their sustenance from their micro components. ... At the micro level change results from the failure of the memories, beliefs, expectations, and networks to perpetuate themselves and this failure occurs because circumstances are altered and the memories, beliefs, expectations, and networks no longer serve the needs to the habit-driven behavior for which they evolved.
>
> (James N. Rosenau, 'Before Cooperation: Hegemons, Regimes, and Habit-Driven Actors in World Politics,' *International Organization* 40(4) (1986): 868–69)

For a sociological study about the micro–macro relationship see Jeffrey C. Alexander, Bernhard Giesen, Richard Munch and Neil J. Semelser, eds, *The Micro–Macro Link* (Berkeley: University of California Press, 1987).

37 Stephen Toulmin, 'Evolution, Adaptation, and Human Understanding,' in Marilynn B. Brewer and Barry E. Collins, eds, *Scientific Inquiry and the Social Sciences* (San Francisco: Jossey-Bass, 1981), 31. To

> understand political choices, we need to understand where the frame of reference for the actors' thinking comes from. ... We need to understand not only how people reason about alternatives, but where the alternatives come from in the first place; [thus] the task of determining how people actually do behave in situations having game-like characteristics must be turned over to empirical research: research that seeks to determine what values people actually act on, and how they form their expectations and beliefs.
>
> (Herbert A. Simon, 'Human Nature in Politics: The Dialogue of Psychology with Political Science,' *American Political Science Review* 79(2) (1985): 300, 302)

38 Joseph S. Nye, Jr., 'Nuclear Learning,' *International Organization* 41(3) (1987): 372.

39 Robert O. Keohane, *After Hegemony: Cooperation and Discord in the World Political Economy* (Princeton: Princeton University Press, 1984).

40 Popper, *Objective Knowledge*, 61, 340–61.

41 *Ibid.*
42 *Ibid.*, 66.
43 *Ibid.*, 24.
44 Arie E. Kruglanski and Icek Ajzen, 'Bias and Error in Human Judgment,' *European Journal of Social Psychology* 13 (1983): 1–44. Kruglanski and Ajzen's argument is an attempt to build an epistemological background to the problems of judgment, heuristics, and biases in cognitive processes, and provide a corrective to the studies of Daniel Kahneman and Amos Tversky (Daniel Kahneman, Paul Slovic, and Amos Tversky, eds, *Judgment under Uncertainty: Heuristics and Biases* (Cambridge: Cambridge University Press, 1982)), who argued, basically, that inference models are normative and that judgments that deviate systematically from such models are 'erroneous' and indicative of bias in the underlying inference process. Kruglanski and Ajzen's 'lay epistemology' should not be interpreted, however, to mean that all knowledge is erroneous. They define bias as a 'subjectively based preference for a given conclusion over possible alternative conclusions.' Error, in turn, is defined as the 'type of experience a person might have following an encountered inconsistency between a given hypothesis, conclusion, or inference, and a firmly held belief' (Kruglanski and Ajzen, 'Bias,' 19, 23).
45 The proof is in the 'numerous recorded instances of "laws" ... that for a time were considered proven beyond the shadow of a doubt, yet were subsequently falsified and replaced by apparently more believable alternatives' (*ibid.*, 12).
46

> The particular inference reached thus depends heavily on a given individual's epistemic process during which alternative cognitions (comprising premises for the person's conclusions) are generated. Such a sequential process during which cognitions are generated and validated has no unique point of termination. In principle, it could continue endlessly, as alternative competing ... cognitions are put forth and validated in timeless succession. In actuality, however, the process does come to a halt at some point. At any given time we seem to have in our possession various items of knowledge without which decision-making and action would be virtually inconceivable.
>
> (*Ibid.*, 15)

47 *Ibid.*, 15–16. The decision to stop the cognitive process that generates alternative sets of understandings can be explained by the person's epistemologically relevant motivations and the availability of given conceptions (*ibid.*, 19).
48 Stephen D. Krasner, 'Approaches to the State: Alternative Conceptions and Historical Dynamics,' *Comparative Politics* 16(2) (1984): 240.
49

> The mere fact that ... experiences emerge continuously within our stream of thought, that previous experiences are permanently receiving additional interpretative meanings in the light of these supervenient experiences, which have, more or less, changed our state of mind—all these basic features ... bar a recurrence of the same. Being recurrent, the recurrent is not the same any more.
> (Alfred Schutz, 'The Homecomer,' in *Collected Papers, II: Studies in Social Theory*, ed. Arvid Brodersen (The Hague: Martinus Nijhoff, 1971), 115)

50 G. John Ikenberry, 'Conclusion: An Institutional Approach to American Foreign Economic Policy,' *International Organization* 42(1) (1988): 234.
51 Edward L. Morse, *Modernization and the Transformation of International Relations* (New York: Free Press, 1976), 180. It should be emphasized, however, that not all cognitive change is episodic. Cognitive structures change continuously, but their effect on political action is better described as episodic, because it is only at those critical moments that a

cognitive threshold is crossed, and decision-makers 'discover' that they have to change their behavior. From a cognitive perspective, then, crises represent the culmination of a gradual process that for most of its course may have remained imperceptible.

52 Krasner, 'Approaches'; Ikenberry, 'An Institutional Approach.'

53 Toulmin, *Human Understanding*, 140.

54 Michael J. Brenner, 'The Theorist as Actor, the Actor as Theorist: Strategy in the Nixon Administration,' *Stanford Journal of International Studies* 7 (1972): 109–10.

55 George Katona, 'Business Expectations in the Framework of Psychological Economics (Toward a Theory of Expectations),' in Mary Jean Bowman, ed., *Expectations, Uncertainty, and Business Behavior* (New York: Social Science Research Council, 1958), 66.

56 I owe this insight to Ashton Carter and Joseph Nye. Nelson Polsby is also aware of it in his description of political innovation in America.

> [What] we normally think of as political innovation can be described as a combination of two processes. The first, the process of invention, causes policy options to come into existence. This is the domain of interest groups and their interests, of persons who specialize in acquiring and deploying knowledge about policies and their intellectual convictions, of persons who are aware of contextually applicable experiences of foreign nations, and of policy entrepreneurs, whose careers and ambitions are focused on the employment of their expertise and on the elaboration and adaptation of knowledge of problems. The second process is a process of systematic search, a process that senses and responds to problems, that harvests policy options and turns them to the purposes, both public and career-related, of politicians and public officials.
> (Nelson W. Polsby, *Political Innovation in America: The Politics of Policy Initiation* (New Haven: Yale University Press, 1984), 173)

57 John G. Ruggie first applied the term epistemic community to International Relations ('International Responses to Technology: Concepts and Trends,' *International Organization* 29(3) (1975): 569–70). See also: Peter M. Haas, 'Do Regimes Matter? Epistemic Communities and Mediterranean Pollution Control,' *International Organization* 43(3) (1989); Emanuel Adler, *The Power of Ideology: The Quest for Technological Autonomy in Argentina and Brazil* (Berkeley: University of California Press, 1987). On a more theoretical basis see Burkart Holzner and John Marx, *Knowledge Application: The Knowledge System in Society* (Boston: Allyn and Bacon, 1979). See also Diana Crane, *Invisible Colleges* (Chicago: University of Chicago Press, 1972). Bureaucracies have also been singled out as a source of political innovation. See, for example, H. Heclo, *Modern Social Politics in Britain and Sweden* (New Haven: Yale University Press, 1974). Peter A. Hall (*Governing the Economy; the Politics of State Intervention in Britain and France* (New York: Oxford University Press, 1986), 274) has emphasized politicians as sources of political innovations. However, he attributes to them the role of choosing among, rather than generating, ideas.

58 Colin A. Gray, *Strategic Studies and Public Policy: The American Experience* (Lexington: University Press of Kentucky, 1982), 26.

59 Douglas C. Bennett and Kenneth E. Sharpe, *Transnational Corporations versus the State: The Political Economy of the Mexican Auto Industry* (Princeton: Princeton University Press, 1985), 250.

60 Graham Allison, *Essence of Decision* (Boston: Little, Brown, 1971).

61 Toulmin, *Human Understanding*, 350.

62 Aaron Wildavsky, 'Choosing Preferences by Constructing Institutions: A Cultural Theory of Preference Formation,' *American Political Science Review* 81(1) (1987): 3–21; Herbert C. Kelman, *International Behavior: A Social-Psychological Analysis* (New York: Holt, Rinehart, and Winston, 1965), 578. For a critique of this approach see Michael Brenner, 'The Ideas of Progress and U.S. Nonproliferation Policy,' in Emanuel Adler and Beverly Crawford,

eds, *Progress in Postwar International Relations* (New York: Columbia University Press, 1991), 174–200.

63 Chih-yu Shih, 'A Cognitive Approach to International Organization: The Process of Seeking Common Cause—Maps in East-Asia,' paper presented at the Annual Meeting of the American Political Science Association, Washington, DC, 1988, 6.

64 Robert Legvold, 'War, Weapons, and Soviet Foreign Policy,' in Seweryn Bialer and Michael Mandelbaum, eds, *Gorbachev's Russian and American Foreign Policy* (Boulder: Westview, 1988), 120–25.

65 *Ibid.*, 121–22.

66 I am aware that the notion of cognitive structures has been widely used in social disciplines with various meanings. See, for example, Zenon W. Pylyskyn and William Demopoulos, eds, *Meaning and Cognitive Structure: Issues in the Computational Theory of Mind* (Norwood, NJ: Ablex, 1986). According to my definition, cognitive structures or collective theoretical understandings, whether or not based on science, when recorded in theories and transmitted can be studied objectively as 'products,' or World 3 objects, independently of the subjective minds that created them. See Bartley, 'Philosophy of Biology,' 20.

67 The concept of the thought collective places the attention on the carriers of collective ideas and was defined by Ludwik Fleck (*Genesis and Development of a Scientific Fact* (Chicago: University of Chicago Press, 1979), 39) as a community of persons mutually exchanging ideas or maintaining intellectual interaction that provides the special 'carrier' for the historical development of any field of thought, as well as for the given stock of knowledge and level of culture.

68 Alexander E. Wendt, 'The Agent–Structure Problem in International Relations Theory,' *International Organization* 41(3) (1987): 352.

69 *Ibid.*; see also Anthony Giddens, *Central Problems in Social Theory* (Berkeley: University of California Press, 1979).

70 Shih, 'A Cognitive Approach,' 14.

71 Wendt, 'The Agent–Structure Problem'; Anthony Giddens, *The Constitution of Society: Outline of the Theory of Structuration* (Cambridge: Polity Press, 1984).

72 Wendt, 'The Agent–Structure Problem,' 354.

73 *Ibid.*, 360.

74 *Ibid.*, 364–65.

75 William E. Connally, *The Terms of Political Discourse*, 2nd edn (Princeton: Princeton University Press, 1983), 46–48.

76 Robert Jervis, 'Realism, Game Theory, and Cooperation,' *World Politics* 40(3) (1988): 344.

77 Rokeach defines human values as 'a relatively small number of core ideas or cognitions present in every society about desirable end-states of existence and desirable modes of behavior instrumental to their attainment that are capable of being organized to form different priorities' (Milton Rokeach, 'From Individual to Institutional Values: With Special Reference to the Values of Science,' in Milton Rokeach, ed., *Understanding Human Values* (New York: Free Press, 1979), 49).

78 *Ibid.*, 50.

79 Robin M. Williams, Jr., 'Change and Stability in Values and Value Systems: A Sociological Perspective,' in Rokeach, *Understanding Human Values*, 16.

80 *Ibid.*, 20–22.

81 Ernst B. Haas and A. S. Whiting, *Dynamics of International Relations* (New York: McGraw-Hill, 1956); Karl W. Deutsch, Sidney A. Burrell, Robert A. Kann, Maurice Lee, Jr., Martin Lichterman, Raymond E. Lindgren, Francis L. Loewenheim, and Richard W. Van Wagenen, *Political Community and the North Atlantic Area* (New York: Greenwood Press, 1957).

82 Norman T. Feather, 'Human Values and the Prediction of Action: An Expectancy-Valence Analysis,' in Norman T. Feather, ed., *Expectations and Actions* (Hillsdale: Lawrence Erlbaum, 1982), 277; Amitai Etzioni, *The Moral Dimension: Toward a New Economics* (New York: Free Press, 1988), 127.

83 Albert O. Hirschman, *The Passions and the Interests: Political Arguments for Capitalism Before Its Triumph* (Princeton: Princeton University Press, 1977), 38.
84 Williams, 'Change and Stability,' 24.

> Japan is now a much more suitable partner for cooperation than it was in the 1930s, and not only because territorial expansion is neither possible nor economically necessary. Something has occurred that is more basic than changes in instrumental beliefs. Rabid nationalism and the drive to dominate have been transmuted. A Japanese nationalist of the 1930s who saw his country today would be horrified. … Because it took a cataclysm to produce such a change, this pattern does not provide an attractive route to a more cooperative world. But it does show both the importance and the mutability of values.
>
> (Jervis, 'Realism,' 343–44)

85 Karl R. Popper, *Unended Quest: An Intellectual Autobiography* (La Salle: Open Court, 1976), 193.
86 Emanuel Adler, 'Seasons of Peace: Progress in Postwar International Security,' in Adler and Crawford, eds, *Progress in Postwar International Relations*, 128–73.
87 Peter M. Haas, 'Making Progress in International Environmental Protection,' in Adler and Crawford, *Progress in Postwar International Relations*, 273–311.
88 Michael Thompson, *The Creation and Destruction of Value* (Oxford: Oxford University Press, 1979), 2.
89 Deutsch *et al.*, *Political Community*, 47.
90 Williams, 'Change and Stability,' 43.
91 Ernst B. Haas, 'Why Collaborate: Issue-Linkage and International Regimes,' *World Politics* 32(3) (1980): 351–405.
92 Herbert A. Simon, *Reason in Human Affairs* (Stanford: Stanford University Press, 1983), 103.
93 *Ibid.*, 104.
94 Thomas C. Schelling, *The Strategy of Conflict* (London: Oxford University Press, 1960), 57.
95 Krasner defined international regimes as 'sets of implicit or explicit principles, norms, rules, and decision-making procedures around which actors' expectations converge in a given area of international relations' (Stephen D. Krasner, 'Structural Causes and Regime Consequences: Regimes as Intervening Variables,' in Krasner, *International Regimes*, 2).
96 Richard N. Gardner, *Sterling–Dollar Diplomacy in Current Perspective: The Origins and the Prospects of Our International Economic Order* (New York: Columbia University Press, 1980).
97 Judith Goldstein, 'Ideas, Institutions, and American Trade Policy,' *International Organization* 42(1) (1988): 179–217; Peter A. Hall, *The Political Power of Economic Ideas: Keynesianism across Nations* (Princeton: Princeton University Press, 1989); Henry R. Nau, *The Myth of America's Decline: Leading the World Economy into the 1990s* (New York: Oxford University Press, 1990); John S. Odell, *U.S. International Monetary Policy: Markets, Power, and Ideas as Sources of Change* (Princeton: Princeton University Press, 1982); John G. Ruggie, 'International Regimes, Transactions, and Change: Embedded Liberalism in the Postwar Economic Order,' in Krasner, *International Regimes*, 195–231; 'Embedded Liberalism Revisited: Institutions and Progress in International Economic Relations,' in Adler and Crawford, *Progress in Postwar International Relations*, 201–34.
98 Raymond Vernon and Debra L. Spar, *Beyond Globalism: Remaking American Foreign Economic Policy* (New York: Free Press, 1989), 78.
99 Robert O. Keohane, 'The Theory of Hegemonic Stability and Changes in International Economic Regimes, 1967–1977,' in Ole Holsti, Alexander George and Randolph Siverson., eds, *Change in the International System* (Boulder: Westview, 1980), 131–62.
100 Ruggie, 'International Regimes,' 202.

101 *Ibid.*, 209.

102 Gardner, *Sterling–Dollar Diplomacy*, 4.

103 Ansel Luxford, as quoted in *ibid.*, xv.

104 Nau, *The Myth of America's Decline*, chs. 3 and 4.

105 Vernon and Spar, *Beyond Globalism*, 54.

106 Gardner, *Sterling–Dollar Diplomacy*, ch. 2.

107 G. John Ikenberry and Charles A. Kupchan, 'The Legitimation of Hegemonic Power,' paper presented at the Center for International Affairs, Harvard University, March 24, 1988, 35; 'Socialization and Hegemonic Power,' *International Organization* 44(3) (1990): 300.

108 *Ibid.*, 302–03.

109 Keohane, *After Hegemony*, 144.

110 *Ibid.*, 184–90.

111 Ernst B. Haas, *When Knowledge Is Power* (Berkeley: University of California Press, 1990).

112 Don Babai, 'International Development Policy in the 1980s—Progress, Statis, or Regress,' unpublished manuscript, Harvard University, 1988.

113 *Ibid.*

114 Keohane, *After Hegemony*, 256.

115 Jock A. Finlayson and Mark W. Zacher, 'The GATT and the Regulation of Trade Barriers: Regime Dynamics and Functions,' in Krasner, *International Regimes*, 313–14; Keohane, *After Hegemony*; Ruggie, 'International Regimes.'

116 Robert O. Keohane ('Theory of World Politics: Structural Realism and Beyond,' in Keohane, *Neorealism and Its Critics*) has already revised three basic realist assumptions dealing with the state, rationality, and power. My proposed assumptions build on Keohane's amended realist position and are inspired by his essay.

117 Toulmin, *Human Understanding*, 84.

118 John G. Ruggie, 'Changing Frameworks of International Collaborative Behavior: On the Complementarity of Contradictory Tendencies,' in Nazli Choucri and Thomas W. Robinson, eds, *Forecasting in International Relations* (San Francisco: Freeman, 1978), 399, 402.

119

> Such complementarity situations appear … within physics; for example in respect to the description of an atom in terms of the quantum state or in terms of the location of its constituents. … There are different ways of perceiving a situation, ways that may be unconnected or even contradictory, but they are necessary for understanding the situation in its totality.
>
> (Weisskopf, 'Frontiers and Limits,' 191–92)

120 Charles F. Sabel, *Work and Politics: The Division of Labor in Industry* (Cambridge: Cambridge University Press, 1982), 131.

121 Kratochwil and Ruggie, 'International Organization,' 764.

122 Robert Jervis, *Perception and Misperception in World Politics* (Princeton: Princeton University Press, 1976).

4 Seizing the middle ground

I am grateful to Michael Barnett, Ernst B. Haas, Peter Haas, Friedrich Kratochwil, Yosef Lapid, Cecelia Lynch, Andy Moravcsik, Nicholas Onuf, John G. Ruggie, and Alex Wendt for their comments on an earlier version of this chapter, as well as to three anonymous referees for their helpful remarks.

1 Realism, neorealism, game theory, and strategic studies, along with neoliberal institutional approaches, share a rationalist approach to states, which they all view as

conscious goal-seeking agents pursuing their interests within an external environment characterized by anarchy and the power of other states. The
paradigmatic question is how states pursue their goals given the constraints
under which they operate. When goals are interdependent, the question
assumes a strategic form: How can one state achieve what it wants, given the
preference and capacities of others?

(James A. Caporaso, 'International Relations Theory and Multilateralism:
The Search for Foundations,' *International Organization* 46 (1992): 605)

2 As represented by the work of Jürgen Habermas: *Knowledge and Human Interests*, trans.
Jeremy J. Shapiro (Boston: Beacon Press, 1971); *The Theory of Communicative Action*, vol.
1, trans. Thomas McCarthy (Boston: Beacon Press, 1984).

3 Notably by Alexander Wendt: 'Anarchy Is What States Make of It: The Social
Construction of Power Politics,' *International Organization* 46 (1992): 391–425;
'Collective Identity Formation and the International State,' *American Political Science
Review* 88 (1994): 384–96; 'Constructing International Politics,' *International Security* 20
(1995): 71–81.

4 See, for example: Emanuel Adler, 'The Emergence of Cooperation: National Epistemic
Communities and the International Evolution of the Idea of Nuclear Arms Control,'
International Organization 46 (1992): 101–46 (chapter 6 in this volume); Michael
Barnett, 'Sovereignty, Nationalism, and Regional Order in the Arab States System,'
International Organization 49 (1995): 479–510; Martha Finnemore, *National Interests
in International Society* (Ithaca: Cornell University Press, 1996); 'Constructing Norms of
Humanitarian Intervention,' in Peter. J. Katzenstein, ed., *The Culture of National
Security: Norms and Identity in World Politics* (New York: Columbia University Press,
1996), 153–85; Peter J. Katzenstein, *Cultural Norms and National Security: Police and
Military in Postwar Japan* (Ithaca: Cornell University Press, 1996); Audi Klotz, *Protesting
Prejudice: Apartheid and the Politics of Norms in International Relations* (Ithaca: Cornell
University Press, 1995); Richard Price, 'A Genealogy of the Chemical Weapons Taboo,'
International Organization 49 (1995): 73–103; Richard Price and Nina Tannenwald,
'Norms and Deterrence: The Nuclear and Chemical Weapons Taboos,' in Katzenstein,
The Culture of National Security, 114–52; Thomas Risse-Kappen, *Cooperation among
Democracies: The European Influence on U.S. Foreign Policy* (Princeton: Princeton University
Press, 1995); Ole Waever, 'Insecurity, Security, and Asecurity in the West European
Non-War Community,' in Emanuel Adler and Michael Barnett, eds, *Security Communities*
(Cambridge: Cambridge University Press, 1998), 69–118.

5 Emanuel Adler and Michael Barnett, 'Governing Anarchy: A Research Agenda for the
Study of Security Communities,' *Ethics and International Affairs* 10 (1996): 63–98;
Katzenstein, *The Culture of National Security*; Wendt, 'Anarchy.'

6 Mitchell M. Waldrop, *Complexity: The Emerging Science at the Edge of Order and Chaos* (New
York: Simon & Schuster, 1992), 232.

7 Morton A. Kaplan, *System and Process in International Politics* (New York: John Wiley,
1957); Hans Morgenthau, *Politics among Nations: The Struggle for Power and Peace* (New
York: Knopf, 1960).

8 Robert Gilpin, *War and Change in World Politics* (Cambridge: Cambridge University
Press, 1981); Kenneth N. Waltz, *Theory of International Politics* (Reading, MA: Addison-
Wesley, 1979).

9 Positivism involves: (a) 'a commitment to a unified view of science, and the adoption of
methodologies of the natural sciences to explain the social world'; (b) 'the view that there
is a distinction between facts and values, and, moreover that "facts" are theory neutral';
(c) 'a powerful belief in the existence of regularities in the social as well as the natural
world. This, of course, licenses both "deductive-nomological" and the "inductive statistical" forms of covering law explanation'; and (d) 'a tremendous reliance on the belief that
it is empirical validation or falsification that is the hallmark of "real" enquiry' (Steve

Smith, 'Positivism and Beyond,' in Steve Smith, Ken Booth, and Marysia Zalewski, eds, *International Theory: Positivism and Beyond* (Cambridge: Cambridge University Press, 1996), 11, 16.

10 With the exception, perhaps, of John J. Mearsheimer, 'The False Promise of International Institutions,' *International Security* 19 (1994/95): 5–49.

11 'Behaviorism: "life is but a motion of the limbs," at any rate for purposes of social science' (Martin Hollis, 'The Last Post?' in Smith, Booth, and Zalewski, *International Theory*, 304).

12 Richard K. Ashley and R. B. J. Walker, eds, 'Speaking the Language of Exile: Dissidence in International Studies,' Special Issue of *International Studies Quarterly* 34 (1990); James Der Derian and Michael J. Shapiro, eds, *International/Intertextual Relations: Postmodern Readings of World Politics* (Lexington: Lexington Books, 1989).

13 Robert W. Cox, 'Social Forces, States and World Orders: Beyond International Relations Theory,' in Robert O. Keohane, ed., *Neorealism and Its Critics* (New York: Columbia University Press, 1986), 204–54; *Production, Power and World Order: Social Forces in the Making of History* (New York: Columbia University Press, 1987); Mark Hoffman, 'Critical Theory and the Inter-Paradigm Debate,' *Millennium* 16 (1987): 231–49; Andrew Linklater, *Beyond Realism and Marxism: Critical Theory and International Relations* (London: Macmillan, 1989); 'The Achievements of Critical Theory,' in Smith, Booth, and Zalewski, *International Theory*, 279–98.

14 Anne Sisson Runyan and V. Spike Peterson, 'The Radical Future of Realism: Feminist Subversions of IR Theory,' *Alternatives* 16 (1991): 67–106; J. Ann Tickner, *Gender in International Relations* (New York: Columbia University Press, 1992).

15 The 'thesis that the natural world and such evidence as we have about the world do little or nothing to constrain our beliefs' (Larry Laudan, *Science and Relativism* (Chicago: University of Chicago Press, 1990), viii).

16 Like 'ethnomethodology' (Harold Garfinkel, *Studies in Ethnomethodology* (Oxford: Polity Press, 1984)), it takes knowledge as a collective accomplishment (Barry Barnes, *The Elements of Social Theory* (Princeton: Princeton University Press, 1995)).

17 Charles Taylor, 'Interpretation and the Sciences of Man,' in Paul Rabinow and William M. Sullivan, eds, *Interpretive Social Science: A Reader* (Berkeley: University of California Press, 1979), 30.

18 Max Weber, 'The Social Psychology of the World Religions,' in H. H. Gerth and C. Wright Mills, eds, *From Max Weber: Essays in Sociology* (New York: Oxford University Press, 1958), 280.

19 By 'cognitive' I mean approaches that study political beliefs and belief systems in International Relations from a perspective that takes individual human acts of cognition, such as perceptions, as independent variables that explain foreign-policy behavior. See, for example, Richard Herrmann, 'The Empirical Challenge of the Cognitive Revolution,' *International Studies Quarterly* 32 (1988): 175–204. Much of the work on cognitive psychology, however, has taken human inference models as normative, in the sense that judgments that deviate systematically from such models are either misperceptions (Robert Jervis, *Perception and Misperception in World Politics* (Princeton: Princeton University Press, 1976)) or 'erroneous,' indicating bias in the underlying inference process (Daniel Kahneman, Paul Slovic, and Amos Tversky, eds, *Judgment under Uncertainty: Heuristics and Biases* (Cambridge: Cambridge University Press, 1982)). For an overview of the field, see: Steve Smith, 'Belief Systems and the Study of International Relations,' in Richard Little and Steve Smith, eds, *Belief Systems and International Relations* (Oxford: Blackwell, 1988), 11–36; Philip Tetlock and Charles McGuire, Jr., 'Cognitive Perspectives on Foreign Policy,' in Samuel Long, ed., *Political Behavior Annual*, vol. 1 (Boulder: Westview, 1986), 255–73.

20 Judith Goldstein and Robert O. Keohane, 'Ideas and Foreign Policy: An Analytical Framework,' in J. Goldstein and R. O. Keohane, eds, *Ideas and Foreign Policy: Beliefs, Institutions, and Political Change* (Ithaca: Cornell University Press, 1993), 3.

21 Robert O. Keohane ('International Institutions: Two Approaches,' *International Studies Quarterly* 32 (1988): 379–96) uses the term 'reflectivist' to describe all interpretive IR scholars, including constructivists, whom he finds antithetical to the rationalist approach.

22 Mearsheimer, 'False Promise.'

23 See, for example: Emanuel Adler, 'Cognitive Evolution: A Dynamic Approach for the Study of International Relations and Their Progress,' in E. Adler and B. Crawford, eds, *Progress in Postwar International Relations* (New York: Columbia University Press, 1991), 43–88 (chapter 3 in this volume); Michael Barnett, 'Institutions, Role, and Disorder: The Case of the Arab States System,' *International Studies Quarterly* 37 (1993): 271–96; 'Sovereignty, Nationalism, and Regional Order'; Finnemore, *National Interests*; 'Constructing Norms'; Katzenstein, *The Culture of National Security*; Klotz, *Protesting Prejudice*; Friedrich Kratochwil, *Rules, Norms, and Decisions* (Cambridge: Cambridge University Press, 1989); Friedrich Kratochwil and John G. Ruggie, 'International Organization: A State of the Art in an Art of the State,' *International Organization* 40(4) (1986): 753–75; Nicholas Onuf, *World of Our Making: Rules and Rule in Social Theory and International Relations* (Columbia: University of South Carolina Press, 1989); Risse-Kappen, *Cooperation among Democracies*; John G. Ruggie, 'Continuity and Transformation in the World Polity: Toward a Neorealist Synthesis,' *World Politics* 35(2) (1983): 261–85; 'Territoriality and Beyond: Problematizing Modernity in International Relations,' *International Organization* 47 (1993): 139–74; Wendt, 'Anarchy'; 'Collective Identity Formation'; 'Constructing International Politics'; *Social Theory of International Politics* (Cambridge: Cambridge University Press, 1999).

24 Karin D. Knorr-Cetina, *Taking the Naturalistic Turn or How Real Philosophy of Science Is Done: Conversations with William Bechtel et al.*, organized and moderated by W. Callebaut (Chicago: University of Chicago Press, 1993), 184.

25 The way we think about International Relations is not unrelated to what we believe about knowledge in general, science, and human understanding. For some general overviews of the philosophy of science, see: A. F. Chalmers, *What Is This Thing Called Science?*, 2nd edn (Indianapolis: Hackett, 1994); Ian Hacking, *Scientific Revolutions* (Oxford: Oxford University Press, 1981); *Representing and Intervening: Introductory Topics in the Philosophy of Natural Science* (Cambridge: Cambridge University Press, 1983); Rom Harré, *The Philosophies of Science* (Oxford: Oxford University Press, 1972).

26 Whose 'scholarship emerges out of the important middle ground between absolutism and relativism' (Paul Howe, 'The Utopian Realism of E. H. Carr,' *Review of International Studies* 20 (1994): 287).

27 E. H. Carr, *The Twenty Years' Crisis, 1919–1939* (New York: Harper & Row, 1964).

28 Martin Hollis and Steve Smith (*Explaining and Understanding International Relations* (New York: Oxford University Press, 1990), 196–216) argue that such a synthesis is impossible. For an accessible introduction to interpretive philosophies of science and sociologies of knowledge as applied to International Relations, see *ibid*. A particularly effective introductory study is Len Doyal and Roger Harris, *Empiricism, Explanation, and Rationality* (London: Routledge and Kegan Paul, 1986).

29 Steve Woolgar, 'Irony in the Social Study of Science,' in Karin D. Knorr-Cetina and Michael Mulkay, eds, *Science Observed* (Beverly Hills: Sage, 1983), 239–66.

30 Stephan Fuchs, *The Professional Quest for Truth: A Social Theory of Science and Knowledge* (Albany: State University of New York Press, 1992), 27.

31 *Ibid*.

32 Because Keohane ('International Institutions') used 'reflective' to describe students of international institutions who take an interpretive perspective, I refrain from using this term.

33 Stephen D. Krasner, 'Westphalia and All That,' in Goldstein and Keohane, *Ideas and Foreign Policy*, 235–64.

34 Goldstein and Keohane, 'Ideas and Foreign Policy.'

35 See, for example, Der Derian and Shapiro, *International/Intertextual Relations*.

36 'Indeed, texts cannot themselves be accepted as representations, even of arbitrarily signified referents. Composed not just of presences but of absences, texts do not exist as complete wholes' (Jeffrey C. Alexander, *Fin de Siècle Social Theory: Relativism, Reduction, and the Problem of Reason* (London: Verso, 1995), 103).

37 Emergence, an increasingly important concept in physics, means that physical and biological systems are partly indeterminate (even though they respond to laws); accordingly, once they cross a threshold of complexity, they can spontaneously organize themselves into more complex, self-sustaining and self-reproducing structures. 'Weather is an emergent property: take your water vapor out over the Gulf of Mexico and let it interact with sunlight and wind, and it can organize itself into an emergent structure known as a hurricane. Life is an emergent property, the product of DNA molecules and protein molecules and myriad other kinds of molecules, all obeying the laws of chemistry' (Waldrop, *Complexity*, 82); see also Stuart Kauffman, *At Home in the Universe: The Search for the Laws of Self-Organization and Complexity* (Oxford: Oxford University Press, 1995), 24. In the social world, I take emergence to mean that 'in contrast to the past which is closed, as it were, the future is still open to influence; it is not yet completely determined' (Karl R. Popper, *The Open Universe: An Argument for Indeterminism*, ed. W. W. Bartley III (Totowa: Rowman and Littlefield, 1982), 56, 130). In other words, the social world is emergent because we humans can reflectively and often surprisingly affect it with formulated human knowledge. Metaphorically speaking, then, human knowledge can produce instabilities that generate the propensity for self-organization.

38 On methodological individualism, see: Max Weber, *Economy and Society: An Outline of Interpretive Sociology*, vol. 1, ed. Guenther Roth and Claus Wittich (New York: Bedminster Press, 1968); Jon Elster, *Explaining Technical Change: A Case Study in the Philosophy of Science* (Cambridge: Cambridge University Press, 1983); *Nuts and Bolts for the Social Sciences* (Cambridge: Cambridge University Press, 1989).

39 See, for example: Peter L. Berger and Thomas Luckmann, *The Social Construction of Reality* (New York: Anchor, 1966); Emile Durkheim, *The Elementary Forms of the Religious Life* (New York: Free Press, 1965); Ludwik Fleck, *Genesis and Development of a Scientific Fact* (Chicago: University of Chicago Press, 1979); Thomas Kuhn, *The Structure of Scientific Revolutions* (Chicago: University of Chicago Press, 1970); Charles Sanders Peirce, *Reasoning and the Logic of Things*, ed. K. Ketner and H. Putnam (Cambridge, MA: Harvard University Press, 1992); Alfred Schutz, *Collected Papers*, vol. 1, ed. Maurice Natanson (The Hague: Martinus Nijhoff, 1962); Peter Winch, *The Idea of a Social Science* (London: Routledge and Kegan Paul, 1958); Ludwig Wittgenstein, *Philosophical Investigations* (Oxford: Blackwell, 1953).

40 Martin Hollis and Steve Smith, 'Beware of Gurus: Structure and Action in International Relations,' *Review of International Studies* 17 (1991): 404.

41 Elster, *Nuts and Bolts*, 13.

42 Elster, *Explaining Technical Change*, 20, 84.

43 Durkheim, *The Elementary Forms of the Religious Life*, 22.

44 Hollis and Smith, 'Beware of Gurus,' 396.

45 Anthony Giddens, *Central Problems in Social Theory* (Berkeley: University of California Press, 1979), 5. For applications of structuration theory to International Relations, see Walter Carlsnaes, 'The Agency–Structure Problem in Foreign Policy Analysis,' *International Studies Quarterly* 36 (1992): 245–70; David Dessler, 'What's at Stake in the Agent–Structure Debate?' *International Organization* 43 (1989): 441–73; Alexander E. Wendt, 'The Agent–Structure Problem in International Relations Theory,' *International Organization* 41(3) (1987): 335–70. According to Wendt, structuration theory 'says something about what kinds of entities there are in the social world and how their relationship should be conceptualized, ... but it does not tell us what particular kinds of agents or what particular kinds of structures to expect in any given concrete social system' (*ibid.*, 355).

46 Ira Cohen, 'Structuration Theory and Social Praxis,' in Anthony Giddens and Jonathan Turner, eds, *Social Theory Today* (Stanford: Stanford University Press, 1987), 302.

47 Hollis and Smith, *Explaining and Understanding International Relations*, 72 (emphasis in the original); Weber, *Economy and Society*.

48 Goldstein and Keohane, *Ideas and Foreign Policy*.

49 Jervis, *Perception and Misperception*.

50 Goldstein and Keohane, 'Ideas and Foreign Policy,' 27.

51 *Ibid*.

52 Wittgenstein, *Philosophical Investigations*; Winch, *The Idea of a Social Science*; Willard van Orman Quine, 'Two Dogmas of Empiricism,' in Willard van Orman Quine, ed., *From a Logical Point of View* (New York: Harper & Row, 1961), 20–46; critical theorists like Jürgen Habermas (*Knowledge and Human Interests*; *The Theory of Communicative Action*); and post-modernists such as Michel Foucault (*The Order of Things: An Archeology of the Human Sciences* (New York: Vintage Books, 1970)) and Jacques Derrida (*Writing and Difference* (Chicago: University of Chicago Press, 1978)).

53 Winch, *The Idea of a Social Science*, 15.

54 Wittgenstein, *Philosophical Investigations*.

55 On the other hand, although Habermas (*The Theory of Communicative Action*), who best represents the Critical Theory school, sees the simple objectivism of positivism as mistaken, he nevertheless believes that 'there are secure foundations for knowledge, and that some versions of the social world are more objective than others' (Steve Smith, 'Positivism and Beyond,' in Smith, Booth, and Zalewski, *International Theory*, 36).

56 Husserl's phenomenology (Edmund Husserl, *General Introduction to Pure Phenomenology*, trans. W. R. Boyce Gibson (New York: Collier, 1962)); Martin Heidegger's concept of *Dasein* (being-in-the-world) (*Being and Time*, trans. John Macquarrie and Edward Robinson (London: SCM Press, 1962)); Alfred Schutz's studies of the commonsense meanings of daily life (*Collected Papers*, vol. 1); George H. Mead's 'symbolic interactionist' construction of social reality (*Mind, Self, and Society*, ed. C. W. Morris (Chicago: University of Chicago Press, 1934)); Harold Garfinkel's 'ethnomethodology' or empirical study of practices (*Studies in Ethnomethodology*); the studies by Peter Berger and Thomas Luckmann of the processes by which bodies of knowledge come to be socially established as reality (*The Social Construction of Reality*); and Clifford Geertz's thickly described 'cultures' (*The Interpretation of Cultures* (New York: Basic Books, 1973))—to mention just a few.

57 Alfred Schutz, 'Concept and Theory Formation in the Social Sciences,' in Fred Dallmayr and Thomas A. McCarthy, eds, *Understanding and Social Inquiry* (Notre Dame: University of Notre Dame Press, 1977), 231.

58 Cohen, 'Structuration Theory,' 287.

59 'In other words, intersubjective meanings quasi-causally affect certain actions not by directly or inevitably determining them but rather by rendering these actions plausible or implausible, acceptable or unacceptable, conceivable or inconceivable, respectable or disreputable' (Albert S. Yee, 'The Causal Effects of Ideas on Policies,' *International Organization* 50 (1996): 97).

60 Stephen Toulmin, *Human Understanding* (Princeton: Princeton University Press, 1972), 35.

61 John R. Searle, *The Construction of Social Reality* (New York: Free Press, 1995), 25.

62 Schutz, *Collected Papers*, vol. 1, 10.

63 Karl W. Deutsch, Sidney A. Burrell, Robert A. Kann, Maurice Lee, Jr., Martin Lichterman, Raymond E. Lindgren, Francis L. Loewenheim, and Richard W. Van Wagenen, *Political Community and the North Atlantic Area* (Princeton: Princeton University Press, 1957).

64 Benedict Anderson, *Imagined Communities: Reflections on the Origin and Spread of Nationalism*, revised edn (London: Verso, 1991).

65 Popper, *The Open Universe*, 118; 'The Place of Mind in Nature,' in Richard O. Elvee, ed., *Mind in Nature* (New York: Harper & Row, 1982), 53–54.

66 Searle, *The Construction of Social Reality*, 41.

67 *Ibid.*, 1, 12.

68 *Ibid.*, 34.

69 *Ibid.*, 74–75.

70 *Ibid.*, 28. Following John Rawls ('Two Concepts of Rules,' *Philosophical Review* 64 (1955): 3–32), Searle distinguishes between regulative and constitutive rules. Regulative rules regulate already existing activities. On the other hand, constitutive rules 'create the very possibility of certain activities. Thus the rules of chess do not regulate an antecedent existing activity. ... Rather, the rules of chess create the very possibility of playing chess' (*The Construction of Social Reality*, 27–28).

71 *Ibid.*, 44.

72 William James, *The Works of William James: Pragmatism*, ed. Fredson Bowers and Ignas K. Skrupskelis (Cambridge, MA: Harvard University Press, 1975); Richard J. Bernstein, *Beyond Objectivism and Relativism: Science, Hermeneutics, and Praxis* (Philadelphia: University of Pennsylvania Press, 1985); Peirce, *Reasoning and the Logic of Things*; Hillary Putnam, *Pragmatism* (Cambridge: Blackwell, 1995).

73 Bernstein, *Beyond Objectivism and Relativism*.

74 Alexander, *Fin de Siècle Social Theory*, 112.

75 John A. Vasquez, 'The Post-Positivist Debate: Reconstructing Scientific Enquiry and International Relations Theory after Enlightenment's Fall,' in Ken Booth and Steve Smith, eds, *International Relations Theory Today* (Oxford: Polity Press, 1995), 228.

76 Alexander, *Fin de Siècle Social Theory*, 117.

77 I thank Cecelia Lynch for this point.

78 Smith, 'Positivism and Beyond,' 13.

79 Katzenstein, *The Culture of National Security*.

80 Hollis, 'The Last Post?', 305.

81 Michael T. Gibbons, 'Introduction: the Politics of Interpretation,' in Michael T. Gibbons, ed., *Interpreting Politics* (New York: New York University Press, 1987), 3.

82 When applying a naturalist and determinist view of scientific causality to social science, positivists should take note of the fact that, by the 1930s, this view had been replaced in physics by the understanding that subatomic relationships are inherently stochastic. In 'recent decades, an entirely new view of uncertainty or chance has emerged under the rubric of chaos theory' (John G. Ruggie, 'Peace in Our Time? Causality, Social Facts, and Narrative Knowing,' *American Society of International Law Proceedings* (1995): 94).

83 Donald Davidson, 'Actions, Reasons, and Causes,' *Journal of Philosophy* 60 (1963): 685–700.

84 Anthony Giddens, *The Constitution of Society: Outline of the Theory of Structuration* (Cambridge: Polity Press, 1984), 345.

85 Rom Harré and Grant Gillett, *The Discursive Mind* (Thousand Oaks: Sage, 1994), 33.

86 Finnemore, *National Interests*, 28.

87 Roy Bhaskar, 'Emergence, Explanation, and Emancipation,' in Paul Secord, ed., *Explaining Human Behavior: Consciousness, Human Action and Social Structure* (Beverly Hills: Sage, 1982), 275–310; Carlsnaes, 'The Agency–Structure Problem'; Finnemore, *National Interests*, 28–29; Giddens, *The Constitution of Society*.

88 Alexander Rosenberg, *Philosophy of Social Science* (Boulder: Westview, 1988), 87.

89 Wendt, *Social Theory of International Politics*, 32.

90 Robert O. Keohane, *After Hegemony: Cooperation and Discord in the World Political Economy* (Princeton: Princeton University Press, 1984); Goldstein and Keohane, 'Ideas and Foreign Policy.'

91 'Methodological individualism is defined primarily by the belief that society consists solely of its members. They alone are real. ... Individualism rules out social structures as supraindividual causes and traces causal inferences to particular individuals or to

individuals in general' (John K. Rhoads, *Critical Issues in Social Theory* (University Park: Pennsylvania State University Press, 1991), 117).

92 Kratochwil and Ruggie, 'International Organization.'

93 Kathryn Sikkink, 'The Power of Principled Ideas: Human Rights Policies in the United States and Western Europe,' in Goldstein and Keohane, *Ideas and Foreign Policy*, 140.

94 Post-modern feminist theory deals with the constitution of International Relations by gender. It argues that International Relations are the result of a hegemonic masculine discourse and that, therefore, 'any claim about "reality" that denies, misrepresents, or simply re-presents women must be thoroughly contested and, thereby, radicalized' (Runyan and Peterson, 'The Radical Future of Realism,' 100).

95 Nick Rengger and Mark Hoffman ('Modernity, Post-Modernism and International Relations,' in J. Doherty, E. Graham, and M. Malek, eds, *Post-Modernism in the Social Sciences* (Basingstoke: Macmillan, 1992), 127–46) classify constitutive approaches into: (a) 'critical interpretative theory' (Habermas, *The Theory of Communicative Action*), which provides a minimal basis of evaluation between different theories; and (b) 'radical inter-pretatism,' which denies even critical theory's minimalist claims about science and the possibility of emancipation.

96 Searle, *The Construction of Social Reality*, 190.

97 J. Baudrillard, *America* (London: Verso, 1989).

98 Pauline M. Rosenau, *Post-Modernism and the Social Sciences: Insights, Inroads, and Intrusions* (Princeton: Princeton University Press, 1992), 110.

99 Fuchs, *The Professional Quest for Truth*, 75.

100 Richard K. Ashley, 'Living on Border Lines: Man, Poststructuralism and War,' in Der Derian and Shapiro, *International/Intertextual Relations*, 259–322.

101 *Ibid.*, 274, 280.

102 Mark Neufeld, *The Restructuring of International Relations Theory* (Cambridge: Cambridge University Press, 1995), 112.

103 Margaret S. Archer, *Culture and Agency* (Cambridge: Cambridge University Press, 1989); *Realist Social Theory: The Morphogenetic Approach* (Cambridge: Cambridge University Press, 1995).

104 Carlsnaes, 'The Agency–Structure Problem.'

105 Yee, 'Causal Effects,' 100.

106 'A semio-critical activity, ever searching for and seeking to dismantle the empirico-rational *positions* where power fixes meaning' (James Der Derian, 'The (S)pace of International Relations: Simulation, Surveillance, and Speed,' *International Studies Quarterly* 34 (1990): 296).

107 David Campbell, 'Violent Performances: Identity, Sovereignty, Responsibility,' in Yosef Lapid and Friedrich V. Kratochwil, eds, *The Return of Culture and Identity in IR Theory* (Boulder: Lynne Rienner, 1996), 178.

108 Jim George and David Campbell, 'Patterns of Dissent and the Celebration of Difference: Critical Social Theory and International Relations,' *International Studies Quarterly* 34 (1990): 269–93.

109 Ashley, 'Living on Border Lines,' 278.

110 Katzenstein, *The Culture of National Security*.

111 Adler and Crawford, *Progress in Postwar International Relations*; Ernst B. Haas, *When Knowledge Is Power* (Berkeley: University of California Press, 1990).

112 Habermas, *The Theory of Communicative Action*.

113 Habermas (*ibid.*) takes the securing of freedom from distorted communication as a progressive enterprise. Post-structuralists and post-modernists, on the other hand, when choosing to highlight some forms of subjective discourse over others, do so randomly and as a reflection of their own personal preferences.

114 Haas, *When Knowledge Is Power*.

115 Cox, 'Social Forces,' 208–09.

116 Alexander Wendt, 'Anarchy.'

117 Ronald L. Jepperson, Alexander Wendt, and Peter J. Katzenstein, 'Norms, Identity, and Culture in National Security,' in Katzenstein, *The Culture of National Security*, 33–75.

118 Gary King, Robert O. Keohane, and Sidney Verba, *Designing Social Inquiry: Scientific Inference in Qualitative Research* (Princeton: Princeton University Press, 1994), 37; see also Herbert Kritzer, 'The Data Puzzle: The Nature of Interpretation in Quantitative Research,' *American Journal of Political Science* 40 (1996): 1–32.

119 For example, Thomas U. Berger, 'Norms, Identity, and National Security in Germany and Japan,' in Katzenstein, *The Culture of National Security*, 317–56. The structured, focused comparison method was described by Alexander L. George, 'Case-Studies and Theory Development: The Method of Structured, Focused Comparison,' in Paul G. Lauren, ed., *Diplomacy: New Approaches in History, Theory, and Policy* (New York: Free Press, 1979), 43–68.

120 For example, Adler and Barnett, 'Governing Anarchy.' It is crucial to remember, however, that constructivism, by assuming that agents and structures constitute each other, goes beyond a linear characterization of causality (Giddens, *The Constitution of Society*; Audi Klotz, 'Reconstituting Interests: Interpretive Analysis of Norms in International Relations,' revised draft, University of Southern California, Los Angeles, 1992, 10).

121 Lars Erik Cederman, 'From Primordialism to Constructivism: The Quest for Flexible Models of Ethnic Conflict,' paper presented at the Annual Meeting of the American Political Science Association, San Francisco, 1996.

122 Lars Erik Cederman, 'Rerunning History: Counterfactual Simulation in World Politics,' in Philip E. Tetlock and Aaron Belkin, eds, *Counterfactual Thought Experiments in World Politics* (Princeton: Princeton University Press, 1996), 247–67.

123 Ruggie argues that

> in the narrative mode … significance is attributed to antecedent events and actions by virtue of their role in some 'human project' as a whole. This mode of explanation comprises two 'orders of information': the descriptive and the configurative. The first simply links occurrences along a temporal dimension and seeks to identify the effect one had on another. The second organizes these descriptive statements into an intersubjective gestalt or 'coherence structure.' These gestalt operations rest on a method of interrogative reasoning that Charles Peirce called 'abduction': the successive adjusting of a conjectured ordering scheme to the available facts, until the conjecture provides as full an account of the facts as possible.
> (Ruggie, 'Peace in Our Time?', 98, citing Donald Polkinghorne, *Narrative Knowing and the Human Sciences* (Albany: State University of New York Press, 1986))

See also Tickner, *Gender*.

124 For example: Adler, 'The Emergence of Cooperation'; Katzenstein, *Cultural Norms*. 'Thick description' has been described by Geertz, *The Interpretation of Cultures*.

125 Tickner, *Gender*; Cynthia Weber, *Simulating Sovereignty: Intervention, the State and Symbolic Exchange* (Cambridge: Cambridge University Press, 1995).

126 Cecelia Lynch and Audie Klotz, 'Constructivism: Past Agendas and Future Directions,' paper presented at the Annual Meeting of the American Political Science Association, San Francisco, 1996.

127 Adler, 'The Emergence of Cooperation'; Barnett, 'Sovereignty, Nationalism, and Regional Order'; Cederman, 'From Primordialism to Constructivism'; Finnemore, *National Interests*; Katzenstein, *The Culture of National Security*; Klotz, *Protesting Prejudice*; Risse-Kappen, *Cooperation among Democracies*.

128 Wendt, 'Anarchy'; 'Collective Identity Formation'; *Social Theory of International Politics*.

129 Cederman, 'From Primordialism to Constructivism'; Waever, 'Insecurity, Security, and Asecurity.'

130 Onuf, *World of Our Making.*

131 Kratochwil, *Rules, Norms, and Decisions.*

132 Lynch and Klotz, 'Constructivism,' 6.

133 Rey Koslowski and Friedrich V. Kratochwil, 'Understanding Change in International Politics: The Soviet Empire's Demise and the International System,' in Richard Ned Lebow and Thomas Risse-Kappen, eds, *International Relations Theory and the End of the Cold War* (New York: Columbia University Press, 1995), 127–66.

134 Tickner, *Gender*; Cecelia Lynch, 'E. H. Carr, International Relations Theory, and the Societal Origins of International Legal Norms,' *Millennium* 23 (1994): 589–620.

135 Tickner, *Gender.*

136 Lynch, 'E. H. Carr.'

137 Ruggie, 'Peace in Our Time?'; Waever, 'Insecurity, Security, and Asecurity.'

138 Price, 'A Genealogy of the Chemical Weapons Taboo': '[H]istory of the present ... looks to the past for insight into today. It focuses on "local, discontinuous, disqualified, illegitimate knowledges." Genealogy dismisses the possibility of any view of history as a "unitary body of theory which would filter, hierarchize, and order ... in the name of some true knowledge and some arbitrary idea of what constitutes a science and its objects"' (Rosenau, *Post-Modernism and the Social Sciences*, xi–xii). See also Michel Foucault, 'Nietzsche, Genealogy, History,' in Paul Rabinow, ed., *The Foucault Reader* (London: Penguin, 1984), 76–100.

139 Thomas J. Biersteker and Cynthia Weber, eds, *State Sovereignty as Social Construct* (Cambridge: Cambridge University Press, 1996).

140 David Strang, 'Contested Sovereignty: The Social Construction of Colonial Imperialism,' in Biersteker and Weber, *State Sovereignty*, 36–37.

141 Mearsheimer, 'False Promise.'

142 Adler and Barnett, 'Governing Anarchy'; Michael C. Williams, 'The Institutions of Security,' paper presented at the Annual Meeting of the International Studies Association, San Diego, 1996.

143 *Ibid.*

144 Adler, 'Cognitive Evolution'; Finnemore, *National Interests*; Jutta Weldes, 'Constructing National Interests,' *European Journal of International Relations* 2 (1996): 275–318.

145 John A. Hall, 'Ideas and the Social Sciences,' in Goldstein and Keohane, *Ideas and Foreign Policy*, 51.

146 For a recent discussion of some of the implications that follow from studying the national interest through constructivist glasses, see Weldes, 'Constructing National Interests.'

147 Kratochwil, *Rules, Norms, and Decisions*; Mearsheimer, 'The False Promise'; Thomas Risse-Kappen, 'Ideas Do Not Float Freely: Transnational Coalitions, Democratic Structures, and the End of the Cold War,' *International Organization* 48 (1994): 185–214.

148 Finnemore, *National Interests*; Katzenstein, *The Culture of National Security*; Klotz, *Protesting Prejudice.*

149 For example, through: (a) the sharing of 'forms of life' and traditions (Wittgenstein, *Philosophical Investigations*); (b) the engagement in 'ideal speech situations,' 'a form of discourse in which there is no other compulsion but the compulsion of argumentation itself' (Jürgen Habermas, 'On Systematically Distorted Communication,' *Inquiry* 13 (1970): 205–18; Richard J. Bernstein, *The Restructuring of Social and Political Theory* (Philadelphia: University of Pennsylvania Press, 1976), 212); and (c) the historical development of 'truth' regimes on the basis of disciplinary knowledge (Michel Foucault, *Power/Knowledge: Selected Interviews and Other Writings, 1972–1977*, ed. Colin Gordon (New York: Pantheon, 1980)).

150 Waltz, *Theory of International Politics.*

151 George Modelski, 'Is World Politics Evolutionary Learning?' *International Organization* 44 (1990): 1–24; 'Evolutionary Paradigm for Global Politics,' *International Studies Quarterly* 40 (1996): 321–42.

152 Stephen D. Krasner, ed., *International Regimes* (Ithaca: Cornell University Press, 1983); Arthur A. Stein, 'Coordination and Collaboration: Regimes in an Anarchic World,' in *ibid.*, 115–40.

153 Peter Hall, 'Conclusion: The Politics of Keynesian Ideas,' in Peter Hall, ed., *The Political Power of Economic Ideas: Keynesianism across Nations* (Princeton: Princeton University Press, 1989), 361–91.

154 Hendrik Spruyt, 'Institutional Selection in International Relations: State Anarchy as Order,' *International Organization* 48 (1994): 527–57; *The Sovereign State and Its Competitors* (Princeton: Princeton University Press, 1994).

155 Spruyt, 'Institutional Selection,' 532.

156 *Ibid.*, 527.

157 *Ibid.*, 555.

158 As opposed to 'analogous'; both concepts are borrowed from biology. 'When similar functions are present in different entities, a homologous account looks to the common ancestry of such a function.' In contrast, an analogous explanation 'provides an account by seeing the similar function as independent responses to similar circumstances' (Amir Pasic, 'Preserving Collective Identity: Lessons from Evolutionary Thought,' paper presented at the Annual Meeting of the American Political Science Association, San Francisco, 1996, 20).

159 Stephen Jay Gould, *Wonderful Life: The Burgess Shale and the Nature of History* (New York: W. W. Norton, 1989); Pasic, 'Preserving Collective Identity.'

160 Hayward R. Alker, *Rediscoveries and Reformulations: Humanistic Methodologies for International Studies* (Cambridge: Cambridge University Press, 1996).

161 Adler, 'Cognitive Evolution'; I owe much of my understanding of cognitive evolution to Ernst Haas. See, for example, Haas, *When Knowledge Is Power*; 'Reason and Change in International Life: Justifying a Hypothesis,' *Journal of International Affairs* 44 (1990): 209–40.

162 Kauffman, *At Home in the Universe*, 300.

163 Mary Douglas, *How Institutions Think* (Syracuse: Syracuse University Press, 1986), 112.

164 Thus, not unlike Foucault's concept of power, which emphasizes the disciplinary effects of bodies of knowledge and discourse, power sets a field of conceptual, normative and practical possibilities that define what is legitimate and illegitimate in international politics (Foucault, *Power/Knowledge*); Price, 'A Genealogy of the Chemical Weapons Taboo'; Williams, 'The Institutions of Security.'

165 Fuchs, *The Professional Quest for Truth*.

166 Toulmin, *Human Understanding*.

167 Klotz, 'Reconstituting Interests,' 11.

168 Barnes, *The Elements of Social Theory*, 77.

169 Alexander Wendt, 'Ideas, Foreign Policy, and Constructivism,' paper presented at the Annual Meeting of the American Political Science Association, New York City, 1994.

170 See note 4.

171 Koslowski and Kratochwil, 'Understanding Change in International Politics.'

172 *Ibid.*, 158–59.

173 Walter W. Powell and Paul J. DiMaggio, eds, *The New Institutionalism in Organizational Analysis* (Chicago: University of Chicago Press), 10–11; Daniel C. Thomas, *The Helsinki Effect* (Princeton: Princeton University Press, 2002).

174 Stephen D. Krasner, *Structural Conflict* (Berkeley: University of California Press, 1985).

175 Roxanne L. Doty, *Imperial Encounters: The Politics of Representation in North–South Relations* (Minneapolis: University of Minnesota Press, 1996).

176 See, for example, Ian H. Rowlands, 'The International Politics of Environment and Development: The Post-UNCED Agenda,' *Millennium* 21 (1992): 209–24.

177 'An epistemic community is a network of professionals with recognized expertise and competence in a particular domain and an authoritative claim to policy-relevant knowledge within that domain or issue area.' Epistemic communities have a shared set of normative and principled beliefs, shared causal beliefs, shared notions of validity, and a common policy enterprise (Peter M. Haas, 'Introduction: Epistemic Communities and International Policy Coordination,' in Peter M. Haas, ed., 'Knowledge, Power, and International Policy Coordination,' Special Issue of *International Organization* 46 (1992): 3).

178 Ron Eyerman and Andrew Jamison, eds, *Social Movements: A Cognitive Approach* (University Park: Pennsylvania State University Press, 1991).

179 Peter M. Haas, *Saving the Mediterranean: The Politics of International Environmental Cooperation* (New York: Columbia University Press, 1990).

180 A security community is a 'group of people which has become integrated,' i.e. 'in which there is real assurance that the members of the community will not fight each other physically, but will settle their disputes in some other way.' Amalgamated security communities involve the 'formal merger of two or more previously independent units into a single larger unit.' Pluralistic security communities, on the other hand, retain the legal independence of separate governments, possess a compatibility of core values derived from common institutions, mutual responsiveness, and a sense of 'we-ness,' and are integrated to the point that they entertain 'dependable expectations of peaceful change' (Deutsch *et al.*, *Political Community*, 5–6).

181 Adler and Barnett, 'Governing Anarchy,' 77.

182 Adler and Barnett (*ibid.*) have categorized pluralistic security communities as loosely and tightly coupled, according to their depth of trust, the nature and degree of institutionalization of their governance system, and whether they reside in a formal anarchy or are on the verge of transforming it. A loosely coupled security community, which refers to a transnational region of sovereign states whose people maintain dependable expectations of peaceful change, is consistent with Wendt's state-centric constructivist approach. On the other hand, a tightly coupled security community is something of a post-sovereign system, endowed with common supranational, transnational and national institutions, and, as such, it exemplifies the emergence of novel political actors on the world scene.

183 *Ibid.*, 76.

184 Katzenstein, *The Culture of National Security*.

185 Jeffrey Legro, *Cooperation under Fire* (Ithaca: Cornell University Press, 1995).

186 Elizabeth L. Kier, 'Culture and French Military Doctrine before World War II,' in Katzenstein, *The Culture of National Security*, 186–215; *Imagining War: French and British Military Doctrine between the Wars* (Princeton: Princeton University Press, 1997).

187 Alastair I. Johnston, *Cultural Realism: Strategic Culture and Grand Strategy in Chinese History* (Princeton: Princeton University Press, 1995).

188 Marc H. Ross, *The Culture of Conflict: Interpretations and Interests in Comparative Perspective* (New Haven: Yale University Press, 1993).

189 Thomas C. Schelling, *The Strategy of Conflict* (Cambridge, MA: Harvard University Press, 1960), 207.

190 *Ibid.*, 106–07.

191 Adler, 'The Emergence of Cooperation.'

192 John Mueller, *Retreat from Doomsday: The Obsolescence of Major War* (New York: Basic Books, 1989).

193 Robert Jervis, 'The Political Effects of Nuclear Weapons: A Comment,' *International Security* 13 (1988): 80–90.

194 Mueller, *Retreat from Doomsday*.

195 Emanuel Adler, 'Seasons of Peace: Progress in Postwar International Security,' in Adler and Crawford, *Progress in Postwar International Relations*, 128–73.

196 Jonathan Mercer, 'Anarchy and Identity,' *International Organization* 49 (1995): 229–52.

197 Campbell, 'Violent Performances.'

198 See, for example, Michael Doyle, 'Liberalism and World Politics,' *American Political Science Review* 80 (1986): 1151–61; Zeev Maoz and Bruce M. Russett, 'Normative and Structural Causes of Democratic Peace, 1946–86,' *American Political Science Review* 87 (1993): 624–38; James L. Ray, 'Wars between Democracies: Rare or Nonexistent?' *International Interactions* 18 (1993): 251–76; Bruce M. Russett, *Grasping the Democratic Peace: Principles for a Post-Cold War World* (Princeton: Princeton University Press, 1993); John M. Owen, 'How Liberalism Produces Democratic Peace,' *International Security* 19 (1994): 87–125.
199 Gabriel A. Almond and Sidney Verba, *The Civic Culture* (Boston: Little, Brown, 1963).
200 Risse-Kappen, *Cooperation among Democracies*.
201 This image is used to socially construct an identity of self and, consequently, an idea of 'the other.' Oren's analysis suggests that Jonathan Mercer's arguments ('Anarchy and Identity') about the formation of identity in-groups ('our-kind') and out-groups ('their kind') can be made amenable to historical–contextual, and thus to constructivist, analysis (Ido Oren, 'The Subjectivity of the "Democratic" Peace: Changing U.S. Perceptions of Imperial Germany,' *International Security* 20 (1995): 150).
202 Toulmin, *Human Understanding*, 371, 486.
203 Yosef Lapid, 'The Third Debate: On the Prospects of International Theory in a Post-Positivist Era,' *International Studies Quarterly* 33 (1989): 235–54.

5 Ideological 'guerrillas' and the quest for technological autonomy

I am grateful to Ernst B. Haas for comments on an earlier version of this chapter and to the anonymous referees for their valuable comments and suggestions. Generous help for this study's research was provided by the Institute of International Studies, Berkeley; the Political Science Department, Berkeley; the Institute for the Study of World Politics in New York; the Center for Latin American Studies at Berkeley, and the Tinker Foundation. I also thank the Instituto Universitário de Pesquisas do Rio de Janeiro and the following Brazilians: J. B. de Abreu Amorim, Mario Bethlem, Paulo Augusto Cotrim, Edison Dytz, Col. Jorge Monteiro Fernandes, Octavio Gennari Netto, Claudio Zamitti Mammana, Ivan de Costa Marques, Marília Rosa Millan, Arthur Pereira Nunes, José Pelúcio, José Ezil Veiga da Rocha, Silvia Helena, Vianna Rodrigues, Ricardo Saur, Manuel F. Lousada Soares, João Paulo dos Reis Velloso, Roberto Zubieta, and, especially, Mário Ripper and Sueli Mendes dos Santos.

1 For example, a relatively poor educational system, scientific and technological underdevelopment, lack of managerial experience and capital, and a strong dependence on the products of multinational corporations (MNCs). The dependency literature has become too large to be summarized in one note. A good article analyzing different approaches and their respective definitions is Gabriel Palma, 'Dependency: A Formal Theory of Underdevelopment or a Methodology for the Analysis of Concrete Situations of Underdevelopment?' *World Development* (August 1978). See also James Caporaso, ed., special issue on dependence and dependency in the global system, *International Organization* 32 (winter 1978). For an analysis of some of the consequences of technological dependency, see Charles Cooper, ed., *Science, Technology, and Development: The Political Economy of Technical Advance in Underdeveloped Countries* (London: Frank Cass, 1973); for a study of Latin America's dependency, see Richard Bath and Dilmus D. James, eds, *Technological Progress in Latin America: The Prospects for Overcoming Dependency* (Boulder: Westview, 1979); and for an analysis of Brazil's technological dependency on MNCs, see Peter Evans, *Dependent Development: The Alliance of Multinational, State and Local Capital in Brazil* (Princeton: Princeton University Press, 1979).
2 See for example: Raymond Vernon, *Storm over the Multinationals: The Real Issues* (Cambridge, MA: Harvard University Press, 1977); Theodore Moran, *Multinational*

Corporations and the Politics of Dependence: Copper in Chile (Princeton: Princeton University Press, 1977); and C. Fred Bergsten, Thomas Horst, and Theodore Moran, *American Multinationals and American Interests* (Washington: Brookings Institution, 1978).

3 For a study showing how the balance of power can shift in favor of developing countries even in high-technology sectors, see Joseph M. Grieco, 'Between Dependency and Autonomy: India's Experience with the International Computer Industry,' *International Organization* 36 (1982). For a more extensive analysis, see Grieco, *Between Dependency and Autonomy: India's Experience with the International Computer Industry* (Berkeley: University of California Press, 1984).

4 For the importance of eclectic ideologies in Latin America, see Charles W. Anderson, *Politics and Economic Change in Latin America* (Princeton: Van Nostrand, 1967), 41.

5 John S. Odell, *U.S. International Monetary Policy: Markets, Power, and Ideas as Sources of Change* (Princeton: Princeton University Press, 1982), 362–63; Lorand B. Szalay and Rita Mae Kelly, 'Political Ideology and Subjective Culture: Conceptualization and Empirical Assessment,' *American Political Science Review* (September 1982): 585.

6 Burkart Holzner and John H. Marx, *Knowledge Application: The Knowledge System in Society* (Boston: Allyn & Bacon, 1979), 82.

7 Odell, *U.S. International Monetary Policy*, 62.

8 *Ibid.*

9 John R. Freeman and Raymond D. Duvall, 'International Economic Relations and the Entrepreneurial State,' *Economic Development and Cultural Change* (January 1984): 375–76.

10 Wando Pereira Borges, president of Digibrás, *Hearings before the Parliament* (Câmara dos Deputados) (mimeo, Brazil, D.F., August 31, 1977); Grieco, *Between Dependency and Autonomy*, 158; Paulo Bastos Tigre, 'Indústria de Computadores e Dependência Tecnológica no Brasil' (Master's thesis, University of Rio de Janeiro, 1978), 75; CAPRE, *Boletim Técnico I* (January–March 1979), 38–39; and G. B. Levine, 'Brazil 1976—Another Japan?' *Datamation* 21 (1975).

11 *SEI Boletim Informativo* 3 (June–September 1983), 10.

12 *Data News*, May 3, 1983, 9; *Brazil Trade and Industry* (May 1982): 11.

13 The SEI (in charge of computer policy since 1979) classifies computers according to their mean value: class 1, US$20,000; class 2, US$90,000; class 3, US$180,000; class 4, US$670,000; class 5, US$1,900,000; and class 6, US$3,000,000 (SEI, *Boletim Informativo* 8 (July–September 1982): 5). Roughly, the six classes stand for microcomputers, minicomputers, small, medium-sized, large, and very large computers. The microcomputer category includes electronic accounting machines and desktop models.

14 SEI, *Boletim Informativo* 3 (June–September 1983): 7.

15 *Dados e Idéias* 5 (April–May 1977): 30.

16 Robert A. Bennett, 'IBM in Latin America,' in Jon P. Gunneman, ed., *The Nation-State and Transnational Corporations in Conflict: With Special Reference to Latin America* (New York: Praeger, 1975), Appendix B, 225.

17 United Nations Center on Transnational Corporations (UNCTC), *Transborder Data Flows and Brazil* (New York: United Nations, 1983), 80; *Brazil Trade and Industry* (May 1982): 12; and information provided to me by IBM do Brasil.

18 *Data News* May 15, 1984, 4.

19 SEI, *Boletim Informativo* 3 (June–September 1983): 11.

20 *Ibid.*, 13, 18.

21 Paulo Bastos Tigre, *Technology and Competition in the Brazilian Computer Industry* (New York: St. Martin's, 1983), 94.

22 *Data News*, November 6, 1984, 6.

23 UNCTC, *Transborder Data Flows and Brazil*, 98.

24 Pedro S. Malan and Regis Bonelli, 'The Brazilian Economy in the Seventies: Old and New Developments,' *World Development* 5 (January–February 1977): 36, 38; United

Nations Industrial Development Organization (UNIDO), *Industrial Priorities in Developing Countries* (New York: United Nations, 1979), 2–3.

25 Success eluded Brazil's attempt to master the nuclear fuel cycle and set up a large number of nuclear plants, despite the agreement signed with West Germany to effect the largest technology transfer in history and despite spending billions of dollars. For an analysis of the Brazilian–West German deal, see Norman Gall, 'Atoms for Brazil, Dangers for All,' *Foreign Policy* 23 (summer 1976). For a description of the Brazilian nuclear power industry and its problems, see Margarete K. Luddeman, 'Nuclear Power in Latin America: An Overview of Its Present Status,' *Journal of Interamerican Studies and World Affairs* 25 (1983).

26 Atul Wad, 'Microelectronics: Implications and Strategies for the Third World,' *Third World Quarterly* 4 (1982): 629.

27 Michael Borrus, James Millstein, and John Zysman, with the assistance of Aeton Arbisser and Daniel O'Neill, *International Competition in Advanced Industrial Sectors: Trade and Development in the Semiconductor Industry* (Joint Economic Committee, 97th Congress, 2nd session, February 18, 1982), 34.

28 Dimitri Ypsilanti, 'The Semiconductor Industry,' *OECD Observer* 132 (January 1985): 14.

29 *Business Week*, August 2, 1982, 55.

30 Grieco, *Between Dependency and Autonomy*, 58; *World Business Weekly*, April 21, 1980, 35.

31 Wad, 'Microelectronics,' 679.

32 For example, a 32-bit microprocessor with the power of a mainframe computer can execute 1 million or more instructions per second; analysts predict it will cost no more than twenty dollars by the end of the 1980s (*Business Week*, July 30, 1984, 56).

33 *Business Week*, May 23, 1983, 53.

34 Borrus *et al.*, *International Competition in Advanced Industrial Sectors*, 123; Ypsilanti, 'The Semiconductor Industry,' 15.

35 *World Business Weekly*, April 20, 1981, 30.

36 *Time*, July 11, 1983, 45; *Business Week*, June 8, 1981, 84.

37 *New York Times*, January 20, 1985, D-5.

38 *Business Week*, July 16, 1984, 61; *Data News*, November 6, 1984, 14.

39 *Business Week*, July 16, 1984, 62, 49.

40 See Francisco R. Sagasti, 'A Framework for the Formulation and Implementation of Technology Policies: A Case Study of ITINTEC in Peru,' in Earl Ingerson and Wayne G. Bragg, eds, *Science, Government, and Industry for Development*, the Texas Forum (Austin: University of Texas Institute of Latin American Studies, 1975), 207–10.

41 'Seriado Estatístico,' *Revista Brasileira de Tecnologia* 13 (April–May 1982): 61; United Nations Educational, Scientific, and Cultural Organization, *Statistical Yearbook 1975* (Paris: UNESCO, 1975), 527; *Statistical Yearbook 1978–79* (Paris: UNESCO, 1979), 845.

42 National Council of Science and Technology (CNPq), *Avaliação e Perspectivas*, vol. 3 (1978), 47.

43 Ricardo A. C. Saur, *Hearings before the Parliament* (Câmara dos Deputados) (mimeo, Brazil, D.F., 1977), 17.

44 CNPq, *Avaliação e Perspectivas*, 47; UNCTC, *Transborder Data Flows and Brazil*, 91, 97.

45 Ferranti built a general purpose and real-time 16-bit computer designed for use in data communications networks, real-time information systems, and process control (Steve Yolen, 'Computer Production Prospects in Brazil Brighten,' *Electronics News*, June 7, 1976, 32).

46 Evans developed the *tripé* thesis in *Dependent Development*.

47 See Jack Baranson, *North–South Technology Transfer: Financing and Institutional Building* (Mt. Airy, MD: Lomand, 1981), 38–42.

48 Paulo Bastos Tigre, 'Brazil: A Future in Homemade Hardware,' *South* (February 1982): 99.

49 Silvia Helena, 'Os Banqueiros e a COBRA,' *Dados e Idéias* 5 (April–May 1977): 35.

50 Grieco, 'Between Dependency and Autonomy,' 625.

51 Saur, *Hearings*, 16.

52 See, for example, Seminario sobre Computação na Universidade, *Recomendações* (Florianópolis, September 29, 1977).

53 Grieco even identified the main 'guerrilleros' when he wrote: 'In 1971, the individual selected to head both the Commission and the Department was M. G. K. Menon, who was until then director of the Tata Institute for Fundamental Research, which is under the Atomic Energy Commission. His key deputy in the Department was A. Parthasarathi, who had been a principal officer in the AEC. An important analyst for the AEC, N. Seshagiri, was chosen to head the Electronics Commission's intelligence-gathering and analysis unit' (Grieco, 'Between Dependency and Autonomy,' 627).

54 *Dados e Idéias* 1 (April–May 1980), 8. For example, in 1976 CAPRE examined 2,000 requests and granted only US$115 million of the US$250 million requested.

55 UNCTC, *Transborder Data Flows and Brazil*, 63.

56 Saur, *Hearings*, 4.

57 CAPRE, *Boletim Informativo* 4 (July–September 1976): 53.

58 Marília Rosa Millan and João Lizardo Hermes de Araújo, 'Na Palavra dos Técnicos, um Ponto de Vista Nacional,' *Cadernos de Tecnologia e Ciência* 1 (December 1978–January 1979): 36.

59 CAPRE, *Boletim Informativo* 4 (July–September 1976): 53.

60 Silvia Helena, 'Minis: A Decisão Final,' *Dados e Idéias* 2 (October–November 1977): 34–35.

61 *Business Latin America*, October 19, 1977, 331.

62 *Conjuntura Econômica* (February 1979): 95.

63 UNCTC, *Transborder Data Flows and Brazil*, 69.

64 SEI, 'Ato Normativo' (mimeo, March and June 1980).

65 But SEI made certain that Model 4331 remained a medium-sized computer by stipulating that its minimum memory power had to be 2 million bytes, that the nationalization index would be set at the 85 percent level established by the Industrial Development Council, and that for each two units sold in Brazil, three had to be exported (*Business Latin America*, October 22, 1980, 344).

66 Coordination of Entities for the Defense of an Informatics National Industry, 'Análise da Decisão da SEI de 6 de Agôsto de 1980' (mimeo, August 14, 1980). According to SEI's secretary general, Octavio Gennari Netto, the decision to allow IBM to manufacture its Model 4331 did not undermine the Model because at the time Brazil did not have the potential to manufacture a computer that size. He stated that the permit was not the result of pressure by IBM but of an understanding at SEI that the market would gain (customers had no Brazilian vendor at that size level) and the Model would not lose.

67 Gennari confided that the statements attributed to him regarding the market reserve were the result of selective editing by the media in order to inflame the controversy between those for and against the market reserve. SEI may also have used these remarks to frighten the domestic industry into becoming more competitive.

68 *Data News*, July 26, 1983, 2.

69 *Data News*, July 24, 1984, 8.

70 *Transnational Data Report on Information Policies and Regulations* 7 (December 1984): 431–32.

71 *Data News*, October 18, 1983, 6.

72 *Data News*, October 9, 1984, 2,

73 *Data News*, August 17, 1977, 1.

74 Steve Yolen, 'Brazil Move May Impact IBM/32 Plans,' *Electronics News*, December 13, 1976, 30, 40.

75 Maria de Conceição, 'Uma Luta Desigual,' *Dados e Idéias* 3 (December 1976–January 1977): 17.

76 UNCTC, *Transborder Data Flows and Brazil*, 78.
77 *Data News*, November 1, 1983, 6; July 24, 1984, 4; *O Estado de São Paulo*, January 13, 1984, 23.
78 Tigre, *Technology and Competition*, 144.
79 Despite all these similarities, the technological and practical outcomes differed in both countries: IBM adapted to Brazil's new reality but left India altogether.
80 I thank Manuel Fernando Lousada Soares (Informatics and Communication Coordinator, CNPq) for calling my attention to this process.
81 The term *subversive* is not intended to be derogatory. I mean it metaphorically, to convey the process by which people who hold certain ideas can influence political action.
82 Odell, *U.S. International Monetary Policy*, 63.
83 Albert O. Hirschman, 'The Turn to Authoritarianism in Latin America and the Search for Its Economic Determinants,' in David Collier, ed., *The New Authoritarianism in Latin America* (Princeton: Princeton University Press, 1979), 86–87.
84 Stephen Toulmin, *Human Understanding: The Collective Use and Evolution of Concepts* (Princeton: Princeton University Press, 1972), 289.

6   The emergence of cooperation

For comments on an earlier version of this chapter I am grateful to the members of the review committee of *International Organization*; to the other contributors to the special issue on 'epistemic communities,' especially Peter Haas and M. J. Peterson; to my colleagues at the Center for Science and International Affairs, especially Joseph Nye; and to Hayward Alker, Stephen Graubard, Joseph Grieco, Ernst Haas, and Thomas Schelling. Research funds were provided by the Center for Science and International Affairs, Harvard University, and by the Leonard Davis Institute for International Relations, the Hebrew University of Jerusalem. An earlier version of this article was presented at the annual meeting of the American Political Science Association, Washington, DC, 1988.

1 An epistemic community is a network of individuals or groups with an authoritative claim to policy-relevant knowledge within their domain of expertise. The community members share knowledge about the causation of social and physical phenomena in an area for which they have a reputation for competence, and they have a common set of normative beliefs about what will benefit human welfare in such a domain. While members are often from a number of different professions and disciplines, they adhere to the following: (1) shared consummatory values and principled beliefs; (2) shared causal beliefs or professional judgment; (3) common notions of validity based on intersubjective, internally defined criteria for validating knowledge; and (4) a common policy project. See Peter M. Haas, 'Introduction: Epistemic Communities and International Policy Coordination,' *International Organization*, 46(1) (1992): 3.
2 Lawrence Freedman, *The Evolution of Nuclear Strategy* (New York: St. Martin's, 1983), 191.
3 See Wesley W. Posvar, 'The New Meaning of Arms Control,' *Air Force Magazine* (June 1963): 38. For another study on intellectuals and nuclear weapons, see Roman Kolkowicz, 'Intellectuals and the Nuclear Deterrence System,' in Roman Kolkowicz, ed., *The Logic of Nuclear Terror* (Boston: Allen & Unwin, 1987), 15–46.
4 Krasner has defined international regimes as 'sets of implicit or explicit principles, norms, rules and decision-making procedures around which actors' expectations converge in a given area of international relations.' Whether the regime concept applies to international security, however, has been debated. On the one hand, Jervis and others have argued that the anarchic characteristics of this issue-area tend to lower incentives for cooperation and regime-building. On the other hand, Nye has shown that, once we take the set of agreements, injunctions, and institutions as forming not just one comprehensive security regime but an incomplete mosaic of partial security regimes, the notion of

security regimes makes sense. These partial security regimes have led to the creation of understandings about what it takes to negotiate security agreements, what type of norms and rules can be applied, and how. In some cases, they have helped institutionalize rules of reciprocity, limit competition, transfer information needed to comply with the agreements, and enhance crisis stability by generating stable expectations, including the expectation that diplomacy and negotiations should not be interrupted in the event of international crises. Taken together, and regardless of their various degrees of success, partial security regimes have amounted to a discreet yet significant effort to limit and control autonomous action in the security area. See: Stephen Krasner, 'Structural Causes and Regime Consequences: Regimes as Intervening Variables,' in Stephen D. Krasner, ed., *International Regimes* (Ithaca: Cornell University Press, 1983), 2; Robert Jervis, 'Security Regimes,' in Krasner, *International Regimes*, 173–94; Joseph S. Nye, Jr., 'Nuclear Learning,' *International Organization* 41 (1987): 371–402.

 5 Robin Ranger, *Arms and Politics, 1958–1978: Arms Control in a Changing Political Context* (Toronto: Macmillan, 1979).

 6 See Robert D. Putnam, 'Diplomacy and Domestic Politics: The Logic of Two-Level Games,' *International Organization* 42 (1988): 434. My approach is further developed in 'Cognitive Evolution: A Dynamic Approach for the Study of International Relations and Their Progress,' in Emanuel Adler and Beverly Crawford, eds, *Progress in Postwar International Relations* (New York: Columbia University Press, 1991), 43–88 (chapter 3 in this volume). See also Emanuel Adler, *The Power of Ideology: The Quest for Technological Autonomy in Argentina and Brazil* (Berkeley: University of California Press, 1987). For other approaches dealing with the role of ideas in world politics, see: Judith Goldstein, 'Ideas, Institutions, and American Trade Policy,' *International Organization* 42 (1988): 179–217; John S. Odell, *U.S. International Monetary Policy: Markets, Power, and Ideas as Sources of Change* (Princeton: Princeton University Press, 1982); John G. Ruggie, 'International Regimes, Transactions, and Change: Embedded Liberalism in the Postwar Economic Order,' in Krasner, *International Regimes*, 195–231; Peter A. Hall, ed., *The Political Power of Economic Ideas: Keynesianism across Nations* (Princeton: Princeton University Press, 1990). For key structural realist studies, see: Kenneth N. Waltz, *Theory of International Politics* (Reading, MA: Addison-Wesley, 1979); Robert Gilpin, *War and Change in World Politics* (New York: Cambridge University Press, 1981).

 7 Steve Weber, 'Realism, Détente and Nuclear Weapons,' *International Organization* 44 (1990): 77.

 8 The conventional structural analysis refers to the approach outlined by Waltz in *Theory of International Politics*. According to Weber, the new structural organizing principle 'follows from joint custodianship, a function that was acquired by the United States and Soviet Union and which fundamentally differentiates them from other states' (Weber, 'Realism, Détente and Nuclear Weapons,' 77).

 9 Structuration theory, as defined by Wendt, is 'a relational solution to the agent–structure problem that conceptualizes agents and structures as mutually constituted or co-determined entities' (Alexander E. Wendt, 'The Agent–Structure Problem in International Relations Theory,' *International Organization* 41 (1987): 350). See also: Anthony Giddens, *Central Problems in Social Theory* (Berkeley: University of California Press, 1979); *The Constitution of Society: Outline of the Theory of Structuration* (Berkeley: University of California Press, 1984).

10 Weber, 'Realism, Détente and Nuclear Weapons,' 69.

11 This framework is partly inspired by Stephen Toulmin's discussion in *Human Understanding* (Princeton: Princeton University Press, 1972), 122–23.

12 J. Rotblat, *History of the Pugwash Conferences* (London: Taylor & Francis, 1962).

13 John G. Ruggie, 'Changing Frameworks of International Collective Behavior: On the Complementarity of Contradictory Tendencies,' in Nazli Choucri and Thomas W. Robinson, eds, *Forecasting in International Relations: Theory, Methods, Problems, Prospects* (San Francisco: Freeman, 1978), 403.

14 Michael J. Brenner, 'The Theorist as Actor, the Actor as Theorist: Strategy in the Nixon Administration,' *Stanford Journal of International Studies* 7 (1972): 109–10.

15 See Wesley W. Posvar, 'The Impact of Strategy Expertise on the National Security Policy of the United States,' *Public Policy* 13 (1964): 39. See also Margaret Gowing, 'An Old and Intimate Relationship,' in Vernon Bogdanor, ed., *Science and Politics* (Oxford: Clarendon Press, 1984), 68. According to Gowing, 'the scientists of the atomic era indeed became acutely conscious of phenomena which rule political life: the conflict of desires and aims, the conflict between the interests of different generations, the difficulty of calculating consequences. In the years of their ascendancy they proved that they were not all-wise nor indeed all-wicked but infinitely human. They could change their minds with devastating speed. They could be both wise and foolish, both myopic and far-sighted, both judicious and ridiculous, both clear-headed and muddled. They turned out to be, indeed remarkably like the politicians.'

16 See Posvar, 'The Impact of Strategy Expertise,' 40. See also John Garnett, 'Strategic Studies and Its Assumptions,' in John Baylis, James Wirtz, Eliot Cohen and Colin Gray, eds, *Contemporary Strategy* (New York: Holmes & Meier, 1987).

17 Charles Reynolds, *The Politics of War: A Study of the Rationality of Violence in International Relations* (New York: St. Martin's, 1989), 28.

18 I owe this insight to Hayward Alker. On the nonscientific basis of strategy, see: Reynolds, *The Politics of War*; Eugene B. Skolnikoff, *Science, Technology and American Foreign Policy* (Cambridge, MA: MIT Press, 1967), 110.

19 Aaron Wildavsky, 'Choosing Preferences by Constructing Institutions: A Cultural Theory of Preference Formation,' *American Political Science Review* 81 (1987): 9.

20 Probably the most succinct and best exposition of Schelling's arms control theory is 'Reciprocal Measures for Arms Stabilization,' in Donald G. Brennan, ed., *Arms Control, Disarmament, and National Security* (New York: Brazillier, 1961), 167–86.

21 Adler, 'Cognitive Evolution,' 61 (79–80 in this volume).

22 These two communities have been the most, though certainly not the only, influential ones from a policy point of view in the nuclear debate. Also involved were communities that strove for nuclear abolition and total disarmament and for solving the nuclear predicament through international institutions and world government. See: Robert A. Levine, *The Arms Debate* (Cambridge, MA: Harvard University Press, 1963); Arthur Herzog, *The War–Peace Establishment* (New York: Harper & Row, 1965); Robert E. Osgood, *The Nuclear Dilemma in American Strategic Thought* (Boulder: Westview, 1988). For example, the peace movement, institutionally represented by the Committee for a Sane Nuclear Policy (SANE), promoted a vision of peace radically different from that of the arms controllers. On some occasions, however, SANE came to the help of arms control. The peace movement also played a significant role in efforts to set aside disarmament ideas and make room for arms control during the period when scientists who were generally favorable to disarmament agreed nevertheless to support arms control as a temporary measure. On SANE, see Milton S. Katz, *Ban the Bomb: A History of SANE, the Committee for a Sane Nuclear Policy, 1957–1985* (New York: Greenwood Press, 1986).

23 Brodie augured this approach, arguing (for the wrong reasons, as it later emerged) that nuclear weapons should be used only to deter the adversary. In what is probably the most quoted sentence in the field of national security, Brodie summarized the message of his book: 'Thus far, the chief purpose of our military establishment has been to win wars. From now on, its chief purpose must be to avert them. It can have no other useful purpose.' See Bernard Brodie, *The Absolute Weapon* (New York: Harcourt Brace, 1946), 76. See also Levine, *The Arms Debate*, 240

24 Robert Jervis, 'Arms Control, Stability, and Causes of War,' *Daedalus* 120 (1991): 172.

25 William Borden's *There Will Be No Time* (New York: Macmillan 1946) also made early references to the usability of nuclear weapons in war, to the expectation that nuclear wars could be won, and to counterforce targeting, active defenses, and intercontinental ballistic missiles (ICBMs). Borden did not expect nuclear weapons to revolutionize

strategy; he expected them only to reinforce some of the oldest and most classic elements of strategy. Believing that the nuclear adversaries would spare each other's cities because of their vulnerability, Borden expected that nuclear weapons would be used against military installations. See: Robert Jervis, 'Strategic Theory: What's New and What's True,' in Kolkowicz, *The Logic of Nuclear Terror*, 48; Levine, *The Arms Debate*, 240.

26 Jervis, 'Arms Control, Stability, and Causes of War,' 173.

27 Levine, *The Arms Debate*, 61, 89–90.

28 Posvar, 'The New Meaning of Arms Control,' 39–40.

29 Thomas Schelling, personal communication.

30 Herzog, *The War–Peace Establishment*, 4.

31 Donald F. Hornig, 'Science and Government in the USA,' in Harvey Brooks and Chester L. Cooper, eds, *Science for Public Policy* (New York: Pergamon Press, 1987), 20.

32 *Ibid.*

33 Posvar, 'The Impact of Strategy Expertise,' 49.

34 See Strobe Talbott, *The Master of the Game: Paul Nitze and the Nuclear Peace* (New York: Alfred A. Knopf, 1988).

35 Jennifer E. Sims, 'The Development of American Arms Control Thought, 1945–1960' (Ph.D. dissertation, Johns Hopkins University, Baltimore, MD, 1985), 284. See also Jennifer Sims, *Icarus Restrained: An Intellectual History of Nuclear Arms Control, 1945–1960* (Boulder: Westview, 1991).

36 Fred Kaplan, *Wizards of Armageddon* (New York: Simon & Schuster, 1983), 123–24.

37 Thomas C. Schelling, *The Strategy of Conflict* (London: Oxford University Press, 1960), vi.

38 See John von Neumann and Oscar Morgenstern, *Theory of Games and Economic Behavior*, 2nd edn (Princeton: Princeton University Press, 1947).

39 The economists tended to treat strategic problems in a formal, detached, and almost apolitical manner. This approach elicited a strong reaction and even led some writers to portray the nuclear strategists as lesser human beings. See, for example: Anatol Rapoport, *Strategy and Conscience* (New York: Harper & Row, 1964); Ralph Lapp, *The New Priesthood: The Scientific Elite and the Uses of Power* (New York: Harper & Row, 1965); Irving L. Horowitz, *The War Game: Studies of the New Civilian Militarists* (New York: Ballantine Books, 1963).

40 Thomas Schelling, cited by Herzog in *The War–Peace Establishment*, 49.

41 Sims, 'The Development of American Arms Control Thought,' 286.

42 Twenty or more physicists were recruited from MIT to participate in Project Charles and work on continental air defense. The project's product was a three-volume report which concluded that a defense of the United States against Soviet bombers was feasible and should be undertaken promptly. Project Vista dealt with the nonnuclear defense of Europe. See Gregg Herken, *Counsels of War* (New York: Oxford University Press, 1987), 61, 63, 65.

43 Experience in one of the major wartime laboratories, especially the MIT Radiation Laboratory and the laboratories of the Manhattan Project, or an apprenticeship with one or more of the military 'summer studies,' still appears to be a useful qualification for scientific advising. See Herken, *Counsels of War*, 116–21; Harold K. Jacobson and Eric Stein, *Diplomats, Scientists and Politicians: The United States and the Nuclear Test Ban Negotiations* (Ann Arbor: University of Michigan Press, 1966).

44 *Business Week*, Special Report, July 13, 1963, 75.

45 Jerome B. Wiesner, *Where Science and Politics Meet* (New York: McGraw-Hill, 1965), 176.

46 Sims, 'The Development of American Arms Control Thought,' 303–04.

47 On the question of whether nuclear strategy is a profession, see E. Licklider, *The Private Nuclear Strategists* (Columbus: Ohio State University Press, 1971), ch. 7. See also Wesley Posvar, 'Strategy Expertise and National Security' (Ph.D. dissertation, Harvard University, Cambridge, MA, 1964).

48 Licklider, *The Private Nuclear Strategists*, 119–22, 130, 135.

49 See Don K. Price, *The Scientific Estate* (Cambridge, MA: Belknap Press, 1965). See also Robert Gilpin and Christopher Wright, eds, *Scientists and National Policy Making* (New York: Columbia University Press, 1964).

50 For a discussion of the group and a description of the RAND Corporation, see Kaplan, *Wizards of Armageddon*, especially 51–73. See also Paul Dickson, *Think-Tanks* (New York: Atheneum, 1971).

51 Wohlstetter was a logician–mathematician at RAND. His studies prompted two important reports, R-266 and R-290, dealing with the vulnerability of bombers and the vulnerability of ballistic missiles, respectively. These studies expressed the triumph of quantitative economics-oriented study at RAND. As Kaplan noted, 'Through Wohlstetter's own personal influence within RAND, vulnerability began to loom as the preoccupying issue, the virtual obsession, of strategic analysis' (Kaplan, *Wizards of Armageddon*, 121–22).

52 Bundy recently characterized the 1955 report as 'one of the most influential in the history of American nuclear policy.' See McGeorge Bundy, *Danger and Survival: Choices about the Bomb in the First Fifty Years* (New York: Random House, 1988), 325.

53 For a discussion of the Gaither Committee report and its influence, see Morton Halperin, 'The Gaither Committee and the Policy Process,' *World Politics* 13 (1961), especially 382–83.

54 James R. Killian, Jr., *Sputnik Scientists and Eisenhower* (Cambridge, MA: MIT Press, 1977), 7.

55 Talbott, *The Master of the Game*, 70.

56 The members of the first PSAC were Robert Bacher, William Baker, Hoyd Berkner, Hans Bethe, Detler Bronk, James Doolittle, James Fisk, Caryl Haskins, James R. Killian, George Kistiakowsky, Edwin Land, Emanuel Piore, Edward Purcell, Isador Rabi, H. P. Robertson, Jerome Wiesner, Herbert York, and Jerrold Zacharias. On the PSAC, see Killian, *Sputnik, Scientists and Eisenhower*, 107–217.

57 Herken quotes Eisenhower's reaction to the idea of a nuclear war: 'You can't have this kind of war; there just aren't enough bulldozers to scrape the bodies off the streets' (*Counsels of War*, 116).

58 Spurgeon Keeny, cited by Herken, *ibid.*, 117. Jerome Wiesner, another community member, offered the following view:

> I first became involved in the disarmament problem as a member of the President's Science Advisory Committee. Prior to that I had been the Staff Director of the Gaither Study. The conclusions of this study convinced me that it was not really feasible to protect the American people if a global nuclear war occurred, and that both the Russians and ourselves would suffer terribly. In fact, I became convinced that as long as the Soviet Union was prepared, as it seemed to be, to attempt to match our military effort, there was no help of avoiding an enormous loss of life in the event of a major nuclear war, *regardless of the magnitude of our defense effort.*
> (Wiesner, *Where Science and Politics Meet*, 174; emphasis added)

59 Saville R. Davis, 'Recent Policy Making in the United States Government,' in Brennan, *Arms Control, Disarmament and National Security*, 385.

60 See Johan J. Holst, 'Strategic Arms Control and Stability: A Retrospective Look,' in Johan J. Holst and William Schneider, eds, *Why ABM? Policy Issues in the Missile Defense Controversy* (New York: Pergamon Press, 1969), 282. On the test-ban conference, see Donald A. Strickland, 'Scientists as Negotiators: The 1958 Geneva Conference of Experts,' *Midwest Journal of Political Science* 13 (November 1964): 372–84.

61 Sims, 'The Development of American Arms Control Thought,' 302.

62 See Holst, 'Strategic Arms Control and Stability,' 268. 'The Westerners,' observed Holst, 'frequently voiced the expectation that they should be able to convince the Easterners by

logical argument' (*ibid.*, 263). Regarding the Soviet reaction to the American technical approach, see *ibid.*, 260.

63 See Bernard G. Bechhoefer, *Postwar Negotiations for Arms Control* (Washington, DC: Brookings Institution, 1961), 475. See also Holst, 'Strategic Arms Control and Stability,' 261, 282.

64 Sims, 'The Development of American Arms Control Thought,' ch. 5.

65 In fact, the majority of the 'brass' thought these theories to be quite 'odd,' since

> it seemed to follow [from the theories] that Soviet forces should perhaps not even be targeted, and maybe American cities should not be defended, even if a defense of populations some day became feasible. For if the vulnerability of our forces made us more trigger-happy and was thus a danger to them, then by the same logic their vulnerability was a danger to us: we should therefore not threaten their strategic forces, either directly, by targeting them, or indirectly, by defending our cities and thus effectively neutralizing them.
>
> (Marc Trachtenberg, 'Strategic Thought in America, 1952–1966,' in
> Marc Trachtenberg, ed., *The Development of American Strategic Thought:
> Writings on Strategy 1961–1969 and Retrospectives*
> (New York: Garland, 1988), 456)

66 See Freedman, *The Evolution of Nuclear Strategy*, 197. The most comprehensive study to date on the intellectual basis of arms control is Sims' 'The Development of American Arms Control Thought.' This section builds substantially on her study.

67 See Hedley Bull, *The Control of the Arms Race* (London: Weidenfeld & Nicolson, 1961); *Hedley Bull on Arms Control*, selected and introduced by Robert O'Neill and David N. Schwartz (New York: St. Martin's, 1987).

68 Norman Cousins, 'Foreword,' in Helen S. Hawkins, G. Allen Greb, and Gertrud Weiss Szilard, eds, *Toward a Livable World: Leo Szilard and the Crusade for Nuclear Arms Control* (Cambridge, MA: MIT Press, 1987), xii.

69 See: Barton J. Berenstein, 'Introduction,' in Hawkins, Greb, and Szilard, *Toward a Livable World*, xvii–xxiv; Leo Szilard, 'Shall We Face the Facts? An Appeal for a Truce Not a Peace,' *Bulletin of the Atomic Scientists* 5 (1949): 269–73. See also Herken, *Counsels of War*, 206, on the Doomsday Machine, a fanciful device to ensure peace by blowing up the world as the penalty for aggression.

70 See: Edward Shils, 'American Policy and the Soviet Policy Ruling Group,' *Bulletin of the Atomic Scientists* 3 (1947): 237–39; William T. R. Fox, 'Atomic Energy and International Control,' in William F. Ogburn, ed., *Technology and International Relations* (Chicago: University of Chicago Press, 1949), 102–25. See also Sims, 'The Development of American Arms Control Thought,' 228, 308. The Acheson–Lilienthal report is cited as US Department of State, Committee on Atomic Energy, *A Report on the International Control of Atomic Energy*, March 1946. Bundy (*Danger and Survival*, 159) described this report as 'the high water-mark of the American effort to grapple with the issue of international control.' See also McGeorge Bundy, 'Early Thoughts on Controlling the Nuclear Arms Race: A Report to the Secretary of State, January 1953,' *International Security* 7 (1982): 3–27.

71 See Robert Gilpin, *American Scientists and Nuclear Weapons Policy* (Princeton: Princeton University Press, 1962), ch. 4. See also Bechhoefer, *Postwar Negotiations for Arms Control*, parts 2 and 3.

72 See: Hans J. Morgenthau, *Politics among Nations*, 5th edn (New York: Alfred A. Knopf, 1978); *Scientific Man versus Power Politics* (Chicago: University of Chicago Press, 1946); Reinhold Niebuhr, 'The Illusion of World Government,' *Bulletin of the Atomic Scientists* 5 (1949): 289; *The Structure of Nations and Empires* (New York: Scribner's, 1959).

73 See: David R. Inglis and Donald A. Flanders, 'A Deal before Midnight,' *Bulletin of the Atomic Scientists* 7 (1951), 305–06, 317; James R. Newman, 'Toward Atomic Agreement,'

Bulletin of the Atomic Scientists 10 (1954): 121–22; David R. Inglis, 'Ban the H-Bomb and Favor the Defense,' *Bulletin of the Atomic Scientists* 10 (1954): 353–56; Hornell Hart, 'The Remedies versus the Menace,' *Bulletin of the Atomic Scientists* 10 (1954): 197–205.

74 See: R. L. Meier, 'Beyond Atomic Stalemate,' *Bulletin of the Atomic Scientists* 12 (1956): 147–53; C. W. Sherwin, 'Securing Peace through Military Technology,' *Bulletin of the Atomic Scientists* 12 (1956): 159–64; Warren Amster, 'Design for Deterrence,' *Bulletin of the Atomic Scientists* 12 (1956): 164–65; Jennifer Sims, 'The American Approach to Nuclear Arms Control: A Retrospective,' *Daedalus* 120 (1991): 258.

75 See Rotblat, *History of the Pugwash Conferences*; Joseph Rotblat, 'Movements of Scientists against the Arms Race,' in Joseph Rotblat, ed., *Scientists, the Arms Race and Disarmament* (London: Taylor & Francis, 1982): 115–57.

76 Thomas Schelling, cited by Herzog, *The War–Peace Establishment*, 52.

77 Rotblat, *History of the Pugwash Conferences*, 14–15.

78 Arthur M. Schlesinger, Jr., *A Thousand Days: John F. Kennedy in the White House* (Boston: Houghton Mifflin, 1965), 301.

79 See: Bechhoefer, *Postwar Negotiations for Arms Control*, part 2; Bundy, *Danger and Survival*, ch. 4. In June 1946, Bernard Baruch, the US negotiator at the United Nations, proposed the following plan for the international control of nuclear energy: the United States would place its entire atomic weapons production under an international authority, and other nations would be barred from producing nuclear weapons and would allow their facilities to be placed under the international authority. The plan also promoted the peaceful use of nuclear energy.

80 Sims, 'The Development of American Arms Control Thought,' 244.

81 Dulles supported arms control only on the condition that the price was right and that American prestige abroad would be enhanced.

82 By developing plans for air reconnaissance, a nuclear freeze, nuclear arms reductions, and a set of objectives for arms control, Stassen augured the 'golden era of arms control.'

83 Schelling, *The Strategy of Conflict*, 207.

84 Freedman, *The Evolution of Nuclear Strategy*, 199.

85 See: Thomas Schelling and Morton Halperin, *Strategy and Arms Control*, 2nd edn (New York: Pergamon-Brassey, 1985); Brennan, *Arms Control, Disarmament, and National Security*; Bull, *The Control of the Arms Race*; Louis Henkin, ed., *Arms Control Issues for the Public* (Englewood Cliffs: Prentice-Hall, 1961); David H. Frisch, ed., *Arms Reduction: Program and Issues* (New York: Twentieth Century, 1961); Ernst W. Lefever, ed., *Arms and Arms Control* (New York: Praeger, 1962). See also Robin Ranger, 'The Four Bibles of Arms Control,' in Susan J. Shepard, ed., *Books and the Pursuit of American Foreign Policy*, special issue of *Book Forum* 6 (1984): 416–32.

86 See Gerald Holton, ed., *Arms Control*, special issue of *Daedalus* 89(4) (1960). The impact of the special *Daedalus* issue on arms control was so great that a revised and enlarged edition was rushed into print in early 1961. After this printing of 20,000 copies was sold out, it went into another printing. Such sales were unprecedented for a specialized work of this kind. See Ranger, 'The Four Bibles of Arms Control,' 417–18.

87 See Thomas C. Schelling, 'What Went Wrong with Arms Control,' *Foreign Affairs* 65 (1985–86): 223. Schelling had made the following statement in 1969:

> Whatever the prospects for successful negotiations with the Soviet Union during the coming months and years, on the subject of strategic weapons, there could not be a greater contrast between the serious and businesslike prospects for realistic negotiations in 1969 and all the fantasy and pretense about 'general and complete disarmament' that characterized the beginning of our decade. ... We think differently now, partly because technological progress obliges us to but partly because we have been thinking and talking and writing and holding hearings and preparing budget justifications and negotiating with allies and enemies during this past decade. ... [The] concern with vulnerability of retaliatory

systems … became the primary criterion for the selection of a weapons system itself [and] it has become also the primary criterion for the design of an arms agreement between the United States and the USSR. … The problem of 'accidental war' was recognized to be primarily one of information and decision rather than sheer mechanical accident, [and the] tradition of non-use, the somewhat self-confirming expectations of non-use, grows stronger every year.

See the testimony of Thomas Schelling, in US Congress, House Committee on Foreign Affairs, *Strategy and Science: Toward a National Security Policy for the 1970s: Hearings before the Subcommittee on National Security Policy and Scientific Developments*, 91st Congress, 1st session, March 1969, 123–24.

88 Colin S. Gray, *Strategic Studies and Public Policy: The American Experience* (Lexington: University Press of Kentucky, 1982), 26.

89 According to Gray, 'Contemporary arms-control theory was an invention of the strategic studies community in the period 1958–60' (*ibid.*, 72).

90 Firestone notes that the Committee of Principals was 'a high-level interagency group designed to coordinate and ultimately ratify arms control policy. Founded in August 1958, the committee was initially composed of the secretary of state as chairman, the secretary of defense, the chairman of the AEC [Atomic Energy Commission], the director of the CIA [Central Intelligence Agency], and the president's special adviser on science and technology' (Bernard J. Firestone, *The Quest for Nuclear Stability: John F. Kennedy and the Soviet Union* (Westport: Greenwood Press, 1982), 76).

91 Licklider, *The Private Nuclear Strategists*, 155.

92 Schlesinger, *A Thousand Days*, 104; William W. Kaufmann, *The McNamara Strategy* (New York: Harper & Row, 1964), 1.

93 Firestone, *The Quest for Nuclear Stability*, 153.

94 Gray, *Strategic Studies and Public Policy*, 97

95 See Steve Weber and Sidney Drell, 'Attempts to Regulate Military Activities in Space,' in Alexander L. George, Philip J. Farley, and Alexander Dallin, eds, *U.S.–Soviet Security Cooperation: Achievements, Failures, Lessons* (New York: Oxford University Press, 1988), 388. On ACDA, see Paul F. Walker, 'The U.S. Arms Control and Disarmament Agency: Policy-Making in Strategic Arms Limitations' (Ph.D. dissertation, MIT, Cambridge, MA, 1978).

96 Herbert F. York, *Making Weapons, Talking Peace: A Physicist's Odyssey from Hiroshima to Geneva* (New York: Basic Books, 1987), 119.

97 Kaplan, *Wizards of Armageddon*, 332–33.

98 Schlesinger, *A Thousand Days*, 494.

99 See: York, *Making Weapons, Talking Peace*, 222–26; Kaplan, *Wizards of Armageddon*, 345.

100 Desmond Ball, *Politics and Force Levels: The Strategic Missile Program of the Kennedy Administration* (Berkeley: University of California Press, 1980), 82–85.

101 My discussion of the hotline idea is based on William L. Ury's *Beyond the Hotline: How Crisis Control Can Prevent Nuclear War* (Boston: Houghton Mifflin, 1985), 142, 144, and on interviews.

102 See: Talbott, *The Master of the Game*, 79; Schlesinger, *A Thousand Days*, 475.

103 See Adler, *The Power of Ideology*. See also William L. Ryland, 'Institutional Impediments,' in Richard Burt, ed., *Arms Control and Defense in the 1980s* (Boulder: Westview, 1982), 101.

104 Schlesinger, *A Thousand Days*, 504.

105 John Newhouse, *Cold Down: The Story of SALT* (New York: Holt, Rinehart and Winston, 1973), 69.

106 Herken quotes some of McNamara's concerns: 'There is a kind of mad momentum intrinsic to the development of all nuclear weaponry. … If a system works—and works well—there is a strong pressure from all directions to procure and deploy the weapon out of all proportion to the prudent level required' (*Counsels of War*, 197–98). Herken

points out that what McNamara termed 'an action–reaction phenomenon' dominated and escalated the arms race.

107 In November 1964, the Soviets first paraded what appeared to be an ABM system. The system, called Galosh, 'was believed to be composed of a network of radars and a two- or three-stage, solid-fueled interceptor missile designed for long-range, ex-atmospheric interception of incoming ICBMs' (Ernst J. Yanarella, *The Missile Defense Controversy: Strategy, Technology, and Politics, 1955–1972* (Lexington: University Press of Kentucky, 1977), 118).

108 On the politics of ABM control up to 1972, see: *ibid.*; Benson D. Adams, *Ballistic Missile Defense* (New York: American Elsevier, 1971); Morton Halperin, *Bureaucratic Politics and Foreign Policy* (Washington, DC: Brookings Institution, 1974); Newhouse, *Cold Down*; Gerard Smith, *The Story of SALT*, 2nd edn (New York: Pergamon-Brassey, 1989); Kaplan, *Wizards of Armageddon*; Herken, *Counsels of War*.

109 See David N. Schwartz, 'Past and Present: The Historical Legacy,' in Ashton B. Carter and David N. Schwartz, eds, *Ballistic Missile Defense* (Washington, DC: Brookings Institution, 1984), 332–33.

110 York, *Making Weapons, Talking Peace*, 222–23.

111 For a discussion of Wiesner and York's article, see Herken, *Counsels of War*, 193. Herken notes that Paul Nitze called the article 'outrageous, an incitement, an example of dirty pool.'

112 Sentinel was a light area missile-defense system set to be deployed in fifteen sites in the continental United States, one site in Hawaii, and one in Alaska. The system consisted of various radars and either a Spartan missile or a Sprint missile, depending on the site. See Adams, *Ballistic Missile Defense*, 177.

113 Newhouse, *Cold Down*, 50, 115–16.

114 Adams, *Ballistic Missile Defense*, 186.

115 Yanarella, *The Missile Defense Controversy*, 144–47.

116 Adams, *Ballistic Missile Defense*, 193.

117 Kahn said that the public debate had been one-sided because about 'ninety percent of the scientists who normally speak in public, or who consult part-time for the government on defense issues, as well as the vast preponderance of the public literature on the subject, opposed ABM' (Herman Kahn, 'The Missile Defense Debate in Perspective,' in Holst and Schneider, *Why ABM?*, 285). For a good source on the involvement of pro- and anti-ABM scientists in the ABM debate, see Anne Hessing Cahn, *Eggheads and Warheads: Scientists and the ABM* (Cambridge, MA: MIT Center for International Studies, 1971). In the 'battle of books,' the counterpart to *Why ABM?* was the anti-ABM work edited by Abram Chayes and Jerome B. Wiesner, *ABM: An Evaluation of the Decision to Deploy an Antiballistic Missile System* (New York: Signet, 1969).

118 Safeguard incorporated both area and terminal defense capabilities, using the same components as Sentinel but deploying these components with the aim of defending Minuteman silos. For command and control reasons, Washington, DC would be defended as well. See Adams, *Ballistic Missile Defense*, 200.

119 According to Brenner,

> each testimony [before Congress] delineated the technical and political aspects of the issue while assiduously drawing the necessary distinctions between those questions amenable to scientific judgment and those requiring subjec-tive estimates. By stipulating the logical connections between acceptance of ABM and its multiple consequences, these analyses heightened awareness of the issue's subtle interdependencies. They discredited the Administration's casual use of the syllogistic argument that in the past had relied successfully on faith (in the simple equation that more arms means more security) and fear (of Soviet aggression).
>
> (Brenner, 'The Theorist as Actor,' 115–16)

120 Sims, 'The Development of American Arms Control Thought,' 13–14.

121 Firestone, *The Quest for Nuclear Stability*, 150.

122 See the testimony of Marshall Shulman, in US Congress, Senate Committee on Foreign Relations, *The Strategic and Foreign Policy Implications of Anti-Ballistic Missile Systems: Hearings before the Subcommittee on International Organization and Disarmament Affairs*, part 1, 91st Congress, 1st session, March 1969, 154. See also the testimony of Vincent P. Rock, in US Congress, *Strategy and Science: Hearings*, 224, which included the following argument: 'In terms of aid, in terms of weapons … there is a great deal of copying, of action and reaction, reciprocal action of a kind, between the nations of the world. … As we know, all nations collect each other's basic and applied scientific output. There is a tremendous interaction going on as a result of having to read and cope with the ideas the other fellow is putting out.'

123 The Soviet–American Disarmament Studies Group, referred to as the Doty group, started to meet in 1965 and met for ten years. The first conference of the Dartmouth group took place in 1959. An official collaboration between the American and Soviet academies of sciences took place under the guidance of W. Panofsky and S. Sagdeev.

124 Walter C. Clemens, Jr., *Can Russia Change? The USSR Confronts Global Interdependence* (Boston: Unwin Hyman, 1990), 67.

125 Holst, 'Strategic Arms Control and Stability,' 258, 264, 268.

126 The Soviet views were cited by Bruce J. Allyn in 'Toward a Common Framework: Avoiding Inadvertent War and Crisis,' in Graham T. Allison and William L. Ury (with Bruce J. Allyn), eds, *Windows of Opportunity: From Cold War to Peaceful Competition in US–Soviet Relations* (Cambridge, MA: Ballinger, 1989), 188.

127 Holst, 'Strategic Arms Control and Stability,' 282.

128 See: Allyn, 'Toward a Common Framework,' 188; John L. Gaddis, *The Long Peace* (Cambridge: Cambridge University Press, 1987), 204.

129 See Peter Stein and Peter Feaver, *Assuring Control of Nuclear Weapons: The Evolution of Permissive Action Links* (Cambridge, MA: Harvard Center for Science and International Affairs, 1987).

130 See Ranger, *Arms and Politics*, 7. Dinerstein and his colleagues at RAND noted in the early 1960s that the technical arms control approach seemed to hold no interest for Soviet military planners. According to Dougherty, however, 'some change was noticeable after the Cuban missile crisis. … During the past decade [1963– 73], there have been signs that the Soviets have begun to take more seriously the Western ideas of "arms control."' See: Herbert S. Dinerstein, Leon Goure, and Thomas W. Wolfe, 'Introduction' to the English translation of *Soviet Military Strategy*, ed. Soviet Marshal V. D. Sokolovskiy (Englewood Cliffs: Prentice Hall, 1963), 77; James E. Dougherty, *How to Think about Arms Control and Disarmament* (New York: Crane, Russak, 1973), 71.

131 Ranger, *Arms and Politics*, 209.

132 Samuel B. Payne, *The Soviet Union and SALT* (Cambridge, MA: MIT Press, 1980), 75.

133 Schlesinger, *A Thousand Days*, 505.

134 See: Michael Mandelbaum, 'Western Influence on the Soviet Union,' in Seweryn Bialer and Michael Mandelbaum, eds, *Gorbachev's Russia and American Foreign Policy* (Boulder: Westview, 1988), 364; Holst, 'Strategic Arms Control and Stability,' 245; Yanarella, *The Missile Defense Controversy*, 197–98.

135 Frank von Hippel, 'Arms Control Physics: The New Soviet Connection,' *Physics Today* (November 1989): 39.

136 See: York, *Making Weapons, Talking Peace*, 223; J. P. Ruina and M. Gell-Mann, 'Ballistic Missile Defense and the Arms Race,' in *Proceedings of the Twelfth Pugwash Conference on Science and World Affairs* (Udaipur, India, January 27–February 1 1964), 232–35; von Hippel, 'Arms Control Physics,' 39; Paul Doty, 'Arms Control: 1960, 1990, 2020,' *Daedalus* 120 (1991): 40.

137 Regarding the Soviet reactions, see Newhouse, *Cold Down*, 102.

138 David Holloway, *The Soviet Union and the Arms Race*, 2nd edn (New Haven: Yale University Press, 1989), 44.

139 See Michael MccGwire, 'Why the Soviets Are Serious about Arms Control,' *Brookings Review* (spring 1987): 11. In a review of MccGwire's book, *Military Objectives in Soviet Foreign Policy* (Washington, DC: Brookings Institution, 1987), Bluth argued that the changes which MccGwire said occurred at the end of 1966 actually started in 1964 and 1965. Bluth's point was indeed proved by a flurry of Soviet articles discussing the possibility of doctrinal change in the 1964–65 period. See Christopher Bluth, 'The Evolution of Soviet Military Doctrine,' *Survival* 30 (1988): 149.

140 Payne, *The Soviet Union and SALT*, 18.

141 *Ibid.*, 7.

142 Georgi A. Arbatov and William Oltman, *Soviet Viewpoint* (New York: Dodd, Mead, 1981), 130.

143 Andrei Kokoshin, personal communication.

144 Payne, *The Soviet Union and SALT*, 46, 59.

145 See *ibid.*, 126. V. V. Larionov made the statement in 'Transformatsiia kontseptsii "strategicheskoi dostatochnosti,"' *SShA* (November 1971). Gromyko later made this same point. It was almost an official statement of the Soviet government's position.

146 Payne, *The Soviet Union and SALT*, 40–41, 47, 76.

147 *Ibid.*, 76.

148 *Ibid.*, 66.

149 Other reasons that led the Soviet leaders to sign a Soviet–US strategic arms control treaty included the following: they perceived that the Americans held a strong edge in the technological race; they realized that multiple independently targetable reentry vehicles (MIRVs) were entering into the strategic equation; they wanted to institutionalize parity with the United States and, if possible, improve their strategic situation in areas unrestricted by SALT; they wanted to project power; they wished to strengthen détente with the West; and they hoped that the resulting economic savings could be directed back to the civilian sector.

150 See: Raymond L. Garthoff, 'Mutual Deterrence and Strategic Arms Limitation in Soviet Policy,' *International Security* 2 (1978): 126; Morton Halperin, 'The Decision to Deploy the ABM: Bureaucratic and Domestic Politics in the Johnson Administration,' *World Politics* 25 (1972): 95.

151 The faces refer to complementary and mutually reinforcing processes. They are ideal types, and 'the distinction between "faces" tends to break down at the margin' (Scott C. James and David A. Lake, 'The Second Face of Hegemony: Britain's Repeal of the Corn Laws and the American Walker Tariff of 1846,' *International Organization* 43 (1989): 4).

152 *Ibid.*

153 Herken, *Counsels of War*, 247.

154 Edward L. Warner III, 'New Thinking and Old Realities in Soviet Defence Policy,' *Survival* 31 (1989): 18–20.

155 Robert Jervis, 'Realism, Game Theory, and Cooperation,' *World Politics* 40 (1988): 325.

156 This awareness of the value of cooperation for national security was essential. According to Davis,

> as the naive type of unsafeguarded arms control of the 1920s became clearly inappropriate to the problems of the next three decades, there developed a relatively harmless tradition in politics of paying it lip service, so as not to offend the gentler elements of public opinion, and of ignoring it in practice. This tradition of the white lie [was] carried over into the nuclear age. ... For several critical years the habit of pretending to work for disarmament served to mask the fact that the political leadership of the United States did not want disarmament. More specifically, those in Washington who considered arms control undesirable or impractical clearly had the upper hand in the process of

> making and administering policy, with the help of others who thought the
> Russians would never sign anyway, or would sign and cheat.
>
> (Davis, 'Recent Policy Making,' 379–80)

157 Walker, 'The U.S. Arms Control and Disarmament Agency,' 13.
158 Gilpin, *American Scientists and Nuclear Weapons Policy*, 299.
159 See Holloway, *The Soviet Union and the Arms Race*, 40.
160 Raymond L. Garthoff, 'On Mutual Deterrence: A Reply to Donald Brennan,' *International Security* 3 (1979): 198.
161 Weber, 'Realism, Détente and Nuclear Weapons,' 72.
162 Terry Nardin, *Law, Morality, and the Relations of States* (Princeton: Princeton University Press, 1984), 14.
163 I owe this insight to Craig Murphy. See Craig N. Murphy, 'Color It Mitrany: Two Patterns of Progress in International Relations' (working paper, Wellesley College, Wellesley, MA, 1989).
164 Nardin, *Law, Morality, and the Relations of States*, 9.
165 Schelling, *The Strategy of Conflict*, 106–07.
166 See Arthur A. Stein, 'Coordination and Collaboration: Regimes in an Anarchic World,' in Krasner, *International Regimes*, 125–27.
167 See Roger K. Smith, 'Explaining the Nonproliferation Regime: Anomalies for Contemporary International Relations Theory,' *International Organization* 41 (1987): 253–81.

7   Imagined (security) communities

I am grateful for comments on an earlier version of this chapter to Hayward Alker, Michael Barnett, Richard Bilder, Beverly Crawford, Raymond Duvall, Ernst Haas, Arie Kacowicz, Peter Katzenstein, Ann-Marie Burley Slaughter, Alex Wendt, and Crawford Young, and to Jeff Lewis for research assistance. I also thank the Davis Institute of International Relations at the Hebrew University of Jerusalem for financial assistance. A draft of this chapter was presented at the Annual Meeting of the American Political Science Association, New York, September 1–4, 1994. Another draft was published as Working Paper 2.28 of the series of the Political Relations and Institutions Research Group, Center for German and European Studies, University of California at Berkeley, January 1995.

1 Italo Calvino, *Invisible Cities*, trans. W. Weaver (San Diego: Harcourt Brace Jovanovich, 1974), 82.
2 Emanuel Adler and Michael Barnett, 'Governing Anarchy: A Research Agenda for the Study of Security Communities,' *Ethics and International Affairs* 10 (1996): 63–98; John G. Ruggie, 'Territoriality and Beyond: Problematizing Modernity in International Relations,' *International Organization* 47(1) (1993): 157.
3 Benedict Anderson, *Imagined Communities: Reflections on the Origin and Spread of Nationalism* (London: Verso, 1983), 15.
4 Zdravko Mlinar, 'Individuation and Globalization: The Transformation of Territorial Social Organization,' in Zdravko Mlinar, ed., *Globalization and Territorial Identities* (Aldershot: Avebury, 1992), 24–25.
5 Until December 1994, the OSCE was the Conference on Security and Cooperation in Europe (CSCE).
6 David Sibley, 'Outsiders in Society and Space,' in Kay Anderson and Fay Gale, eds, *Inventing Places: Studies in Cultural Geography* (Melbourne: Longman Chesire, 1992), 107.
7 John Agnew, 'The Territorial Trap: The Geographical Assumptions of International Relations Theory,' *Review of International Political Economy* 1(1) (1994): 54. For the

conventional view, see Kenneth E. Waltz, *Man, the State and War* (New York: Columbia University Press, 1959).

8 Agnew, 'The Territorial Trap,' 60–61; Alexander Wendt, 'Collective Identity Formation and the International State,' *American Political Science Review* 88(2) (1994): 384–96.

9 Agnew, 'The Territorial Trap,' 62. For counter arguments against the conventional view, see David Mitrany, *A Working Peace System* (Chicago: Quadrangle Books, 1966).

10 For an example of this, see: Hans J. Morgenthau, *Politics among Nations: The Struggle for Power and Peace* (New York: Knopf, 1948); E. H. Carr, *The Twenty Years' Crisis, 1919–1939: An Introduction to the Study of International Relations* (New York: Harper & Row, 1964). Corporate identity refers to 'the intrinsic self-organizing qualities that constitute actor individuality. For human beings, this means the body and experience of consciousness; for organizations it means their constituent individuals, physical resources, and the shared beliefs and institutions in virtue of which individuals function as a "we."' Social identity is the 'sets of meanings that an actor attributes to itself while taking the perspective of others, that is, as a social object. … [S]ocial identities [are] at once cognitive schemas that enable an actor to determine "who I am/we are" in a situation and positions in a social role structure of shared understandings and expectations' (Wendt, 'Collective Identity Formation,' 385). In other words, for a state, corporate identity refers to its constituent individuals, physical resources, and institutions which generate interests of physical security, recognition by other actors, and economic development. On the other hand, in its relations with other states, a state may have many social identities, such as those of 'liberal,' 'democratic,' and 'balancer,' which generate interests of preserving liberal values, democracy, and the balance of power.

11 Wendt, 'Collective Identity Formation.'

12 Ruggie, 'Territoriality and Beyond,' 165. See also Agnew, 'The Territorial Trap'; Wendt, 'Collective Identity Formation'; R. B. J. Walker, *Inside/Outside: International Relations as Political Theory* (Cambridge: Cambridge University Press, 1993). See also the contributions in Mlinar, *Globalization and Territorial Identities.*

13 Ruggie, 'Territoriality and Beyond,' 165.

14 Wendt, 'Collective Identity Formation,' 392.

15 Ruggie, 'Territoriality and Beyond,' 165.

16 Ronnie D. Lipschutz, 'Reconstructing World Politics: The Emergence of Global Civil Society,' *Millennium* 21(3) (1992): 389–420.

17 Lee Cuba and David M. Hummon, 'Constructing a Sense of Home: Place Affiliation and Migration across the Life Cycle,' *Sociological Forum* 8(4) (1993): 549.

18 See, for example: William Bloom, *Personal Identity, National Identity and International Relations* (Cambridge: Cambridge University Press, 1990); Ruggie, 'Territoriality and Beyond'; Iver B. Neumann, 'A Region-Building Approach to Northern Europe,' *Review of International Studies* 20(1) (1994): 53–74; Walker, *Inside/Outside*; Wendt, 'Collective Identity Formation.' See also Alexander Wendt, 'Anarchy Is What States Make of It: The Social Construction of Power Politics,' *International Organization* 46(2) (1992): 391–425.

19 Leo R. Chavez, 'The Power of the Imagined Community: The Settlement of Undocumented Mexicans and Central Americans in the United States,' *American Anthropologist* 96(1) (1994): 52–73.

20 A region is 'a set of countries that are more markedly interdependent over a wider range of different dimensions—and usually also transactions—than they are with other countries. In many ways, therefore, regions are made by culture, history, politics and economics rather than by geography alone' (Karl W. Deutsch, 'On Nationalism, World Regions and the Nature of the West,' in Per Torsvik, ed., *Mobilization, Center–Periphery Structures and Nation-Building: A Volume in Commemoration of Stein Rokkan* (Bergen: Universitetsforlaget, 1981), 54). An interpretation of community, closer to that used in the present study, emphasizes meaning and symbolic interaction. It refers to 'a system of values, norms, and moral codes which provides a sense of identity within a bounded whole to its members' (Peter Hamilton, 'Editor's Foreword,' in Anthony P. Cohen, *The*

Symbolic Construction of Community (New York: Tavistock, 1985), 9). Deutsch defined a political community as social groups with a process of political communication, some machinery for enforcement, and some popular habits of compliance; see Karl W. Deutsch, Sidney A. Burrell, Robert A. Kann, Maurice Lee, Jr., Martin Lichterman, Raymond E. Lindgren, Francis L. Loewenheim, and Richard W. Van Wagenen, *Political Community and the North Atlantic Area* (Princeton: Princeton University Press, 1957), 3. See especially Andrew Linklater, 'The Problem of Community in International Relations,' *Alternatives* 15(2) (1990): 135–53; 'Citizenship and Sovereignty in the Post-Westphalian State,' *European Journal of International Relations* 2(1) (1996): 77–103. See also Haskel Fein, *Normative Politics and the Community of Nations* (Philadelphia: Temple University Press, 1987).

21 A 'multiperspectival polity' refers to a system of rule where national, supranational, and transnational identities share the same cognitive space. Hence it is at odds with the 'single point,' state-centered, Westphalian geographic perspective. See Ruggie, 'Territoriality and Beyond,' 172.

22 John A. Agnew and James S. Duncan, eds, *The Power of Place: Bringing Together Geographical and Sociological Imaginations* (Boston: Unwin Hyman, 1989); Agnew, 'The Territorial Trap'; Cuba and Hummon, 'Constructing a Sense of Home'; and Sibley, 'Outsiders in Society and Space.' For two very useful studies connecting the notion of place to politics, see Walker, *Inside/Outside*; and Ivo D. Duchacek, *The Territorial Dimension of Politics: Within, among, and across Nations* (Boulder: Westview, 1986).

23 Michael N. Barnett, 'Identity and Alliances in the Middle East,' in Peter J. Katzenstein, ed., *The Culture of National Security* (New York: Columbia University Press, 1996), 400–47.

24 Bruce Bueno de Mesquita and David Lalman, *War and Reason* (New Haven: Yale University Press, 1992), ch. 4; Harvey Starr, 'Democracy and War: Choice, Learning and Security Communities,' *Journal of Peace Research* 29(2) (1992): 210–11.

25 Deutsch *et al.*, *Political Community*, 5.

26 *Ibid.*, 6.

27 *Ibid.*, 36, 66–67. By 'we-feeling,' Deutsch refers to cognition rather than affection.

28 Adler and Barnett, 'Governing Anarchy,' 73. See also Emanuel Adler and Michael Barnett, eds, *Security Communities* (Cambridge: Cambridge University Press, 1998).

29 Adler and Barnett, 'Governing Anarchy,' 73.

30 Barry Buzan, 'From International System to International Society: Structural Realism and Regime Theory Meet the English School,' *International Organization* 47(3) (1992): 339.

31 Ronald Beiner, *What's the Matter with Liberalism* (Berkeley: University of California Press, 1992), 105. See also Linklater, 'Citizenship and Sovereignty.'

32 With respect to NATO, see Joseph Lepgold, 'The Next Step toward a More Secure Europe,' *Journal of Strategic Studies* 17(4) (1994): 7–26.

33 Paul W. Schroeder, 'The New World Order: A Historical Perspective,' *Washington Quarterly* 17(2) (1994): 30.

34 See Barbara A. Misztal, *Trust in Modern Societies* (Cambridge: Polity Press, 1996).

35 *Constructivism* denotes the view that social reality is constructed when individuals come into contact with each other and interact. Constructivists assert that to understand the social world, one must begin with shared understanding and knowledge and, in particular, practices, and investigate how they help to define the institutional and material worlds. Cognitive and institutional structures give meaning to the material world. They provide people with reasons for the way things are and indications as to how they should use their material capabilities and power. In turn, changes in the identities and interests of the agents involved continually transform cognitive and institutional structures. Constructivists do not deny the reality of the material world. They merely point out that the manner in which the material world shapes, modifies, and affects human interaction, which in turn affects it, depends on prior dynamic epistemic and normative interpretations of the material world. See: Emanuel Adler, 'Seizing the Middle Ground:

Constructivism in World Politics,' *European Journal of International Relations* 3(3) (1997): 319–63 (chapter 4 in this volume); Friedrich Kratochwil, *Rules, Norms, and Decisions* (Cambridge: Cambridge University Press, 1989); Ruggie, 'Territoriality and Beyond'; Wendt, 'Anarchy.' For an alternative view on the construction of security communities, see Ole Waever, 'Insecurity, Security, and Asecurity in the West European Non-War Community,' in Adler and Barnett, eds, *Security Communities*, 69–118.

36 Wendt, 'Collective Identity Formation.'

37 For the ideational effect of American hegemony, see John G. Ruggie, 'Multilateralism: The Anatomy of an Institution,' in John G. Ruggie, ed., *Multilateralism Matters: The Theory and Praxis of an Institutional Form* (New York: Columbia University Press, 1993), 3–47.

38 For the 'democratic peace' thesis, see: Michael W. Doyle, 'Kant, Liberal Legacies, and Foreign Affairs: Part I,' *Philosophy and Public Affairs* 12(3) (1983): 205–35; Bruce Russett, *Grasping the Democratic Peace* (Princeton: Princeton University Press, 1993).

39 See Amitav Acharya, 'Collective Identity and Conflict Resolution in Southeast Asia,' in Adler and Barnett, eds, *Security Communities*, 198–227.

40 Ronald Inglehart, *Culture Shift in Advanced Industrial Societies* (Princeton: Princeton University Press, 1990), 396–97. See also Diego Gambetta, ed., *Trust: Making and Breaking Cooperative Relations* (New York: Blackwell, 1988).

41 Gabriel A. Almond and Sidney Verba, *The Civic Culture: Political Attitudes and Democracy in Five Nations* (Boston: Little, Brown, 1963).

42 Robert D. Putnam, *Making Democracy Work: Civic Traditions in Modern Italy* (Princeton: Princeton University Press, 1993).

43 *Ibid.*

44 Starr, 'Democracy and War,' 210.

45 *Ibid.*; Bueno de Mesquita and Lalman, *War and Reason*.

46 Starr, 'Democracy and War,' 211.

47 See, for example, Patricia Chilton, 'Mechanisms of Change: Social Movements, Transnational Coalitions, and the Transformation Processes in Eastern Europe,' in Thomas Risse-Kappen, ed., *Bringing Transnational Relations Back in: Non-State Actors, Domestic Structures and International Institutions* (Cambridge: Cambridge University Press, 1995), 189–226.

48 Lipschutz, 'Reconstructing World Politics.'

49 Kathryn Sikkink, 'Human Rights Issue-Networks in Latin America,' *International Organization* 47(3) (1993): 411–42; Margaret E. Keck and Kathryn Sikkink, *Activists beyond Borders: Transnational Advocacy Networks in International Politics* (Ithaca: Cornell University Press, 1998).

50 Chilton, 'Mechanisms of Change'; Daniel Thomas, 'Social Movements and International Institutions: A Preliminary Framework' (paper presented at the annual meeting of the American Political Science Association, Washington, DC, 1991).

51 See: Doyle, 'Kant, Liberal Legacies, and Foreign Affairs'; Russett, *Grasping the Democratic Peace*.

52 Emanuel Adler and Michael Barnett, 'A Framework for the Study of Security Communities,' in Adler and Barnett, *Security Communities*, 29–65.

53 Deutsch *et al.*, *Political Community*, 38; emphasis added.

54 See, for example, Kenneth Waltz, *Theory of International Politics* (Reading, MA: Addison-Wesley, 1979).

55 Steven Lukes, *Power: A Radical View* (London: Macmillan, 1974).

56 For an exception, see Stefano Guzzini, 'Structural Power: The Limits of Neorealist Analysis,' *International Organization* 47(3) (1993): 443–78.

57 John R. Searle, *The Construction of Social Reality* (New York: Free Press, 1995).

58 Adler and Barnett, 'Governing Anarchy'; Michael C. Williams, 'The Institutions of Security' (paper presented at the annual meeting of the International Studies Association, San Diego, April 16–21, 1996).

59 Williams, 'The Institutions of Security.' See also: Michel Foucault, *Power/Knowledge: Selected Interviews and Other Writings, 1972–1977*, ed. C. Gordon (New York: Pantheon Books, 1980); Richard Price, 'A Genealogy of the Chemical Weapons Taboo,' *International Organization* 49(1) (1995): 73–103.

60 Adler, 'Seizing the Middle Ground,' 336–37 (104–05 in this volume).

61 Ira J. Cohen, 'Structuration Theory and Social Praxis,' in Anthony Giddens and Jonathan Turner, eds, *Social Theory Today* (Stanford: Stanford University Press, 1987), 287.

62 David Laitin, 'Political Culture and Political Preferences,' *American Political Science Review* 82(2) (1988): 591. However, instrumental reasoning may be the first stage of a socialization process that leads people to internalize an identity.

63 Cohen, 'Structuration Theory,' 297.

64 For the role of positive images of material progress, see Ernst B. Haas, *Nationalism, Liberalism and Progress: The Rise and Decline of Nationalism* (Ithaca: Cornell University Press, 1997).

65 Adler and Barnett, 'Governing Anarchy,' 83.

66 Guzzini, 'Structural Power,' 471.

67 See Antonio Gramsci, *Selections from the Prison Notebooks of Antonio Gramsci*, trans. Q. Hoare and G. Nowell Smith (New York: International Publishers, 1971). See also: Robert W. Cox, 'Social Forces, States and World Orders,' *Millennium* 10(2) (1981): 126–55; Stephen Gill, *American Hegemony and the Trilateral Commission* (Cambridge: Cambridge University Press, 1990).

68 Adler and Barnett, *Security Communities*.

69 R. Tuomela, 'Actions by Collectives,' in J. E. Tomberlin, ed., *Philosophy of Mind and Action Theory* (*Philosophical Perspectives*, vol. 3) (Atascadero: Ridgeview Publishing Company, 1989), 471–96.

70 See, for example, John C. Turner, 'Towards a Cognitive Redefinition of the Social Group,' in Henry Tajfel, ed., *Social Identity and Intergroup Relations* (Cambridge: Cambridge University Press, 1982), 15–40.

71 *Ibid.*

72 *Ibid.*, 16.

73 *Ibid.*, 18.

74 See: Henri Tajfel, *Human Groups and Social Categories: Studies in Social Psychology* (Cambridge: Cambridge University Press, 1981); Henry Tajfel, ed., *Differentiation between Social Groups: Studies in the Social Psychology of Intergroup Relations* (London: Academic Press, 1978); Henry Tajfel and John C. Turner, 'The Social Identity Theory of Intergroup Behavior,' in Stephen Worchel and William G. Austin, eds, *Psychology of Intergroup Relations*, 2nd edn (Chicago: Nelson-Hall, 1986), 7–24; Jonathan Mercer, 'Anarchy and Identity,' *International Organization* 49(2) (1995): 229–52. For the view that genuine conflict of interest generates intergroup competition, see Muzafer Sherif, *Group Conflict and Co-operation: Their Social Psychology* (London: Routledge and Kegan Paul, 1966). For the importance, as well as the limitations, of social-psychological explanations, see Herbert C. Kelman, *International Behavior: A Social-Psychological Analysis* (New York: Holt, Rinehart and Winston, 1965).

75 Turner, 'Towards a Cognitive Redefinition,' 31.

76 James S. Coleman, *Nigeria, Background to Nationalism* (Berkeley: University of California Press, 1958); Richard A. Higgott and Kim R. Nossal, 'Australia and the Search for Security Community in the 1990s,' in Adler and Barnett, *Security Communities*, 265–94.

77 Anthony D. Smith, 'National Identity and the Idea of European Unity,' *International Affairs* 68(1) (1992): 59.

78 Anthony Black, 'Nation and Community in the International Order,' *Review of International Studies* 19(1) (1993): 87.

79 Buzan, 'From International System to International Society.' The reference is to Ferdinand Tönnies, *Community and Association* (Gemeinschaft und Gesellschaft), trans. C. P. Loomis, (London: Routledge and Kegan Paul, 1955).

80 Buzan, 'From International System to International Society,' 336.

81 *Ibid.*, 339.

82 John G. Ruggie, 'Continuity and Transformation in the World Polity: Toward a Neorealist Synthesis,' *World Politics* 35(2) (1983): 280.

83 For sovereignty, see Thomas J. Biersteker and Cynthia Weber, eds, *State Sovereignty as Social Construct* (Cambridge: Cambridge University Press, 1996).

84 Linklater, 'The Problem of Community,' 145; Hedley Bull, *The Anarchical Society* (New York: Columbia University Press, 1977).

85 Anthony Giddens, *The Constitution of Society* (Berkeley: University of California Press, 1984), especially ch. 1.

86 Anne-Marie Burley and Walter Mattli, 'Europe before the Court: A Political Theory of Legal Integration,' *International Organization* 47(1) (1993): 41–42.

87 Thomas Buergenthal, professor of international law (George Washington University) and US delegate to the CSCE negotiations, interview with author, October 1993. See also Thomas Buergenthal, 'The CSCE Rights System,' *George Washington Journal of International Law and Economics* 25(2) (1991): 352.

88 See F. H. Hinsley, *Sovereignty*, 2nd edn (Cambridge: Cambridge University Press, 1986).

89 David Jacobson, *Rights across Borders: Immigration and the Decline of Citizenship* (Baltimore: Johns Hopkins University Press, 1996).

90 Thomas M. Franck, 'The Emerging Right to Democratic Governance,' *American Journal of International Law* 86 (1992): 46–91.

91 Ruggie, 'Territoriality and Beyond,' 172.

92 Adler and Michael Barnett, 'A Framework.'

93 Linklater, 'Citizenship and Sovereignty,' 97–98.

94 Dennis F. Thompson, *The Democratic Citizen* (Cambridge: Cambridge University Press, 1970), 2. Instead, Jean Bodin argues that what 'makes a man a citizen [is] the mutual obligation between subject and sovereign' (Jean Bodin, *Six Books on the Commonwealth* (London: Blackwell, 1967), 21).

95 Examples of this are the OSCE, the European Union, and the Council of Europe, as well as, lately, NATO and ASEAN.

96 For studies on the CSCE/OSCE, see: Stefan Lehne, *The CSCE in the 1990s: Common European House or Potemkin Village?* (Vienna: Braumuller, 1991); Michael Lucas, ed., *The CSCE in the 1990s: Constructing European Security and Cooperation* (Baden-Baden: Nomos, 1993); Vojtech Mastny, *The Helsinki Process and the Reintegration of Europe 1986–1991: Analysis and Documentation* (New York: New York University Press, 1992); Alexis Heraclides, *Security and Cooperation in Europe: The Human Dimension, 1972–1992* (London: Frank Cass, 1993); Arie Bloed, *The Conference on Security and Cooperation in Europe: Analysis and Basic Documents, 1972–1993* (Dordrecht: Kluwer Academic, 1993); Victor-Ives Ghebali, *L'OSCE dans l'Europe post-communiste, 1990–1996: Vers une identité pan-Européenne de sécurité* (Brussels: Bruylant, 1996); Diana Chigas, with Elizabeth McClintock and Christophe Kamp, 'Preventive Diplomacy and the Organization for Security and Cooperation in Europe: Creating Incentives for Dialogue and Cooperation,' in Abram Chayes and Antonia H. Chayes, eds, *Preventing Conflict in the Post-Communist World* (Washington, DC: The Brookings Institution, 1996), 25–97.

97 For additional information on the CSCE/OSCE, see: Conference on Security and Cooperation in Europe, *Charter of Paris for a New Europe* (Paris: CSCE, 1990); *The Challenges of Change: CSCE Helsinki Document 1992* (Prague: CSCE Secretariat, 1992); *Toward a Genuine Partnership in a New Era: Budapest Document 1994* (Prague: CSCE Secretariat, 1994); Organization for Security and Cooperation in Europe, *Lisbon Document 1996* (Lisbon: OSCE, 1996); Chigas, McClintock, and Kamp, 'Preventive Diplomacy.'

98 See James E. Goodby, 'The Diplomacy of Europe Whole and Free,' in Samuel F. Wells, Jr., ed., *The Helsinki Process and the Future of Europe* (Washington, DC: The Wilson Center Press, 1990), 59. Note that I do not claim that there is already a security community, or

that the OSCE will ultimately succeed in establishing a security community, in the *entire* OSCE region.

99 Conference on Security and Cooperation in Europe (CSCE), 'Toward a Genuine Partnership in a New Era,' Budapest Document, 1994 (Budapest: CSCE, 1994). See also a statement made by the head of the US delegation to the CSCE, Ambassador John Kornblum, at the CSCE Seminar on Early Warning and Conflict Prevention, Warsaw, January 20, 1994, to the effect that CSCE practices 'are designed to be part of a process of community building.'

100 Marianne Hanson, 'Democratization and Norm Creation in Europe,' *Adelphi Papers* 284 (London: Brassey's for the International Institute for Strategic Studies, 1994), 34.

101 *Ibid.*

102 Heraclides makes a similar point. See Heraclides, *Security and Cooperation in Europe*, 15.

103 Janie Leatherman, 'Conflict Transformation in the CSCE: Learning and Institutionalization,' *Cooperation and Conflict* 28(4) (1993): 413–14. Transparency, the absence of nuclear deterrence, intensive and regular communications, diffuse reciprocity, and a set of interlocking security, human-rights, economic and environmental organizations characterize a fully developed model of cooperative security. For cooperative security, see Janne E. Nolan, ed., *Global Engagement: Cooperation and Security in the 21st Century* (Washington, DC: The Brookings Institution, 1994).

104 See, for example, Arnold Wolfers, *Discord and Collaboration* (Baltimore: Johns Hopkins University Press, 1962), ch. 10.

105 Buergenthal, 'The CSCE Rights System,' 382; emphasis added.

106 *Ibid.*, 380–1.

107 Lehne, *The CSCE in the 1990s*, 5. For the human dimension, see Heraclides, *Security and Cooperation in Europe*; Arie Bloed and Pieter van Dijk, eds, *The Human Dimension of the Helsinki Process: The Vienna Follow-up Meeting and Its Aftermath* (Dordrecht: Martinus Nijhoff, 1991). On the HCNM, see Alexis Heraclides, *Helsinki-II and Its Aftermath: The Making of the CSCE into an International Organization* (London: Pinter Publishers, 1993).

108 Lehne, *The CSCE in the 1990s*, 62.

109 *Ibid.*, 15.

110 For OSCE institution-building, see Heraclides, *Helsinki-II*.

111 For a critical account of OSCE institutional processes, see Richard Weitz, 'Pursuing Military Security in Eastern Europe,' in Robert O. Keohane, Joseph S. Nye, and Stanley Hoffmann, eds, *After the Cold War: International Institutions and State Strategies in Europe, 1989–1991* (Cambridge, MA: Harvard University Press, 1993), 342–80.

112 Mastny, *The Helsinki Process*, 2.

113 US Commission on Security and Cooperation in Europe, *Beyond Process: The CSCE's Institutional Development, 1990–92* (Washington, DC, 1993). For social movements, see Thomas, 'Social Movements and International Institutions.'

114 *Ibid.*

115 For the quote, see Lehne, *The CSCE in the 1990s*, 73. The 'consensus-minus-one' provision from 1992 refers only to the human dimension and not to all the commitments and principles of the OSCE. However, in practice, the provision has been used more widely. On paper, at least, there also exists a 'consensus-minus-two' provision in the case of directed conciliation procedure, directing two disputants to seek conciliation irrespective of their will. See Heraclides, *Helsinki-II*, 179–80.

116 Heraclides, *Security and Cooperation in Europe*, 51.

117 Mastny, *The Helsinki Process*, 3.

118 Manfred Woerner, 'NATO Transformed: The Significance of the Rome Summit,' *NATO Review* 39(6) (1991): 5. The North Atlantic Cooperation Council was replaced and upgraded by the Euro-Atlantic Partnership Council in May 1997.

119 Martha Finnemore, 'International Organizations as Teachers of Norms: The United Nations Educational, Scientific, and Cultural Organization and Science Policy,' *International Organization* 47(3) (1993): 565–97.

120 Conceptually, seminar diplomacy stands on similar but broader grounds than Herbert Kelman's social-psychological 'Problem-Solving Workshop' approach for settling international conflicts. See Herbert C. Kelman and Stephan P. Cohen, 'The Problem-Solving Workshop: A Social-Psychological Contribution to the Resolution of International Conflict,' *Journal of Peace Research* 13(2) (1976): 79–90.

121 See Ruggie, *Multilateralism Matters.*

122 Adler and Barnett, 'Governing Anarchy,' 77.

8 Condition(s) of peace

1 See for example: Thucydides, *History of the Peloponnesian War*, trans. Rex Warner (Baltimore: Penguin Books, 1972); Niccolò Machiavelli, *The Prince*, trans. Henry C. Mansfield, Jr., (Chicago: University of Chicago Press, 1985); Thomas Hobbes, *Leviathan*, ed. C. B. MacPhearson (Harmondsworth: Penguin Books, 1954); Jean-Jacques Rousseau, 'Judgment on Perpetual Peace,' in *A Project of Perpetual Peace*, trans. Edith M. Nuttall (London: Richard Cobden-Sanderson, 1927); Hans J. Morgenthau, *Politics among Nations: The Struggle for Power and Peace* (New York: Alfred A. Knopf, 1948); Robert Gilpin, *War and Change in World Politics* (Cambridge: Cambridge University Press, 1981).

2 Johan Galtung, 'Violence, Peace, and Peace Research,' *Journal of Peace Research* 6 (1969): 167–91; *Essays in Peace Research*, vol. 1 (Copenhagen: Christian Ejlers, 1975); Kenneth E. Boulding, *Stable Peace* (Austin: University of Texas Press, 1978). See also Arie Kacowicz, *Zones of Peace in the Third World: South America and West Africa in Comparative Perspective* (Albany: State University of New York Press, 1998).

3 During the 1960s and 1970s, Galtung and Boulding conducted a lively debate on the meaning of peace, which centered in part on Galtung's notions of 'negative' and 'positive' peace. See Kenneth E. Boulding, 'Twelve Friendly Quarrels with Johan Galtung,' *Journal of Peace Research* 14 (1977): 75–86. Whereas Galtung defined 'negative peace' as the absence of physical violence, Boulding argued that the concept of negative peace is a 'complete misnomer': 'Peace ... is not just "not-war" any more than water is "not ice"' (Boulding 'Twelve Friendly Quarrels,' 78). A year later, however, Boulding himself referred to peace's 'negative side' as 'the absence of turmoil, tension, conflict, and war' (Boulding, *Stable Peace*, 3). According to Herbert C. Kelman, the concept of negative peace is valuable because it stresses the avoidance of violence and destruction. See Herbert C. Kelman, 'Reflections on the History and Status of Peace Research,' *Conflict Management and Peace Science* 5 (1991): 105.

4 Galtung is mostly in a category of his own when he defines 'positive peace' as the absence of something else, i.e., 'structural [socioeconomic] violence' (Galtung, 'Violence, Peace, and Peace Research,' 167–91; *Essays in Peace Research*). See also Heikki Patomaki and Ole Waever, 'Introducing Peaceful Changes,' in Heikki Patomaki, ed., *Peaceful Changes in World Politics* (Research Report no. 71, Tampere Peace Research Institute, University of Tampere, 1995). Boulding, on the other hand, correctly defined 'positive peace' in positive terms, i.e., as a 'condition of good management, orderly resolution of conflict, harmony associated with mature relationships, gentleness, and love' (Boulding, *Stable Peace*, 3).

5 'In this sense [positive peace] peace is one of the ultimate time's arrows in the evolutionary process, an increasing product of human development and learning' (*ibid.*, 3). According to Kacowicz, positive peace 'includes also social and economic justice, and some kind of world order that meets the needs and interests of the human population as a whole' (Kacowicz, *Zones of Peace in the Third World*).

6 See, for example: Isaiah 1:16–17, 2:2–4, 11:1–4, 6, 9, and 42:5–7; Matt. 5:3–11 ('The Beatitudes'); Dante Alighieri, *Monarchy and Three Political Letters*, trans. Donald Nicholl and Colin Hardie (London: Weidenfeld & Nicolson, 1954); Emeric Cruce, *The New Cyneas*, trans. C. Frederick Farrell, Jr., ed. Edith Farrell (New York: Garland, 1972);

William Penn, *An Essay toward the Present and Future Peace of Europe* (Washington, DC: American Peace Society, 1912); Abbé de Saint Pierre, *Ouvrages de Politique*, 16 vols (Rotterdam, 1733–41); Antoine-Nicolas de Condorcet, *Sketch for a Historical Picture of the Progress of the Human Mind*, trans. June Barraclough, intro. Stuart Hampshire (London: Weidenfeld & Nicolson, 1955); Immanuel Kant, *Perpetual Peace and Other Essays*, trans. Ted Humphrey (Indianapolis: Placket 1983); Jeremy Bentham, *Plan for a Universal and Perpetual Peace* (London: Grotius Society, 1927); Norman Angell, *The Great Illusion* (London: Penguin Books, 1908); A. Zimmern, *The League of Nations and the Rule of Law* (London: Macmillan, 1939); Grenville Clark and Louis Sohn, *World Peace through World Law*, 3rd edn (Cambridge, MA: Harvard University Press, 1973); Philip Noel-Baker, *The Arms Race: A Program for World Disarmament* (London: Stevens and Sons, 1958); Richard A. Falk, *A Study of Future Worlds* (New York: Free Press, 1975).

7 Kant, 'Perpetual Peace.'

8 Michael W. Doyle, 'Kant, Liberal Legacies, and Foreign Affairs: Part 1,' *Philosophy and Public Affairs* 12 (1983): 205–33; Bruce M. Russett, *Grasping the Democratic Peace: Principles for a Post-Cold War World* (Princeton: Princeton University Press, 1993).

9 Boulding, *Stable Peace*, 13.

10 Karl W. Deutsch, Sidney A. Burrell, Robert A. Kann, Maurice Lee, Jr., Martin Lichterman, Raymond E. Lindgren, Francis L. Loewenheim, and Richard W. Van Wagenen, *Political Community and the North Atlantic Area* (Princeton: Princeton University Press, 1957); Richard W. Van Wagenen, *Research in the International Organization Field: Some Notes on a Possible Focus* (Princeton: Center for Research on World Political Institutions, Princeton University, 1952); Emanuel Adler and Michael Barnett, eds, *Security Communities* (Cambridge: Cambridge University Press, 1998). See also E. H. Carr, *Conditions of Peace* (London: Macmillan, 1942). According to Kelman, 'positive peace does not imply an ideal utopian situation, but merely a livable one' (Kelman, *Reflections on the History and Status of Peace Research*, 108).

11 Deutsch *et al.*, *Political Community*, 5.

12 'If we can speak of violent practices, or of practices based on (threats) of violence … we can also speak of making practices more peaceful' (Patomaki and Waever, 'Introducing Peaceful Changes,' 10).

13 My approach follows a 'constructivist' line of reasoning. On constructivism, see: Alexander Wendt, 'Anarchy Is What States Make of It: The Social Construction of Power Politics,' *International Organization* 46 (1992): 391–425; David Dessler, 'What Is at Stake in the Agent Structure Debate?' *International Organization* 43 (1989): 441–74; Emanuel Adler, 'Seizing the Middle Ground: Constructivism in World Politics,' *European Journal of International Relations* 3 (1997): 319–63 (chapter 4 in this volume). On the reality of 'social facts,' such as practices, see John Searle, *The Construction of Social Reality* (New York: Free Press, 1995).

14 Patomaki and Waever, 'Introducing Peaceful Changes,' 16.

15 Hedley Bull, *The Anarchical Society* (New York: Columbia University Press, 1977).

16 Andrew B. Schmookler, *The Parable of the Tribes* (New York: Houghton Mifflin, 1984).

17 There is a growing attention in the IR literature to the role played by agents in the constitution of international practices. One such type are known as 'moral entrepreneurs.' See, for example, Ethan Nadelmann, 'Global Prohibition Regimes: The Evolution of Norms in International Society,' *International Organization* 44 (1990): 479–526.

18 On learning, see Ernst B. Haas, *When Knowledge Is Power* (Berkeley: University of California Press, 1990).

19 Although I prefer the expression 'condition of peace,' to avoid confusion with the 'conditions of (for) peace' I shall refer instead to the 'state of peace.'

20 Searle, *The Construction of Social Reality*, 43–51. See also the comments by Ian Hacking, Mary Midgley, Thomas Osborne, and John R. Searle in 'Review Symposium on John R. Searle,' *History of the Human Sciences* 10 (1997): 83–110.

21 E. H. Carr, *The Twenty Years' Crisis: 1919–1939* (New York: Harper, 1964).

22 Carr, *Conditions of Peace*, 123, 274.

23 *Ibid.*, 273.

24 *Ibid.*, 102–25.

25 Carr, *The Twenty Years' Crisis*, 92.

26 Charles Taylor, 'Interpretation and the Sciences of Man,' in Fred R. Dallmayr and Thomas A. McCarthy, eds, *Understanding and Social Inquiry* (Notre Dame: University of Notre Dame Press, 1977), 127.

27 *Ibid.*, 123.

28 Deutsch *et al.*, *Political Community*, 5.

29 *Ibid.*, 5; Emanuel Adler and Michael Barnett, 'Security Communities in Theoretical Perspective,' in Adler and Barnett, *Security Communities*, 3–28. To measure this 'sense of community,' Deutsch and his associates quantified transaction flows, with particular emphasis on their volume, within and among nation-states. A relative growth in transaction flows between societies, as contrasted against flows within them, was thought to be a crucial test for determining whether new 'human communities' might be emerging. See, for example, Deutsch's essays in Philip E. Jacob and James V. Toscano, eds, *The Integration of Political Communities* (Philadelphia: Lippincott, 1964): 'Communication Theory and Political Integration,' 46–74; 'Transaction Flows as Indicators of Political Cohesion,' 75–97; 'The Price of Integration,' 143–78; 'Integration and the Social System,' 179–208. For incisive analyses of Deutsch's contribution to integration theory, see Donald J. Puchala, 'Integration Theory and the Study of International Relations' and Arend Lijphart, 'Karl W. Deutsch and the New Paradigm in International Relations,' both of them in Richard Merritt and Bruce M. Russett, eds, *From National Development to Global Community* (London: George Allen & Unwin, 1981), 145–64, 233–51.

30 Karl W. Deutsch, *Political Community at the International Level: Problems of Definition and Measurement* (New York: Doubleday, 1954), 41.

31 'His [Carr's] readers, overwhelmingly realists, have pounced upon his attack on utopianism but generally have failed to note his … criticism of realism and his positive comments about utopianism' (Ken Booth, 'Security in Anarchy: Utopian Realism in Theory and Practice,' *International Affairs* 67 (1991): 531). There is a relatively large literature dealing with Carr's writings and ideas. On the realist side see, for example: Hans J. Morgenthau, 'The Political Science of E. H. Carr,' *World Politics* 1 (1948): 127–34; William T. R. Fox, 'E. H. Carr and Political Realism: Vision and Revision,' *Review of International Studies* 11 (1985): 1–16. On the Grotian side see, for example: Hedley Bull, 'The Twenty Years' Crisis Twenty Years On,' *International Journal* 24 (1969): 625–38; Booth, 'Security in Anarchy.' For constructivist and critical theory critiques see, for example: Cecelia Lynch, 'E. H. Carr, International Relations Theory, and the Societal Origins of International Legal Norms,' *Millennium* 23 (1994): 589–620; Paul Howe, 'The Utopian Realism of E. H. Carr,' *Review of International Studies* 20 (1994): 277–97. For strong criticism of Carr's work, see Whittle Johnston, 'E. H. Carr's Theory of International Relations: A Critique,' *Journal of Politics* 29 (1967): 861–84.

32 Carr, *Conditions of Peace*, xxiii.

33 *Ibid.*

34 *Ibid.*, 275.

35 *Ibid.*, 62.

36 *Ibid.*, 273.

37 *Ibid.*, 117–25. On leadership, see 123.

38 The failure to create modern mass democracy, Carr thought, had to do, first, with the 'failure to give adequate social and economic content to the concept of equality'; second, with the fact that political rights became 'a sham,' because economic power exercised a predominant influence on political affairs; and third, with the removal of issues of great importance from popular control, because of the technocratic nature of the machinery of government (*ibid.*, 35–36).

39 *Ibid.*, 50.

> Shorn of its moral foundation ... nationalism, as the history of the last twenty years has shown, could lead only to the doctrine of the morally purposeless super-nation or *Herrenvolk*. ... The 'good' nationalism of the nineteenth century ... has been transformed into the 'bad' nationalism of the twentieth century, the fertile breeding-ground of 'economic nationalism,' racial discrimination, and war.
>
> (*Ibid.*, 106–07)

40 *Ibid.*, 101. 'Our most urgent economic problem is no longer to expand production, but to secure a more equitable distribution of consumption and a more regular and orderly utilization of our productive capacity' (*ibid.*, 80).

41

> Liberal democracy assumed that individual citizens would recognize the exis-tence of a fundamental harmony of interest between them and would adjust apparent differences of interest on particular points by a process of give-and-take to their mutual advantage. ... National self-determination was the sure basis for an international community because each nation, in pursuing its own highest interest, was pursuing the interest of the world as a whole, so that nationalism was the natural stepping-stone to internationalism. Laissez-faire economics assumed that by promoting their own interest individuals were doing all they could to promote that of the community.
>
> (*Ibid.*, 102).

42 Carr, *The Twenty Years' Crisis*, 220 (emphasis added).
43 Carr, *Conditions of Peace*, 63.
44 *Ibid.*, 272.
45 *Ibid.*, 242–70.
46 See Ole Waever, 'Insecurity, Security, and Asecurity in the West European Non-War Community,' in Adler and Barnett, *Security Communities*, 69–118.
47 Carr, *Conditions of Peace*, 117–24.
48 Deutsch *et al.*, *Political Community*; Ernst B. Haas, *Nationalism, Liberalism, and Progress: The Rise and Decline of Nationalism* (Ithaca: Cornell University Press, 1997); Taylor, 'Interpretation and the Sciences of Man.'
49 *Ibid.*, 122.
50 Norbert Wiener, cited by Karl W. Deutsch, *The Nerves of Government* (New York: Free Press, 1966), 77.
51 Deutsch, *Political Community*, 36. See also Adler and Barnett, 'Security Communities in Theoretical Perspective.'
52 Deutsch, *Political Community*, 47.
53 Emanuel Adler and Michael Barnett, 'A Framework for the Study of Security Communities,' in Adler and Barnett, *Security Communities*, 29–65.
54 Deutsch, *Political Community*, ch. 2; *Political Community at the International Level*, 37.
55 Deutsch, *Political Community*, 91.
56 *Ibid.*, 47
57 *Ibid.*, chs 2 and 3.
58 Haas, *Nationalism, Liberalism, and Progress*, 19–20
59 *Ibid.*, 323.
60 *Ibid.*, 14–21, 59, 342, 351–52.
61 Ernst B. Haas, 'Nationalism: An Instrumental Social Construction,' *Millennium* 22 (1993): 541.
62 *Ibid.*, 543–45.
63 Haas, *Nationalism, Liberalism, and Progress*, 19.
64 Adler and Barnett, 'A Framework for the Study of Security Communities.'

65 See, for example: Waever, 'Insecurity, Security, and Asecurity'; Guadalupe Gonzalez and Stephan Haggard, 'The United States and Mexico: A Pluralistic Security Community?' in Adler and Barnett, *Security Communities*, 295–332.

66 Adler and Barnett, 'A Framework for the Study of Security Communities'; Emanuel Adler, 'Imagined (Security) Communities: Cognitive Regions in International Relations,' *Millennium* 26 (1997): 249–77 (chapter 7 in this volume).

67 Adler and Barnett, 'A Framework for the Study of Security Communities.'

68 *Ibid.* Trust is a social phenomenon that depends on the assessment that another actor will behave in ways that are consistent with normative expectations. Identities are 'images of individuality and distinctiveness ("selfhood") held and projected by an actor and formed (and modified over time) through relations with significant "others"' (Ronald L. Jepperson, Alexander Wendt, and Peter J. Katzenstein, 'Norms, Identity, and Culture in National Security,' in Peter J. Katzenstein, ed., *The Culture of National Security: Norms and Identity in World Politics* (New York: Columbia University Press, 1996), 59). Collective identities require people not only to identify (positively) with the destiny of other people but also to identify themselves and those others as a group in relation to other groups.

69 Deutsch, *Political Community*, 37–39; Adler and Barnett, 'A Framework for the Study of Security Communities.'

70 *Ibid.*

71 Jürgen Habermas, *The Theory of Communicative Action: Reason and the Rationalization of Society*, trans. T. McCarthy (Boston: Beacon Press, 1984); *Between Facts and Norms: Contributions to a Discourse Theory of Law and Democracy*, trans. William Rehg (Cambridge, MA: MIT Press, 1996).

72 When we scratch the 'surface' of strategic rational choice, we realize that it is enabled and mediated by communicative action. For example, a closer look at Thomas Schelling's strategic and bargaining theory shows that its rational-choice assumptions can work only in the context of a process of social communication (Schelling's innovation was pointing out the tacit and implicit manifestations of such processes). See Thomas C. Schelling, *The Strategy of Conflict* (New York: Oxford University Press, 1960).

73 Thomas Risse, "Let's Talk!": Insight from the German Debate's on Communicative Behavior and International Relations,' paper presented to the annual Convention of the American Political Science Association, Washington, DC, August 27–31, 1997, 8; later published as "Let's Argue!": Communicative Action in World Politics,' *International Organization* 54 (2000): 1–40.

74 Andrew Moravcsik, 'A Liberal Theory of International Politics,' *International Organization* 51 (1997): 513–53.

75 On Soviet ideas, technocrats, and the end of the Cold War, see Thomas Risse-Kappen, 'Ideas Do Not Float Freely: Transnational Coalitions, Domestic Structures, and the End of the Cold War,' *International Organization* 42 (1994): 185–214. See also Jeffrey T. Checkel, *Ideas and International Political Change: Soviet/Russian Behavior and the End of the Cold War* (New Haven: Yale University Press, 1997).

76 I take these subcommunities to perform a role similar to that of epistemic communities. On epistemic communities, see 'Knowledge, Power and International Policy Coordination,' *International Organization* 46 (1992), ed. Peter M. Haas. On security issues, see Emanuel Adler, 'The Emergence of Cooperation: National Epistemic Communities and the International Evolution of the Idea of Nuclear Arms Control,' *ibid.*, 100–45 (chapter 6 in this volume).

77 On the incipient security community in South America, see Andrew Hurrell, 'An Emerging Security Community in South America,' in Adler and Barnett, *Security Communities*, 228–64.

78 On NATO as a security community-building institution, see Emanuel Adler, 'Seeds of Peaceful Change: The OSCE's Security Community-Building Model,' in Adler and Barnett, *Security Communities*, 119–60. See also Thomas Risse-Kappen, *Cooperation among*

Democracies: The European Influence on US Foreign Policy (Princeton: Princeton University Press, 1995).

79 John Mueller, *Retreat from Doomsday: The Obsolescence of Major War* (New York: Basic Books, 1989).

80 Emanuel Adler, 'Seasons of Peace: Progress in Postwar International Security,' in Emanuel Adler and Beverly Crawford, eds, *Progress in Postwar International Relations* (New York: Columbia University Press, 1991), 128.

81 Robert Jervis, 'The Political Effect of Nuclear Weapons: A Comment.' *International Security* 13 (1998): 80–90.

82 Waever, 'Insecurity, Security, and Asecurity.'

83 Michael Howard, 'The Causes of Wars,' *Wilson Quarterly* 8 (1984): 92. See also: Mueller, *Retreat from Doomsday*; F. H. Hinsley, 'Peace and War in Modern Times,' in Raimo Vayrynen, ed., *The Quest for Peace* (Beverly Hills: Sage, 1987), 77–78.

84 See Doyle, 'Kant, Liberal Legacies, and Foreign Affairs.'

85 Gabriel A. Almond and Sidney Verba, *The Civic Culture* (Boston: Little, Brown, 1963).

86 Margaret Keck and Kathryn Sikkink, *Activists beyond Borders: Advocacy Networks in International Politics* (Ithaca: Cornell University Press, 1998).

87 On the role of Great Powers in regional security, see Paul A. Papayoanou, 'Great Powers and Regional Orders: Possibilities and Prospects after the Cold War,' in David A. Lake and Patrick M. Morgan, eds, *Regional Orders: Building Security in a New World* (University Park: Pennsylvania State University Press, 1997), 125–39.

88 On ASEAN as an emerging security community, see Amitav Acharya, 'Collective Identity and Conflict Resolution in Southeast Asia,' in Adler and Barnett, *Security Communities*, 198–227.

89 Dorothy V. Jones, *Code of Peace: Ethics and Security in the World of the Warlord States* (Chicago: University of Chicago Press, 1991).

90 *Ibid.*, 159–66; Adler, 'Seeds of Peaceful Change'; 'Imagined (Security) Communities,' 268–75 (199–204 in this volume).

91 *Ibid.*, 268–70 (199–200 in this volume).

92 *Ibid.*, 271 (201 in this volume). See also Marianne Hanson, 'Democratization and Norm Creation in Europe,' *Adelphi Papers* 284 (London: Brassey's for the International Institute for Strategic Studies (IISS), 1994): 34.

93 Thomas Buergenthal, 'The CSCE Rights System,' *George Washington Journal of International Law and Economics* 25 (1992): 380–81.

94 Thomas M. Franck, *The Power of Legitimacy among Nations* (New York: Oxford University Press, 1990), 196.

95 Nadelmann, 'Global Prohibition Regimes.'

96 Robert Wuthnow, 'The Foundations of Trust,' *Report from the Institute for Philosophy and Public Policy* 18 (Maryland: University of Maryland, 1998), 4. On trust, see also Barbara Mistzal, *Trust in Modern Societies* (Cambridge: Polity Press, 1996).

97 Adler, 'The Emergence of Cooperation.'

98 John G. Ruggie, ed., *Multilateralism Matters: The Theory and Praxis of an Institutional Form* (New York: Columbia University Press, 1993); Michael Barnett, 'The New UN Politics of Peace,' *Global Governance* 1 (1995): 79–98.

99 Janie Leatherman, 'Conflict Transformation in the CSCE: Learning and Institution-alization,' *Cooperation and Conflict* 28 (1993): 414.

100 Samuel Huntington, 'The Clash of Civilizations?' *Foreign Affairs* 72 (1993): 22–49; *The Clash of Civilizations and the Remaking of World Order* (New York: Simon & Schuster, 1996).

101 On the construction of the Mediterranean region see, for example: Roberto Aliboni, George Joffe, and Tim Niblock, *Security Challenges in the Mediterranean Region* (London: Frank Cass, 1996); Alberto Bin, ed., *Cooperation and Security in the Mediterranean: Prospects after Barcelona* (Malta: Mediterranean Academy of Diplomatic Studies, University of Malta, 1996); Antonio Marquina and Hans Gunter Braude, eds, 'Confidence Building and Partnership in the Western Mediterranean: Tasks for

Preventive Diplomacy and Conflict Avoidance,' UNISCI Papers no. 1 (Madrid: UNISCI, 1994); Fred Tanner, 'An Emerging Security Agenda for the Mediterranean,' *Mediterranean Politics* 1 (1996): 279–94.

102 On Europe, see Waever, 'Insecurity, Security, and Asecurity'; on ASEAN, see Acharya, 'Collective Identity and Conflict Resolution in Southeast Asia.'

103 The following three paragraphs rely in part on Emanuel Adler and Beverly Crawford, 'Regional Security through Integration: Constructing the Mediterranean Region,' draft proposal, December 1997; and on Emanuel Adler, 'The Cooperative Security Way to Stable Peace: Constructing Regional and Global Security Communities,' paper commissioned by the Swedish Ministry of Foreign Affairs, August 1996.

104 Victor-Yves Ghebali, 'Toward a Mediterranean Helsinki-type Process,' *Mediterranean Quarterly* 4 (1993): 92.

105 *Ibid.*, 93–97.

106 Barcelona Declaration adopted at the Euro-Mediterranean Conference (Barcelona, November 28, 1995).

107 On economics, see George Joffe, 'The Economic Factor in Mediterranean Security,' *The International Spectator* 31 (1996): 75–87. On regional security, see Aliboni *et al.*, *Security Challenges in the Mediterranean Region*.

108 See, for example, Laura Guazzone, 'The Evolving Framework of Arab Security Perceptions: The Impact of Cultural Factors,' *The International Spectator* 31 (1996): 63–74

109 See, for example: Roberto Aliboni, Abdel Monem Said Aly, and Alvaro Vasconcelos, *Joint Report of EuroMeSCo's Working Group on Political and Security Co-operation* (second draft), April 1997; Maria-Angels Roque, *Forum Civil Euromed: Towards a New Scenario of Partnership in the Euro-Mediterranean Area* (Barcelona: Institut Catala de la Mediterrania d'Estudios y Cooperacio, 1997).

110 Jones, *Code of Peace*.

111 Benedict Anderson, *Imagined Communities: Reflections on the Origin and Spread of Nationalism* (London: Verso, 1983).

112 Haas, *Nationalism, Liberalism, and Progress*, 40.

113 *Ibid.*, 21, 336.

114 Philip Shabecoff, *A New Name for Peace: International Environmentalism, Sustainable Development, and Democracy* (Hanover: University Press of New England, 1996).

115 Carr, *Conditions of Peace*, 275.

9   A Mediterranean canon and an Israeli prelude to long-term peace

This is a revised transcript of a talk given at the conference on 'Current European and Israeli Perspectives on the Mediterranean Concept' held at the Van Leer Jerusalem Institute on March 8, 2001. The conference was sponsored by the EU–Israel Forum, the Interdisciplinary College Herzliya, and the Van Leer Jerusalem Institute. The talk grew out of my project with Beverly Crawford, 'The Convergence of Civilizations: Building Security in a Mediterranean Region.' I would like to thank the Institute of Global Conflict and Cooperation (the University of California, San Diego) for financial support and Ronald Bee for helping organize the project.

1 Emanuel Adler and Michael Barnett, eds, *Security Communities* (Cambridge: Cambridge University Press, 1998).

2 Samuel Huntington, *The Clash of Civilizations and the Remaking of World Order* (New York: Simon & Schuster, 1996).

3 Kalypso Nicolaidis used this concept at a conference on 'Constructing a Mediterranean Region: Cultural and Functional Perspectives,' University of California, Berkeley, November 18–19, 1999.

4 Karl W. Deutsch, Sidney A. Burrell, Robert A. Kann, Maurice Lee, Jr., Martin Lichterman, Raymond E. Lindgren, Francis L. Loewenheim, and Richard W. Van Wagenen, *Political Community and the North Atlantic Area* (Princeton: Princeton University Press, 1957).
5 I owe this observation to Raffaella del Sarto.
6 See David Ohana, 'Israel towards a Mediterranean Identity,' in Shlomo Avineri and Werner Weidenfeld, eds, *Integration and Identity: Challenges to Europe and Israel* (Bonn: Europa Union Verlag, 1999), 81–99.
7 Charles Taylor, 'Interpretation and the Sciences of Man,' in Paul Rabinow and William Sullivan, eds, *Interpretive Social Science: A Reader* (Berkeley: University of California Press, 1979).

10 Changing identities

1 Uzi Benziman, 'It Is Not a Personal Conflict,' *Ha'aretz*, January 27, 2002.
2 Baruch Kimmerling, *The Invention and Decline of Israeliness: State, Society, and the Military* (Berkeley: University of California Press, 2001).
3 Yaron Ezrahi, *Rubber Bullets: Power and Conscience in Modern Israel* (Berkeley: University of California Press, 1997).
4 John Hall, 'Ideas and the Social Sciences,' in J. Cooldstein and R. O. Keohane, eds., *Ideas and Foreign Policy: Beliefs, Institutions and Political Change* (Ithaca: Cornell University Press, 1993), p. 51.
5 Ruth Gavison, 'Jewish and Democratic? A Rejoinder to the "Ethnic Democracy" Debate,' *Israel Studies* 4(1) (spring 1999): 44–72.
6 Kalypso Nicolaidis used this concept at a conference on 'Constructing a Mediterranean Region: Cultural and Functional Perspectives,' University of California, Berkeley, November 18–19, 1999.
7 David Ohana, 'Israel towards a Mediterranean Identity,' in Shlomo Avineri and Werner Weidenfeld, eds, *Integration and Identity: Challenges to Europe and Israel* (Bonn: Europa Union Verlag, 1999), 81–99.
8 Translated from Hebrew by Chaya Galai, copyright ACUM Ltd. Israeli Ministry of Foreign Affairs website, http://www.mfa.gov.il/mfa/history/modern+history/israel+at+50/50+years+of+hebrew+song.htm.

INDEX

Abdullah, King of Jordan 248
ABM treaty (1972) 147, 148, 164, 171, 173, 179
accountability norm: OCSE 201–2, 203; peace 224; security communities 231
Acheson, Dean 161
Acheson-Lilienthal Report (1946) 161
action, human vs. social origins 94–5
Adams, Benson 170
Adelman, Kenneth 154
Adler, Emanuel 189, 208, 217, 263n107, 265n135, 287n120, 290n182, 310n65, 313n122, 317n67, 319n1
agency: communities of practice 16, 17, 25; constructivist approach 6, 8, 11–12, 94–5, 101, 106–7; peace 209, 225; state and pluralistic security communities 197–9; and structure 4, 16, 78–9, 94–5
Ajzen, Icek 275n44, n46
al-Aqsa Intifada (2000-) 237, 244, 247, 249
Al Qaeda 240
Alexander, Jeffrey C. 283n36, 285n74
Algeria 227, 240
Almond, Gabriel A. 272n9
amalgamated security communities 189, 212, 238, 290n180
American Academy of Arts and Sciences 164, 173
American Association for the Advancement of Science 178
Amir, Yigal 248, 252
Amorim, José Bonifacio de Abreu 143
Amster, Warren 162
analytic perspective 3, 4, 5, 6, 8, 11–13, 27–8
analytical complexity 60
anarchy 218, 221
Anderson, Benedict 96, 185, 263n112
anthropology 57

anti-dependency guerrillas, Brazilian computer industry 22, 119–46
Arab-Israeli peace process see Middle East peace process
Arab League 227–8
Arab states: Mediterranean identity 236; nuclear balance of power 52–3
Arafat, Yasser 246, 247, 248
Arbatov, Iu. 174
Aristotle 9
arms control 22, 80, 107; constructivist approach 104
Artsimovich, Lev 173
ASEAN 25, 27, 239; security communities 190, 211, 217, 223, 226, 235, 241, 311n95
Ashkenazi Jews 241, 256
Ashley, Richard K. 7, 8, 10, 259n8, 286n109
Asia-Pacific region 239, 240
Association of Data-Processing Professionals 139, 141
Association of Data-Processing Service Enterprises 139, 144
Association of Southeast Asian Nations see ASEAN
Atlantic community see Euro-Atlantic community; NATO
Atoms for Peace (1953) 163
Australia 189
authority 25–6

Bacher, Robert 299n56
Baert, Patrick 262n82, n83
Baker, William 299n56
balance of power 35–7, 46–7, 66–7, 238; nuclear 50–3
banking 24
Barak, Ehud 247, 248, 252, 253